the Parables

of Christ

the Parables

of Christ

E. X. Heatherley

BALCONY PUBLISHING

AUSTIN, TEXAS 78734

Abbreviations
for Versions of the Bible

ANT   *The Amplified New Testament*
ASV   *The American Standard Version*
AV   *The Authorized (King James) Version*
ATR   A. T. Robertson's *The Four Gospels Paralleled*
CBW   Charles B. William's *The New Testament in the Language of the People*
JBR   Joseph B. Rotheram's *The Emphasized Bible*
KSW   Kenneth S. Wuest's *Expanded Translation of the Greek New Testament*
NASB *The New American Standard Bible*
NEB   *The New English Bible*
RFW   Richard F. Weymouth's *The New Testament in Modern Speech*
RV   *The Revised Version of 1881*
TCNT *The Twentieth Century New Testament*

Note that quotations not otherwise credited are from the Authorized (King James) version.

Balcony Publishing, Inc., Austin, Texas

Library of Congress
Catalog Card Number (Applied For)
ISBN 0-929488-98-9

Printed in the United States of America

To William J. Woody,
a prince of princes in
his own domain.

"Truly, I say unto you, many prophets and righteous men longed to see what you see, and did not see it, and to hear what you hear and did not hear it."

~Matthew 13:17 (RV)

CONTENTS

A THEMATIC GUIDE
TO CONTENTS

A THEMATIC GUIDE TO CONTENTS

A THEMATIC GUIDE TO CONTENTS (continued)

ACKNOWLEDGMENTS

Almost every book owes a degree of its quality to its editor. That statement is especially true of this work. Faithfully preserving the author's content, meaning, and style, Connie Giles massaged this manuscript into the superb reading experience that will be discovered in these pages. The author and publisher are indebted to this skilled and committed artisan.

"There is no question about Christ's constant, predominant aims and purposes. He was intent on saving the lost, promoting their spiritual interests, and fashioning them into the nucleus of a new Theocracy. Thus, we may safely assume that every parable He spoke was meant to advance or defend some phase of that undertaking."

INTRODUCTION

Preliminary Thoughts on the Interpretation of Parables

When we speak of the "parables" of Christ, we are of course referring to all of His major illustrations, regardless of their rhetorical nuances. While most of these object lessons are more or less parabolic, many of them are largely allegorical, and some of them are hardly more than similitudes, expandable into full-blown parables only by visualizing their various implications.

For our present purposes, it is not necessary to define or press these distinctions except as they affect the question of interpretation. It will suffice to use the following distinctions:

1. a **parable** is a story or an object lesson involving a real-life situation; it is meant to illustrate a single moral or spiritual truth, or a composite truth;

2. an **allegory** is a story which in itself may or may not be strictly true to fact, but in which a factual lesson touching on any number of related truths is veiled and blended in a narrative; and

3. a **similitude** is almost any rhetorical device that brings a truth to light by pointing out its likeness to some more familiar circumstance by use of an analogy.

These peculiarities, though otherwise of no great importance, call for somewhat different approaches to the interpretation of various types of illustrations.

In seeking the correct interpretation of a simple **parable**, we should examine the context to discover the speaker's current theme and its major point of emphasis, and construe all the details in keeping with the obvious end in view. The same is true of a

similitude the implications of which invest it with the character of a parable. In an **allegory,** however, every item in the story has a significance of its own. We must round out its interpretation by relating its parts to similar truths revealed elsewhere in the Scriptures. Often, our task as interpreters is more complicated than these simple rules make it appear to be, for in many instances we find both parabolic and allegorical elements, sometimes mingled with similitudes, in the same illustration. In such a case, we must discriminate among these diverse components and deal with each according to its own requirements. But as they often tend to overlap, how are we to determine which is which?

Perhaps we cannot always be sure, but we can stay on the safe side by exercising ordinary spiritual discernment and due discretion. Such discretion demands that we always give priority to the theme suggested by the **context,** construing whatever is allegorical as best we may, but never in a way that blunts the main edge of the illustration or contradicts any of the rest of the Scriptures at any point.

Thus, granted that we are familiar with the basic rules and tools of interpretation, our first concern is to discern the primary purpose and focal point of any given illustration. This task usually entails little or no difficulty. Often, the purpose can be gathered from the general drift of the accompanying narrative. Occasionally, it is suggested by a sort of prologue or postscript in the record. But there are instances in which no such clues are apparent either in the context or the text itself. What then?

Perhaps the simplest and best approach—in connection, of course, with the generally accepted procedures of Biblical interpretation—is to deduce X, the thematic thrust of a particular parable, from four primary considerations:

(a) the known aim of the **speaker,**
(b) the known needs of the **audience,**
(c) the known character of the local situation or **place,** and
(d) the known issues of the **time** when the parable was spoken.

These four known factors, in any given case, are fairly certain to identify X.

In this book, the **speaker** in every instance is, of course, the

Lord Jesus Himself. There is no question about Christ's constant, predominant aims and purposes. He was intent on saving the lost, promoting their spiritual interests, and fashioning them into the nucleus of a new Theocracy. Thus, we may safely assume that every parable He spoke was meant to advance or defend some phase of that undertaking. This knowledge may not *pinpoint* the specific lesson of every particular parable, but it narrows down the possibilities considerably.

They are narrowed down still further by considering the likeliest needs of Jesus' **audience** at the time, for invariably the purpose of His teaching was to minister to people's needs. We can scarcely go wrong by assuming that He tailored a specific parable to fit the particular needs of those people to whom it was addressed.

The local setting, or **place**—not the setting of the parable itself, but the place where it was spoken—frequently provides additional clues to its leading theme. The circumstances under which the Master spoke (and under which His hearers *must* have considered what He had to say) may also suggest the theme of a parable—in other words, the parable may have been designed to fit a specific situation.

This last concept is especially true with respect to the **time** of the parable's delivery. Granted that one is familiar with the major epochs in Jesus' earthly career (and the corresponding attitudes of those to whom He preached at various stages of His ministry), these circumstances tend to suggest the most probable burden of His teaching from time to time—and hence, the corresponding lessons of His respective illustrations.

For the foregoing described reasons, in this work I have examined the Savior's parables in their several chronological settings with special reference to speaker, audience, time, and place. To grasp these basic principles from the start is to be better prepared for an understanding of our Lord's inimitable parables.

SECTION ONE
THE KINGDOM MESSAGE

"He was not a reformer, but a revolutionist: He had come not to repair the old order, but to create a new one. The marriage of the Lamb was to be not a natural, but a spiritual, transaction."

1

OLD THINGS AND NEW

The Mutual Exclusiveness
of Law and Grace

Primary text: Luke 5:33–39
Cf. Matthew 9:14–17; Mark 2:18–22

Our Lord gave these illustrations to the scribes, the Pharisees, and certain disciples of John the Baptist— at Capernaum—about a year after the beginning of His public ministry.

Introduction and background. Our text presents a series of brief but pregnant illustrations, each of which is the kernel of an unelaborated parable. These illustrations, considered as a whole, contribute to the development of a single theme: the radical difference between the old things of the Law and the new things of the Gospel—and hence, the incongruity of any effort to mingle Judaism and Christianity.

Here, as in a good many other cases, the Savior's discourse was elicited by a knotty question. This time, Matthew says, it was raised by "the disciples of John"; Mark includes those "of the Pharisees"; and Luke says the "scribes and Pharisees."

From all accounts, it appears that the scribes and Pharisees were trying to incite the disciples of John the Baptist to find fault with Jesus and His followers for feasting in the house of

7

Levi the publican, possibly during a stated fast, while John himself was languishing in prison.

"Why," they murmured (verse 33), "do the disciples of John fast often, and make prayers, and likewise the disciples of the Pharisees; but thine eat and drink?"

In Jesus' reply, He confined His remarks to the conduct of His own disciples, for whom He presumably was responsible. But His defense of their behavior was an implicit indictment of their critics, who pursued an opposite course. He voiced no objection to fasting if practiced voluntarily as an expression of penitence or sorrow, or when incurred by one's preoccupation with prayer, but He disavowed it as a meritorious act of piety. The practices in question were of little moment except as they reflected opposing sides of a larger issue—Jesus' Messianic claims. The real issue at stake was not a matter of observing or disregarding proprieties, but of believing or not believing the Gospel. Our Lord's disciples felt no need for fasting because they believed their Messiah had come, their sins were forgiven, and the promised Kingdom was at hand.

The Pharisees continued fasting and uttering repetitious prayers because, in their distrust of Jesus' good offices, they hoped to escape God's wrath and earn favor by multiplying their abstemious devotions. The disciples of John the Baptist wavered between the limited light they had and the legalistic notions with which their master had never been completely disenthralled.

Obviously then, fasting itself was not the issue, except as it focused attention on the chasmal rift between the slavish spirit of traditional Judaism and the buoyant freedom of Christ's message. If Judaism were right, then Jesus and His followers should have adhered to the customs and regulations of the old rabbinical order. But if He was right, His critics should have abandoned their servile chores to celebrate the inauguration of a "better covenant" (Hebrews 7:22, ASV).

To this point, God had represented Himself as a husband to Israel. And, although He had found it necessary to put away the natural nation as an adulterous wife, He had promised to betroth its faithful remnant to Himself forever (cf. Hosea 1–2).

Now He had appeared on earth, in the person of His Son, to fulfill that promise. It was time, not to fast, but to rejoice. Thus, Jesus retorted to His critics, "Can ye make the children of the bridechamber fast, while the bridegroom is with them?" (verse 34).

John the Baptist, when told of Jesus' growing popularity, had used remarkably similar language to his disciples:

> He that hath the bride is the bridegroom: but the friend of the bridegroom, which standeth and heareth him, rejoiceth greatly because of the bridegroom's voice: this my joy therefore is fulfilled (John 3:29).

Because John recognized Jesus as God's Messiah, the heavenly Bridegroom, he considered himself merely the "friend of the bridegroom," or best man—an intermediary. Thus, once he had introduced Jesus to the believing remnant, he found sufficient satisfaction in the assurance that his own mission had been fulfilled.

Interpretation. Against this background, it appears that the "marriage of the Lamb," like the Messianic Kingdom itself, was "at hand" only in a provisional way. Equally clear, just as the Kingdom was to be rejected and deferred, the Bridegroom was to be detained from His wedding until a later day. "But," Jesus went on to say, "the days will come, when the bridegroom shall be taken away from them, and then shall they fast in those days" (verse 35). He knew that after His death and ascension to heaven His followers would fast—not as a legal formality, but because of their grief at His protracted absence.

Meanwhile, He would have both friends and foes know they should not expect Christianity to fit into the antiquated molds of Judaism. He never intended it should. He was not a reformer, but a revolutionist: He had come not to repair the old order, but to create a new one. The marriage of the Lamb was to be not a natural, but a spiritual, transaction. And in this wedding ceremony, "the bride, the Lamb's wife," would be arrayed, not

The Mutual Exclusiveness of Law and Grace

in the patched tatters of decadent legalism, but in the pristine livery of righteous grace. By any manner of reasoning, it was preposterous for His critics to demand conformity between two belief systems so radically at odds.

"No man," He replied, "putteth a piece of a new garment upon an old" (verse 36). Who would think of taking material from a brand-new wedding gown to patch an older garment that had outlasted its usefulness? Besides clashing with the faded texture of the older fabric, the patches would shrink and thus tear the gown even worse than before. It would have been just as illogical and futile for Jesus to mutilate the Gospel in an effort to salvage an obselete legal system which, having served its purpose, was "ready to vanish away" (Hebrews 8:13).

Our Lord was by no means dealing with an isolated local situation, but with a timeless, universal principle. Judaism is identified with the old creation; Christianity, with the new. They stand in the same relation to each other as that of Adam to Christ, Old Covenant to New, the natural to the spiritual. What must be said in every such case is ". . . that was not first which is spiritual, but that which is natural; and afterward that which is spiritual" (I Corinthians 15:46). Everything natural—the Adamic race or Judaism or the physical creation as a whole—is temporary and must pass away. Only the spiritual will abide (cf. Hebrews 12:27). "The first man is of the earth, earthy," that is, mortal, doomed to die; "the second man is the Lord from heaven," that is, *immortal, alive forever* (I Corinthians 15:47).

As for the two Covenants? "He taketh away the first, that he may establish the second" (Hebrews 10:9). The two creations? "Heaven and earth shall pass away" (Matthew 24:35); "the heavens shall pass away with a great noise, and the elements shall melt with fervent heat, the earth also and the works that are therein shall be burned up" (II Peter 3:10). "Nevertheless [that is, *despite the impending dissolution of the natural order*], we, according to his [God's] promise, look for new heavens and a new earth, wherein dwelleth righteousness" (II Peter 3:13). Since that "which is born of the flesh is flesh, and that which is born of the Spirit is spirit" (John 3:6), clearly human destiny will involve either consummate death or "eternal life through

Jesus Christ our Lord" (Romans 6:23).

These opposing categories are mutually exclusive. They may exist together only in an unresolved state of probation and conflict during this transitory phase we call "history." In every case the alternative to survival is ultimate extinction. Nor is there any doubt about the final outcome: the old must give place to the new. All that is sustained by Nature must perish in the coming conflagration. Only what has been recreated and eternalized by Christ will share His immortality. Unlike the first man Adam, Christ is not a mortal soul, but a "life-giving spirit" (I Corinthians 15:45 ASV); therefore, "if any man be in Christ, he is a new creature: old things are passed away; behold, all things are become new" (II Corinthians 5:17). This scripture means that one must be born again, through faith in Christ, if he is to survive the old order and live on to inherit the new one (cf. I Peter 1:3, 23).

The "old" was never intended to endure, but simply to be used, disused, and "done away" (II Corinthians 3:7, 11, 14). And this statement applies to Nature, natural Israel, and the Levitical Law alike. They who dream of "natural immortality" delude themselves, and they hope in vain who barricade their souls within the insubstantial shadows of Law instead of seeking refuge in Him through whom alone the Law's aspirations are realized (cf. John 1:17; Colossians 2:17; Hebrews 10:1). There is no basis for "life and immortality" except in "the gospel" (cf. II Timothy 1:10). According to the Gospel, the "hope of Israel" resides, not in any carnal achievement, but in the regeneration and eventual glorification of "Israelites indeed" (cf. Acts 26:6-8; 28:20).

This scripture points up a strange bit of irony—that those who undertake to rectify their fallen nature by observing the carnal ordinances of the Law are actually lingering in the fleshly sphere, which is under sentence of death. As we are told . . .

> . . . they that are after the flesh do mind the things of the flesh; but they that are after the Spirit the things of the Spirit. For to be carnally

minded is death; but to be spiritually minded is
life and peace (Romans 8:5–6).

It is one thing for a child of God to "mortify the deeds of the
body" (Romans 8:13) by "walking in the Spirit" (Galatians 5:16).
It is quite another for a natural, unregenerate man to depend on
subjecting his flesh (his body) to ceremonial rites—putting it on a
special diet, resting it on certain days, or forbidding it to touch or
taste a convenient assortment of innocuous taboos—to win favor
with God. As if a leopard could change its spots by practicing
self-discipline! (Cf. Colossians 2:16-23.) We are Galatianists if we
think that, "having begun in the Spirit," we are "made perfect by
the flesh" (Galatians 3:3). No one is foolish enough to try such
folly in the bridal shop, yet that is just what legalists would have
us all do in the wardrobe of religious experience.
 Any attempt to mend the flaws of legalism by patching it
with Gospel here and there serves only to rend its threadbare
tissue more and more. Incalculably worse, the new wedding
gown is ruined in the process. The Gospel of Grace cannot be
altered to accommodate any system of "dead works" without
being robbed of its intrinsic character. As Paul so emphatically
declares, if salvation is . . .

> . . . by grace, then it is no more of works: other-
> wise grace is no more grace. But if it be of works,
> then it is no more of grace: otherwise work is no
> more work" (Romans 11:6).

Patchwork is a destructive liability both to the Law and to the
Gospel, each being weakened in proportion as it is confused
with the other. This concept, in Jesus' mind, was a matter of
such profound importance that He went on to reiterate His
warning with another simile:

> . . . And no man putteth new wine into old
> bottles; else the new wine will burst the bottles,
> and be spilled, and the bottles shall perish. But
> new wine must be put into new bottles; and both

are preserved (verses 37–38).

We know, of course, that such "bottles" were bags made from animal skins, usually of goatskin (the torso, with the legs tied and cut off); the wine was poured in or out through the neck. It was common knowledge to Jesus' audience of the time that a fresh wineskin would expand as the grape juice fermented, but a used one, already having been stretched to the limit, would burst if subjected to the same process anew. In such a case, both the   wineskin and its contents would be a total loss. So it is, according to Jesus, with the Law and the Gospel. Each is good for its purpose, but the merciless exactions of the legal code have nothing in common with the unconditional magnanimity of grace. The Gospel fulfills the requirements of the Law, but it does much more than that. "For" we are told, "the Law entered, that the offense might abound. But where sin abounded, grace did *much more* abound" (Romans 5:20). Although "the Law is holy, and the commandment holy, and just, and good" (Romans 7:12), grace is so much more than the Law metes out for mere obedience that no natural "wineskin" could contain the overplus of blessedness.

What we have in Jesus Christ is as much better than the optimum benefits of legal righteousness as He is greater than Adam—or as His redemptive achievement is greater than Adam's failure. The Law could only guarantee the life of the obedient and penalize the disobedient with death; Christ, when He endured our death, did infinitely more than simply restore our life. Since it was a finite man who sinned, all the Law could demand was the death of that finite man. But since it was a divine Human Being with a life of infinite worth who paid our penalty, He earned for us a heritage of glory as great as the gap between His merits and our ill deserts.

Law and Grace are incompatible only when their functions are confounded. As long as the Law is viewed as a conductor to Christ, and Grace as unmerited favor bestowed through Christ's redemptive ministry, the integrity of both is preserved. As independent consecutive factors in our experience, they are not at all contradictory. But they cannot be mingled without frustrating the aims and purposes of both. Why should one persist on such a futile course? Having heard the Gospel, why should one fast in the presence of such a feast?

We have our answer in the current text: "No man having drunk old wine straitway desireth new: for he saith, The old is better" (verse 39). How hard it is for an earthbound legalist to forsake his putrid cup for one that "runneth over" with "joy unspeakable and full of glory"! (Cf. Psalms 23:5; I Peter 1:8.)

Yet, if and when he does, he, like another diner at another wedding feast, will be shouting, "Thou hast kept the good wine until now" (John 2:10).

2

SALT AND LIGHT

The Genius of Discipleship

Primary text: Matthew 5:11-16
Cf. Mark 4:21–22; 9:49–50; Luke 8:16-18; 11:33-36; 14:34–35.

Our Lord gave these illustrations to His disciples, in the presence of a mixed multitude—probably at Qurn-Hattin, about five miles northwest of Tiberias, but possibly in the vicinity of Capernaum—in the early summer of the second year of His public ministry.

Introduction and background. The similitudes in this sketchy passage with its loosely connected metaphors cannot be said to form a full-orbed parable—yet they are of such a nature as to admit of no other classification. The same, for that matter, might be said of most of our Lord's earlier illustrations, some of which are even less elaborate than these. With two or three exceptions, they are transparent analogies dramatizing simple statements of fact. Several, including the current story, were repeated from time to time with modifications suitable to the needs of different situations. Here is a cluster of germinal parables, each of which could be developed separately, but all of which actually cling like so many petals around a common stem. All these terms—*the salt of the earth, the light of the world, a city that is set on a hill,* and *a candle*—point up various aspects of a single theme: the character and purpose of discipleship.

15

Our Lord had just prefaced His Sermon on the Mount with a series of beatitudes in which He had mentioned some of the distinctive characteristics of those regenerate believers who were to inherit the felicity of His Kingdom. They were . . .

- *poor in spirit*: lowly of mind, in view of their conscious neediness;
- *often made to mourn*: crushed between contrition and vexation, yet hoping against hope;
- *meek*: unassuming, nonaggressive, and submissive to their providential lot;
- *habitually hungering and thirsting after righteousness*: earnestly longing for moral harmony with God;
- *merciful*: compassionate, forgiving toward all mankind;
- *pure in heart*: holy, unsullied, and sincere in their affections, motives, and attitudes; and
- *peacemakers*: not merely peaceable, but active advocates, architects of amicable relations throughout their societal community (cf. verses 3-9).

Rare virtues, these! What more could make a person an ideal neighbor or fellow citizen?

Yet Jesus, knowing even such exemplary saints would find themselves as sheep among wolves, had gone on to add an alarming remark: "Blessed are they which are persecuted for righteousness' sake: for their's is the kingdom of heaven" (verse 10).

Examination and interpretation. Then, speaking directly to His disciples, He continued:

> Blessed are ye, when men shall revile you, and persecute you, and shall say all manner of evil against you falsely, for my sake. Rejoice, and be exceeding glad: for great is your reward in heaven: for so persecuted they the prophets which were before you (verses 11–12).

The experience of the prophets had proved that
- in a world that loves darkness not light, it is perilous to be a

living testimony for the truth;
- the more one loves God, the more he will be hated by the world's godless men; and
- no one can be a faithful witness to his generation without being willing to risk making himself an object of contempt, to risk hazarding his fortunes, his reputation, even his life.

Jesus knew well that such disciples were indispensable to the advancement of His Kingdom. He already had a good many nominal followers, but it remained to be seen how they would react to the fiery trials that lay ahead. That was the question, and He would have them know that their profession would be meaningless unless they held fast, against all odds, up to the bitter end.

Salt and discipleship. It was no minor matter to be a servant of this King. "Ye are the salt of the earth" (verse 13), our Lord declared—and to reverent Jews, this was a solemn statement with profound implications. Throughout the East, salt had long been a symbol of hospitality, friendship, and fidelity. Parties to an important contract duly pledged their faithfulness with a "covenant of salt"—an exchange of oaths that were solemnized by participation in a sacrificial feast hallowed by salt. After that rite, their mutual obligations were considered binding and inviolable. Significantly, such also had been the character of the covenant-relationship between God and Israel, in token of which every proper sacrifice had required salt before it could be offered on the altar, maintaining a constant reminder of the original vows exchanged at Sinai (cf. Leviticus 2:13; Numbers 18:19).

Additionally, then as now, salt was universally valued for its more apparent qualities, especially its aseptic, preserving, and seasoning properties. The Jews used salt in washing their newborn babies, curing their meats, and flavoring their meals. In light of these various usages, it is evident that our Lord's language was meant to characterize His disciples as a divinely appointed agency for purifying and preserving society—in keeping with the intent of the Everlasting Covenant: which is to say, the evangelization of the world at large in order to gather out a chosen people who, as the true "Israel of God," are to inherit the Kingdom prepared for them before the foundation of the world.

Clearly, Jesus, even at that early date, was contemplating a universal Kingdom embracing the whole earth, not merely a little Jewish monarchy in Palestine. Above everything else, He was stressing the vital role of His disciples in that tremendous undertaking. They were to infiltrate the masses like so much salt in a kneading trough. Like salt, they would have to retain their distinct character while exerting strength, influencing their environment, resisting its temptations, and losing themselves in these accomplishments. That mission would demand total consecration to the fires of the altar, and Jesus warned them that there was no alternative short of losing their discipleship.

"If," He said, "the salt have lost its savour, wherewith shall it be salted?" (verse 13). Salt is unique; it has no substitute. It can impart its virtue to many other substances, but once its peculiar pungency is spent, it cannot be recovered from any other source. Salt is no longer really salt if it loses its strength. Only its appearance remains, mocking it as a sheer illusion of its former self. It is literally "good for nothing, but to be cast out, and to be trodden under foot of men" (verse 13). Jesus was pointing out that, likewise, a disciple is no longer truly a disciple if he ceases to perform his appointed functions in the fire.

Christian discipleship, also, is unique—one of the highest and noblest of all callings. However, once nullified by personal apostasy, its privileges and powers are virtually irrecoverable— because it is identified so closely with its testimony, without which "disciple" is only an empty name. A disciple's testimony may be impaired by human frailty and then restored by due amendment, but once renounced, it is never effective again. The world puts no faith in the word of a person unwilling to stake his fortunes—and, if need be, his life—on what he preaches. He may be a sincere believer, ever so strong in his faith, but the "salt has lost its savour" where his influence is concerned.

And *that*—the loss of one's discipleship, not his salvation—

is the point in focus here. Here, as in many similar contexts, nought but confusion will result if this distinction is overlooked.

One's *salvation* is, according to the consistent teaching of the Scriptures, provided and sustained by sovereign grace. Its endurance depends entirely on the constancy of God, whose promises never lose their savor. However, one's capacity for effective witnessing diminishes proportionately as he shirks its concomitant sacrifices and responsibilities. He may even become a castaway from the sphere of service (cf. I Corinthians 9:22), though "he himself shall be saved; yet so as by fire" (I Corinthians 3:15).

No one ever escapes the fires of trial by shunning them. Our Lord declares in another connection, "For every one shall be salted by fire" (Mark 9:49), that is, we must all be fitted for our destiny in the crucible of suffering. As Job says, "Man that is born of a woman is of few days, and full of trouble;" as one of his comforters puts it, "man is born unto trouble, as sparks fly upward" (Job 14:1; 5:7). This statement is true, sooner or later, of all humanity without exception. We are all sinners in a moral universe controlled by moral laws that penalize us— and that will finally eliminate everything that cannot be brought into harmony with God. In the realm of the spiritual, the believer's penalty is remitted and he himself conditioned for the enjoyment of eternal life. In his natural state, however, he must endure all the reactions of divine holiness against the sinfulness of the fallen race to which he belongs—though, in his case, the afflictions of the flesh contribute to his spiritual discipline, refinement, and development. For this reason, it is written of Christians in general that "we must through much tribulation enter into the kingdom of God" (Acts 14:22). True disciples "count it all joy" when they submit to the rigors and exactions of their calling (cf. James 1:2; I Peter 4:12-14). Less faithful saints who have sought to avoid the "afflictions of the righteous" will be saved "as by fire."

Those who reprobate themselves by outright rejecting the provisions of grace also will endure fire—the fires of hell— until their punishment issues in "everlasting destruction from the presence of the Lord" (II Thessalonians 1:9). We all pass through the fire, with different results. With the processes of judgment grinding out the grist for which the mill of destiny was made, we all find ourselves between the upper and nether millstones of probation. No one is exempted from the friction or the heat, though some emerge as wheat for the garner and others forfeit their souls like chaff to the all-consuming flames (cf. Matthew 3:12). Is this not another way of describing those who would rather enter the Kingdom of God with one hand or foot or eye than, having two hands or feet or eyes, be cast into hell? (Cf. Mark 9:43-48.)

Paul remarks, "if we would judge ourselves, we should not be judged." Yet, knowing there are delinquent saints who quail before self-discipline, he adds, "But when we are judged, we are chastened of the Lord, that we should not be condemned with the world" (I Corinthians 11:32). Though true believers are self-committed to "crucify the flesh" with its "affections and lusts" (Galatians 5:24), not a few of us sometimes allow self-indulgence or carelessness to stultify our resolution and destroy our usefulness, thus making it necessary for God to correct us with His rod to save us from the terrible fate of the impenitent.

Once again it is clear that a saint may lose the savor of his discipleship, but not his soul. Late in the first half of Jesus' public career, according to Matthew, He compared the disciples themselves to salt, warning them of the danger of losing their usefulness (verses 13-16). Then Mark tells us that, some months later during a visit in Capernaum, the Savior likened salt to the nature of moral judgment that either purifies or destroys, depending on one's willingness to break with mortal sin (cf. Mark 9:49–50). In the Gospel of Luke, we are told that, during the closing weeks of Jesus' ministry while teaching in Perea, He employed salt as a symbol of discipleship as such.

> Salt is good, but if the salt have lost its savour, wherewith shall it be seasoned? It is neither fit for the land, nor yet for the dunghill; but men cast it out. He that hath ears to hear, let him hear (Luke 14:34–35).

In this scripture, also, Jesus was discussing qualifications for discipleship, not personal salvation as such.

"Great multitudes" (Luke 14:25), impressed by His miracles and fascinated by their mistaken conceptions of His Messianic aims, were rallying around Him hoping to share the privileges and honors of an earthly Kingdom which they thought would soon be established by some sort of *coup d'etat.* Foreknowing all that both He and His followers would have to suffer before attaining to their promised glory (cf. Luke 24:26), Jesus frankly and openly challenged the impulsive throngs to reconsider His requirements before committing themselves to a course for which most of them were utterly unprepared. He cautioned:

> If any man come to me, and hate not his father, and mother, and wife, and children, and brethren, and sisters, yea, and his own life also, He cannot be my disciple. And whosoever doth not bear his cross, and come after me, cannot be my disciple (Luke 14:26–27).

Like salt, discipleship is a good thing if it is genuine, but it is only a sterile sham if it lacks the intrinsic character of what it purports to be.

Light and the mission. Not to introduce a new subject, but to expand and emphasize His foregoing remarks, our Lord went on to revamp His language with several new figures of speech.

> Ye are the light of the world. A city that is set on a hill cannot be hid. Neither do men light a candle, and put it under a bushel, but on a candle-stick (verses 14–15).

All three of these terms—*the light of the world, a city that is set on a hill,* and *a candle*—represent the disciples collectively, though the character of the group was presumably shared by each of its members. Their mission was to lavish the light of the Gospel upon a resentful world that fears and hates the truth. They would be exposed, like the spires of a lofty mountain city, to the gaze of all humanity. No inconsequential matter of chance, this was their divinely appointed lot. Rather than hide their light, like a lamp under a bushel, to escape persecution, they would have to mount the lampstand and proclaim the message of salvation to the ends of the earth. This ministry would prove to be a thankless—even perilous—undertaking. But only through such good works and selfless sacrifices on behalf of their assailants could they convince and capture the hearts of those who were to greet their kindness with stones and lashes. Only thus could they prevail on others to glorify God by seeking refuge in His fatherly arms.

Now, this message was not a new revelation; neither is its relevance confined to any particular age. The missionary torch has always been a target. The witness (or, literally, *martyr*) has often baptized his detractors with his blood. But, as Daniel described saints of a future day, "they that be wise disciples [meaning, *they who are faithful witnesses*] shall shine as the brightness of the firmament; and they that turn many unto righteousness as the stars for ever and ever" (Daniel 12:3). Is this not the blessedness of which Jesus spoke to His disciples, the reward in view of which He told them to "rejoice, and be exceeding glad"? (Cf. verses 11–12).

Peter thought so. After many rugged but glorious years of faithful discipleship, He cherished the privilege of suffering, in view of its reward, taking both for granted, one as much as the other. How like his Master's teaching about the ministry of salt and light are these words from the aged apostle's pen!

> Beloved, think it not strange concerning the fiery trial which is to try you, as though some strange thing happened unto you: but rejoice, inasmuch as ye are partakers of Christ's sufferings; that when his glory shall be revealed, ye may be glad also with exceeding joy (I Peter 4:12–13).

Again, the message is a restatement of a timeless, universal principle, known even to the ancient psalmist who declared:

> They that sow in tears shall reap in joy. He that
> goeth forth and weepeth, bearing precious seed,
> shall doubtless come again rejoicing, bringing his
> sheaves with him (Psalms 126:5–6).

3

An Admonitory Parable

THE MOTE AND THE BEAM

The Evangelical Basis of the Sermon on the Mount

Primary text: Matthew 7:1-5
Cf. Luke 6:37–42.

Our Lord gave this illustration to His disciples, in the presence of a mixed multitude—probably at Qurn-Hattin, about five miles northwest of Tiberias, but possibly in the vicinity of Capernaum—early in the summer of the second year of His public ministry.

Introduction and context. Although this text does not contain a complete parable, its metaphors imply all the features of a parable that are lacking in the text as it stands. We find here a typical example of the Savior's earlier illustrations, most of which are casually woven into the fabric of extended discourse and characterized by forthright simplicity. We must in this case, however, be on our guard against the all-too-common tendency to oversimplify the matter of interpretation. If we consider the immediate text apart from its overall setting, we are likely to miss the point of Jesus' argument altogether—or at minimum, obscure it by placing too much emphasis on its minor details. Neglectful of this precaution, a good many expositors find in this passage little more than a warning . . .

- that uncharitable criticism eventually boomerangs against the critic; or
- that faultfinding often proves to be a greater fault than the fault it finds; or
- that, in the words of a familiar proverb, "It ill becomes the pot to call the kettle black."

Granted that all these observations are true, must we—*dare* we—suppose that so great a teacher deliberately (or casually) interjected such shallow platitudes into the Sermon on the Mount, the manifesto of His Kingdom, of which this passage is a part? Can we believe that He digressed from such a weighty message, on such a solemn occasion, to chide His audience with a caricature of a petty backbiter?

I, for one, think not.

Doubtless this and many similar applications may readily be drawn from the imagery of this parable if it is taken alone, with no regard for its contextual connections. But surely it must be obvious to any discerning Bible student that we must look farther and deeper than this surface analysis to find a serious interpretation that is worthy of the name. Nor is it difficult to determine *where* to look, for it should go without saying that the actual teaching of this passage is bound to tie in with the central issues embodied in the more comprehensive discourse to which it belongs.

Examination and interpretation. In the Sermon on the Mount, Jesus speaks with utmost candor as a realist with no illusions about the relevance and inexorability of the Law—or about the culpability of fallen humanity.

Insisting He has come not to destroy but to fulfill the Law, and knowing well that all of us are Lawbreakers, even so, He proposes to lavish the highest privileges of the Kingdom on those who repent. These promises run parallel throughout His sermon, demonstrating that—intending neither to circumvent the demands of the Law nor to base our salvation on human righteousness—He anticipated—presupposed—a dispensation of justifying grace on the moral ground of His imminent death for the sins of the world. The cross stood behind every word

He spoke. There was no other way for Him to uphold the Law and at the same time offer eternal life and blessing to sinful men. Since the manifesto of His Kingdom necessitated totally unimpeachable righteousness as a prerequisite of citizenship, it would be a commonwealth of pardoned sinners accredited solely by the righteousness of faith (cf. Galatians 3:9).

For now, the Law is satisfied and the believer's position in the Kingdom is maintained by divine intervention. We are urged to deal with one another as God deals with us, based on the principle that sinners saved by grace should esteem one another as we are severally esteemed of God. It is evident that the seemingly superficial aspects of Jesus' illustration were intended to dramatize a much more profound matter than is usually supposed: the danger of alienating oneself from the purview of righteous Grace by relegating one's brethren to the jurisdiction of the Law.

This admonition follows quite naturally from our Lord's understanding of our mutual identification as sinners, all alike dependent on pure grace. Given the same light, we must, in view of our common guilt and the common provision made for our redemption, stand or fall together. Mercy is available to every man, but if one person arraigns another before the bar of naked justice, he exposes himself to like condemnation. Such is the basic nature of moral government: one's responsibility before the Law, as well as his amenability to redeeming grace, are proportionate to his light. One must know the Law to be held liable to its penalties (cf. Romans 4:15; 5:13), and one must know and believe the Gospel to be free of legal condemnation and saved by grace.

Because Law and grace apply to all alike, one cannot claim the merciful provisions of grace for himself while denying it to others—else he repudiates the only means whereby he is saved! As the Apostle Paul declares,

> ... thou art inexcusable, O man, whosoever thou art, that judgest: for wherein thou judgest another, thou condemnest thyself; for thou that judgest doest the same things (Romans 2:1).

Judging others was precisely what the adherents of Judaism, in general—and the Pharisees, in particular—were in the habit of doing, and, as do their kind in all generations, they depended on casuistry to justify their inconsistencies. Though professing to keep the Law, they interpreted and applied it in ways that excused their own transgressions while condemning everyone else! Their hypocrisy was what Jesus had in mind when He warned—

> Judge not, that ye be not judged [or, in other words, *Stop judging other people by the Law, lest you subject yourselves to the same treatment when you stand before God*].

—not the language of a rabbi scolding petulant faultfinders for impugning the motives or sizing up the personal defects of their fellows! No, it is a divine indictment against sinners who take it upon themselves to pass judgment on other sinners' souls.

Of course, from their point of view, the judgments of the scribes and Pharisees were anything but frivolous. They saw the glaring indiscretions of their carnal neighbors and took for granted that such transgressors were utterly lost. But by this manner of thinking, they placed their own souls in jeopardy, since the standard by which they judged their fellow men also condemned themselves.

"For," Jesus went on to say, "with what judgment ye judge, ye shall be judged: and with what measure ye mete, it shall be measured to you again" (verse 2)—adding nothing to what had already been said, but simply spelling out the message with explicit finality:

> If you regard your brother as being under the Law, it is because you yourselves are lingering on legal ground; in that case, you are liable to the same condemnation you impute to him. But if you look upon him as an object of grace, it shows that you believe the Gospel, in which case you yourselves are assured of the same mercy that is granted to him. If under

Law, your brother is a guilty sinner. If under grace, He is a justified saint. Which, in your estimation, is the case? Your answer is the verdict you will get, measure for measure—judgment for judgment, or grace for grace.

This basic thesis pervades the Sermon on the Mount, in which the righteousness of the Kingdom is viewed—implicitly, if not explicitly—as a vicarious achievement in the Pauline sense of justification by grace through faith. Accordingly, the citizens of the Kingdom are told to regard one another as beneficiaries of sovereign mercy.

As the Father "maketh his sun to rise on the evil and the good, and sendeth rain on the just and the unjust," we must be like-minded if we are to deport ourselves as His children (cf. Matthew 5:45). On this same principle, the disciples were told to pray, "forgive us our debts, as we forgive our debtors." Jesus added . . .

> if ye forgive men their trespasses, your heavenly Father will also forgive you; but if ye forgive not men their trespasses, neither will your Father forgive your trespasses (Matthew 6:12, 14–15).

The message, far from establishing "legal ground," as some expositors insist, does precisely the opposite: It admonishes us not to withhold forgiveness on legal grounds. We are told, not that God forgives us because we forgive others, but that He will not forgive us if we refuse to forgive others. If we, on legal grounds, refuse to forgive an erring brother, we renounce the principle of grace for that of Law, thus rendering ourselves incapable of receiving God's forgiveness on the principle of grace.

Such contempt for the spirit of the Gospel reveals the worst kind of unbelief—an incomparably greater sin than any moral failure on our brother's part. Jesus asks, "And why beholdest thou the mote that is in thy brother's eye, but considerest not the beam that is in thine own eye?" (verse 3). A censorious attitude is, in comparison with the offense it condemns, like a sawlog that dwarfs a speck of sawdust. Yet the legalist gazes with horror at his brother's motelike fault, unmindful of his own beamlike implacability.

That person may affect concern for his brother's well-being and even propose to come to his aid, but according to Jesus, any such show of solicitude is altogether vain. For, He demands, "how wilt thou say to thy brother, Let me pull out the mote that is in thine eye; and, behold, a beam is in thine own eye?" (verse 4). The implication is that it cannot be done, that one who turns from grace to Law can render no spiritual service to anyone. Nor can he. A man on death row can scarcely help another prisoner to break out of jail. A drowning man is in no position to teach another person how to swim. A dying man can hardly administer first aid to someone else. Nor can an unbeliever do anything whatever to relieve the plight of other wayward men. Thus the "beam" that blinds and incapacitates the legalist is nothing more nor less than his own unbelief.

The only reason one sinner writes off another sinner is that he himself does not believe the Gospel of the Grace of God. Even his zeal for the Law is affected and spurious. It was to such men as he that Jesus was to say a short while afterward, "Did not Moses give you the law, and yet none of you keepeth the law?" (John 7:19). And again He would chide them, "Do not think that I will accuse you to the Father: there is one that accuseth you, even Moses, in whom ye trust" (John 5:45). In a word, such a person is a consummate fraud, an actor who plays a role contrary to his character.

The Lord continues,

> Thou hypocrite, first cast out the beam out of thine own eye; and then shalt thou see clearly to cast out the mote out of thy brother's eye (verse 5).

This last statement can mean only one thing: the legalist must renounce his unbelief and throw himself upon the mercy of God before he can be an instrument of grace, ministering to the spiritual needs of his fellow men. There is no hope for any of us except in the Gospel, and only those of us who believe it are in a position to administer its benefits.

Nor only so; cleansing another person's eye is such a delicate operation that only the most spiritual Christian has either enough compassion or insight to undertake it successfully. Just as Paul entreats us:

> Brethren, if any man be overtaken in a fault, ye which are spiritual, restore such an one in the spirit of meekness; considering thyself, lest thou also be tempted (Galatians 6:1).

This parable demonstrates, once more, the essential unity of the Gospel as it was revealed by the Lord Jesus and preached by Paul, underscoring the evangelical basis of the Sermon on the Mount. As for the unity of that matchless sermon itself, is there any difference between warning, "Judge not, that ye be not judged," and promising, "Blessed are the merciful: for they shall obtain mercy"? (Cf. Matthew 5:7.) The warning and the promise are based on the assumption that one's attitude toward others reflects his estimate of God's attitude toward himself.

4

DOGS AND SWINE

The Futility of Trying to Evangelize Apostates

Primary text: Matthew 7:6.

Our Lord gave these illustrations to His disciples, in the presence of a mixed multitude—probably at Qurn-Hattin, about five miles northwest of Tiberias, but possibly in the vicinity of Capernaum—early in the summer of the second year of His public ministry.

Introduction and context. Whatever this text lacks being a fully developed parable is easily supplied by one's imagination. To find a reliable clue to its interpretation, we need only relate the spiritual meaning of its metaphorical terms to the drift of Jesus' teaching at the time.

All that was said about the contextual background of the foregoing parable is equally pertinent here, since this passage is a closely connected sequel of that one. There, Jesus cautioned His disciples to avoid the legalistic spirit of the scribes and Pharisees. Here, He warns that any effort to convert the false shepherds of Israel would be improper, unavailing, and even dangerous. The disciples, naturally inclined to be censorious, were, as tractable saints, amenable to correction. And there were hosts of uncommitted sinners still amenable to persuasion. But

---

31

it should never be supposed for one moment that the apostate
Jewish leaders could ever be prevailed upon to choose a better
course. In effect, Jesus was telling them:

> You may as well know, to begin with, that you must never
> give what is holy to dogs, never cast your pearls before hogs,
> lest they trample them and, turning in revulsion, mangle
> you.

Interpretation. Some respectable commentators to the contrary,
I must insist this passage does not present an exception to the
rule, "Judge not, that ye be not judged"—as if to say, *You must
not pass judgment on anyone except the "dogs" and the "swine,"
but you are fully justified in judging them!* That interpretation, I
believe, stems from a mistaken notion that the judging under
discussion is of a superficial nature, meaning only to criticize,
find fault with, or impugn the motives of, another person—at
most, to disparage a person's character—whereas it actually
means to condemn a person's soul. Jesus was referring to
people who had advertised their reprobation by deliberately,
publicly, rejecting the Gospel. Even so, He was not discussing
judging them, but recognizing that, by their own testimony,
they had judged and condemned themselves. Nor did Jesus
advise His disciples to sit in judgment even on such flagrant
unbelievers; He simply warned that any further attempt to
evangelize such incorrigible blasphemers would only inflame
their contempt for the Gospel and incite violence against the
saints.

Obviously, His advice, construed in context, is in no way
inconsistent with the Great Commission. The dogs and swine
were not unevangelized heathen, but enlightened Jews who
had already "rejected the gracious purposes of God on behalf
of themselves" (Luke 7:30, RV). They were under the wrath of
God, having committed the "unpardonable sin" (cf. John 3:18,
36). All this, as we see in the book of Acts, became a matter of
public record in time, for each time the chief priests and elders
were confronted with vibrant Christian testimony, they reacted
with blasphemy against the Lord and then with violence

against His witnesses. That has been true of such hardened disbelievers, as a class, in succeeding generations. Wherever the Gospel has become an issue, history has always confirmed the wisdom of Jesus' prophetic admonition.

My interpretation is also supported by Biblical arguments from the traditional connotations of the terms Jesus used: *dogs, swine, holy things,* and *pearls.* Let's look at the use of these terms in the Scriptures.

Dogs were regarded not only as unclean beasts, unfit for food or sacrifice, but as special objects of contempt, so much so that the word *dog* became a byword for everything that is mean, depraved, and altogether despicable (cf. Deuteronomy 23:18; Revelation 22:15). The Jews reviled the uncircumcised Gentiles as "dogs," and they occasionally hurled that derisive epithet at degenerate Israelites who were regarded as being uncircumcised of heart despite their outward identification with the Covenant People. Isaiah reproached the faithless prophets of Israel when He wrote:

> His watchmen are blind: they are all ignorant, they are all dumb dogs, they cannot bark; sleeping, lying down, loving slumber. Yea, they are greedy dogs which can never have enough, and they are shepherds that cannot understand: they all look to their own way, every one for his gain, from his quarter (Isaiah 56:10–11).

What an appropriate description of the bestial hirelings who, in another evil day, rejected and crucified the Prince of Life! Surely, it was to them our Lord alluded when He described His passion in this prophetic prayer recorded by the psalmist:

> For dogs have compassed me: the assembly of the wicked have inclosed me: they pierced my hands and my feet. . . . Deliver my soul from the power of the dog (Psalms 22:16-20).

Paul also used this metaphor for unbelieving Jews. "Beware

of dogs," he warned the Gentile saints at Philippi, "beware of evil workers, beware of the concision" (Philippians 3:2). To Paul these terms were synonyms: circumcised unbelievers were evil workers, spiritual dogs, not really circumcised in any proper sense, but, in the absence of saving faith, only mutilated in their flesh. *Concision* means merely a physical amputation. The Judaizers at Philippi had stigmatized the Gentile Christian saints as dogs, uncircumcised heathen. Paul replied that they, "the concision," were really the dogs, and believers were "the circumcision, which worship God in spirit, and rejoice in Christ Jesus, and have no confidence in the flesh" (cf. Philippians 3:3).

Thus—like David, Isaiah and Paul—when our Lord spoke of "the dogs," He referred, not to heathen, nor to unsaved people in general, but to the reprobate Jews who, despite their seemingly unimpeachable outward credentials, were inwardly as foul and vicious as "ravening wolves (cf. Matthew 7:15)—though what He said concerning them is equally applicable to their spiritual posterity in all nations and generations.

Swine. It does not appear that Jesus, in His reference to swine, intended to designate a second class of reprobates, but rather that His object was to intensify His characterization of the apostate Jews, showing them to be as unspiritual as they were unholy. Dogs and hogs are thus classed together in at least two other passages.

1. God, in disgust at the empty formalism of ancient Jewry, pronounced this terrible indictment against the soulless worship of Isaiah's time (although this, no doubt, has a future reference also):

> He that killeth an ox is as if he slew a man; he that sacrificeth a lamb, as if he cut off a dog's neck; he that offereth an oblation, as if he had offered swine's blood; he that burneth incense, as if he blessed an idol. Yea, they have chosen their own ways, and their soul delighteth in their abominations (Isaiah 66:3).

This text strikes a trenchant blow at any form of spurious

worship, discriminating the false by placing it in contrast with the true. In legitimate worship, his faith identifies the penitent offerer with his flawless sacrifice, thus enabling God to accept the offerer along with the offering. But in the absence of penitence and faith, the transaction is reversed: the sacrifice is identified with the offerer's unbelief, and is rendered as unacceptable as He is. In the passage before us, we are told God regarded the pretentious sacrifices of Isaiah's generation as abominations, and that He looked upon the worshipers as if they were pagans who offered unclean beasts instead of the lambs and oblations actually brought. The enormity of false worship lay in themselves, not in what they offered. They themselves were unclean. Their attitudes and motives were abominable. They, and therefore the sacrifices they offered, were just as detestable as dogs and hogs in the sight of God.

2. And if this pronouncement was true of the Jews of Isaiah's day, how much more so of that "wicked and adulterous generation" that professed so much zeal for God, all the while rejecting His Son! The pious hypocrites who hated Jesus were not just unbelievers, but were disbelievers who had known and forsaken the way of truth—an earlier brood of the same stripe as the renegades of Christendom who were soon to share their folly and their fate.

As Peter declares

> For it had been better for them not to have known the way of righteousness, than, after having known it, to turn from the holy commandment delivered unto them. But it is happened unto them according to the true proverb, The dog is turned to his own vomit again; and the sow that is washed to her wallowing in the mire (II Peter 2:21–22).

Holy things and pearls. Now that we know the metaphorical significance of the dogs and the swine, it should no longer be difficult to see the impropriety and uselessness of pampering them with holy things and pearls. The better we understand the nature of the gifts the disciples were told to withhold, the more we shall be convinced that it was right and best for them to do so.

"That which is holy," (or *the holy thing,* to be exact) was, in this case, something edible. A number of passages in Leviticus expressly designate the holy things as sacrificial foods, the flesh and bread left over from offerings made to God, a part of which was legally allotted to the priests, and the remainder to the worshiper. Consumption of that food was strictly, repeatedly forbidden to any person who was ceremonially unclean (cf. Leviticus 22:6 ff), and to animals of any kind (cf. Exodus 22:31). Nor is the reason difficult to find, since every offering was a symbolical representation of some particular aspect of the Gospel, and all together, they presented a full-orbed depiction of Christ's redemptive ministry. Obviously, then, the proceeds of such sacrifices typified the benefits of righteous grace, which, though provided for all men alike, may be enjoyed by only those who repent of sin and place their trust in Christ.

Pearls likewise are symbolic of the riches of grace which abound in the Gospel. This usage is reflected in the books of Job and Proverbs. Precious gems stand for the multifaceted wisdom of God as it was to be personified in Christ (cf. Job 28:18; Proverbs 3:15, 8:11, 20:15). In the Book of Matthew, our Lord alludes to Himself as a "pearl of great price" (Matthew 13:46). However conceived, the Gospel is the wisdom and power of God unto salvation (cf. I Corinthians 1:24), but only to "everyone that believeth" (Romans 1:16), never to those who greet His mercy with contempt (cf. Hebrews 10:29). Since the Gospel enables God to "be just, and the justifier of him which believeth in Jesus" (Romans 3:26), it must not be misused as a devious device to condone the wickedness of unbelievers. Its pearls must never, not once, be made to adorn the conceit that willful unbelief may somehow be forgiven either in this world or in that to come (cf. Exodus 34:7; Matthew 12:32).

Thus, viewed within the framework provided by Jesus' metaphors as illustrated in other places throughout the Bible, this parable clearly yields the interpretation suggested at the beginning of this discussion. Such is the nature of the human heart and its relation to moral government that when a person who has heard the Gospel deliberately rejects it, He thereby confirms himself in unbelief and forfeits his susceptibility to the attractions of saving grace. It is therefore not only useless and dangerous, but also irrational, unethical, and irreverent, to offer salvation to a self-confessed apostate assuming God may somehow find a way to pardon him despite his rejection of Christ. To offer hope to one who has renounced the Gospel is to misrepresent God as some sort of compassionate but amoral pushover who would rather incriminate Himself than give a rebel his just deserts.

On one hand, the religious infidel is like a dog wanting nothing more than to gorge itself on flesh from the altar; on the other, he is like a hog loathing what the altar represents. As dogs, the ancient scribes and Pharisees vied with each other for the honors and profit of religion; and as swine, they trod "under foot the Son of God" and did "despite unto the Spirit of grace" (Hebrews 10:29). And so the story goes, down through the years, until this day: The pampered dog ere long turns out to be a hog with terrible tusks!

5

THE TWO WAYS

The Righteousness of Faith
versus
The Righteousness of the Law

Primary text: Matthew 7:13–14
Cf. Luke 13:24-30.

Our Lord gave this illustration to His disciples, in the presence of a mixed multitude—probably at Qurn-Hattin, about five miles northwest of Tiberias, but possibly in the vicinity of Capernaum—early in the summer of the second year of His public ministry.

Introduction and background. This passage is, in spite of its brevity, quite remarkable for the rich diversity of its content, at once comprising literal statements of fact, poetic similitudes, several radical antitheses, an urgent invitation, and a terrible warning— all within the compass of a single sentence.

Although it can hardly be classified strictly as a parable, its metaphors, as in most of Jesus' earlier illustrations, combine to create a mental picture which is undeniably of a parabolic character. It presents a graphic view of the world at large with two divergent roads stretching out through the reaches of time to different destinations in eternity—one to everlasting life and immortality, one to eternal death and "everlasting destruction

---

from the presence of the Lord . . ." (cf. II Timothy 1:10; II Thessalonians 1:9).

Interpretation. This depiction of "two ways" was not a new concept, but a timely adaptation of an old familiar portrayal of the alternatives of human destiny.

Moses. A reading of this parable immediately recalls the words of Moses in his farewell message to Israel on the plains of Moab, where he admonished his fledgling nation:

> See, I have set before thee this day life and good, and death and evil; in that I command thee this day to love the LORD thy God, to walk in his ways, and to keep his commandments and his statutes and his judgments, that thou mayest live . . . I call heaven and earth to record this day against you, that I have set before you life and death, blessing and cursing: therefore choose life, that thou and thy seed may live: that thou mayest love the LORD thy God, and that thou mayest obey his voice, and that thou mayest cleave unto him: for He is thy life, and the length of thy days . . . (Deuteronomy 30: 15-20).

These words, construed spiritually in the light of the Gospel, have virtually the same meaning as those of Jesus concerning the two ways:

* *Moses,* having rehearsed the obligations and privileges of Israel's Covenant relationship with God, summed up with a momentous challenge. If the Children of Israel kept faith with God, depending on the blood of the Covenant to atone for their human frailties, they would live and prosper. But if they flouted the provisions of the Covenant, they would be cursed and left to perish in their sins.
* *Jesus,* having shown that the Law's requirements are met only through the Gospel, ended His Kingdom manifesto with an admonition much like that of Moses, insisting that those who obeyed the Gospel would live and reign with Him eternally,

---

The Righteousness of Faith vs. the Righteousness of the Law

but those who persisted in unbelief would be destroyed.
In both cases, one as much as the other, the appeal was to the
heart, not merely to the hands. In Moses' case, his approach
was necessarily like that of a teacher using object lessons in a
kindergarten class. Jesus' lot was to interpret the Law to Moses'
nearsighted pupils who had never come to see beyond their
building blocks.

The demands of the Law and the provisions of grace have
always operated in tandem in God's dealings with men, though
that was not so manifest in former ages as it is in ours. The
necessity of obedience, the culpability of sin, and the grounds
of divine forgiveness never change. In Moses' day obedience
was rendered, sin was judged, and forgiveness was received,
by believing and relying on the available revelation of God's
redemptive purposes, just as in our own dispensation—but the
believer's faith could be assisted only by the ceremonial
foreshadowings of realities which have since been fully revealed
to us in the Gospel (cf. John 1:17; Colossians 2:17; II Timothy
1:10; Hebrews 9:1-12). All that the moral Law demanded was
supplied by what the ceremonial law prefigured concerning
Christ's redemptive ministry. The believing Israelite met the
Law's moral demands observing its ceremonial regulations—
not mechanically with his hands alone, but also discerningly
with his heart, just as we now "discern the Lord's body" in the
Eucharistic loaf (cf. I Corinthians 11:29). Everything we have
in Christ today was represented in the anticipatory types and
shadows of the Law. Clearly, God never expected ancient Jews
to rely upon their own ability to satisfy the Law; rather, that
they should look through its ceremonies to their fulfilment in
and by Jesus Christ and to claim the benefits of His vicarious
achievements for themselves. For them, obeying the Law was
"the obedience of faith" (cf. Romans 16:26) whereby they
"obeyed the gospel" (cf. Romans 10:16). However, over time,
vast numbers of them, as sacramentalists of Christendom later
on would do, perverted the vehicles of faith into idolatrous
fetishes, putting their trust in the Law itself instead of trusting
Him to whom it testified.

That is the besetting sin of Judaism: that misdirection of

religious faith from the object of the Law to the Law itself—hence, to one's ability to save himself by keeping the Law instead of trusting Christ. By practicing their religion in this manner, the scribes and Pharisees virtually had rejected Jesus even before He came. When He did appear, the reflex action of their unbelief was almost automatic. Nor were they moved to repentance by exhibition of His personal virtues and mighty works; just the opposite, they were inflamed with resentment by every evidence of His integrity because it threw their own hypocrisy into bold relief. Despite their affected zeal for the Law, they were actually evading its real demands in an effort to enter the Kingdom without renouncing their sins. Parading their ostensible orthodoxy, at the same time they muzzled the law in which they boasted, by interpreting it to suit themselves. Thus they could . . .

- hate and slander their fellow men without committing murder (cf. Matthew 5:21–22);
- divorce their wives at will without stooping to outright adultery (cf. Matthew 5:27–28);
- perjure themselves without taking God's name in vain (cf. Matthew 5:33-37); and
- exact "an eye for an eye, and a tooth for a tooth" without transgressing the law of love (cf. Matthew 5:38-45).

In short, they made the Word of God of no effect by watering it down with their own traditions (cf. Matthew 7:13).

The rebelliousness of religious unbelief, not the remissness of open sin, is the "wide gate" Jesus described as leading to destruction. Its opposite, repentance and the obedience of faith, is the "narrow gate" that leads to life. It is not one's moral failures, but his willful unbelief, that damns his soul. It is not through one's personal merits, but through his faith in Christ, that his soul is saved. Christ died and paid for all the sins of all the sinners of all the world, and therefore, "All manner of sin and blasphemy shall be forgiven unto men" (Matthew 12:31). Sin is no longer the issue; Christ Himself is; the alternatives are limited to faith and unbelief. The only way to be saved is to trust in Jesus; the only way to be damned is to reject Him. And each of us must sooner or later commit himself one way or the other. Much more might be said about just how this fateful decision is effected, or allowed to come about, but this much is true as it stands.

This choice is what Jesus had in mind when He besought His listeners to enter the narrow gate. He was not urging the Jews to be better Jews, or the Pharisees to be better Pharisees, but was exhorting all His hearers to renounce their Judaistic delusions and place their trust in Him.

David. First Psalms likewise underscores the distinction between the way of the righteous (justified believers) and the way of the wicked (confirmed unbelievers) by describing their respective destinies:

> Blessed is the man that walketh not in the counsel of the ungodly, nor standeth in the way of sinners, not sitteth in the seat of the scornful. But his delight is the law of the LORD; and in his law doth he meditate day and night. And he shall be like a tree planted by the rivers of water, that bringeth forth his fruit in season; his leaf also shall not wither; and whatsoever he doeth shall prosper. The ungodly are not so; but are like the chaff which the wind driveth away.
>
> Therefore the ungodly shall not stand in the judgment, nor sinners in the congregation of the righteous. For the LORD knoweth the way of the ungodly shall perish (Psalms 1:1–6 AV).

This psalm is, in fact, an epitome of the Sermon on the Mount as a whole, summing up in a few short phrases the distinctive characteristics of those who obey, and those who disobey, the Gospel. Like Jesus' sermon, this first psalm makes no sense whatever except on the presupposition that believing sinners are justified through faith in Christ and willful unbelievers are reprobated by rejecting Him. Both the psalmist and the Savior testify in other connections that all men are sinners by nature and, as such, utterly dependent on the vicarious provisions of "the redemption that is in Christ Jesus" (Romans 3:24).

In every case—Moses' farewell message, David's psalm, and the Lord Jesus' sermon—the cross stands in the background, and the careers and destinies of men are seen as the results of faith or unbelief. God has never conditioned salvation on the meritorious works of sinful creatures. The Scriptures consistently—always, invariably—present a believer's obedience as evidence of divinely given faith. Thus, the Sermon on the Mount was not intended, as some interpreters suppose, to establish the Kingdom of Heaven on "legal grounds"—as if the legalists of unbelieving Jewry might enter the Kingdom by being somewhat stricter legalists than they already were! Had that been the case, the scribes and Pharisees would have been among the first to follow Jesus, whereas, they actually spurned His Messianic claims because He denounced their efforts to justify themselves on "legal grounds." "Except your righteousness shall exceed the righteousness of the scribes and Pharisees," He cautioned His prospective followers, "ye shall in no case enter the kingdom of heaven" (Matthew 5:20). In view of the Pharisees' unrivaled reputation as sticklers for the letter of the Law, these words can mean only that (a) there is no hope for anyone, or else (b) we must somehow be *given* the righteousness the ceremonial Law prefigured but could not impart—which is to say, the righteousness of Christ Himself.

And yet, alas, some of our popular expositors construe the teaching of this parable (and the entire Sermon on the Mount, for that matter) as if Jesus had meant to take the Pharisees' side against Himself! Such interpretation of this passage would, if it were correct, doom all of us. Paradoxically, the common use of that misinterpretation serves, rather, to demonstrate the exceeding breadth of the way that leads to destruction, just as Jesus forewarned. Had He not expressly declared that this would be the case, it would be strange indeed to find so many misguided interpreters recommending, in His name, the very course He took so much trouble to warn against—insisting, as they do, that we must save ourselves by being more pharisaic than the Pharisees!

The narrow way, they tell us, is a life of personal holiness, and the broad way is a life of open sin—or, in other words, good people go to heaven and bad people go to hell.

Never was Biblical interpretation more plausible—nor more misleading! It lifts a vast body of wholesome instruction out of its proper context and injects it into an immensely different connection in a way that makes one truth appear to nullify another one.

We are all aware that sin is obnoxious to the Law and the Gospel alike, and that it never finds any condonation in the Scriptures. Every thoughtful person, whatever be his spiritual condition, knows sin tends toward death and righteousness tends toward life. Certainly, every serious Bible student knows that sin must be judged and that salvation entails the eventual attainment of personal holiness. Every sincere Christian knows that sin is utterly incompatible with the intent of saving grace.

But—granting all the provisions of the foregoing paragraph (as we readily do) sin simply is not under consideration here. Here, Jesus is warning against a deadly error at the opposite end of the scale, the heresy of Judaism, and of Pharisaism in particular: the conceit that we are saved by what we do for God, rather than by what He does for us.

Bear in mind that our text belongs to the Sermon on the Mount, which, though delivered in the hearing of "the people" (cf. Matthew 7:28), was addressed, not to flagrant sinners, but to Christ's own disciples (cf. Matthew 5:1, 2). It does not evade, but frankly faces up to, the universal guilt and impotence of humanity as a whole. It insists there can be no salvation apart from the realization of all that the Law requires. But, far from demanding personal righteousness, it calls for self-effacement, presupposes the provisions of redeeming grace, and conditions acceptance with God on the righteousness of faith. This is a repudiation of Judaism, Pharisaism, Sadduceeism, and every other "-ism" that claims sinners can justify themselves by their own religious efforts. It calls us away from the whole legalistic concept to that of justification through faith in Christ alone (though it envisages the believer's eventual sanctification as a result of his new relationship with God).

Against this contextual background, it is absurd to construe the narrow way as a good life that entitles a religious sinner to salvation, or the broad way as a bad life that disqualifies an erring saint for heaven.

The narrow way is . . .
- the Jesus way, as opposed to the self way;
- the way of the cross, as opposed to that of legalistic hypocrisy; and
- the way of faith, as opposed to that of meritorious works.

We marvel at the lawyers and doctors of Jewry for being so blind, so stupid, and yet so smug in their delusions. But are we being any more perceptive when we misconstrue our Lord's denunciation of Judaism as if He meant to teach what those critics already believed, rather than urge them to "repent from dead works" and place their trust in Him?

Let us be objective, candid, honest, with ourselves. If Jesus taught (as we are frequently told) that only good people are saved, how many of us, with all our faults and failings, are really in the narrow way? How "good" was . . .
- *Noah,* when he debauched himself and exposed his shame?
- *Abraham,* when he forsook the Promised Land and fled to Egypt, when he lied to save his neck at the expense of Sarah's virtue, or when he humbled Hagar at his wife's request?
- *Jacob,* when he cheated Esau, taking advantage of his aging father's blindness to perpetrate a fraud?
- *Samson,* the Lazarite, when he violated his vows in the arms of a harlot?
- *David,* when he seduced Bathsheba and murdered Uriah?
- *John the Baptist,* when, in a moment of discouragement, he chided God's Messiah?
- *Peter,* when he denied his Lord with a perjurer's oath?
- *Thomas,* when he questioned the Savior's resurrection?
- *Mark,* when he forsook his calling?
- *Barnabas,* when he quarreled with Paul?
- *Paul,* when, after denouncing Judaism for a quarter of a century, he compromised his testimony by participating in the offering of an animal sacrifice?

And what about the rest of us? Are we any better than those

The Righteousness of Faith vs. the Righteousness of the Law

ancient heroes of the faith? Have we no carnal failings? no
emotional distempers? no intellectual vices? Worse, have we
no spiritual sins—no envy? no pride? no rancor?—staining our
consciences and marring our fellowship with one another or
with God? Oh, it's easy enough to prate about the *desirability*
of being good, and it's all too easy to *affect* the goodness we
extol—but are we really good? Or are we just making believe?

The truth is, human goodness is at best a relative matter,
always falling short of the glory of God and, hence, providing
no ground whatever for acceptance in His sight. Because the
Lord Jesus Christ was the only man whose righteousness was
(is) absolute, unfailing, and unimpeachable, only as we are in
union with Him can we possibly measure up to God's demands.

Not to say that the legalists of Jesus' day were altogether
insincere. No; in deluding themselves, they were simply being
themselves—hypocrites, yes, but doubtless, for the most part,
conscientious hypocrites. As sinners by nature, it was perfectly
natural for them to practice deceit and delude themselves, for
as Jeremiah says, "The heart is deceitful above all things, and
desperately wicked" (Jeremiah 17:9). Nor is it strange that such
a course appeals to fallen men in general, seeing that it cuts
God down to the pretender's size and brings the tree of life
within the hypocrite's reach. Those features are what makes
the broad way so attractive to the masses; it offers so much for
so little, all at God's expense, and gives the religious sinner
credit for it all! To be "righteous," all an ancient Pharisee had
to do was wash his hands or write a bill of divorcement or
mutter *Corban;* all a modern Pharisee has to do is to subscribe
to a few sectarian taboos and pay his tithes—as if a leopard
could change its spots by switching from meat to grass and
entering the zoo!

"There is a way," we are told, "which seemeth right unto
man, but the end thereof are the ways of death" (Proverbs
14:12). No one, however wicked, thinks it right to wallow in
vice, but there are legions who see nothing wrong with trying
to bribe the Holy One of Israel with their "filthy rags" (cf. Isaiah
64:6). That act, not the obliquity of the rabble, is the way that
ends in death.

Conversely, entering the narrow gate means—
- repenting of our sins instead of protesting our innocence;
- confessing our impotence instead of insisting on our self-sufficiency; and
- trusting in Christ instead of fondling the delusion that we can save ourselves.

Certainly, this choice does involve a desire, a willingness, and a resolution to break with sin and lead a holy life, but it in no way hazards our salvation on our own ability to persevere. It throws the entire responsibility for our eternal welfare on the Lord. We accept the consequences—discipline, chastisement, personal sacrifices, and all the rest—not as exactions in return for grace received, nor as means of retaining the grace we have, but as efficient guarantees of all the grace we shall need in times to come.

This is not a flattering view, but it is realistic, being founded
- not on human presumption, but on divine revelation;
- not on the illusion that we are good, but on the assurance that God is gracious;
- not on our precarious faithfulness, but on the constancy of Him who is "able to keep [us] from falling, and to present [us] faultless before the presence of his glory with exceeding joy" (Jude 24).

Our security is in Christ, for we are assured that "by him all that believe are justified from all things, from which [we] could not be justified by the law of Moses" (Acts 13:39). Even so, being still embodied in sinful flesh, we often find ourselves in conflict with the lingering tugs of our fallen nature. We hate the sins that tempt our carnal appetites, yet we sometimes yield to the lures we loathe. "For," we must, all too often, confess with the Apostle Paul, "that which I do I allow not: for what I would, that do I not; but what I hate, that do I" (Romans 7:15). Nor is this confession as enigmatic as it at first appears to be; it is a simple statement of fact. The Christian actually has two opposing natures. As a child of God who resides in a natural body, He can truthfully say, "I delight in the law of God after the inward man" (Romans 7:22), but at the same time, it must be said of his Adamic nature that "it is not subject to the law of

God, neither indeed can be" (Romans 8:7). But no true believer, even in moments of defeat, is guilty of willful lawlessness, for He agrees with the law that condemns what his lower nature does. As Paul reasons:

> If then, I do that which I would not, I consent unto the law that it is good. Now then it is no more *I* that do it, but *sin* that dwelleth in me. For I know that in me (that is, in my flesh), dwelleth no good thing: for to will is present with me; but how to perform that which is good I find not. For the good that I would I do not: but the evil which I would not, that I do. Now if I do that I would not, it is no more *I* that do it, but *sin* that dwelleth in me (Romans 7:16-20; *italics added*).

And Paul's admission, far from being abnormal, is in fact a universal phenomenon in Christian experience.

Meanwhile, the Holy Spirit is working mightily within us, purging away the "dross" and preparing us for an abundant entrance into the Kingdom of heaven when only the "gold" remains. The gate is narrow, and the road is hard, but "our light affliction, which is but for a moment, worketh for us a far more exceeding and eternal weight of glory" (II Corinthians 4:17).

The way of life begins with the pangs of a new birth; it entails a subsequent struggle that is often painful, sometimes defeating, and always humiliating. Constant self-examination, confession, and rededication are required. But "we all, with open face beholding as in a glass the glory of the Lord, are changed into the same image from glory to glory even as by the Spirit of the Lord" (II Corinthians 3:18).

When Jesus taught this unpopular doctrine, He was outlawed by the horrified ecclesiastics of Jerusalem as "gluttonous, and a winebibber, a friend of publicans and sinners" (Matthew 11:19).

When Paul proclaimed it, He was slanderously accused of holding that it is perfectly all right to "do evil that good may come" (cf. Romans 3:8; 6:1 ff).

But *who* ever lived a holier life than the Lord Jesus or Paul or the early saints who sat at their feet? No one can possibly find any fault with this doctrine unless He assumes, without any warrant, that it was recommended to the unregenerate masses as a license to sin and, hence, that it was an artifice to condone deliberate lawlessness—when it was simply meant to explain the actual facts of Christian experience. If a person is a Christian, this truth will commend itself to his conscience, rebuke his failures, and relieve his doubts, strengthening his determination to press forever upward to higher ground. If he is not a believer, it has no relevance for him, that is, not until He is enrolled in the school of grace. At any rate, this is the narrow way; and if there be few that find it, that is just what Jesus told us to expect.

There are two gates, two roads, two destinies: Christ and life—or unbelief and destruction. These are the alternatives, and sooner or later each of us must make his fateful choice. This is the human side of divine election—and the only way we can make our calling and election sure is to cast our vote with the minority.

The Righteousness of Faith vs. the Righteousness of the Law

6

A Hortatory Parable

ROCK AND SAND

The Test of Christian Profession

Primary text: Matthew 7:24-27
Cf. Luke 6:47-49.

Our Lord spoke this parable to His disciples, in the presence of a mixed multitude—probably at Qurn-Hattin, about five miles northwest of Tiberias, but possibly in the vicinity of Capernaum—early in the summer of the second year of His public ministry.

Introduction and background. This passage, which concludes the Sermon on the Mount, must be understood in light of the preceding sayings of the Master, sayings to which it explicitly refers. The text begins with the significant word *therefore,* which, besides its general reference to the larger discourse, introduces an illustration of an immediately foregoing assertion.

Having just declared that He will refuse to acknowledge many of His nominal followers in the day of judgment, Jesus went on to show why, *therefore,* that refusal will take place:

> Not everyone that saith unto me, Lord, Lord, shall enter into the kingdom of heaven. Many will say unto me in that day, Lord, Lord, have we not prophesied in thy name? and in thy name have cast out devils? and in thy name done many

wonderful works? And then will I profess unto
them, I never knew you: depart from me, ye that
work iniquity (Matthew 7: 21-23).

Then, rather than leave this startling declaration hanging in
the air, He proceeded to illustrate the difference between true
and false disciples. Because only those who by faith translate
the Kingdom message into personal experience, and thus
realize the will of God, are truly saved; *therefore* those who are
not "doers of the word," but "hearers only" (James 1:22), have
no valid basis for hope of eternal life. The immediate connection to Jesus' foregoing statements is provided in these verses.
    Also evident is that Jesus' introductory *therefore* serves to
summarize the general arguments of His sermon as a whole,
thus:
- *Because* superficial piety is vain,
- *because* the spirit of the Law requires implicit heart-obedience,
  and
- *because* the perfect will of God can be realized only through
  faith in the vicarious merits of Christ,
- *therefore* one must either obey the Gospel or lose his soul.
This explanation serves to reiterate that, as I have insisted all
along, Jesus' Kingdom message presupposed His subsequent
redemptive ministry and the provisions of righteous grace as
they were to be expounded later on in the Apostolic Epistles.

Therefore, this parable was certainly not intended, and must
not be construed, to foster the fallacious notion that we are
saved by anything we do. It does, indeed, make *doing* the test
of Christian profession, but in no sense does it make *doing* a
basis of salvation. In fact, the context shows that doing the will
of God is a matter of heart-obedience, "the obedience of faith,"
not of legal works. That was the basic thrust of Jesus' entire
sermon. After insisting repeatedly that the Law requires far
more than man is able to perform, He urged His hearers to act
on the principle of faith. It was altogether as if He had said (as
He did have Paul say a few years later) that "a man is judged
by faith without the deeds of the law" (Romans 3:28).

Examination and interpretation. "Therefore," Jesus begins this parable, this portion of his sermon, "whosoever heareth these sayings of mine, and doeth them, I will liken him unto a wise man, which built his house upon a rock" (verse 24).

This language designates a hearer who takes the Kingdom message to heart and acts on what he has heard—he, a penitent believer having turned from the "dead works" of legalism, is "serving the living God" (Hebrews 9:14) "in spirit and in truth" (John 4:24). He is no longer working for salvation, but is now working out the salvation he has freely received (cf. Philippians 2:12). Herein is his wisdom, that he is building his hope on the rock of Christ and Christ alone.

"For other foundation can no man lay than that is laid, which is Jesus Christ" (I Corinthians 3:11). So spoke the Apostle Paul, in concurrence with all the other apostles and, indeed, the holy prophets of former times. Nor is there any question but that the *rock* in this parable represents Jesus Himself. It will not do to construe the rock as the hearer's obedience, as if he were, after all, depending on his own good deeds; that is just what Jesus was urging His hearers not to do. The thought is, rather, that it is naturally part of the obedience of faith to build on Christ rather than anyone or anything else—although, undoubtedly, here as elsewhere, real faith is contemplated as issuing in a course of conduct consistent with its profession. Our personal works and merits contribute nothing whatever toward the procurement of our salvation, but faith would be utterly vain if it did not produce new moral inclinations which result in a new way of life. Not to say that we are saved by faith plus its resultant works, but through faith "which worketh by love" (Galatians 5:6). God does the saving, on the moral ground of Christ's redemptive ministry. He imparts His grace through faith engendered for that purpose, and He thereby creates us "in Christ unto good works" (Ephesians 2:10). It therefore follows that, in the long run, although we are not saved by anything we do, the general tenor of our deeds will either confirm or refute our profession of faith.

This rule, despite whatever appearances there may be to the contrary, is unexceptionable.

As free moral beings confronted by countless duties and temptations, we can by no means escape the trial of our faith. Turbulence and tensions are inevitable. Yet, come what may, if our faith is grounded on Christ, it keeps us true and steadfast when the storms of life unleash their pent-up fury on our souls. We shall be like the wise man whose house stood firm and fast in the midst of the angry elements:

> And the rain descended, and the floods came, and the winds blew, and beat upon that house; and it fell not: for it was founded upon a rock [literally, *upon the rock*] (verse 25).

It is just the other way round with the nominal "disciple" who, in keeping with his characteristic stupidity, fails to act on the Gospel after hearing it. He is like the "foolish man" who "built his house upon sand," with the result that under the pounding of the ensuing storm "it fell: and great was the fall of it" (verses 26–27). Such a person, despite his profession of faith, actually is guilty of practical infidelity. His life belies the faith he feigns. To him, the Apostle James would say:

> Even so faith, if it has not works, is dead, being alone ... Thou believest that there is one God; thou doest well: the devils also believe, and tremble. But wilt thou know, O vain man, that faith without works is dead? (James 2: 17-20).

In few words, this parable ...
* identifies Christ as the object and ground of saving faith;
* underscores the importance of acting on the truth we hear;
* commends the wisdom of those who take the Gospel seriously;
* exposes the folly of complacency;
* assures the true believer of his security; and
* warns the trifler of his impending doom!

SECTION TWO
KEYS TO THE KINGDOM

"In the eyes of the world, a man is great in proportion as he senses and satisfies the world's prevailing moods.... True greatness is characterized by a disposition to do what is right and best ...regardless of the cheers or jeers of the fickle throngs."

7

An Admonitory Parable

THE CHILDREN IN THE MARKETS

Christ's Appraisal of His Critics

Primary text: Matthew 11:16-19
Cf. Luke 7:31-35.

Jesus spoke this parable to the multitudes—somewhere in Galilee—most likely during the summer of the second year of His public ministry.

Introduction. Thus far in our study of the Savior's earlier parables, we have found one all-pervading truth standing out above everything else: The Gospel provides the only moral ground on which a penitent believer may enter the Kingdom of God. This was the keynote of Jesus' first message to Israel, when He pleaded, "The time is fulfilled, and the kingdom of God is at hand: repent ye, and believe the gospel" (Mark 1:15). All that He taught and preached thereafter was based on the yet-to-be-expressed premise that the Gospel of Christ is "the power of God unto salvation" (Romans 1:16). Nor can we qualify His presentation of the Gospel, as if its content were somewhat different from that of Peter, John, and Paul—for who can believe that the gospel of Christ was unknown or altered or diluted by Christ Himself?

No, if what the apostles have said about the Gospel is true, then it has always been true, and there has never been any other way of salvation.

Granted that Jesus Christ deferred the full revelation of many things until later generations were prepared to bear them (cf. John 16:12), the basic essence of the Apostolic doctrines of Sovereign Grace, Redemption, and Justification by Faith is clearly perceptible throughout the Savior's oral teaching, as recorded by the four Evangelists. We'll do well to recognize, once and for all, that there is only one authentic Gospel—and one saving message—found in the Scriptures. True, it has many different aspects and may be contemplated from various points of view, but all of its facets reflect the indivisible unity of an integral gem. The light of that gem irradiates Jesus' teaching, through and through.

We may, therefore, expect this parable to shed additional light on the evangelical nature of Jesus' Kingdom message— and that it will do—but if we are to grasp its full significance, we must first examine the connection in which it occurs.

Contextual background. Our Lord was now approaching the first major crisis in His public career; tensions confronted Him on every hand. Since delivering His Sermon on the Mount, He had devoted Himself to an extensive healing ministry, which excited so much notoriety that even John the Baptist, who had been in prison for several months, heard reports of his Master's growing popularity. Nor was he altogether pleased by what he heard.

John the Baptist was, instead, perplexed by an unexpected course of events which, to his human heart, seemed strangely inconsistent with the Messianic role. From the beginning of his ministry, he had warned that the coming Messiah would wield the axe of judgment, hew down the wicked, and purge His realm with fire (cf. Matthew 3:10-12). Now, instead of wreaking vengeance on the false shepherds of Israel, Jesus was only ministering to the sheep. What kind of King was this, who substituted meekness for the axe, compassion for fire? Just as well-meaning but not-so-gracious reformers of later times were to do, John, with his legalistic background and zeal for naked righteousness, had overlooked other prophecies in which the "sure mercies of David" are vouchsafed to children

---

Matthew 11:16–19   *Admonitory*

of the Kingdom (cf. Psalms 89:30 ff). Nor only so. Evidently, John was peeved—offended at the mercy being lavished on others, even sinners—while he himself, who was so faithful, lay month after month in a miserable dungeon, abandoned and apparently forgotten! If Jesus could deliver others from disease and death, why had He not delivered His own devoted forerunner from the clutches of Herod? Thus, John had lost not his faith, but his perspective. Feeling as he did, he sent two of his disciples to Jesus to protest his bewilderment.

"Art thou He that should come," he chided the Master, "or do we look for another?" (verse 3).

And *chided*, I devoutly believe, is the right word. John was not really challenging Jesus' Messiahship, but was posing a purely rhetorical question meant to prod the Savior into the assertion of His Messianic authority. John's question might be freely rendered: *As for You, are You really the one who was to come? Or should we be looking for another of a different kind?* If taken alone as it stands, this language certainly seems to imply that John had fallen into doubt. But in consideration of our Lord's ensuing remarks, I believe we must understand this event, rather, as the protest of a troubled but unswerving heart. From Jesus' answer, we can see that He construed His impatient suppliant's message as a mere protest, for instead of taking it as an expression of waning confidence, He assumed that John's misgivings were prompted by genuine concern for his Master's honor. Not denying that He must eventually judge impenitent Jewry (as both John and a number of the former prophets had foretold), the Savior simply replied that He was, meanwhile, working miracles of mercy, saving penitent sinners in keeping with certain other, more benign prophecies which John would do well to remember along with the more severe ones (cf. Isaiah 35:3-10: 61:1-3).

Then, lest the onlooking crowd should misinterpret John's remonstrance as a sign of wavering faith, our Lord at once proceeded to repudiate that faulty inference. John the Baptist, He insisted, was not "a reed shaken with the wind" (verse 7), was not retracting his former testimony, but was only urging the Master to assert His kingly power. Nor did this mean that

John, ambitious for personal promotion and a place of ease in the coming Kingdom, was prodding Jesus to seize His throne precipitately by devious means. That type of opportunist would already have been courting the favor of current rulers, not enduring the rigors of a Roman prison for the cause of righteousness (cf. verse 8). No, John was indeed a prophet and more—exalted of God to see and herald the promised King of whom former prophets had been allowed only a foreglimpse from afar. Though no mere man had ever been honored with a higher calling, John—with all his faith, but a still imperfect comprehension of the grace of God—was for the time at hand less privileged than the least of Jesus' humble followers (cf. verse 11).

The preparatory function of Law and prophets terminated with the ministry of John the Baptist (cf. verse 4). Then "Christ . . . brought life and immortality to light through the gospel" (II Timothy 1:10). The unbelieving Jews, deluding themselves that they could somehow earn salvation by simply observing the external regulations of the rabbinic code, refused to repent and believe the message of grace. As shown by their contempt for the baptism of John, which symbolized submission to the reign of Christ, they willfully rejected the merciful counsels of God on their behalf (cf. Luke 7:30). Thus, they flouted God's appointed means of grace and undertook to force their way into the Kingdom on their own terms. They resorted to "moral violence" in a presumptuous effort to take the Kingdom by storm.

This moral violence is obviously what Jesus meant when He declared that "from the days of John the Baptist until now the kingdom of heaven suffereth violence, and the violent take it by force" (verse 12)—or, as Luke reports the same saying in another connection, "The law and the prophets were until John: since that time the kingdom of God is preached, and every man presseth into it" (Luke 16:16).

According to an allowable rendering of Matthew's account, Jesus was saying that since the beginning of John the Baptist's ministry, the Kingdom of Heaven had been invaded, and that invaders were seizing it. According to Luke, everyone was invading it. Both writers use the same word meaning "forcible invasion," and in both cases, the context alludes primarily to the unbelieving legalists among the Jews. Our Lord expressed the same idea, in a different way, when He declared on a later occasion: "Verily, I say unto you, He that entereth not by the door into the sheepfold, but climbeth up some other way, the same is a thief and a robber" (John 10:1). Unwilling to enter the Kingdom through the good offices of Christ, who is the only legitimate door of the sheepfold, the unbelieving Jews were trying to "climb up some other way"—by pretending to keep the letter of the Law while violating its real demands.

Examination and interpretation. In this rebellious frame of mind, the Jews found themselves at odds with John and Jesus alike. John's asceticism was too genuine and, hence, too stern for them. John's standards were too high; his demands, too exacting. As for Jesus, in their minds He was not abstemious enough—too indifferent to their rabbinical taboos, and much too indiscriminate in His associations with the common horde. They saw nothing in either John or Jesus that corresponded with their own conceits, but much in both that filled them with resentment and uneasiness. For this reason Jesus likened that generation to . . .

> . . . children sitting in the markets, and calling unto their fellows, and saying, We have piped unto you, and ye have not danced; we have mourned unto you, and ye have not lamented (verses 16–17).

The scene is the marketplace of an Oriental town; the time, perhaps evening, after business hours. Some little children have gathered there, and are playing games—in this case, acting out familiar social functions they doubtless have seen their elders perform in real life. Some of them propose to mimic the celebrants of a wedding feast. But when they pipe, the others refuse to dance; when they mourn, the others refuse to lament.

Whereupon, the children who suggested the game take their fellows to task for not following their lead.

That is the story, and, some commentators to the contrary, we must, in my opinion, interpret its details just as they stand. To begin with, we must discriminate between the *children*, who are likened to "this generation," and *their fellows*, who stand in the place occupied by John and Jesus. A glance at the text will show that this is a valid distinction, for the language states that "this generation ... is like unto children sitting in the markets." It does not include *their fellows* in that particular group (cf. verse 16). In fact, the original language explicitly differentiates *their fellows* as "others of another kind." No, the petulant children who wanted to direct the games represent the "evil and adulterous [meaning, *faithless*] generation" (cf. Matthew 12:39) determined to intrude itself into the Kingdom without obeying the Gospel. "Others of another kind" stand for the elect in general, specifically John the Baptist and Jesus— those who refused to join the willful gamesters of Jewry in their pretentious parodies.

When the hypocritical legalists would fain have rejoiced in the delusion that they were about to inherit the Kingdom, John not only refused to join them, but besought them to repent. When, in keeping with their contempt for the grace of God, they bewailed the hopeless depravity of the publicans and the sinners, our Lord replied by attending the joyous celebrations of His lowly followers.

> ... John came neither eating nor drinking, and
> they say, He hath a devil. The Son of man came
> eating and drinking, and they say, Behold a man
> gluttonous and a winebibber, a friend of publicans
> and sinners (verses 18–19).

This comment clearly shows it was the Jews, the children of that generation, who did the piping, the mourning, and the complaining—not John and Jesus; and that John and Jesus were the fellows of a different kind who refused to dance to Jewry's tune or mourn at its behest—not the willful children thwarted in their play. As for those willful children,

they wanted . . .	*instead . . .*
John to endorse their illusory dream of being exalted as the bride of Jehovah (cf. Hosea 2:20 ff) in the coming Kingdom.	John upbraided them for their spiritual infidelity; moreover, he commanded them to repent.
they wanted . . .	*instead . . .*
Jesus to sanction their spurious piety.	He admonished them to seek the righteousness of faith.

The point is that the Jews were utterly implacable when they could not have their way. John and Jesus, notwithstanding their dissimilar emphases, were, each in his own way, insisting on compliance with the will of God. When the Jews berated Jesus and John the Baptist, they were opposing God and betraying their own unfitness for a place in His Kingdom. Ironically, John and Jesus were actually vindicated by opposition from such a source, for had they not been in the will of God, they would not have been so vehemently resented by His enemies.

Refusing to take their cues from the ruling clique, John and Jesus had not only kept faith with God, but also exemplified the mark of true greatness. The appraisal of human greatness is always a relative matter, depending largely on the appraiser's point of view. The aspiring demagogue who manages to project the kind of image the public demands is almost certain to win the adulation he wants. In the eyes of the world, a man is great in proportion as he senses and satisfies the world's prevailing moods. He dances when the public pipes and weeps when it mourns, for he is, after all, a servant of its whims. To him, the voice of the people is the voice of God. He knows no other God.

True greatness is characterized by a disposition to do what is right and best—therefore truly wise—regardless of the cheers or jeers of the fickle throngs. I think this is what Jesus had in mind when He said that "wisdom is justified of her children" (verse 19). It is a moot question whether, in the original text, this last remark employs the word for "children" or that for "works," for in either case the meaning is virtually the same. The children of wisdom demonstrate their legitimacy by what they do—or refuse to do. As such, both John the Baptist and Jesus discharged their distinctive missions faithfully in spite of the many pressures and blandishments of their times. John the Baptist, with his limited knowledge of the Gospel, invoked the Law to convict the consciences of open sinners and hypocrites alike. Our Lord Jesus, knowing that grace supplies far more than even the Law demands, went forth as a Man among men to seek and save the lost. Thus wisdom forbade John to dance with the dying—the unbelieving Jews—and forbade Jesus to mourn with the living— the converted publicans and sinners. Still, in spite of the murmurs of her critics in succeeding generations, wisdom is vindicated by both her works and her children as, in time, all those who repent and believe the Gospel are given "beauty for ashes, the oil of Joy for mourning," and, of course, "the garment of praise for the spirit of heaviness" (Isaiah 61:3).

8

THE TWO DEBTORS

Gratitude's Response to Grace

Primary text: Luke 7:41–42.

*Our Lord spoke this parable to Simon the Pharisee—
in his house, somewhere in Galilee—probably in late
summer of the second year of His public ministry.*

Background. Here the illustration is a part of the narrative in
which it occurs, and is inseparable from it. Moreover, there was
a close connection between the accompanying incidents and a
major crisis in the Savior's career. Having been tacitly rejected
by the Jewish hierarchy, He turned His attention mainly to the
masses who at least regarded Him as a prophet sent from God.
The tenor of His message from that time forth is epitomized in
the tender invitation recorded by Matthew:

> Come unto me, all ye that labour and are heavy
> laden, and I will give you rest. Take my yoke
> upon you, and learn of me; for I am meek and
> lowly in heart: and ye shall find rest unto your
> souls. For my yoke is easy, and my burden is light
> (Matthew 11:28-30).

These gracious words were gladly received by many people—

among others, by an errant woman who, having found the promised rest for her soul, was eager for an opportunity to express her gratitude to the compassionate Nazarene.

Now, to find such an occasion was, in view of prevailing customs, practically impossible for any strange woman, let alone a person of her reputation, but as the saying goes, "Love found a way," despite the rigid social inhibitions of the times.

Story. Upon learning that one Simon the Pharisee had invited the Lord Jesus Christ to dine at his house, this penitent woman took it upon herself to slip into the festive chamber of Simon's house, without any formal ado, carrying with her an alabaster box of ointment. Whereupon, having found her way into the shadows behind the reclining guest, she wept her heart out and "began to wash his feet with tears, and did wipe them with the hairs of her head, and kissed his feet, and anointed them with ointments" (verse 38).

That touching display of devotion should have been enough to break the proud Pharisee's heart. Not so; he could interpret the situation only in keeping with those suspicions natural to his depraved mentality. Reasoning as only a Pharisee could, He

> ... spake within himself, saying, This man, if
> he were a prophet, would have known who and
> what manner of woman this is that toucheth him:
> for she is a sinner (verse 39).

Although he was aware that Jesus was popularly regarded as a prophet, Simon had "leaned over backward," so to speak, in entertaining Him even as a teacher—and that he did, no doubt, so he could scrutinize Him as closely and critically as possible. Now he thought "the cat was out of the bag." No respectable Jew would knowingly allow a harlot to caress his feet, and any real prophet would at once have discerned this woman's sordid and sinful character and therefore shunned her very undesirable attentions. It apparently didn't occur to Simon's callous heart that Jesus was deliberately permitting what was taking place.

But there was a sobering surprise in store for Simon. "Jesus answering said unto him, Simon, I have somewhat to say unto thee" (verse 40)—somewhat more, no doubt, than Simon had expected to hear! The skeptical host was about to learn that not only this woman's reputation, but his own vile thoughts, were an open book to the piercing eyes of his mysterious guest. For the moment, however, Simon answered unsuspectingly, "Master, say on" (verse 40).

Our Lord proceeded to explain His conduct by telling the story of the two debtors:

> There was a certain creditor which had two debtors: the one owed him five hundred pence, and the other fifty. And when they had nothing to pay, he frankly forgave them both. [That was the parable, but Jesus sharpened its point with this concluding question:] Tell me therefore, which of them will love him more? (verses 41–42).

Had Simon cautiously acknowledged Jesus as a mere teacher? Then he must learn that he was dealing with a Teacher indeed!

Here was a parable so transparent that even the dullest of pupils could scarcely miss its meaning. In addition, lest the wily Pharisee might feign to do so, Jesus had handed him the key in the form of a leading question—practically forcing him to turn the lock. Moreover, the problem Jesus had posed was carefully worded to turn Simon the Pharisee's own manner of reasoning to good account.

Ah, if one debtor were to be forgiven ten times as much as another one, which would love the forgiving creditor more?

That was the question, and what rigid legalist could forego the conclusion for which it called?

So Simon answered that, in his opinion, the man who had been forgiven more would love his benefactor more (cf. verse 43).

Whereupon, the Master replied, "Thou hast rightly judged," and, turning toward the woman He continued:

Gratitude's Response to Grace

Simon, Seest thou this woman? I entered into
thine house, and thou gavest me no water for
my feet: but she hath washed my feet with tears,
and wiped them with the hairs of her head. Thou
gavest me no kiss: but this woman since the time
I came in hath not ceased to kiss my feet. My
head with oil thou didst not anoint: but this
woman hath anointed my feet with ointment.
Wherefore I say unto thee, her sins, which are
many, are forgiven; for she loved much: but to
whom little is forgiven, the same loveth little
(verses 44-47).

Application. As to the immediate application of this parable,
our Lord's own comments are so explicit that little more need
be said. He Himself was the *creditor*; the woman was the *debtor*
who "owed five hundred pence"; and Simon was the one who
owed only fifty. Of both debtors alike, it could be said that
"they had nothing to pay," each being as bankrupt of personal
merits as the other—but, likewise, both were freely forgiven
despite their ill deserts. Hence, the conduct of each reflected
his or her response to mercy in terms of grateful love—or the
want of it. How could Simon be so blind as to misunderstand
his fellow debtor's chastened ardor brimming over in the acted
language of a broken and contrite heart? He, also, was acting
out his heart—not, indeed, with tears and ointment, but with
grudging hospitality void of warmth, chilled with disrespect.
Two needy souls, not merely one, were on display.

Faulty Inference 1. It is critical that we understand the full
significance of this text, else we shall not only miss one of the
leading points of the parable, but also leave our minds wide
open to an untenable inference. Jesus was not teaching that
one must be a flagrant sinner to be more grateful for having
been forgiven much, but that one's own estimate of his debt
determines the measure of his gratitude on being forgiven.
Doubtless, the proportions of indebtedness mentioned in the
parable are intended to be considered as representing the

Pharisee's own manner of reckoning. Simon thought it thus, in view of the ostensible contrast between himself and the former harlot as measured by human standards. In God's sight, there was no difference between their hearts (cf. Romans 3:22–23)—any more than there is between a rattlesnake that has bitten many times and another that has bitten only once, or possibly never at all.

In this case, one snake had bitten five hundred times; the other, only fifty. The former felt that she was exceedingly bad, and the latter considered himself fairly irreprehensible, whereas there was actually no essential difference between the two. In view of their appraisals of themselves, the woman loved much because she had been forgiven much—whereas Simon loved less because he had been forgiven less. (Even so it must be noted to Simon's credit that, unlike the Pharisees in general, he was not altogether unmindful of his obligation to the Lord. On that slender basis, it may not be too much to hope that he eventually broke some alabaster boxes of his own.)

Faulty Inference 2. It would not be necessary to warn against another faulty inference sometimes extorted from this story except for the fact that there are some interpreters who attempt to dignify it with the guise of scholarship, surmising that the woman was forgiven *because* she loved the Lord. Such an idea militates against the teaching of the remainder of the Bible. According to our popular version, the record says, "Her sins, which are many, are forgiven; for she loved much" (verse 47). Now, there is nothing really wrong with this translation if we construe it naturally in its context, which explicitly asserts that the woman had been saved through faith (cf. verse 50). But if taken alone as it stands—and if the word *for* is mistaken as a synonym for *because*—the passage can thus be made to imply that she was forgiven in view of, and by virtue of, her love. To accept this interpretation is to ignore the actual language of the original text and contradict the Gospel of the Grace of God as set forth in many other passages.

In Greek as in all other languages, the precise meaning of many, if not all, words is affected by their usage in various contexts. Although the Greek word here translated *for* often does mean "because," in other usages it is purely explanatory of some result, and has the converse meaning "on account of which." Similarly, in English one might say, for example, "It's been raining, for the ground is wet." Here, three points must be made:

a. The word *for* in the English example sentence is used as a conjunction to introduce evidence ("the ground is wet") for the foregoing statement ("It's been raining"). This is a clearly recognized usage of the English word *for*.[1]

b. In this usage, the word *for* certainly does not indicate "It's been raining *because* the ground is wet," which would be to say that the wet ground *caused* the rain. (One sometimes hears even this incorrect usage, "It's been raining, because the ground it wet," but what the speaker actually means is "I know it's been raining because the ground is wet." The clause *because the ground is wet* tells how "I know.")

c. And, putting the actual meaning of the original sentence into another correct English construction, one might say "It's been raining, *on account of which* the ground is wet."

That "on account of which" is the sense of *for* in our parable is borne out further by the tense of the verb in the original Greek. It is not said that the woman's sins were forgiven on the spot, but that they had been forgiven beforehand. Thus, a literal rendering must be substantially as follows: "Therefore, I say to thee, her many sins have been forgiven, on account of which she loved much."

Just a bit later, addressing the woman directly to the same effect, the Savior said, "Thy faith hath saved thee; go in peace" (verse 50). Her love for Jesus was a result, not the cause, of her salvation. Just as most new converts do, the woman needed such reassurance, but according to Jesus' actual language, she had already been restored to God's favor through her faith, before she loved at all.

---

[1] *Webster's New World Dictionary, Third College Edition*. New York: Simon & Schuster, 1988.

Deeper significance. Far from skirting the fringe of spiritual experience, the story depicts two representative types of pious people discernible in every area of religious profession. Notice how different their characteristics are in the following columns:

Those who propose to pay their paltry favors to God in a perfunctory way.	*Those who* bubble up and over with eager, grateful, loving spontaneity.
They include: • respectable churchmen, • rigid sectarians, • slavish Sabbath-keepers, • grudging tithers.	*They include:* • jubilant saints, • freedmen of Christ's, • joyous worshipers, • hilarious givers.
They are characterized by cringing duty born of fear and working for hire.	*They are characterized by* the sweet aroma of lives poured forth like precious ointment from an alabaster box.

With all this discussion, we have scarcely touched on the basic argument underlying all the other lessons of this parable: the real identity of the *creditor*. Simon, though evidently impressed by the exalted character of Jesus' teaching, had nevertheless hesitated to acknowledge Him even as a prophet. Entertaining Him as a teacher of indisputable eminence, even so Simon had been very careful to avoid the extension of any courtesy that might have been construed as an endorsement of His higher claims. We have seen exactly how Jesus responded to Simon's unspoken doubt about His prophetic gifts by exposing the haughty Pharisee's innermost thoughts. But, not content with that exposure alone, He went on to assert His own essential deity—first, by representing Himself as the forgiving Creditor, and then, by assuring the penitent woman of the remission of her sins.

There can be no doubt that the other guests perceived the full significance of this procedure, for they "began to say within themselves, Who is this that forgiveth sins also? (verse 49), meaning, *Who is this who presumes to grant what only God can give?*

As for Simon—though the record is silent here—he must have known that, if this remarkable man were all He claimed to be, the Lord of Glory had been exceedingly patient with a wretched host that day!

9

An Admonitory Parable

THE DISARMING OF
THE STRONG MAN

The Impossibility of Prolonged Neutrality

Primary text: Matthew 12:29
Cf. Mark 3:27; Luke 11:21–22.

*Our Lord spoke this parable to the scribes and the
Pharisees—somewhere in Galilee—in Capernaum,
perhaps—most probably during late summer in the
second year of His public ministry.*

Introduction and background. This very casual illustration is,
despite its brevity and informality, too important to be passed
over in a survey of Jesus' parables. Occurring with slight yet
significant variations in all three Synoptic Gospels, it reflects
the Savior's familiarity with Old Testament prophecy and is
doubtless the source of a good many germinal ideas which were
later expounded at considerable length in the Apostolic Epistles.
It epitomizes the general teaching of Scripture with respect to
the all-decisive conflict between Christ and Satan.

Here again, the context dictates the interpretation of the
text; yet, as is quite often the case, the parable supplies the key
to the situation described in the accompanying narrative. In
this case it shows that Jesus' foes were courting destruction by
misjudging and opposing Him. Up to this time, they had been

content to ignore the implications of His mighty works and to shrug off His teaching as an irritating but not yet intolerable nuisance, without going so far as to openly renounce His claims. Inflamed with resentment at His rising popularity, they were now about to cast their die, dash across their Rubicon to the point of no return (cf. Matthew 12:14). In this state of mind, having steeled themselves against the truth until their hearts were insensible to divine persuasion, they could go no further without abandoning themselves to unbelief, without placing themselves forever beyond the reach of grace. Jesus warned them that such a step could never be retraced (cf. Matthew 12:32). He knew that once that step had been taken, it would precipitate a national crisis which only the cross, on His part, and centuries of bitter chastisement, on theirs, would be able to resolve.

Alas! His warning went for nought, and His critics lost no time in sealing their fateful "covenant with death" (cf. Isaiah 28:15, 18). On seeing Him heal a blind and dumb man who had been possessed by a demon, they couldn't deny a notable miracle had been wrought, but rather than acknowledge this act as proof of Christ's Messiahship, they instead accused Him of collaborating with the devil! "This fellow," they grumbled, "doth not cast out devils, but by Beelzebub the prince of the devils" (Matthew 12:24). This charge meant, in effect, that they and Jesus were, Godwise, on opposite sides; thus, whatever His own relation to God or Satan, they deliberately placed themselves on the other side. At last, a definite commitment on their part—one that, regardless of other points at issue, drove an inexorable wedge between themselves and whoever enabled the Man of Nazareth to perform His miracles. That much they could do; no one could stop them. However, such a desperate course of action, far from proving their point, still left untouched the question as to who was of God, and who of Satan. They assumed, as they meant their accusation to imply, that their own allegiance to God should be taken for granted as a matter of common knowledge—but, for all their religious zeal, another question remained to be settled: Who was the God for whose sake they denounced this holy Nazarene?

The Scriptures teach and history proves that many religious people have worshiped demons, deluding themselves that they were serving the true and living God. The ancient Israelites kept a "feast to the LORD" before a golden calf (cf. Exodus 32:5), and the apostate Jews of later generations "built altars for all the hosts of heaven in the two courts of the house of the LORD" (II Chronicles 33:5). Again, now, the false shepherds of Israel were likewise doing Satan's bidding in the name of God.

This truth would become apparent to whatever extent the Savior was able to vindicate Himself against the charges of His foes: if, as they contended, He was in the service of one God and they another, then as far as He could clear Himself of any connection with Satan, they themselves would be shown to be Satan's tools. Nor was there want of proof at His command. Had He not just demonstrated His opposition to the Evil One by breaking his cruel hold on a helpless demoniac?

As for the fatuous notion that the devil had sponsored that work of mercy, it was ridiculous to suppose that Satan would make war against himself (cf. Matthew 12:25–26). And the Pharisees could not attribute expulsion of demons to the power of Satan without dividing themselves, for their own disciples were constantly claiming similar cures.

No, Jesus had evidently wrought His miracle "by the Spirit of God" (cf. Matthew 12:27) or, as Luke reports it, "with the finger of God" (Luke 11:20). Therefore, it was obvious that His accusers had, in opposing Him, gone over to the Enemy. The Jewish leaders found they could not answer such arguments; they were unanswerable.

Examination and interpretation. Not content with having shut His critics' mouths, our Lord went on to show that His mission was unfolding in the current situation precisely as it had been forecast in a number of Messianic prophecies.

> Or else how can one enter into a strong man's house, and spoil his goods, except he first bind the strong man? and then he will spoil his house (verse 29).

While Jewry (and the world at large) lay in the clutches of the strong man, a "stronger than he" (cf. Luke 11:22) had appeared, unexpectedly, to set the captives free. The Kingdom of God had taken the Chosen Nation unaware (cf. Luke 11:20).

It was a common practice for the ancient prophets to extol the coming Messiah's superiority over His adversaries; and whatever form the adversary took in any particular case, it was always Satan who stood in the background, destined to defeat. On this subject, Isaiah had prophesied:

> Shall the prey be taken from the mighty, or the lawful captive delivered? But thus saith the LORD, Even the captives of the mighty shall be taken away, and the prey of the terrible shall be delivered: for I will contend with him that contendeth with thee, and I will save thy children (Isaiah 49:24–25).

Then, just a bit later, in concluding a marvelous description of Christ's redemptive ministry, the same prophet, speaking for God, declared: "Therefore will I divide him [Christ] a portion with the great, and He shall divide the spoil with the strong [Satan] . . ." (Isaiah 53:12). Surely this language is too much like that of Jesus' parable for the similarity to be mistaken as a sheer coincidence. True, it envisages the Savior's sharing of the spoils as a result of His sacrificial death, which had not yet taken place; but were not all the benefits of Calvary retroactive from the start? Assuredly, as to the case in point, the healing of the blind and dumb man was, like the rest of Jesus' miracles, a foretaste of His impending victory on the cross.

Every tiny detail in the current parable makes a significant contribution to the development of this general theme. The *strong man* is Satan—apostate Lucifer, variously described as "the prince of this world," "the prince of the power of the air," and "the god of this world" (cf. Isaiah 14:12; Luke 11:15, RV; John 12:31; Ephesians 2:2; and II Corinthians 4:4, respectively). He has serpentlike subtlety and demoniacal powers, and he is armed with a dreadful array of destructive devices (cf.

II Corinthians 11:3, 14; Ephesians 6:12; II Corinthians 2:11). His *house*, or estate, is the world over which he usurps authority during this present evil age (cf. I John 5:19; Galatians 1:4). And his *goods*, so long as he can keep them in his grip, are the souls of fallen men (cf. Ephesians 2:1-3).

But in the course of time One "stronger than he," the Lord Jesus Christ, having through His incarnation entered into the strong man's guarded house, conquered the mighty usurper with one fell blow at Calvary. There and then the prince of this world was judged (John 16:11), defeated once and for all in open court before the bar of sovereign justice. Thenceforth, he is being stripped of all his armor as the forces of darkness give way before the advancing light of truth. Meantime, just as God decreed through the mouth of Isaiah, Christ is "dividing the spoil with the strong"—saving those who heed the Gospel, and leaving the rest to perish with their fallen god.

The "Son of God was manifested, that He might destroy the works of the devil" (I John 3:8), or to be even more specific, Paul puts it this way in his epistle to the Colossians:

> ... and you, being dead in your sins and the uncircumcision of your flesh, hath He [God] quickened together with Him [Christ], having forgiven you all trespasses; blotting out the handwriting of ordinances that was against us, which was contrary to us, and took it out of the way, nailing it to his cross; and having spoiled principalities and powers [the forces of Satan], He made a shew of them openly, triumphing over them in it [*it* being *the cross*] (Colossians 2:13-15).

This passage emphasizes the centrality of the cross in both our deliverance and Satan's defeat. But in general terms reflecting the believer's point of view, the Savior's parable could scarcely be paraphrased more strikingly than in the following passage from the book of Hebrews:

> Forasmuch then as the children [that is, reborn

believers] are partakers of flesh and blood, He
[Christ] also himself likewise took part of the
same; that through death He might destroy him
that had the power of death, that is, the devil;
and deliver them who through fear of death were
all their lifetime subject to bondage (Hebrews 2:
14–15).

Considering all that the Scriptures have to say on this subject,
it is clear that the binding of the strong man entails at least
two definite measures—one at the outset, the other at the close,
of the present age. He was bound in a strictly moral sense when
the Lord Jesus redeemed mankind at Calvary, thus breaking
the Wicked One's hold on God's elect. He will be bound again,
in a personal and local sense, upon the Lord's return—and will
be prevented from deceiving nations during the Millennium
(cf. Revelation 20:1-3). Then, finally, in connection with the Last
Judgment, he will be bound and cast to his destruction in the
"lake of fire" (cf. Revelation 20:10).

So much for the interpretation of the parable itself, but one
additional word is almost mandatory: The Lord Jesus, having
turned His critics accusation against themselves, went on to
warn His uncommitted listeners that they could not for long
maintain a neutral attitude. "He that is not with me" our Lord
insisted, "is against me; and he that gathereth not with me
scattereth abroad" (Matthew 12:30).

That awful warning is as pertinent and urgent today as it
was back then. Once having heard the Gospel, we must either
take our stand with Christ or else pursue the course that the
apostate leaders of ancient Jewry followed to their doom.
Wherefore, it is written: "Today if ye will hear his voice, harden
not your hearts . . ." (Hebrews 3:15).

10

THE UNCLEAN SPIRIT

The Fateful Consequences of Apostasy

Primary text: Matthew 12:43-45
Cf. Luke 11:24-26.

Our Lord spoke this parable to the scribes and the Pharisees—in Galilee, perhaps in Capernaum—most probably late in the summer of the second year of His public ministry.

Introduction and background. A very important passage is this, terrible in all its implications, but fraught with much needful instruction. There is no doubt about its primary application, for in a closing comment our Lord expressly indicated that He was illustrating the spiritual experience of the unbelieving Jews: "Even so shall it be unto [or, *shall be with respect to*] this wicked generation" (verse 45). But, in principle at least, this parable is more or less applicable to every apostate religious group or individual who commits the unpardonable sin—underlying all, its theme is the suicidal results of rejecting the Holy Spirit's testimony concerning Christ.

This parable is a sequel of the former one, "The Disarming of the Strong Man," which, with its context, is the background for this text. This base we must keep in mind to follow the drift of the larger narrative, in which the Jewish ecclesiastic leaders are shown to have been moving steadily toward the brink of hopeless apostasy, which situation prompted Jesus' additional

---

word of warning.

Clearly, then, this parable was not intended as an excursus
on demonology—as if meant to explain what normally occurs
after a demon's expulsion—any more than Jesus' illustrations
taken from Nature were technical disquisitions on agriculture
or meteorology. It is a hypothetical case illustrating the lesson
the Savior had in mind at the time. Having just cast a demon
out of a man who was blind and dumb (cf. verse 22), He uses
that occasion as a *psychological springboard* for His story—but
that is the *only* connection. He makes no reference whatever,
here, to demons as such, certainly none to demons of disease.
Rather, He specifies an "unclean spirit," one particular lewd or
adulterous spirit that had left and reentered one particular man.
It had wanted a resting place, a permanent abode congenial to
its own nature and designs. After failing, at first, to realize its
ambition in that intended victim, it had sought a more propitious opportunity elsewhere, in "dry places" (verse 43). At last,
it returned in desperation to its former home, where it now
found just what it had wanted from the start: a dwelling place
swept and tidied up but left unoccupied. In the absence of
opposition from within, it recruited "seven other spirits" more
wicked than itself, and together they invaded the empty "house"
and settled down to stay.

We have described the background and substance of the
story, but what does the parable mean?

Examination and interpretation. We have already seen that this
parabolic *man* represents the Jewish nation, particularly that
"wicked generation" of Jews who rejected Christ. The context
shows the *unclean spirit* as a personification of their idolatry,
which, in view of Israel's covenant-relationship as Jehovah's
"wife," involved her in spiritual adultery (cf. Hosea 1–2), for
which Jesus called His contemporaries an "evil and adulterous
generation" (verse 30). These facts, considered in the light of
Jewish history, make the matter of interpretation a fairly easy
task. It was common knowledge that the Chosen People, by
and large, had often struggled under the spell of some heathen
superstition up until the time of the Babylonian Captivity, but

that in post-Exilic times from Ezra's day and onward, they had outdone themselves in a superb effort to banish every vestige of idolatry from their midst. Having "swept and garnished" their house, they were now, by rejecting its rightful occupant, virtually inviting His enemy to fill the resultant void.

Nature abhors a vacuum no less in the heart than in the laboratory; wherever Christ is shut out, the devil is at perfect liberty to take over. Thenceforward, Satan has done just so in unbelieving Israel, intensifying his influence—her corruption—sevenfold. First apparent at Calvary, when the Jews renounced and crucified the Lord of Glory, Satan's work is seen today in their continued opposition to the Gospel. And according to the consistent testimony of the Scriptures, it will culminate in their seduction by Antichrist. Jesus warned them of this eventuality on a previous occasion: "I am come in my Father's name," He said, "and ye receive me not: if another shall come in his own name, him ye will receive" (John 5:43). Thus, an enlightened nation's willful unbelief is to plunge it deeper into idolatry than heathendom itself has ever sunk.

Such degradation is, in fact, impossible in the absence of sufficient light to make apostasy a willful choice of darkness. This interpretation explains why the parabolic *unclean spirit* could find no rest in "dry places." In a more literal translation of the original, *waterless places* might be used, a term which corresponds with Isaiah's description of Babylon, alluding to the sterility of religion in the absence of special revelation—since *water* is a symbol for the Word of God (cf. Isaiah 13:19–22; 55:11). The heathen were too irresponsible for even Satan to use them to his best advantage. But Judaism, having a form of godliness without its power, was and is ideally suited to his purposes. Only those who have heard the Gospel and have "done despite unto the Spirit of grace" are irrevocably lost (cf. Hebrews 10:29).

Given that at the time it was spoken this parable contemplated the fate of unbelieving Israel, no discerning Bible student who is also familiar with Church history can doubt that it contains a needful lesson for Christians as well. Just as our Lord and

His apostles repeatedly forewarned, many early churches were engulfed by a tidal wave of pseudo-Christian superstition and idolatry. From that time onward for a thousand years or more, an "unclean spirit" dominated most of Christendom. Then came a season of reformation. One zealot swept the house, another one garnished it, and others have taken their turns with the broom and the brush. Now, alas! the ghost of paganism has returned with a host of demons, which—for all their seeming sophistication, are more pernicious than itself. Superstitions once discredited are now dignified as infallible dogmas, and rationalism has spawned an evil brood of atheistic philosophies, right in the pulpit, that put medieval fictions in the shade. The Master's name still meets us on the bulletin board, but all too often our gilded creeds hang on the walls of an unholy house while He stands in the cold outside the door (cf. Revelation 3:20). The Bible has been "demythologized," and "God is dead." Christendom, never so enlightened nor ever so blind, is being readied for the Man of Sin. The "mystery of iniquity" working as never before, the great Apostate Church of the Apocalypse is taking shape before our very eyes (cf. II Thessalonians 2:7; Revelation 17). The faithless bride degenerates into a spiritual harlot—worse for having soiled her garments in the light than had she remained in darkness and taken no vows at all.

In the final analysis, this parable, as the rest of Jesus' teaching, poses a challenge to the individual, since any corporate group— the Church no less than Jewry—is composed of responsible human beings, each of whom must answer for himself before the Lord. Nor is the issue here as mysterious or rare as most of us seem to think. It is as simple as the choice between life and death, as universal as mankind's confrontation with a holy God.

As sinners by nature, we are all enslaved by the unclean spirit when we leave the womb. Sooner or later, somewhere, somehow, we all come under the influence of the Gospel, and our wills are liberated to resist or acquiesce in the overtures of grace. If we acquiesce, the Holy Spirit enables and inclines us to repent of sin and place our trust in Christ of our own accord. However, if we resist, we make it morally impossible for Him to engender repentance and faith in our hearts. This, as may be seen from numerous Biblical examples, is seldom—if ever—an absolutely punctiliar occurrence, but comes about gradually as a self-willed person becomes more and more impervious to the truth. Quite often, those who thus resist the Gospel try to quiet their consciences by adopting convenient reforms, professing religion, or by devoting themselves to some particular system of doctrine or philosophy. They would rather do anything else than die to sin and the world by casting their lot with Christ, but once He is rejected, all other courses lead to the same end: consummate depravity and inevitable doom. It is as simple as that. The unpardonable sin—the only sin that damns—is the human will's defiance of the Holy Spirit when He undertakes to impart the gift of grace. It is resisting the truth instead of acquiescing in its power. It is one's abuse of his freedom until He becomes impersuasible and thus confirmed in incorrigible unbelief.

And such resistance cannot take place until one hears the Gospel. It never happens, nor can it happen, accidentally or unconsciously. Just as the only way to be saved is to accept Christ on purpose—likewise, the only way to be damned is to reject Him on purpose. There comes a time when everyone, on having heard the Gospel, must make a definite, all-decisive, irrevocable response. Woe to him who, in that crucial moment of truth, makes the wrong response!

> For it is impossible for those who were once enlightened, and have tasted the heavenly gift, and were made partakers of the Holy Ghost, and have tasted the good word of God, and the powers of the world to come, if they shall fall away, to renew them again unto repentance; seeing they crucify to themselves the Son of God afresh, and put him to an open shame . . . For if we [in this way] sin willfully after we have received the knowledge of the truth, there remaineth no more sacrifice for sins, but a certain fearful looking for of Judgment and fiery indignation, which shall

devour the adversaries. He that despised
Moses' law died without mercy under two or
three witnesses: of how much sorer punishment,
suppose ye, shall He be thought worthy, who
hath trodden under foot the Son of God, and
hath counted the blood of the covenant, wherewith He was sanctified, an unholy thing, and
hath done despite unto the Spirit of grace?
(Hebrews 6:4-6; 10:26-29).

Verily, "the last state of that man is worse than the first" (verse
45).

SECTION THREE
THE KINGDOM MISSION

The new disclosure would unveil the outlines of a Mystery. ... It had always been a definite part of God's great dispensational program, but unlike many other major epochs of history, it was not made known until the time came for it to be fulfilled.

Preliminary Thoughts on the Mystery Parables

Introduction and background. We have seen that our Lord's illustrations often reflect the progressive development of His teaching ministry, which in turn reflects the salient epochs of His public career. Most of His teaching and all of His parables were concerned, directly or indirectly, with the explication and establishment of a Kingdom—one which, having been foretold by the Hebrew prophets, was now "at hand." At least, Jesus, like John the Baptist before Him, had been proclaiming that the promised Kingdom was at hand. Now, having pleaded with the Chosen Nation for about eighteen months or more, He had been rebuffed by unbelief at almost every turn. The natural heirs of the Davidic Covenant were in no way ready to accept their national heritage on the terms of the Gospel. What then? Had the promised King been sent in vain? Would God have to alter His sovereign plan?

The seven parables of Matthew 13 were given to meet and answer these knotty questions. To understand them, it will be helpful to inquire, in advance, into aspects of their "mystery" or "secrets," beginning with a significant incident recorded in the preceding chapter. There we find our rejected Lord and King surrounded by His disciples as He teaches in a house in the city of Capernaum. He is interrupted by the announcement that His mother and brethren—His biological relatives—have just arrived outside and wish to speak to Him. They seem to have concluded that He is beside Himself and have come to take Him home. Jesus makes use of this occasion to prepare His disciples for one underlying secret of the forthcoming parables:

> He answered and said unto them that told him,
> Who is my mother? and who are my brethren?
> And He stretched forth his hands toward his
> disciples, and said, Behold my mother and my
> brethren! For whosoever shall do the will of my
> Father which is in heaven, the same is my
> brother, and sister, and mother (Matthew 12:46-
> 50).

These words clearly imply that He is now renouncing all purely temporal relationships and aspirations, and is introducing a spiritual Kingdom which is to consist of those—whoever they may be—who are wholeheartedly submissive to the will of God. He is preparing the way to inform His disciples that the Kingdom of God must pass through a previously unrevealed mystery phase before it is finally manifested in its originally expected form upon the earth.

Against this background and from this point of view, Christ presents, and we must understand, the mystery parables.

Examination. To this end, it may be well to begin with a few observations about the "Kingdom idea" and why our Lord was justified in introducing the new Mystery Kingdom while still declaring that the traditionally expected Davidic order was at hand. God's Kingdom has so many different aspects that an undiscriminating Bible 101 student may become confused by the various terms by which it is designated in the Scriptures; and the Christian public's perplexity on this subject has been aggravated, more than relieved, by many popular expositors.

Sometimes the doctrine of the Kingdom is generalized at the expense of dispensational considerations essential to any well-rounded interpretation. Alternately, it is subjected to so much meticulous hairsplitting that the doctors cannot agree among themselves. Perhaps it will be best for us to attempt to ascertain the usual meaning of the Kingdom idea as it finds expression in the Scriptures—without insisting on anything more or less than the Bible actually reveals about its relevance to various stages of human history.

To find this meaning, we must begin by contemplating God Himself, for the Kingdom idea derives from a consideration of who and what He is.

Apart from the various names identifying God with His several attributes, it will suffice to say that, as the almighty Creator and Judge of the world, He is a peerless Sovereign over His domain. Whatever else he is, he is a King. This statement being true, His Kingdom, in its broadest sweep, is obviously coextensive with the entire area under His control. In this sense, all the universe—including every man, angel, demon, and even Satan—belongs to the Kingdom of God.

However, in a stricter sense, the Kingdom of God consists of those who are voluntarily submissive to His will. Under the old Theocratic Covenant, the nation of Israel occupied that nominal position in the world (cf. Exodus 19:5–6). Moreover, God promised to send His Messiah to Israel to be the head of an abiding royal theocracy on earth (cf. Micah 5:2). This verse referred to the Kingdom that both John the Baptist and Jesus declared to be at hand at the time of the Savior's first advent. Jesus called it the "kingdom of heaven;" He contemplated it as a system in which the will of God would be as truly supreme as it is in heaven.

The Jews were slow to apprehend and unwilling to accept this moral and spiritual aspect of the Kingdom. The Kingdom Jesus proposed was not to be just a political state, but a holy commonwealth completely dedicated to the service of God in the person of His Messiah. It was not to entail a reign of law, but a realization of the Law's ideal through the achievements of a righteous grace. This Kingdom could not be entered by merely subscribing to the formal requirements of a ceremonial code, but only through repentance toward God and trustful submission to the lordship of Christ. This idea, utterly foreign, was obnoxious to the carnal expectations of the Jews.

The Jews were heartily in favor of establishing a temporal empire in which they would enjoy supremacy over the rest of the world, if that could be brought about on their own terms.

But they had no proper conception of the ethical nature of the promised Messianic Kingdom, nor any sympathy whatever with its exalted spiritual aims.

This is not to say that Jesus did not originally offer Israel the earthly Kingdom of which their prophets had spoken: He did—but on the terms of the Gospel (cf. Matthew 12:28). The promise was made to "the lost sheep of the house of Israel" (Matthew 10: 5–6). But to inherit it, they would have to show themselves to be sheep in deed as well as in name. They would have to measure up to Jesus' teachings in the Sermon on the Mount by trusting Him to satisfy the Law on their behalf and bring them into full conformity with its demands. After long centuries of lip service to the Law, the nation for the most part rejected God's appointed means of realizing its aims. Making the most of their privileged position under the legal Covenant, the rank and file of the Jews persisted in spiritual anarchy. Exploiting their advantages as defenders of the ancient faith, the ruling cliques interpreted the Mosaic Code to suit themselves—thus managing to go to almost any excess with complete impunity and little loss of respectability. They viewed the Gospel as a kiss of death to their venerated status quo, a menace to their personal liberties, and a mortal threat to their vested interests.
     As for Jesus, the Jews could never feel at ease as long as He remained alive to challenge their hypocrisy.
     Of course, Jesus knew from the outset what the outcome would be. Yet in all good faith, He offered them the promised Kingdom, knowing all the while that they would take His life instead of bowing to His claims (cf. Matthew 12:40; 16:21). Nor did this lay Him liable to a charge of inconsistency, for, sharing the mind of God, He understood, as no mere human being ever could, how God permits the freedom of the human will and at the same time overrules and sometimes even utilizes its rebellious choices in a way that achieves His own overriding purposes. In this case, Jesus knew that, by dying at the hands of His unruly subjects, He would make it morally possible for them, along with the rest of us, to be forgiven and received into the Mystery Kingdom on the terms of the Gospel.

Preliminary Thoughts on the Mystery Parables

Now the time had come to inform His disciples of what was about to take place. They must understand that the earthly Kingdom would be deferred—their King would be crucified, and His Kingdom would take on a hitherto unrevealed form until the time arrived when Israel would be morally prepared for her belated exaltation. The disciples needed to know these things, lest they be overwhelmed with disappointment in the tragic days that lay ahead. Here is the purpose of the Mystery Parables: to brief the disciples on the course of Christianity during the interval between Christ's rejection and His return in glory at the end of this age (cf. verses 11, 16–17).

The new disclosure would unveil the outlines of a Mystery design which had not been expressly revealed before that time (cf. verses 34–35). It had always been a definite part of God's great dispensational program, but unlike many other major epochs of history, it was not made known until the time came for it to be fulfilled. Prophets had foreseen the establishment of the Messianic Kingdom, but they were not aware that it would pass through an intermediate phase before its eventual manifestation on earth—the coming of this phase being part of the Mystery. Doubtless, God's reason for this arrangement was to leave the way open for the Jews of that day to exercise uninhibited freedom in rejecting the proffered Kingdom, just as He knew they would—and this event, too, was part of the Mystery.

It was not a question of Jesus' undertaking the impossible or overpledging Himself, for He could and would have done what He proposed on the terms He proposed. His terms were part of His offer. Therefore, though it was morally impossible for Him to fulfill His offer on any other terms, He was in no wise being disingenuous in making it. Nor was He taken by surprise when Jewry's unbelief precipitated the ensuing crisis. Knowing the Jews, being what they were, could not because they would not meet His terms, He had resolved to lay down His life to redeem all mankind, to ensure the salvation of His elect in the course of time (cf. John 5:34, 40).

Sidelights. All background discussion so far is revealed in the first twelve chapters of Matthew. To complete our preliminary work, let us glance at several accompanying sidelights in the thirteenth chapter, where the Mystery Parables are found.

1. The first parable occurs in the opening verse, where we are told that Jesus delivered these parables on the same day that He renounced His natural relationships with Mary and His brethren, acknowledging His moral and spiritual ties with believers in general. This timing is a matter of critical significance; if the Mystery Parables were spoken immediately after our Lord had disavowed an exclusive relationship with natural Israel, this circumstance indicates that they were meant to illustrate subjective and objective aspects of the Mystery Kingdom as complementary parts of a spiritual order flourishing in the milieu of a natural world. Our Lord's eyes were on the future, and His parables envisioned the characteristic features of a new Theocracy both as to its intrinsic nature and its external form. Thus, the timing of their delivery provides a helpful clue to their interpretation.

2. The reason Jesus gave for His extensive use of parables on this occasion (cf. verses 10-17) also sheds a good deal of light on how they should be interpreted. He had employed a number of similitudes before, but occasionally, without much elaboration, to illustrate truths which were otherwise more or less self-evident. But now the disciples noticed that whereas most of His former teaching had been remarkably plain, He was couching almost all of His current lessons in conundrum-like analogies that seemed to conceal as much as, or more than, they revealed.

    When His disciples asked Him why He was adopting this new procedure, He answered "Because it is given unto you to know the mysteries of the kingdom of heaven, but to them [the skeptical crowd] is not given" (verse 11). He had been speaking plainly to the masses, and most of His audience had willfully "closed their eyes" to the truth (verse 15). Even though Jesus had addressed them in the familiar language of the prophets of the old Theocracy, they had not understood (verses 12–13). Still, among the heedless

Preliminary Thoughts on the Mystery Parables

"children of the flesh" (cf. Romans 9:8), our Lord had found some true "Israelites" who had "ears to hear (verse 9). *They* were "children of the promise" (cf. Romans 9:8), true Jews (cf. Romans 2:28, 29), and members of the true "Israel of God" (cf. Galatians 6:16). They must be initiated into the mysteries of the Kingdom. They could learn its secrets. The King would not cast such pearls before swine; from now on He would veil His language in way that reserved its secrets for believing ears. The skeptical throngs would hear, but not understand; would see, but not perceive (cf. verses 11-15).

3. Why did Jesus change His basic method of teaching at this particular time, henceforth confining Himself to the use of parables that no one but His closest followers could totally understand?

   His object was to divulge some needful information to His disciples while—for the time at hand—withholding it from the unbelieving crowd. The disciples must be prepared for the terrible shock awaiting them at Calvary and assured that the Kingdom would survive in a new, unexpected form, despite the postponement of our Lord's Davidic reign. They needed to know what issues, what opposition, and what progress to look for in the days that lay ahead. Meanwhile, nothing should be said to give the fickle throngs an excuse for refusing to accept a Kingdom admittedly in abeyance at the time. In His earlier addresses Jesus had hinted at some of these disclosures, but never plainly: His allusions had always been in side remarks not fully understood in the absence of further details. Now He was confiding those additional details to His disciples alone, still leaving the uninitiated masses where they were from the start, that is, confronted with a Kingdom still at hand as far as they knew. But to His followers, who had committed themselves to Him already, for better or worse, these Mystery Parables unlocked the dark secrets of the future—and opened a vista of hope through the coming storm. We should keep this situation in mind as we begin to interpret them.

4. We find, also, the following word of explanation injected

into the record by Matthew himself:

> All these things spake Jesus unto the multitudes
> in parables; and without a parable spake He not
> unto them: that it might be fulfilled which was
> spoken by the prophet, saying, I will open my
> mouth in parables; I will utter things which have
> been kept secret from the foundation of the world
> (verses 34–35).

Aside from this text's obvious reference to the parables in
this series that were addressed to a general audience, this
inspired commentary is doubtless equally applicable to
those which were shortly to be spoken to His disciples in
private. Matthew was quoting from Asaph, in Psalms 78:2,
ascribing the psalmist's words to the inspiration of Christ.
This scripture tells us, again, that the Mystery Kingdom
was incorporated at the beginning in the secret counsels of
God, though it remained for Christ to make it known to
men at this particular time. Foreknowing all that would
happen, God had planned for Jesus to offer the Kingdom
to Israel on the terms of the Gospel and then, when she
refused to accept it on those conditions, to introduce this
Mystery Kingdom as a protemporaneous arrangement for
the benefit of all who do submit to Jesus' lordship during
the present age. But, to ensure the genuineness of the
Savior's offer and uninhibited freedom in Israel's response,
this phase of God's redemptive program was never meant
to be revealed until the time came for Christ to accomplish
it—and even then it was to be divulged to believers alone.

The question might be raised whether this Mystery is
the same as that which Paul declares to have been "kept
secret since the world began" (Romans 16:25). In a general
sense, with certain qualifications, yes—although definitely
Paul's "mystery" is not the immediate reference of these
parables. The "mystery" in each passage has to do, more
or less, with the same historical era. Here, in Matthew, the
reference is to the Kingdom of Heaven; in the Pauline

Epistles, attention is focused on the Church. Of course, we are now aware that the Mystery Kingdom and the Church are inseverably related, so much so that both are involved in a single composite Mystery. However, in this section of Matthew, there is no allusion whatever to the Church as such. We shall do well to recognize that the Mystical Body of Christ, as such, is *not* the subject of these Kingdom parables, though it is certainly discernible here by many Bible students who are familiar with the Pauline passages that are related, as seen in retrospect.

5. Of considerable significance is that the disciples were able to grasp at least the basic meaning of these revolutionary disclosures. "Have ye understood all these things?" Jesus asked at the conclusion of the series. "Yea, Lord," was their reply, with which He implicitly concurred (verse 51). Not to say that they understood all the ramifications of this new revelation, as they were to be elaborated in the Apostolic Epistles later on, but it certainly indicates that they were beginning to see at least the general drift of Jesus' current teaching.

Obviously, then, the Savior's metaphors were meant to be taken in their ordinary sense, familiar to the common folk of ancient Palestine, not to be scrutinized and analyzed, as some expositors do, in a scientific manner that His lowly unsophisticated followers never dreamed of—for example, alluding to the chemical processes by which a pearl is formed within an oyster. This intent, also, we must take into account, or else run the risk of losing our way in a maze of speculation and artificiality.

6. There is a good deal of auxiliary information in the Master's concluding words to His disciples on this occasion. After they had professed to understand His Mystery Parables, He went on to explain His reason for taking them into His confidence.

> Therefore every scribe which is instructed unto the kingdom of heaven is like unto a man that is an householder, which bringeth forth out of his

treasure things new and old (verse 52).

Now, having learned the secrets of the Kingdom, each of the disciples occupied the position of a scribe, or official teacher. As such, He should minister those truths to his fellow saints, like a well-to-do host who treats his guests to a variety of wholesome foods, some fresh from the fields and others aged and mellowed in the storage bins.

The disciples were to go forth, serving as "stewards of the mysteries of God" (cf. I Corinthians 4:1), to proclaim a message which was at once both new and old—that is, the Gospel as it had just been reinterpreted by Christ Himself. This message did no violence at all to the old revelations, but it presented them in a light that was altogether new. Hence, it is evident that any correct interpretation of the Mystery Parables must be compatible with the whole sweep of Bible prophecy in the Old and the New Testaments alike.

7.   The fact that the first four of these parables were spoken in public to the multitude, but the remaining three in private to the disciples, provides a valuable clue to their several purposes. It indicates that those reserved for believing ears were meant to instruct the saints by dramatizing their own experience from first to last, whereas the others portrayed the whole sphere of profession, warning or encouraging every man in keeping with his peculiar needs. Thus, all of the Mystery Parables depict the *nominal* membership of the Mystery Kingdom, more or less objectively, as a society of mingled saints and hypocrites. The three private Mystery Parables represent that Kingdom's *actual* constituency, more or less subjectively, as a spiritual commonwealth composed exclusively of regenerate believers.

8.   Finally, it should hardly need to be said that our Lord's own explanatory remarks on the sower (verses 18–23) and on the tares (verses 36–43), as well as on the dragnet (verse 49), are of utmost value as a key, not only to the first four of these parables, but also to the series as a whole. They set forth certain basic principles which both facilitate and restrict the interpretation of the rest. For example,

Preliminary Thoughts on the Mystery Parables

- His comments on the sower forbid us to construe either this or any of the rest of these illustrations as teaching that there will be a universal acceptance of the Gospel during this age;
- His comments on the tares discredit any interpretation that contemplates a converted world before the Lord's return; and
- His remarks on the dragnet invalidate the notion that even all those who *profess* faith will be genuinely saved.

We cannot afford to disregard the Teacher's own yardstick, if we are to "rightly divide" the lessons He has given us.

All discussion so far has been introductory exposition to prepare us for understanding the mystery parables. We have just been getting our shop in order and assembling our tools. Having thus prepared ourselves, it is now a relatively simple matter to perform the task itself.

Now we must project ourselves into the Biblical setting, listen as if through the ears of those who sat at Jesus' feet, and evaluate the teaching of our rejected Lord and King against the background from which He spoke. And, of course, we have the advantage accruing from more than 1,900 years of research and observation on this scene in which the "secrets" of the Kingdom are currently unfolding before our eyes.

11

THE SOWER

The Propagation of the Kingdom

Primary text: Matthew 13:3-8; 18-23
Cf. Mark 4:1-20; Luke 8:4-15.

Our Lord spoke this parable to the multitudes, in the presence of His disciples—beside the Sea of Galilee, near Capernaum—during the autumn of the second year of His public ministry.

Introduction. The Savior obviously intended this parable to acquaint His disciples with the method by which the Mystery Kingdom was to be promoted, and to show them what results they should and should not expect. At the same time, He meant it to warn the multitudes against the danger of ignoring or responding halfheartedly to the Gospel. The warning had to be delivered in a way that would give the crowd no pretext for refusing to own Him as their promised King on grounds that it would not make sense to accept a king who was admittedly about to die, or to yield allegiance to a Kingdom that was to be deferred. To accomplish both of these purposes at a single stroke, He addressed the whole crowd with a parable designed to cut like a two-edged sword.

Examination and interpretation. "Behold, one sowing went forth to sow" (verse 3, *literal*). This is the actual form of the opening statement in the original, showing the emphasis is not on the identity of the sower, but on the act of sowing, whoever the sower may be. Emphasis is further suggested by the predominance of verbal action in Jesus' language: "one *sowing* went forth to *sow*, and when He *sowed* . . ." Of course, we know that Jesus Himself was the principal Sower. His disciples, too, were sowers; but the identity of the sower in this parable is not asserted either here or in our Lord's ensuing interpretation. Here the sowing itself is stressed as the means by which the Kingdom must be advanced, and that text is followed by a graphic depiction of the results which must be expected, wherever and whenever that method is employed.

There has to be a sower—a preacher, teacher, personal witness, or missionary—who goes forth to disseminate the Gospel. But whoever does the sowing, the results will very likely be about the same.

The seeds represent the "word of the kingdom" (verse 19), from which explanation it is apparent that, although this parable lacks the usual introduction, "The kingdom of heaven is like unto thus and so," it is nevertheless as much concerned with Kingdom truth as any of the rest. Still, it does not describe the Kingdom itself, but rather the manner in which the Kingdom is to be propagated and the normal response to be expected. It shows, among other things, that the Kingdom is not to be established by the sword, nor by any other such means, but by the preached word—with the result that only those who hear and obey the gospel will survive all odds and bring forth fruit, making their "calling and election" sure (cf. II Peter 1:8–10).

Primarily, this parable taught the disciples (and teaches us) that the Mystery Kingdom is to be promoted by the preaching of the Gospel, and that whenever and wherever it is preached, the results will reflect the responses of those who hear it, depending on whether, and to what extent, they resist or acquiesce to the message of grace.

What results? The results depend on *where* the seeds fall,

that is, on *who* hears the message in any given case.

In this parable before us, Jesus provides four examples of where the seeds may fall and what results to expect in each case.

1. Some of the seeds fall "by the way side" (verses 4, 19), which is to say, alongside the road or perhaps beside a footpath that runs through a field—not on it, but beside it. They fall upon, but not into, the neglected border ground. There is no penetration whatever. Although there is definitely an encounter between seeds and soil, no interaction occurs— no response, no growth, no fruit—because the edges along the pathway have not been broken by the plow.

    Jesus, in His ensuing comments, shows this situation is like the case of a man whose heart has never been stirred and harrowed by conviction, and who therefore, when He hears the Gospel with only his ears, "understandeth it not" (verse 19). He hears the words but does not perceive their spiritual meaning or experience their quickening power. The message, obstructed by an indifferent attitude, never finds its way into the subsoil of his heart. To him the Bible may be good literature, a treasury of ancient lore, or even a valuable manual on religion or ethics, but little or nothing more. So the precious seeds of life and immortality are left to the birds, or "fowls."

    The seeds do not succumb to *chance*. There are no birds of chance, not in the Master's reckoning. Everything has a cause. God works, and the devil works—both on purpose. Jesus tells us that the Wicked One snatches away the seeds that fall beside the road. The devil uses "fowls" such as subversive institutions, skeptical teachers, or apostate preachers—also doubt, fear, indifference, lust, and pride— all kinds of agents—but it is Satan, a personal adversary, who lurks in ambush to exploit the impenitence of men. What makes a heart impervious to truth is this impenitence, born of deliberate impersuasibility. Nor are there exceptions to this rule. Whoever preaches the word of the kingdom, he will find no convert where human *will* meets sovereign mercy with sullen contempt—not even Christ nor His apostles, much less the rest of us. In so many words, the Savior seems to have been telling His disciples:

We have a tremendous audience here today, but entertain no illusions about its reaction to the Gospel. Much of what I am saying is "going to the birds." It is falling on apathetic ears that have little if any spiritual perception and will soon have even less, so stupefying is the effect of willful unbelief. And so it will be when you go forth to preach; never become discouraged if—when—the "birds" invade, distract, and alienate the fickle crowd.

2. Some of the seeds fall "upon stony places where they [have] not much earth"—on shallow soil underlain by a hidden sheet of solid rock. These seeds spring up quickly, but, having no roots, they soon are "scorched by the sun" and are "withered away" (verses 5–6, 20–21). There are many such "stony places," we are told, in the farm lands of Palestine, and in our parable a plural term is used— not one, but numerous, stony areas.

   Likewise, there are many such hearts wherever the Gospel is preached. Such a person, says the Master, "heareth the word, and anon with joy receiveth it; yet he hath no root in himself, but dureth for a while" (verses 20–21). In this part of the parable, it seems to me, Jesus is telling His disciples:

Do not be deceived by the momentary enthusiasm of many here today. They are novelty-seekers who delight in immediate advantages of the Gospel, but, alas, they have no spiritual depth. Beneath their superficial zeal lie hearts of selfish, stubborn, stony unbelief. They are opportunists, "fair-weather saints"; therefore, when tribulation or persecution arises because of the Word, they'll soon become offended and forsake the faith as readily as they seemed to welcome it at the start. And so it will be when you go forth to evangelize the nations; do not become disheartened when such "converts" lose their ardor and belie their profession.

3. Still other seeds fall "among thorns,"—that is, they fall in soil cluttered with the roots and spores of briars, which may have been chopped down and burnt over but not completely destroyed the year before—"and the thorns [spring] up, and [choke] them" (verse 7). This falling among thorns, we learn from the accompanying explanation, represents the heart of a person who "heareth the word," but with scanty results—because "the care of this world, and the deceitfulness of riches, choke the word, and it becometh unfruitful" (verse 22).

In this case, there is nothing necessarily wrong with the soil itself. For all we know, it may be good, deep, harrowed ground, in excellent condition—except for the lingering thorns. Now, this imagery, illuminated as it is by our Lord's accompanying comments, pictures the heart of a "double minded man" (cf. James 1:8) who receives the Gospel without renouncing his former attachments to the world. He is a "carnal" Christian (cf. I Corinthians 3:1-3), who allows fleshly interests to hamper his spiritual growth and limit his fruitfulness.

On one hand, He enervates himself with anxiety about temporal things; on the other, he exhausts his strength in pursuit of material wealth that will only mock him in the course of time. Thus, while paying so dear a price for the "pleasures of this life" (cf. Luke 8:14), he loses the joy of his salvation and "becometh unfruitful" (verse 22). Not that He is utterly fruitless; the "grain" no doubt heads out at the start, but it is eventually sapped by the burgeoning "thorns," and therefore fails to mature.

This pictures early promise and then later deterioration owing to a lack of singleness of heart. "And this," the Lord seems to have been forewarning His disciples, "must still be expected when you go forth to preach . . ."

4. However, other seeds fall "into good ground, and [bring] forth fruit . . ." (verse 8). This ground is characterized by its unlikeness to the rest; its relative "goodness," then, is manifested by its yield.

- Unlike the inhospitable wayside, it is ready, waiting to receive the newly planted seeds.
- Unlike the superficial, stony ground, it is deep and nourishing.
- Unlike the briar-infested ground, it is not encumbered by any competitive growth.

And the same is the case with corresponding audiences of the Gospel, to wit:

- Unlike the callous unbeliever represented by the ground along the wayside, the good-ground hearer understands (literally *takes in* or *absorbs*) the glorious Kingdom message (verse 23).
- Unlike those who exhibit superficial, stony-ground emotionalism, he perseveres just as vigorously as he first responds.
- Unlike the double-minded, thorny-ground believer, he is unreservedly consecrated to the will of God.

Still, it is obvious that these classifications leave room for overlapping variables. Even among the good-ground saints, there are varying degrees of faithfulness reflected in the harvests' yields, "some an hundredfold, some sixty, some thirty" (verse 23).

Thus, while forewarning His disciples (and the rest of us) that faithful preaching will meet with disappointments, the Master insists that the harvest will be successful enough to justify the efforts of those who sow. Though much labor may *seem* to be wasted along the wayside, in stony places, and among thorns, God's Word will not "return unto [Him] void" (Isaiah 55:11).

A goodly remnant will respond (cf. Romans 9:29). As many as are "ordained to eternal life" will believe (Acts 13:48). And some of these will give convincing proof of their calling and election by yielding abundant fruit (cf. II Peter

1:8-10). So far, so good.

Faulty Interpretation 1. This passage makes perfect sense as long as it is construed in keeping with its central theme—but only confusion will follow if we attempt to extort a message of salvation from its details. By such mistaken interpretations:

a. a hyper-Calvinist can "prove," from the soil's passivity, that this parable teaches the doctrine of Irresistible Grace;

b. an Armenian can "prove," from the withered wheat-stalk on stony ground, that a regenerate believer can fall from grace; and

c. a Pelagian can "prove," from the naked language of the text, that a still unregenerate sinner has "an honest and good heart" (cf. Luke 8:15).

However, most (if not all) of these anomalies vanish when we recognize that they are induced by drawing inferences from details which have no essential connection with the primary lesson of the parable.

Dual purpose. No *one* parable illustrates all the peripheral connotations of its dominant theme, nor is this one meant to spell out every item (or even all the major items) in a complete theology regarding salvation. Its dual purpose is:

• to show that the Kingdom is to be extended through the propagation of the Gospel; and

• to forecast the normal results of personal witnessing.

The parable serves that dual purpose; it neither purports nor pretends to do anything else.

Necessarily, it does exhibit various points of contact with related truths operating outside the scope of the illustration itself, but its imagery is meant to elucidate one basic theme, with no apparent adaptation to any synthetic scheme. This is a fact to be recognized and reckoned with, regardless of one's predilections to the contrary. It is so because it *is* so, and that is well enough. It eliminates difficulties which would otherwise be well-nigh insuperable.

Faulty Interpretation 2. Less serious—rather amusing, in fact— is the way some commentators insist on dividing the soil into four *equal* parts, surmising that one-fourth, and only one-fourth, of those who hear the Word are good-ground saints. Whereas, if we press the question of proportions, considering the intent of the sower, it would seem most likely that relatively few of the seeds fell beside the road, as few as possible on the stony or the thorny soil, and most of them on the choicest ground. That would certainly be the case as far as any competent sower could have his way about it in actual practice. But all these speculations are beside the point! Our Lord did not introduce the idea of proportions at all. He only emphasized the varied responses of several different kinds of soil and left the matter there. We see these four types reflected in our congregations from year to year. It is neither within our province, nor within our power, to separate and classify them statistically.

Back to basics. It is seriously doubtful that most, if any, of these lateral questions so much as crossed the minds of the disciples. To them this parable simply revealed the secret that the Mystery Kingdom would be promoted by the preaching of the Gospel, with the result that, though many of those who heard it would be unresponsive and unfruitful, a good many others would gladly receive it and go on to demonstrate its wonderworking power in their lives.

The Book of Acts records precisely the events this parable visualized. From first to last, the Kingdom was expanded by means of "sowing," that is, preaching, teaching, and personal witnessing. The results were, by and large, about the same in every case: some mocked, others postponed decision, others believed (cf. Acts 17:32-34).

Moreover, those who did respond exhibited various degrees of fruitfulness:

- some (such as Alexander and Hymenaeus) forsook the faith;
- some (such as Demas) were overcome by ambitions of the worldly sort;
- some (such as young John Mark) relaxed their efforts and retreated under pressure; but
- others (such as Peter, James, and Paul, as well as most of the other apostles) were faithful even unto death.

So it has been down through the centuries to the present day. Of those who hear the Gospel, some reject it, some embrace it temporarily, some hold on to it halfheartedly. But *some* obey it with such unstinted devotion that they themselves personify its inseminating and fructifying power!

12

THE TARES

The Heterogeneous Character of the Kingdom

Primary text: Matthew 13:24-30; 36-43.

Our Lord spoke this parable to the multitudes, in the presence of His disciples—beside the Sea of Galilee, near Capernaum—during the autumn of the second year of His public ministry.

Introduction. To discover the principal "Kingdom secret" in this parable, let us survey it by the following method: we will look first at the details of the story, then at their significance as revealed by Jesus' own explanatory remarks. Having completed our examination, we shall draw conclusions from our findings in both of those areas.

Examination of the story. In following this procedure, we shall consider, in order, these features of the story: the characters; various items in the general setting; and the development of events.

A. *The characters*

   1. *The sower* is the leading character, of course—the man who sowed the "good seed," or wheat (verse 24). He is a person of considerable means; he owns the field and barn; the servants and the reapers are, evidently, his personal slaves. As the householder, he appears to be a

---

man of known authority in his domain: he commands, and others obey. That he is alert and industrious is seen from the fact that he himself both tends his field and exercises careful supervision over his whole estate. Moreover, he exhibits patience, foresight, and prudence to meet a vexing situation with a definite plan, at once safeguarding his crop and resolving a serious problem without resorting to rash or self-defeating expedients.

He is not, however, a storybook tyrant who succeeds by arbitrarily suppressing every potential opponent. He does have an *enemy* (verse 25) whom he allows to work without restraint until his evil devices are thwarted by the inexorable laws of a moral universe.

2. *The enemy* is a sower, also, but a malicious one who, under cover of darkness, defiles his neighbor's field with noxious seed and then flees from the scene of his crime to conceal his connection with the mischief he has wrought. He is a cunningly wicked scoundrel who takes delight in the prospect of another man's embarrassment or loss.

3. *The servants* are the householder's loyal bondsmen; their chief duty is to promote his interests by attending to the cultivation of his land (cf. verse 27).

4. *The reapers* are bondsmen of another cast, charged with the special task of harvesting the crop (cf. verse 30).

B. *The setting (circumstantial items)*
   1. *The field.* Unlike the field in the former parable, which might have been just any piece of arable land, this one is expressly identified as the householder's property (cf. verse 24). There can be no doubt about that—or, if its possession is shared by the servants and reapers, that is only because they, too, belong to him.
   2. *The good seed* (verse 24) is wheat, each grain of which is identified by the plant it produces.
   3. *The tares* (verse 25) are wild "bastard wheat," or, as it is sometimes called, "cheat;" it also reproduces itself in its issue.
   4. *The blade* is the initial foliage grown on the planted

grain, either wheat or tare, with the two varieties being so similar in appearance during their early stages of growth that no difference is readily discernible.

5. *The fruit.* Only when the "fruit" (verse 26), or "ears," begin to appear are wheat and tares distinguished easily, by sight.

6. *The harvest* (verse 30) is the ingathering of the crop at the end of the growing season.

7. *The bundles* (verse 30) are loosely bound sheaves of grain.

8. *The barn* (verse 30) is the householder's storage house, or granary.

C. *Development of events*

As to the element of time, this parable covers a normal crop year, and only four events are mentioned:

1. the sowing of the wheat;
2. the surreptitious oversowing of the tares;
3. the servants' discovery of the enemy's deviltry; and
4. the final harvesting.

Jesus' interpretation. Now let us see how our Lord interprets these particulars. Worthy of notice, to begin with, is the fact that He applies the principal reference of the story to Himself. When the disciples ask Him to explain the "parable of the tares of the fields" (verse 36), He ignores their preoccupation with the tares and answers, "He that soweth the good seed is the Son of man" (verse 37). True, the disciples are quite correct when they connect this parable's specific revelation with the appearance of evil in the Master's realm. But our Lord's reply suggests that such a turn of events, however significant, must be regarded as deriving its importance from its meaning to Himself. The principal character is *the sower,* the householder, the Son of man—not His enemy. Whatever the enemy does is relatively insignificant—except as it affects the Householder's personal interests. With the Son of Man on the scene, whoever else appears is necessarily relegated to a subordinate role. The enemy deserves no particular notice except as *His* enemy; the tares are notable only as an affront to *Him.*

Nor is it mere coincidence that the legitimate sower is made to represent the Son of man. The word for "man" in both of these parables is the generic term, for "Son of man" designates not only an individual human being, but a *human* individual. The planting was done by the "Son of man," not as the Eternal Son of God, but as the Word of God Incarnate. The planting was done when He died and rose again, as He Himself was to declare at a later time: "Except a corn of wheat fall into the ground and die, it abideth alone; but if it die, it bringeth forth much fruit" (John 12:24). What is the Gospel, or the "word of the kingdom," if not a verbal embodiment of that reality? The Son of God became a man, and as such, He died and rose again. It was a *Man* who planted the seeds that "bringeth forth much fruit," and He did so by "offering himself' (cf. Hebrews 9:14). I do not suggest that the disciples, at this early stage in their spiritual training, were able to perceive this meaning of the sowing, but that this truth was in Jesus' mind. It is reflected in what He actually said. The rejected King had to die, but in doing so, He would "sow" Himself in the "field" so that the "children of the kingdom" might become the spiritual issue of His triumph over death.

A larger purpose *would be* achieved, in spite of any and all machinations of *the enemy*, whom Jesus expressly identified as "the devil" (verse 39). This foe, having wrought his pernicious mischief, hides himself; the servants are totally unsuspecting of his personal agency on the scene. The *servants* are obviously the ministers of Christ, but since their role is incidental to the major lesson of this parable, they are not even mentioned in our Lord's interpretation. On the other hand, He tells us that the *reapers* are His angels (verse 39), information we need to know because of their prominence in the closing harvest scene.

The significance of the field, the tares, and the harvest is clearly defined—and the remaining details, explained—in their connection with ensuing events. The *field* is "the world" (verse 38), that is, the cosmos, the orderly sphere of civic life, the human community as an organized society in a moral universe. And it is "his" (verse 24); it belongs to the Son of man—not only as His creation, but also as His purchased possession. Although it is true that He, as the inseparable son of God, created the world, He is represented here as Christ the *Man* who, as such, claims it as His own by right of redemption.

The *good seed*, or *wheat*, is "the children [or, literally, *the sons*] of the kingdom" (verse 38). In the former parable the seed was the "word of the kingdom," but here the Word (contemplated as the Kingdom message or as its personification in Christ) is viewed as the begetting seed embodied in it's issue. James tells us that God, of his own will, "begat . . . us with the word of truth, that we should be a kind of firstfruits of his creatures" (James 1:18). Thus, regenerate believers—having been "born again, not of corruptible seed, but of incorruptible, by the word of God, which liveth and abideth for ever" (I Peter 1:23)—are, as both faithful hearers and the spiritual generation of a risen Lord, the true "sons of the kingdom."

The *tares* are "the children [or, literally, *the sons*] of the wicked one" (verse 38). Not only unregenerate sinners, but—in some sense—"regenerate *un*believers," the seed of the Serpent, the spawn of their "father the devil," born below (cf. John 8:44). But they may easily be mistaken for wheat until their evil *fruit* eventually betrays their real identity (cf. John 3:10).

The *harvest* is "the end of the world" (verse 39)—that is, the consummation of the present age—an end that will disclose the aggregate of all the cumulative issues remaining unresolved until intervening processes of history reach a climactic crisis at our Lord's return.

Analysis. Clearly, this parable contemplates the entire course of the present era. It fits into an overall chronological program in connection with the other six parables, and like each of the rest, it has a point of contact with every epoch of this entire age. More than any other, it delineates the general trend of the entire Christian dispensation.

As we have already pointed out, the original planting was done by Christ Himself, both actually (through His death and resurrection) and orally (through His proclamation of the Gospel). But Satan, by counter-sowing Christendom with pernicious error, has from the outset infiltrated the sphere of Christian profession with unregenerate hypocrites. Wherever the Gospel is proclaimed, Satan proliferates insidious heresies. Just as truth has brought about the begettal of real believers, his deceptive propaganda has interspersed the Kingdom with spurious "sons." Satan's deviltry is always indiscernible for a while, since nominal converts of every kind typically subscribe to more or less the same externals. However, in keeping with the thematic thrust of this parable, the mounting evidence of insincere profession on almost every hand goes to show that there must be a great many tares among the wheat.

Leave them alone. However—and this message is critically important—our Lord commands us, His ministers, to leave the "tares" alone rather than undertaking to weed them out—lest, in our well-intentioned but misdirected zeal, we should "root up also the wheat with them" (verse 29). In fact, just as we learn from the bitter lessons of ecclesiastical history, too often it is the *tares themselves* who propose to purge the field! Hence, we are told to "let both grow together until the harvest" (verse 30), when Christ Himself will separate the evil from the good.

The harvest. For this harvest He will employ His angels (verse 41) as the *reapers* (verse 30). At Christ's command, they will first gather up the tares and "bind them in bundles," but after that they will burn, or, literally, "set them on fire" (verse 30). In fact, it appears that even now the stage is being set for just such a consummation. Right now, in our own generation, all sorts of bundles—apostate councils and federations, as well as other organizations—are being bound together in readiness for the "furnace of fire" (verse 42).

But not so with the wheat! It will be safely garnered into glory while the wrath of God consumes His enemies. When all of Satan's baseborn sons are wailing and gnashing their teeth in "the lake of fire," then "shall the righteous shine forth in the kingdom of their Father" (verse 43).

The Mystery Kingdom. So, in what respect may the Kingdom of Heaven be likened to the situation we are considering in this parable? Evidently, in some *particular* sense.

However, such a vast, prolonged plan could scarcely be fully illustrated within the compass of a sketchy little story in a single paragraph.

It should be so obvious as to need no proof that no specific *one* of these parables presents a *complete* analogy of the interim Mystery Kingdom, but that each of them is meant to bring into focus some special single *aspect* of Kingdom truth.

We have seen that the first one stressed the method by which the Kingdom is to be promoted, as well as that method's anticipated results. The current parable, while assuming all that the first contained, introduces an additional, altogether new revelation: that there is a counter-sower, a counter-planting, and a counter-crop. The Mystery Kingdom is, in some sense, to have a heterogeneous character; there are to be within it many wicked people along with the good.

This new revelation must have come as an unexpected shock to Jesus' disciples, for hitherto, He had insisted that only those who do the will of God can enter the Kingdom. Now He was admitting—nay, *declaring*—that some people who were by no means *of* it would be *in* it, notwithstanding their palpable ineligibility. As with so many other apparent paradoxes in the Scriptures, there was nothing in this new disclosure that was actually inconsistent with previous revelations, in which this one was neither precluded nor divulged. Only now did the disciples *need* to be informed of all the facts, to see how the silence of the Scriptures allows latitude for the occurrence of formerly unpredicted events.

Certainly, only the righteous could belong to the Kingdom in an ethical or *spiritual* sense, but the disciples needed to be warned that there would be many impostors in the *nominal* realm. The Son of Man would seed His Kingdom with wheat, but the devil would oversow the field with cheat—that is the principal "secret" this parable was meant to bring to light.

To the crowd, this story was a simple warning against the wiles of Satan and the fate of those who allow themselves to be used in his opposition to Christ. Thus, while it put the Jews on notice that to reject the Savior would be to share the guilt and the penalty of Satan's deed, it disclosed nothing that could

The Heterogeneous Character of the Kingdom

be used to excuse their rejection of Jesus on the ground that a foredoomed "king" could not be God's Messiah. However, to the disciples, it conveyed a much deeper meaning: namely, the prospect of a mystical *interim* Kingdom, an internal conflict, and a final victory that would usher in the reign of glory which was, for the moment, being deferred.

Serious interpretation guide. Inasmuch as both of the first two Mystery Parables, though spoken publicly, were interpreted privately to the disciples, it is only reasonable to assume their interpretation was intended to furnish a key to the general teaching of the other five as well. Any correct exposition of the others certainly must at least be compatible with our Lord's own comments on the former two. Any manipulation of the rest which contradicts Jesus' authoritative explanation here is bound to be wrong.

Why does this point deserve special emphasis? Because, if duly considered, it will forestall a needless misunderstanding of several of the following Mystery Parables: especially the notion that the whole world will eventually convert, before the Lord's return. Such an idea flies in the face of all that we have learned so far.

According to Jesus' own interpretation of the parable of the sower, only a fraction of those who hear the Gospel will bring forth sufficient fruit to demonstrate genuine profession. According to His interpretation of the parable of the tares, there will be legions of religious unbelievers throughout the course of this age, right up to the end.

Else, what are the tares? And why are they to be burned? And why did Jesus give us this parable at all?

13

THE MUSTARD SEED

The Phenomenal Growth of the Kingdom

Primary text: Matthew 13:31–32
Cf. Mark 4:1-32.

Our Lord spoke this parable to the multitudes, in the presence of His disciples—beside the Sea of Galilee, near Capernaum—during the autumn of the second year of His public ministry.

Introduction. The best way to find the correct interpretation of this passage is to first ascertain what the language actually *says,* and what it *means* by what it actually says—instead of taking for granted that it says what we want it to say. To interpret in this way, we must first identify the principal item in our Lord's analogy, thus putting our fingers on the actual subject of this illustration.

Examination and interpretation. What, then, does our Savior, in this parable, say that the Kingdom of Heaven is like?

Not a man. Not a field. Not an act of sowing, nor anything else that is merely incidental to His central theme. Instead, He tells us, "The kingdom of heaven is like to a grain of mustard seed" (verse 31). This is a *certain* grain of mustard seed, but one which He proceeds to describe as a *typical* specimen of such seeds. However important the other details may be in their respective connections, they occupy a subordinate place in the overall setting of this particular parable.

Now, what is affirmed of the mustard seed in question?

The only direct assertion is that the man took it and sowed it in his field, but clearly implied is that it, like any other ordinary mustard seed, though proverbially smaller than those of other herbs, grew up into a "tree" so large and strong that birds made their roosts in its branches (verse 32). In other words, it is described as having the *usual* features and potentialities known to be characteristic of the species to which it belongs. Instead of being a freakish monstrosity, as some interpreters imagine, it was actually distinguished by its normality—whereby it exhibited the customary size and development of mustard seed in general.

The foregoing paragraph undoubtedly summarizes what the language of this passage says, and it ill becomes those of us who profess to believe in the accuracy of the sacred text to wrest from it substantiation of some cherished theory, even if the theory itself is otherwise unassailable.

Here it is simply said that a certain mustard seed, when planted, displayed the same remarkable growth that any other mustard seed will achieve under similar circumstances. The results of the planting mentioned here are tacitly equated with those known to be commonplace. The subject of this object lesson is a grain of mustard seed; the emphasis is on its phenomenal growth—in keeping with the characteristic tendency of its kind—so that "the least of all seeds" becomes "the greatest among herbs," or a veritable "tree." Not only is this the meaning of the actual language; it is essential to the basic lesson of the parable. The force of the illustration lies in the contrast between the *usual* size of such a seed and the *usual* growth of the plant it produces.

It was precisely because of His audience's familiarity with the normal propensities of a common mustard seed that our Master made use of this particular simile. Nor has Jesus' imagery suffered from the lapse of time; most of us have witnessed this phenomenon in our own backyards. And, travelers tell us that in some parts of Palestine, as well as in certain other countries such as Chile, mustard plants grow vastly taller than here in the United States. It has even been reported that men can ride on horseback under the luxuriant mustard trees in modern Galilee. Biblical evidence of the plant's astonishing size and strength is indicated by the allusion to its branches becoming a habitual lodging place for birds. This is not directly affirmed in the case before us, but it is definitely implied.

Terms. As to the adjunctive terms employed in the main assertion, we find, once again, a *man* and a *field*; a man took the mustard seed and sowed it in "his field." In this parable, the man's identity is not the paramount consideration, nor does the *field* have any special bearing on the principal emphasis here. However, in view of this parable's connection with the preceding one, who can suppress the natural inference that this sower also represents the "Son of man" and that this field also represents "the world"? All the pertinent considerations require acceptance of such an interpretation, for what "man" except the Lord Jesus can be said to have sown a single seed—*the* Seed—that has developed into *His* Kingdom? And where does this Seed bring forth its—His—issue, if not in the world as is also indicated in the former parable? (Cf. verse 38.) However inferential, these conclusions are inherent in the context; they defy refutation.

But let us go on. Can any reverent Christian conversant with the rest of the Scriptures believe that Jesus planted something inherently bad or "monstrous," when He Himself descended into the grave and rose again? (Cf. John 12:24.) This mustard tree depicts the issue of the Savior's own sowing; it cannot represent a monstrous *sphere of profession* in which both good and evil intermingle. No, it represents the regenerate segment of the Mystery Kingdom. It is a heavenly society in an earthly environment: "in the world," but not "of the world," and hence is essentially good, not bad.

The fowls. The foregoing assertion, however, is not to deny that there is indeed a mixed condition in the *visible* Kingdom. Thus, the allusion to birds' seeking shelter in the mustard tree's branches indicates just such a heterogeneous character.

However incidental it may seem, this added detail could not have been introduced except by deliberate design—not in a parable spoken by Jesus to Scripture-conscious Jews. Both He and they were much too familiar with the figure of birds, or *fowls,* for it to have been used without suggesting its ordinary metaphorical connotations to their minds.

For examples, look at the unsavory implications of birds in Ezekiel 31:3-9; Daniel 4:20-22; and Revelation 18:2, where John employs the identical metaphor in his denunciatory description of Babylon. It is incredible that a Jew addressing Jews could have used such imagery without intending His hearers to construe it as meaning that wicked men would seek refuge in the Kingdom "tree," vying with one another for the choicest perches among its limbs. Even in this very chapter, in the parable of the sower, Jesus has represented the agents of the Wicked One as "fowls" (cf. verse 4).

And how history, in succeeding centuries, has confirmed (just as modern history still confirms) that deplorable fact!

This parable, in its connection with the former two, reveals the "secret" that
• although only a fraction of those who hear the Gospel will render a proper response,
• although Satan will infiltrate the *visible* Kingdom with presumptuous impostors,
• the true Kingdom will exhibit marvelous growth—in spite of the parasitic worldlings intent on exploiting its temporal advantages without possessing its moral and spiritual character.

To the carnal crowd, this third parable simply indicated the inevitable ascendancy of an imminent Kingdom and warned against false profession. It divulged no explicit information about the Kingdom's mystical origin in Jesus's death and resurrection that would give the impenitent masses pretext for rejecting the Kingdom of Heaven which was still—for the moment—"at hand," as far as they were concerned.

To the disciples, it held forth the prospect of Christianity's amazing growth from exceedingly small beginnings. It also forewarned of the depredations of "false brethren unawares brought in" (Galatians 2:4). That dual message, it seems to me, sums up the basic teaching of this parable.

14

THE LEAVEN

The Corruption of the Kingdom

Primary text: Matthew 13:33
Cf. Luke 13:20–21.

Our Lord spoke this parable to the multitudes, in the presence of His disciples—beside the Sea of Galilee, near Capernaum—during the autumn of the second year of His public ministry.

Introduction. This is the final one of the four Mystery Parables spoken in public. More so than any of the others in this series, it has become a battleground of perennial controversy. And indeed, if considered alone, apart from its connection with the rest of the Mystery Parables (and with the Bible in general), it can be used as a plausible proof-text for almost any argument ever extorted from it!

A popular but misguided interpretation. One theory often advanced is that the *leaven* symbolizes the Gospel, which will eventually permeate—and Christianize—the whole of human society during the present age. That unfortunate argument forces this passage to belie what it actually affirms!

Such an interpretation unblushingly contradicts Christ's own explanation of the first two parables in this series, denies the corresponding implications of the third, and refutes His comments on the seventh. Moreover, such a view *ignores* the unexceptionable symbolical significance of leaven in every other Scripture. My allegations are founded on sober facts which, given due attention, speak for themselves.

Examination and interpretation. First of all, inasmuch as this parable expressly contemplates the Kingdom of Heaven, we are obligated to construe this depiction in keeping with all the foregoing descriptions of the Mystery Kingdom.

Nature of the Mystery Kingdom. What, then, according to the three preceding parables, is the Kingdom of Heaven?

Broadly speaking, it is
• a field comprising various types of ground.
• a mingled crop of wheat and tares.
• a mustard tree infested with vagrant birds.

In short, it is a nominally Christian realm in which both believers and unbelievers ostensibly pass as citizens. Now, who can honestly visualize a converted *world* in such an anomalous society as that which is pictured here? Moreover, here the imagery is still more explicit. We are told that "The kingdom of heaven is like unto leaven . . ."

As we have already seen, no specific *one* of these parables illustrates *all* the various facets of the Mystery Kingdom, but each of them portrays some particular characteristic of the composite whole. As the typical mustard tree represents the true constituency of the Kingdom (disregarding its baser elements), *leaven* here depicts the Kingdom's baser elements commingled with the true—although it also *characterizes* the nature and influence of what it represents.

So, in this particular sense, one aspect of the Mystery Kingdom is likened to a common household item with a well-known symbolical significance, more specifically to "leaven, which a woman took, and hid in three measures of meal, till the whole was leavened" (verse 33). Anything short of this entire description proves inadequate to the overall design of the parable.

If we bear in mind that leaven here symbolizes certain people characterized by their leavening qualities, we easily see that the question of interpretation, then, hinges on the symbolical meaning of the term *leaven* in the Scriptures as a whole. Nor, with an open Bible before us, should this be hard to determine. Since the real significance of any term depends on what the term means to the one who uses it and to his or her hearers, our task is to find out what leaven meant to Jesus and His audience.

Here a Jewish teacher was addressing orthodox Jews. It is only reasonable to assume that His use of a familiar figure of speech was, in the absence of any hint to the contrary, intended to convey its ordinary, traditional meaning. This being so, do we need to convince any serious student of the Scriptures that ancient Jewry always looked upon leaven as a symbol of *evil*?

Who does not know that . . .

- leaven was strictly forbidden in every Levitical offering that typified Christ? (Cf. Leviticus 2:11; 7:12.)
- sacrificial use of leaven was allowed only in exceptional cases in which *imperfect* worshipers were contemplated in the types? (Cf. Leviticus 7:13; 24:17.)
- Christ Himself often used the term *leaven* as an epithet to designate the doctrine and hypocrisy of the Pharisees, the Sadducees, and the Herodians? (Cf. Matthew 16:6-12; Mark 8:15-21; Luke 12:1.)
- Jesus never employed the term *leaven* in any other than a pejorative sense?
- Paul equated the moral turpitude within the Corinthian church to leaven? (Cf. I Corinthians 5:6-8; Galatians 5:9.)

No, most interpreters—even those holding the mistaken view under discussion—readily admit that leaven retained its evil connotations in every *other* case. How, then, can they seriously contend that here, where a Jew was addressing Bible-reading Jews, it was invested with another, better sense? Especially if they consider that here it was being used to illustrate one of the predominant features of an admittedly imperfect society!

The view of leaven as signifying evil is implied, moreover, by the association of leaven with the *woman* who mixed it in the meal; it is obvious that the woman, too, must be construed in an odious sense. No matter how unpopular now, we must concede that, at the time, it was only natural that a woman be represented as preparing the meal; as to the quantity, "three measures of meal" was most likely the amount ordinarily prepared for a typical Oriental household. Both of these details undoubtedly reflected normal practices among the Jews.

Why, if it would sharpen the point of a lesson, shouldn't Jesus make use of ordinary customs to illustrate spiritual truths?

Sowing and reaping were commonplace in Palestine, and it is recognized on every hand that Jesus, in His teaching, frequently invested these and many other familiar practices with spiritual significance. So it is with both the *woman* and the *meal*. These details are not just so much stage drapery; they are, rather, of the very essence of the play. But what do they mean?

1. *The meal.* Naturally, it represents food; spiritually, it symbolizes the regular diet of the Levitical priests, who subsisted largely on meal-offerings (cf. Revelation 2). Since priests typified saints in general as believer-priests (cf. I Peter 2:9), it clearly represents the *spiritual food* of a believing brotherhood—meaning, the Word of God.

   Hence, Christ, accordingly, agrees with Moses that "Man shall not live by bread alone, but by every word that proceedeth out of the mouth of God" (Matthew 4:4). The *meal*, then, is the Christian message.

   But . . .

   • just as the Kingdom's true citizens are characterized by and identified with the mustard tree, and

   • just as the Kingdom's baser element is characterized by and identified with the leaven,

   • those who believe and preach the Word of God are identified with, and characterized by, their *message*.

   Thus there is a sense in which the *meal* stands not only for the Gospel, but also for individuals who believe and propagate the Gospel.

2. *The woman.* No woman, among the Jews *or* in the early Christian churches, was authorized to administer the Word of God in an official way. So, in any truly spiritual

application of this parable, we must see the *woman* as an unauthorized agent employing religious unbelievers to mix human error with divinely given truth, with the result that nominal Christianity as a whole is vitiated with pernicious heresies. True, our Lord's disciples were not in a position to identify the woman—"that woman Jezebel" (Revelation 2:20), the Apocalyptic harlot (cf. Revelation 17)—as, in the light of subsequent history, we are.

Still, according to their own testimony, the disciples understood the fundamental implications of all the symbols Jesus employed (cf. verse 51). Therefore they were, at minimum, aware from this parable that some unhallowed tool of Satan would diffuse the leaven of error and hypocrisy within the spiritual food that was meant for a "kingdom of priests" (cf. Revelation 1:6; 5:10). That is the secret this parable evidently was meant to reveal.

To the Pharisees, the Sadducees, the Herodians, and their followers, this parable was a veiled indictment of their own perversion of the Law. To the disciples, it contained a warning that the Gospel itself also would be perverted in the days ahead.

Far from encouraging us to believe that the world will be converted during the current age, this parable raises—and leaves with us—the solemn question: "Although the Son of man come, will he, after all, find the faith on the earth?" (Luke 18:8, JBR).

15 & 16

THE HIDDEN TREASURE
AND
THE MERCHANTMAN

The Mystery of the
True Israel of God

Primary text: Matthew 13:44–46.

*Our Lord spoke these two parables to His disciples
in private—at a house in Capernaum—during the
autumn of the second year of His public ministry.*

Introduction. Two Mystery Parables, "The Hidden Treasure"
and "The Merchantman," are so similar in some respects and
so different in others that I have thought it best to treat them
together, in order to examine how both their similarities and
their differences contribute to understanding the message they
convey overall.

Evidently Christ spoke these parables only to His disciples.
They were addressed to and for believing ears, their message
intended for the saints alone. Moreover, they were aptly
phrased to meet the special needs of the disciples at the time.

The disciples, abruptly disillusioned by the apparent shift
in the Savior's teaching, were doubtless in a quandary. We may
even imagine that they were, in their minds, asking:

What is to become of Israel if her Messiah, upon being officially rejected, is to establish this mystical Kingdom altogether independent of Jewish nationalism?

Hasn't Jehovah declared that Israel shall be a "kingdom of priests"? Hasn't He called her His own "peculiar treasure . . . above all people"? (Cf. Exodus 19:5.)

Hasn't He made with her an "everlasting covenant" to that effect? (Cf. Jeremiah 32:40.) Will He now disown His treasure and retract His promises?

How could the disciples, with their Jewish background, have reconciled the prospect of Christ's humiliation—and of Israel's suspension as a Theocratic race—with Messianic prophecies of former times?

Examination and interpretation. Jesus divulged to His disciples the solution to these difficulties with a parable the meaning of which would be spelled out later by the Apostle Paul:

God hath not cast away his people which he fore-knew.

[It is] not as though the word of God hath taken none effect. For they are not all Israel, which are of Israel: neither, because they are the seed of Abraham, are they all children: but, In Isaac shall thy seed be called. That is, They which are the children of the flesh these are not the children of God: but the children of the promise are counted for the seed (Romans 11:2; 9:6-8).

The Hidden Treasure

What the Lord meant this parable to teach His disciples was, apparently, this: Although the unbelieving Jews were about to disqualify themselves as heirs of the promise made to *national*

Israel, the Everlasting Covenant would be fulfilled on a higher plane to the *spiritual seed* of Abraham among both Jews and Gentiles who, as regenerate believers, are, after all, the true "Israel of God" (cf. Galatians 6:16).

The impenitent Jews were merely "children of the flesh;" they were not God's true Israel, not His "peculiar treasure" at all. Though rejected by that carnal nation, Christ had found a "treasure hid in a field"—that is, a believing remnant destined to inherit a thitherto-unheard-of "Mystery Kingdom," in which all of His "sheep" from various "folds" would be united within a single "flock" (cf. John 10:16, RFW).

The *field*, as in the second Mystery Parable, is doubtless the world (cf. verse 38). The Messiah had come "unto his own [things], and his own [people]" had refused to receive Him. Yet He found a chosen remnant that was glad to welcome Him, and "to them gave he power to become the sons of God" (John 1:12). In this respect, then, the Mystery Kingdom is "like unto treasure hid in a field." The *treasure* consists of all true sons of the Kingdom.

The believing remnant was truly hid in the field. Natural Israel was never hid in the world, nor is it now. It has always been decidedly conspicuous, either for good or bad. Under Solomon, it startled the nations with its temporal glory. Since then it has often been the world's sore thumb, "a burdensome stone" (cf. Zechariah 12:3). A perpetual issue, it will not and cannot be ignored.

How astonishing that some otherwise outstanding Bible scholars insist that the *hidden treasure* in this story represents unbelieving Jewry! Several even equate it with the "lost tribes of Israel." What "lost tribes"? The Scriptural record knows nothing of that popular fancy.

Nor are the natural Jews, as such, a factor in the Mystery Kingdom any more than other believers or unbelievers, as the case may be. The idea that natural Israel could be the hidden treasure not only is unfounded, but also is incongruous and utterly unscriptural. Historically, Christ's Mystery Kingdom consists neither in the Jews nor in the Gentiles, as such, but in regenerate believers, regardless of their racial origins. Certainly

God has no hidden treasure made up of people who *renounce* the Lord Jesus Christ! Any *saved* Jews are part of the treasure only because they are Christians, therefore, *spiritual* children of Abraham, as are rest of God's believing elect (cf. Romans 2:28–29; 4:12; Philippians 3:3).

From the beginning, those belonging to the chosen remnant were quite literally hid in the field. They were like Nathanael, who, though an "Israelite indeed" (John 1:47), was commonly looked upon as just another Jew.

Jesus found them scattered among the masses, and He could recognize them as His "sheep." But to any ordinary observer, they were part of the common horde. As elect believers, they were incognito to every eye but that of Christ—thus, they were *hidden* in the sense of being unrecognized by an unbelieving world.

- Hence, John declares that although we are "sons of God," nevertheless "the world knoweth us not, because it knew him not" (I John 3:1).
- According to Paul, although "The Lord knoweth them that are his," the world will never recognize the saints for what they truly are until "the manifestation of the sons of God" at Christ's return (II Timothy 2:19; Romans 8:19).

The next thing this story reveals is the manner in which the hidden treasure is redeemed. The man who finds it is so overjoyed that he immediately sells all his possessions to buy the field in which the treasure is concealed. Now, the *man* in this parable can represent none other than our Lord Himself, for He, also, has bought the "whole field" to acquire the treasure for Himself—redeemed the whole world to establish a valid claim on His elect.

Here, incidentally—or *is* it incidental?—we find a valuable clue to the main problem that exercises those who hold, and those who challenge, the "Limited Atonement" theory. And the solution suggested by this clue is corroborated by numerous assertions to the same effect in various doctrinal passages. Christ died for the entire human race, thus making salvation possible for all who are willing to accept it on the terms of the Gospel, and He did this to ensure the salvation of His elect, the only ones who can be brought to acquiesce in His good offices.

Christ Himself, in His high-priestly prayer, declared to the Father:

> . . . thou hast given him [the Son, as our racial Redeemer] power over all flesh, that he should give eternal life to as many as thou hast given him (John 17:2).

In other words, the redemptive death of Christ, in keeping with the "predeterminate counsel and foreknowledge of God" (Acts 2:23), established the Savior's moral claim on the whole field, thus enabling Him to save all true believers who are in the field. Hence, it may be said of Him, as well as of the Father, that He *potentially* is the "Saviour of all men," but *actually* is Savior of only "those that believe" (I Timothy 4:10).

In light of these and numerous related passages, it becomes obvious that Jesus meant this parable to prepare His disciples for the critical days ahead. He was assuring them that, although He was to be rejected by unbelieving Jews, through that tragic turn of events—in fact, through His death at their hands—He would redeem all the subjects of a Kingdom made up of "the children of promise," who, unlike mere "children of the flesh" would (through divine persuasion and the Savior's enablement) be prevailed upon to accept Him of their own accord.

Summary. So far, then, the Savior's current disclosures to His disciples may be summarized substantially as follows:

1. Officially rejected by the Jews, He was going to establish a provisional interim Kingdom, which had not been expressly revealed to the prophets of former times (although nothing in it was *incompatible* with prophesied promises).
2. This Kingdom would not be propagated by the sword, but by the preached Word; not all its hearers would "believe to the saving of the soul" (Hebrews 10:39).

The Mystery of the True Israel of God

3. The devil, or Satan, would try to subvert God's plan by mixing impostors among loyal subjects and by corrupting its doctrine with pernicious heresies.
4. In all events, Christ's death at the hands of apostate Israel would seal His claim on those who were Israelites indeed; they, His "peculiar treasure," would be secure until the day of His return.

This parable revealed the secret that sovereign grace, through the redemptive death of Christ, ensures eventual fulfillment of the Everlasting Covenant to the "children of the promise," notwithstanding the reprobation of the "children of the flesh."

The Merchantman

Love-begotten love constrains every heir of redeeming grace, of his own free will, to apprehend that for which he has been apprehended (cf. Philippians 3:12). "Deep calleth unto deep" (Psalms 42:7); the Shepherd finds and ransoms His sheep (cf. John 10:11, 17). In turn, the sheep, on finding its finder (cf. John 10:14; Galatians 4:9) counts nothing inexpendable in its devotion to Him. Jesus reveals this aspect of the Kingdom in the parable of the merchantman. Notice how differently these two parables are introduced:
- The former one tells us that the kingdom of heaven is "like unto treasure," a particular treasure-trove purchased by a certain man.
- This second one declares that the kingdom of heaven is "like unto a merchant man," an itinerant gem-dealer who found and bought a certain exceedingly precious pearl.
- It does *not* say that the Mystery Kingdom is like unto a pearl. The subject is "a merchant man" who gave up his entire estate for one incomparable gem.
In one sense the Kingdom is like a treasure; in another, like a merchantman. It is not in any sense likened to a pearl. No, the

---

constituency of the Kingdom is a treasure—God's elect, the heirs of grace, redeemed by the blood of Christ. Then here, one of these true sons of the kingdom is contemplated as a devoted disciple, one willing to go to any length, willing to make any sacrifice, that allows him to sing,

> Thou, O Christ, are all I want
> More than all in Thee I find . . .

Any interpretation that likens the Kingdom (or the Church) to the "pearl of great price" is palpably in error. The text both fails to support that popular misapprehension and definitely *excludes* it. Indeed, at the stage in history when Jesus spoke this parable, the Mystical Church, as such, had never yet been explicitly revealed. Hence, the Church as such can hardly be in view, inasmuch as the disciples are said to have understood all these things (verse 51).

Instead, a certain aspect of the Mystery Kingdom is before us. In my considered opinion, those who insist on reading the Church as such into this parable are well-nigh as far afield as those who would force the parable of the leaven to prop up the Social Gospel theory. A true son of the Kingdom, an Israelite indeed, an incipient believer is like a merchantman who searches for beautiful pearls.

What pearls?

- In the book of Job, pearls are associated metaphorically with wisdom (cf. Job 28:18).
- Throughout Proverbs, precious gems are invested with the same significance, especially in Chapter 8, where Christ Himself is personified as wisdom (cf. Proverbs 3:15; 8:11; 20:15).
- In the book of Matthew, our Lord mentions pearls in a figurative allusion to spiritual truth (Matthew 7:6).
- In the Apocalypse, the entrance into the New Jerusalem has gates of pearl (cf. Revelation 21:21).

A *pearl*, then, connotes wisdom and truth, or access to God through wisdom and truth. This connotation is personified in Him who is "the way, the truth, and the life" (John 14:6).

Here, in keeping with Proverbs 23:23 ("Buy the truth, and sell it not"), a merchant seeks goodly pearls, or, a potential believer is on the lookout for truth wherever he finds it.

When, with God's help, he discovers the Lord Jesus Christ, he looks no farther. He has found what he wants, all he wants, and he gladly sacrifices everything else to possess this one magnificent Pearl. Now, of course, nobody can actually *buy* either Christ or salvation in a literal sense. But one can give up every seemingly precious earthly bauble in his search for God's "unspeakable gift" (cf. II Corinthians 9:15)—or, as Isaiah puts it, "buy wine and milk without money and without price" (Isaiah 55:1). This *buying* is precisely what Jesus calls on us to do. It is what He means when He says—not once, but time and time again:

> He that taketh not his cross, and followeth after me, is not worthy of me. He that findeth his life shall lose it: and he that loseth his life for my sake shall find it (Matthew 10:38–39).

In "The Hidden Treasure"	*In "The Merchantman"*
. . . Jesus condescends to bear a cross for His disciples' sake.	. . . a disciple responds to love with love, shouldering a cross of his own in order to "know Christ and the power of his resurrection, and the fellowship of his sufferings" (Philippians 3:10).
. . . Jesus redeems His elect, His "hidden treasure."	. . . an elect believer counts "all things but loss for the excellency of the knowledge of Christ: for whom I have suffered the loss of all things, and count them but dung, that I may win Christ" (Philippians 3:8).

And so we understand what it means to sell all else and buy the Pearl of Great Price. The Savior is speaking privately to His disciples. What He says pertains primarily to them alone. It is personal. It is beyond the ken of, the comprehension of, the outside, uninitiated world. In the former parable, He has etched out the redemptive aims and ends of sovereign elective grace; now He goes on to illustrate an elect believer's response to the effectual call. In these two parables, divine sovereignty and human free agency meet and embrace.

Jesus, in the parable of the hidden treasure, says:

> I gave My life for thee,
> My precious blood I shed,
> That thou might'st ransomed be,
> And quickened from the dead.

A grateful saint, in the parable of the merchantman, replies:

> When I survey the wondrous cross,
> On which the prince of glory died,
> My richest gain I count but loss
> And pour contempt on all my pride.
>
> Were the whole realm of nature mine,
> That were a present far too small;
> Love so amazing, so divine,
> Demands my soul, my life, my all.

17

THE DRAGNET

The Mission of the Kingdom

Primary text: Matthew 13:47-50.

*Jesus spoke this parable to His disciples, in private—
at a house in Capernaum—during the autumn of the
second year of His public ministry.*

Introduction and background. To discern the primary lesson
embodied in the imagery of this particular Mystery Parable,
we must of necessity consider it against its general background
in the book of Matthew and in connection with the drift of its
immediate context. Since it occupies a climactic position as the
closing item in a comprehensive series of related illustrations,
we can scarcely err in expecting it to supply the denouement
anticipated by the rest.

In the background lie the Savior's all-but-officially rejected
proposal to restore the Davidic Theocracy and His consequent
determination to establish an interim Kingdom pending Israel's
national conversion at a later time. In the local narrative, we
find our Lord, in view of this state of affairs, forecasting the
course and characteristics of His Kingdom during the present
age, but in a manner formulated to reorient the expectations of
His disciples without retracting His original offer to the nation
at large.

The initial four of the seven parables in this series, spoken

---

but not explained in public, were meant to acquaint believers with the missionary *modus operandi* of the Mystery Kingdom and to warn them that the Gospel message would meet with different reactions—various forms and degrees of incredulity, subversion, dissimulation, and apostasy. The latter three parables, being addressed to believers only, were also mainly concerned (however indirectly in the first two of the three) with the same evangelistic emphasis, especially with the importance of personal discipleship and faithful witnessing.

In reality, the same theme—less perceptible in one, more prominent in another—pervades all seven of the Mystery Parables. Jesus was informing His disciples of the following:

> Totally dedicated disciples were to carry out a vigorous missionary effort, despite any and all opposition, in pursuance and after the manner of our Lord's own ministry.
>
> Our Lord Himself was to suffer and die for bearing witness to the truth and, through this personal sacrifice, redeem the subjects of His realm.
>
> His disciples would have to devote themselves to an utterly self-sacrificial ministry to mediate the saving knowledge of His act to their fellow men.

In "The Hidden Treasure," the Savior depicted Himself as the Missionary *Par Excellence* who redeemed us all alike, thereby ensuring the salvation of His elect. In "The Merchantman," where the disciple dominates the scene, He pictured gratitude's response to grace—the disciple returns love for love with no consideration for the cost. Now it only remained for Him to define the disciples' assignment and urge them to obedience.

Examination and interpretation. Such defining and urging is obviously what the parable of the dragnet was designed to do— a fact further confirmed by what might be called a kind of quasiparabolical postscript on the series as a whole:

The Mission of the Kingdom

On being asked by Jesus whether they understood all these things, the disciples answered
confidently in the affirmative; whereupon, the
Lord went on to tell them that a well-informed
disciple is like the master of a house who sets
before his guests a variety of wholesome foods
and refreshments, some of which are new and
fresh and others mellow with age (cf. verse
52).

The implication of this "postscript" is that Jesus had been
instructing His followers in order that they, in turn, might
proclaim the Kingdom message, in its various dispensational
aspects, to their fellow men.

Elsewhere, the Lord Jesus used several different terms
in pointing out the various duties involved in the disciples'
mission, some specific and others rather general. They were
to be *fishers of men, reapers, witnesses.* On different occasions
they were told to be disciples, to preach, or to teach. Here,
all these ideas are comprised within a single all-inclusive
metaphor: the Kingdom of Heaven, as a missionary force
including all true disciples with their several gifts, was to
be like a *net*—a dragnet, or seine—the peculiar function of
which is *to catch as many fish as possible.*

Here the particular duties of individual workers are not
directly in view. In this case, Christ's disciples are not called
"fishermen;" instead, all of them together comprise the
meshwork of a single net—an integral evangelistic agency
supervised by angels under Christ's command.

The fishermen are not identified in the parable itself, but
in His comment on the closing scene, our Lord assigned
that role, implicitly at least, to angels—thus, like Ezekiel,
recognizing them as ministers of providential government,
managing unseen "wheels" and "inner-wheels" of destiny
(cf. Ezekiel 1). And why not? "Are they not all ministering
spirits, sent forth to minister for them who shall be heirs of
salvation?" (Hebrews 1:14).

But why did Jesus' disciples *need* to be reminded of their

missionary calling and to be urged to accept their appointed role as so many pliable cords in the meshwork of a single, all-inclusive net?

A number of likely reasons may be inferred from the record. Such imagery is certainly suggestive of the ideal integrality of Christianity and our mutual interdependence as witnesses of Christ. The *net* also suggests that we, as instruments, are totally dependent on the Lord; therefore, our usefulness takes its measure from our yieldedness.

However, from the standpoint of those who heard this parable on the spot, it doubtless had some very practical implications intended for their immediate instruction.

How easy it might have been for the disciples, faced with the obstacles of which they had been so frankly forewarned, to throw up their hands in despair and thenceforth attempt to excuse themselves from their responsibilities!

Just imagine how easily they might have thought:

> *What's the use of sowing the seed, the "word of the kingdom," if so much of our effort will be spent along the barren wayside, in stony places, and among thorns?*
>
> *What's the use of forsaking secular careers and sowing the Word, in hope of stumbling on a little fertile soil here and there?*
>
> *What's the use of sacrificing all our earthly interests to preach the Gospel, if there are to be odious tares among the wheat, abominable birds in the mustard tree, and unholy leaven in the meal?*
>
> *What's the use, in face of these odds?*
>
> *Besides, since God is working omnipotently to secure possession of a treasure that is already redeemed and destined for glory, then why shouldn't we relax our efforts and simply wait for irresistible grace to seize its inevitable prize?*
>
> *After all, we have no way of knowing just*

*where to plant, or whether we're cultivating wheat
or tares.*

Misgivings such as these invariably assail *our* minds today
as we ponder the risks and count the costs of being faithful
witnesses. Often, instead of recognizing divine election as
the supreme incentive for sustaining our evangelism, we
choose to misconstrue the guarantees of sovereign grace as
an excuse for indolence and complacency.

But Jesus would have us know that whatever mysteries
baffle our comprehension at any particular moment, God
has ordained us, the net, as His effective instrument for the
accomplishment of His gracious purposes. The sea must, in
all events, be seined until the net is full.

We are the net; the sea is the world; and every current,
gulf, and estuary from pole to pole must be carefully
dragged.

Not ours the task of selecting the catch, but of catching
all we can. It matters little that we are unable to discriminate
between the good and the worthless fishes, for this net
sweeps everything before it, gathering fish of every kind,
so as to leave no good ones. When the angels of judgment
haul the mingled draught ashore, the Lord, who "knoweth
them that are his" (II Timothy 2:19), will see that the good
are salvaged and the bad committed to their proper fate (cf.
verses 48-50).

All things considered, here we find a lesson for disciples
on the urgent need for unremitting cooperative evangelism.
However similar in some respects to the parable of the tares,
this one has a peculiar purpose and emphasis of its own.
The former pointed out the heterogeneous composition of
the visible Kingdom and forecast an all-resolving crisis at
the end of the age, whereas the missionary motif, though
implicit, was not so prominent. This last parable stresses
the *indispensability* of selfless dedication to God's appointed
"fishing program," in view of the precious souls at stake, as
well as the *propriety* of leaving the separating process to the
Lord.

True, in its broadest application, this parable envisages an agelong missionary enterprise. However, lest we weary of the work before us, let us remember this: According to the Master's own explanatory remarks, this His parable also anticipates the ultimate triumph, in the long run, of all the true sons of the kingdom, and the expulsion of all impostors, preparatory to Christ's eventual inauguration as "King of kings, and Lord of lords" (cf. Revelation 19:16).

SECTION FOUR
KINGDOM VALUES

"This is the prospect with which the Lord of the harvest encourages our hearts. The growing season exposes our souls to many torrid days, chilly nights, and stormy blasts, but 'when the fruit is brought forth, immediately he putteth in the sickle, because the harvest is come.' "

18

THE MYSTERIOUS SEED

The Miracle of Spiritual Development

Primary text: Mark 4:26-29.

Jesus spoke this parable to His apostles and certain other disciples—somewhere in Galilee—during the autumn of the second year of His public ministry.

Introduction and contextual background. This parable, found only in Mark, is a kind of excursus on the parable of the sower, elaborating on the nature of the seed that falls on good ground. The record does not explicitly identify Jesus' audience at the time, but we may safely infer He addressed this illustration to some of His closest followers because it . . .

a. is especially adapted to the instruction of believers;

b. is obviously irrelevant to the unspiritual masses; and

c. bears similarity to the parable of the sower, which we know was interpreted privately to the disciples (cf. Matthew 13:10-20).

Because Mark omits the parable of the tares, recording this one instead, some scholars have wondered, Might these two passages present different versions of a single story? However, this speculation overlooks the fact that Jesus quite often used similar, sometimes identical, metaphors in various connections. It is true both parables in question involve a *sower*, a *sowing*, and a *harvest*. Apart from these basic narrative circumstances

---

(which, for that matter, occur in the parable of the sower as well), their other details and distinctive emphases are much too dissimilar to admit of the aforesaid theory.

Examination and interpretation. To discover what particular aspect of the Kingdom of God our Lord meant this parable to illustrate, we need only ponder the simple text until we sense its basic thrust. Its essential details include the *man* who does the sowing (verse 26), the *seed* that is planted (verse 26), and the final *harvest* (verse 29). But what it stresses is the gradual development of the germinal life of the seed, in stages, between the sowing season and the harvest (cf. verse 28). To anticipate the matter of interpretation, this parable was evidently intended to reassure those who preach the Gospel . . .

- that the moral order is organized to ensure that God's elect, having heard and been begotten "with the word of truth" (cf. James 1:18), will "grow in grace" (cf. II Peter 3:18) until we receive an "abundant entrance" into "the everlasting kingdom of our Lord and Saviour Jesus Christ" (II Peter 1:11); and
- that therefore we may be "confident of this very thing, that he which hath begun a good work in [us] will perform it until the day of Jesus Christ [*the harvest*]" (Philippians 1:6).

This lesson was needed then, and it is needed just as much so now.

In the Parable of the Sower, our Lord has revealed that much of our effort—spent along the wayside, in stony places, and among thorns—seems to go for nought. Here, He assures us that, given due time, the good ground *will* reward patience with abundant fruit. This assurance serves a number of useful purposes, which we will now explore.

Processes of spiritual development. The processes of spiritual development are usually so slow and imperceptible that, in the absence of visible evidence, we may become discouraged. Such misgivings, in turn, tend to foster erroneous ideas about regeneration and spiritual growth, in turn tempting some of us to resort to unscriptural methods in an effort to get quicker results. Moreover, such discouragement undoubtedly accounts for a great deal of faulty preaching on the part of zealous but indiscriminating evangelists, who seem to think any teaching that produces nominal professions is justified by its ostensible success. As a result, more than a little harm is done to genuine converts, who find their experience at variance with what they hear. Such evangelists themselves may become bewildered by the quite anomalous fruitage of their misguided enthusiasm.

Among other things, this parable exposes the fallacy of such notions as that—

- the new birth is a magical emotional experience, more or less unrelated to the law of cause and effect;
- it is invariably instantaneous, and its manifestations are the same for everyone; or
- it suddenly endows its recipient with spiritual maturity.

In fact, while leaving the ultimate mysteries of life and growth as inscrutable as ever, this passage depicts regeneration as—

- a *gradual* process, as conformable to moral and spiritual law as a seed of wheat is to the laws of nature;
- a work of sovereign, unassisted grace; and
- an event certain *in time* to culminate in personal perfection and glorification.

Let us see.

Stage 1: The seed is sown. In this parable, Christ says, "So is the kingdom of God, as if a man should cast a seed into the ground . . ." (verse 26). As in the parable of the sower, the man who does the sowing here is not identified, nor is his identity essential to the principal lesson of the illustration. There, the emphasis was on the *sowing*; here, it is on the gradual *growth* and *development* of the seed. In each case, the sower is merely an accessory to the leading theme. Even so, he is a most needed accessory, whose identity cannot be completely ignored, but must be inferred from the teaching of the foregoing parables. We have seen that our Lord Himself was the original Sower, and also that the sowing was subsequently carried on by His disciples. This *sower* must, therefore, represent both Christ and His followers—neither in particular, but both in a general way.

And that is just what the language indicates.

Verse 27 implies sheer *human* agency, for it cannot be said of Christ that "he knoweth not how" the seed develops—but verse 29 ascribes the reaping to the *parabolic sower,* and that prerogative, in what ever manner it is implemented, belongs to Christ alone. As in New Testament Greek a neuter pronoun is sometimes used to refer to an antecedent idea, regardless of the gender of the terms by which it is expressed (e.g., Ephesians 2:8), here the overall context refers to that which is human in one aspect and divine in another.

Stage 2: The ground accepts the seed. In the original text, this man is said to cast *"the* seed [singular] *upon* the ground" (verse 26). We have already learned from our Lord's own explanation of the Sower that the *seed* stands for the Word (cf. Mark 4:14) or the Gospel message; and the *ground*—in this case, the "good ground"—for the hearer's heart (cf. verse 15). This imagery shows how the Gospel produces a new birth by impregnating the believer's soul with the seed of eternal life (cf. I Corinthians 4:15; James 1:18; I Peter 1:23).

The Christian witness, as a human agent, sows the seed *upon* the ground in the sense of presenting the Gospel *to* the hearer (cf. Mark 16:15). But only the Holy Spirit can cause it actually to penetrate the *ground,* the hearer's heart, and thus engender growth and fruit, in the sense of repentance, faith, and everlasting life (cf. II Thessalonians 2:13, 14). So, as far as winning souls is concerned, our task, then, is to *proclaim* the Gospel—not to try to *implement* its effectiveness by carnal means.

To apply the imagery of the parable: After planting the seed, the sower "should sleep, and rise night and day, and the seed should spring and grow up, he knoweth not how" (verse 27). Thus, he resumes the routine of his daily life, leaving the seed to germinate and grow according to the invisible processes of nature—no assistance, or even understanding, of nature's work is required of him. So it is with us: the operation of the Holy Spirit whereby He begets life and promotes spiritual growth is both independent of human assistance and totally beyond our comprehension (cf. John 3:8).

Stage 3: The seed germinates. The sower's knowledge and his ability are limited to the duties of his appointed task, yet "the earth bringeth forth fruit of herself; first the blade, then the ear, after that the full corn in the ear" (verse 28). This verse is phenomenal language—that is, language that discusses facts as they *appear* to be—and it must be understood as such. It certainly doesn't teach that the the earth itself produces life, but that nature (which, in the final analysis, means nature's God) produces an interaction between the seed and its earth environment which results in germination and consequent growth. Applying this concept to witnessing, the text signifies that the Holy Spirit employs all the stimuli of the moral order needed to produce an interaction between the believer's heart and the Gospel, which results in regeneration and spiritual development.

This interaction is not accomplished arbitrarily. It is not done by simple fiat. It is indeed miraculous, but in no sense magical. It is achieved by divine power in keeping with all the requirements of a God-ordained moral system the "laws" of which are actually God's attributes in action. Nor is it by any means instantaneous, any more than the sprouting of a seed or the procreation of an animate body is instantaneous. There is, indeed, a protracted "moment" wherein a sprout breaks through the surface of the soil, or wherein a baby proceeds from the womb, or wherein a believer first becomes aware of his new life and relationship with God—but in every such case the critical moment is preceded by ample cause and followed by its quota of effects. And, not a single aoristic effect, it is a continuity of effects. No sprout emerges from the soil with "full corn in the ear"; no babe is born full-grown; and no child of God begins his new career as a "perfect man" possessing the measure of the stature of the fullness of Christ" (cf. Ephesians 4:13).

Stage 4: The seed grows and develops in phases. Relating to the *blade, ear,* and *full corn* stages in the growth of wheat, the

Apostle John mentions three successive phases in the course of Christian experience, analogous to childhood, adolescence (or early adulthood), and mellow age (cf. I John 2:12-14). In this passage, John

- calls *immature* believers "little children, or born ones" (as the Scots say, *bairnies*), who, forgiven of their sins, may be considered minors under the discipline of their Heavenly Father.
- addresses *more mature* Christians as "young men" (one might say youthful adults), brimming with vigor, zealous for the truth, and waging a victorious struggle with the Wicked One.
- refers to *seasoned veterans* of the faith as "fathers," who, no longer preoccupied with their spiritual adolescence, are primarily absorbed in the unspeakably intense satisfaction of ever-increasing fellowship with Christ.

No one who has risen from grade to grade in the school of grace can question the accuracy of these classifications.

It is characteristic of "babes in Christ" to rejoice for the most part in their newly found freedom from condemnation and to concentrate their attention on the rudimentary dos and don'ts which normally exercise the awakened consciences of children under parental discipline. In time, on reaching what might be called their "prime of life," they learn to depend on the Word of God for moral strength to overcome temptation and achieve their spiritual aspirations. Finally, as superannuated soldiers of the Lord, who take all lesser gains for granted, they neither know nor want any greater joy than that of leaning on His breast!

Only then can one say: "For to me to live is Christ, and to die is gain" (Philippians 1:21). Only then can he or she shout:

Thou, O Christ, art all I want;
More than all in Thee I find.

Stage 5: The harvest comes. This is the prospect with which the Lord of the harvest encourages our hearts. The growing season exposes our souls to many torrid days, chilly nights,

and stormy blasts, but "when the fruit is brought forth, immediately he putteth in the sickle, because the harvest is come"
(verse 29). In the light of this assurance we sing:

> Through many dangers, toils, and snares
> I have already come;
> 'Tis grace that brought me safe thus far,
> And grace will lead me home.

19

THE UNMERCIFUL SERVANT

The Unforgivable Guilt of Unforgivingness

Primary text: Matthew 18:23-35.

*Our Lord spoke this parable to Peter—somewhere in
Galilee, probably at Capernaum—late in the summer
of the third year of His public ministry.*

Introduction. It is sometimes said—by devout Bible students—
that the Gospel is not to be found in the writings of the four
Evangelists. Not without considerable reason, there are others
who object to that unqualified assertion. It is, however, one of
those half-truths which tend to provoke a too-hasty rejection
of its actual merits. In this case as in so many others, a flat
denial hardly does full justice to all the facts.

The four Evangelists do not record a formal definition of
the Gospel, nor did the Lord in His recorded teaching present
any systematic analysis of Gospel truth. However, the sum and
substance of the first four books of the New Testament is as
thoroughly evangelical as that of the following twenty-three.
Jesus, during the transition from the Mosaic Economy to the
Dispensation of Grace, preached and illustrated fundamental
principles of the revolutionary Christian message *before* they
were objectified at Calvary and Pentecost. After those events,
the apostles correlated and expounded these same principles
in light of the Savior's triumphant bout with death and the

Holy Spirit's ensuing ministry within the Church. Thus, the basic assumptions of the Gospel were presented to faith *before* their moral grounds and spiritual dynamics were actualized in historical experience, and the Gospel as a historical verity was proclaimed and explained *after* its accomplishment. The Gospel was preached in progressive stages, to fit the spiritual apprehension of corresponding eras. Throughout the Savior's teachings, one can hear in the background the echo of His words, "I have many things to say unto you, but ye cannot bear them now" (John 16:12). In the preaching of the Apostles, we are constantly reminded that

> [God's] grace, which was given us in Christ Jesus before the world began ... is now made manifest by the appearing of our Saviour Jesus Christ, who hath brought life and immortality to light through the Gospel (II Timothy 1:9–10).

And so, if our Lord's preparatory message was meant to give His hearers a foreglimpse of the Gospel as we have come to know it, it should be much easier for us, with hindsight, to detect in His illustrations the kernels of Gospel truth that have been unfolded in subsequent Scriptures.

It is a mischievous thing to contrast the teachings of Jesus with those of Paul, as far as their essentials are concerned. As to the substance, there is no contradiction whatever, only a forward development by the selfsame author, who spoke here and guided there.

Actually, the teaching of Jesus *includes* the writings of Paul, and all of the Christian Scriptures, fulfilling His promise when He prophesied:

> Howbeit when he, the Spirit of truth, is come, he shall guide you into all truth: for he shall not speak from himself; but what things soever he shall hear, these shall he speak: and he shall declare unto you the things that are to come (John 16:13. RV).

The Unforgivable Guilt of Unforgivingness

The pertinence of these remarks will be seen as we proceed, for our Lord, in this parable, goes far beyond His immediate subject to point out a truth which is given elaborate treatment in the Apostolic Epistles: a *real* experience of grace involves not only justification and forgiveness, but regeneration and sanctification—without which justification and forgiveness would have no practical, experiential value.

Background. This parable was delivered in connection with an extended discourse at Capernaum, during the third and final period of the Savior's Galilean ministry, rather late in the last summer before His crucifixion. With a view toward the maintenance of fellowship among His followers, He had just been telling His disciples how to deal with a delinquent brother in faith. The injured person should make a private effort to bring the offender to repentance and effect a reconciliation. If that effort failed, he should try again, accompanied by two or three witnesses. If this attempt also proved unsuccessful, he should arraign the offender before the church, which entity was fully competent to take appropriate action. If the offender *still* refused to repent, he was then to be treated "as a heathen man and a publican" (verse 17). Far from being recriminative, the main purpose of this procedure was to bring about the restoration of the erring saint, that he might immediately and wholeheartedly be forgiven.

Thus, even before we get to the parable, we learn a good deal about disciplinary policy in the local church. Fellowship with one another, and with God, rests on an ethical basis; it cannot flourish in the presence of unconfessed or unforsaken sins. The one who has erred must own his fault, and he who has been wronged must forgive it, before real communion can be restored. These principles are forever—universal, absolute, and unexceptionable on both sides. One simply must confess his sin before it is morally possible for forgiveness to be either bestowed or received. On the other hand, however penitent an erring person may be, the breach of fellowship can never be healed unless and until the one who has been wronged is willing to forgive.

It was evidently a heightened appreciation of this latter fact that prompted Peter to rise above the customary legalistic point of view—though as yet not far enough!. Peter made the following query.[2]

> Q. Lord, how oft shall my brother sin against me, and
> I forgive him? till seven times? (verse 21).

There was a saying current among the Jewish rabbis that a wrongdoer should be forgiven three times and no more. Now, under the influence of Jesus' teaching, Peter seems to have sensed the stinginess of such a rule of conduct among those whom God has forgiven all their own trespasses. Still, not as yet perceiving the unbridgeable gulf between law and grace, he evidently felt he was stretching charity to a magnanimous limit when he ventured to suggest that a Christian might even forgive a penitent brother as many as *seven* times. But despite his fancied generosity, this suggestion showed that he had still to learn the measure of the obligation grace imposes upon its beneficiaries. Jesus answered:

> A. I say not unto thee, Until seven times; but, until sev-
> enty times seven (verse 22).

For those who have been saved by the grace of God, there should be no bounds to the grace they show others, provided only that it is preceded by genuine penitence. As the Savior says in another place:

> Take heed to yourselves: If thy brother trespass
> against thee, rebuke him; and if he repent, forgive
> him. And if he trespass against thee seven times
> in a day, and seven times in a day turn again to
> thee, saying, I repent; thou shalt forgive him
> (Luke 17:3–4).

---

[2] Inset text preceded by a Q may indicate a direct question, an indirect question, a request, or even an implied question—something requiring an answer. Likewise, A (answer) text may be direct or indirect—*either* a quoted or rephrased scripture *or* a summary of the Scriptural answer.

The Unforgivable Guilt of Unforgivingness

This language assumes, of course, that such repentance is truly heartfelt, not merely a perfunctory gesture.

If it should seem unlikely that such habitual repentance could be altogether sincere, it might help to ask ourselves, *How many times a day do we call on God for forgiveness?* And again, *Do we ask Him for justice, or do we plead for mercy?*

Now, to the parable itself.

Examination and interpretation. The parable contemplates the Kingdom of Heaven, hence all *professing* Christians, true or false. Jesus said:

> Therefore is the kingdom of heaven likened unto a certain king, which would take account of his servants. And when he had begun to reckon, one was brought unto him, which owed him ten thousand talents (verse 24).

This scene could have occurred in almost any Oriental court, but a number of details reflect heathen practices which would scarcely have been found among the ancient Jews. The servant (or literally, *bondservant*) in question appears to have been a state official who evidently had misappropriated a huge amount of tax receipts belonging to the royal treasury—else it would be hard to account for his owing the king such a huge sum as ten thousand talents (about $10–12 million).

The language indicates that the occasion involved a more or less normal accounting to the king by the various officials of his realm and permits us to assume that this particular man had been in regular standing with his sovereign until now.

> . . . But forasmuch as he had not to pay, his lord commanded him to be sold, and his wife, and children, and all that he had, and payment to be made (verse 25).

We have to realize that such a punishment would have been customary in such a case at that time. It is not the purpose of this parable to weigh the moral propriety of such household slavery; it simply presents the facts as they would ordinarily have occurred.

The meaning is that the defaulting servant and his property, including his family, were confiscated by the king for what they were worth, that he exacted the greatest possible reparation for the unpaid debt. Such was the royal sentence, subject to no court of appeal besides that of the king himself.

"The servant therefore fell down, and worshiped him, saying, Lord, have patience with me, and I will pay thee all" (verse 26). This statement prepares the way for what follows. Up to this point, every stroke of the Savior's brush has been spent on the background, but here we see the debtor himself with his heart laid bare. Despite his cowering worship and his plea for patience, he is by nature a rigid legalist who neither asks nor expects to be treated graciously. Pure mercy is foreign to his thoughts. Assuming his master a person of like character, he doesn't even think of asking him for anything more than an extension of time so that he might pay his debt in full.

"I," he says, "will pay thee all." Unfortunately, this is also precisely the attitude of professing Christians who outwardly fawn before God but inwardly rely on their own resources, imagining that, given ample opportunity, they can "live down" their sins, buying God's favor with an overplus of meritorious penance. It is Galatianism: the notion that God exhausts His grace in giving us a chance to save ourselves. It is, therefore, *unbelief*, refusing to recognize God's estimate of sin, the real demands of His righteousness, and the all-sufficiency of Christ's redemptive ministry. Still, God extends His mercy even to those who ask for less . . . "Then the lord of that servant was moved with compassion, and loosed him, and forgave him his debt" (verse 27).

Since it is clear from what follows that this wicked servant does not represent a real believer, how, then, may it be said that he was forgiven his debt? Is it possible for such a legalistic unbeliever to be an object of saving grace?

Paul replies that "God was in Christ, reconciling the world unto himself, not imputing their trespasses unto them"

(II Corinthians 5:19).

As far as the king in the parable was concerned, he *extended* his forgiveness to his faithless servant. And, so far as God is concerned, He *extends* His grace to the world at large. But the reception and enjoyment of such unmerited favor is another matter, as we shall see. Justification and pardon are *available* to all of us by virtue of the fact that Christ redeemed us all; but only through personal faith do we *experience* the proffered mercy. Also, genuine faith invariably results in regeneration, in turn disposing those who are saved by grace to be gracious toward others. Not so in this case:

> But the same servant went out, and found one of his fellowservants, which owed him an hundred pence: and he laid hands on him, and took him by the throat, saying, Pay me that thou owest (verse 28).

The same man whose $10- or $12-*million* debt had been freely remitted immediately dunned a fellow servant who owed him about $15 or $20! Was he trying to raise enough money to settle his own obligation, eventually, as he had pledged to the king? If so, it is obvious that the royal pardon had fallen on deaf ears, that it was simply too much for the legalistically minded debtor to accept at face value. We are not told. Whatever may have been *his* reasons, we know there are certainly legions of nominal Christians who nourish such delusions, who are fully convinced (notwithstanding God's assurance to the contrary) that His grace affords only a respite during which they must redeem themselves! As the servant in the parable, such people are never satisfied with anything less than a "pound of flesh" dealing with anyone else! There are none so ungracious as those who have received the grace of God in vain (cf. II Corinthians 6:1). Note the merciless servant's response to the very same plea he himself had so recently made on his own behalf:

> And his fellowservant fell down at his feet, and besought him, saying, Have patience with me,

> and I will pay thee all. And he would not: but
> went and cast him into prison, till he should pay
> the debt (verses 29–30).

Having just been forgiven a fantastic sum, not only did the servant refuse to remit a pittance; he even denied his debtor the patience he had asked for himself!

This parable constitutes a depiction of spiritual experience, showing that unless divine forgiveness is received by faith and accompanied by a new birth, profession is a meaningless farce that leaves one still in the "gall of bitterness" and the "bond of iniquity." It is not that our salvation *depends upon*, but that it is *tested by*, our attitude toward others. No real Christian, assured of having been forgiven so much, can refuse to forgive so little. No one who has been transformed by the Spirit of Grace can act so ungraciously.

The servant's actions reveal his true status, for how can any sinner who dares to dream of meeting God on *legal ground* deal with his fellow men on *kindlier* terms?

All the moral sensibilities of the human heart revolt when a redeemed sinner insists on exacting naked justice. The world as well as heaven was looking on when the forgiven debtor pressed charges against his unfortunate comrade.

> So when his fellowservants saw what was done,
> they were very sorry, and came and told unto
> their lord all that was done. Then his lord, after
> that he had called him, said unto him, O thou
> wicked servant, I forgave thee all that debt, be-
> cause thou desiredst me: Shouldest not thou also
> have had compassion on thy fellowservant, even
> as I had pity on thee? And his lord was wroth,
> and delivered him to the tormentors, till he
> should pay all that was due him (verses 31-34).

The first accounting had been a routine procedure, but now the unforgiving servant was summoned to a special hearing before the king. Before, upon the discovery of his shortage, he was not upbraided, but was merely sentenced as a matter of course. Now he was publicly denounced for his wickedness. Before, the king, on being asked for no more than patience, had found it in his heart to remit the whole of a colossal debt. Now, on finding the freely forgiven man insisting on *his* legal rights, the lord indignantly decreed the maximum penalty. Hence our Lord's concluding comment:

> So likewise shall my heavenly Father do also unto you, if ye from your hearts forgive not every one his brother their trespasses (verse 35).

> Q. What was it that moved the king to anger? What is it that likewise provokes the displeasure of God in such a case?
> A. Not a mountainous debt—but a pardoned sinner's insistence on his right to bring a fellow sinner to justice.

Now, we know that God through Christ has balanced the scales of justice on our behalf, thus making forgiveness possible for all of us alike. For one of us to withhold forgiveness from a penitent brother (for whom, also, Christ died) is to repudiate the principle of redeeming grace that undergirds the only hope there is for anyone. Refusing to forgive in that case is practical infidelity! An unforgiving spirit betrays an absence of saving faith—thus, an unregenerate heart is laid bare.

Not that God forgives us *because* we forgive one another, but that we who are truly saved simply will forgive. Not that the parabolic servant is wicked because he was unforgiving, but that he was unforgiving because he is wicked. He does not represent a child of God who "falls from grace" (Galatians 5:4), but an unbeliever who "receives the grace of God *in vain*." A real believer is saved, however poorly he understands his own experience. However, saving grace is rendered ineffectual by unbelief.

To insist on legal justice is, therefore, to commit oneself to pay the "uttermost farthing" required by Law (cf. Matthew

5:26)—payment which, in the last analysis, is eventual death, or "everlasting destruction from the presence of the Lord." (II Thessalonians 1:9).

When we consider this parable in context and in light of the more definitive disclosures of the Apostolic Epistles, we must conclude it was meant not only to inculcate a forgiving spirit among the saints, but also to test the genuineness of Christian profession. Jesus wanted His disciples to understand that forgiveness is normal in Christian experience and that an unforgiving spirit is alien to the Kingdom of Grace. Paul was assuming the salvation of his readers, when he wrote: "Be ye kind one to another, tenderhearted, forgiving one another, even as God for Christ's sake hath forgiven you" (Ephesians 4:32). He could have added, as he does indeed exhort us in another place: "Examine yourselves whether ye be in the faith . . ." (II Corinthians 13:5).

20

A Vindicative Parable

THE SHEPHERD OF THE SHEEP

The Moral Grounds of Jesus' Messianic Claims

Primary text: John 10:1-18, 26-30 (ASV).

This passage contains two related discourses. Our Lord addressed the first one to the Pharisees—at Jerusalem—shortly after the Feast of Tabernacles, in October of the third year of His public ministry, and the second one to the Jewish elders—in the court of the temple—at the Feast of Dedication, during the latter part of the following December.

All quotations in this parable are from the American Standard Version unless otherwise noted.

Introduction. We simply must classify this text as a parabolic allegory. However, although it is definitely allegorical in the main, in some ways it does display certain distinctive features. The address to the Pharisees is a composite illustration of a parable consisting in at least three telescoping parts which share the same basic ideas, but with different emphases. They are followed by a concluding address to the Jewish elders.

Part I (verses 1-5), germinal to all of the rest, describes two contrasting characters in a general way, identifying neither: a true "shepherd of the sheep," who has all the hallmarks of legitimacy; and a "stranger," who affects the role of a shepherd to exploit the sheep.

Part II (verses 7-10) explains, and elaborates on, particular aspects of the first, identifying our Lord as the legitimate Shepherd, who is "the Door of the sheep" and exposing the Pharisees as evil pretenders who are out "to steal, and to kill, and to destroy."

Part III (verses 11-18), again represents Christ as "the good shepherd" and the Pharisee as a "hireling;" dealing with their respective encounters with "the wolf" and explaining the implications of that telltale test.

Part IV, *Jesus' summation.* As a peroration on His protracted discourse as a whole (verses 26-30), our Lord points to His achievement in and on behalf of His "sheep" as crowning proof that He, and He alone, is God's appointed Shepherd.

Although these passages touch on a good many lateral truths, some of which lie at the very heart of the Gospel, they were chiefly a continuation of the Savior's defense of His Messianic claims against the attacks of His enemies.

Background. This discourse has a twofold background, (a) in the writings of the prophets and (b) in the local narrative.

As to (a) the prophets' portrayal of Christ as a shepherd, we immediately think of the lovely imagery of the twenty-third Psalm. Or of those beautiful lines from the Book of Isaiah:

> He shall feed his flock like a shepherd: he shall
> gather the lambs with his arms, and carry them
> in his bosom, and shall gently lead those that
> are with young (Isaiah 40:11).

The prophets also foresaw and described the false shepherds of Israel, whom Jesus denounced as "thieves and robbers" (verses 1, 8) and as "hirelings" (verse 12). One cannot examine passages such as Jeremiah 23, Ezekiel 34, and Zechariah 11 and not visualize the contest between the Savior and the faithless pastors of His day, as recorded in John 5–9.

That section of the book of John also provides (b) the local background against which the allegory on the Shepherd of the sheep must be understood. Beginning with the Jewish rulers' first open opposition when He had healed an impotent man on a Sabbath day nearly two years earlier (cf. John 5:16), it records the ensuing controversy between Him and His critics until the time of the uproar over His healing a congenitally blind man, again on a Sabbath, about five months before the Crucifixion (cf. John 9).

This latter incident prompted Him to answer His foes with the discourse we are now considering. Because the formerly blind man rebuffed their questioning with an expression of amazement at their unbelief, the ruling Jews had summarily excommunicated him (cf. John 9:34). Our Lord, construing that high-handed measure for what it was—a blow at Himself—then proceeded openly to challenge their authority and vindicate His own.

Part I: "The shepherd enters by the door" *and*
"Seven characteristics of the true shepherd"
(verses 1–5)

The shepherd enters by the door. "Verily, verily, I say unto you," the Savior continued, "He that entereth not by the door into the fold of the sheep, but climbeth up some other way, the same is a thief and a robber" (verse 1). Now, the expression *Verily, verily* carries all the solemnity of an oath, and inasmuch as Jesus never used those words to introduce a new subject, it is evident His intention here was to remonstrate with those arrogant elders who imagined they could excommunicate His followers from the Theocratic fold. Although certain of His disciples, as well as the man who had just been healed, were in His audience, the context shows He was addressing the Pharisees and their confederates among the ruling Jews.

It is also clear to us, although His opponents could not perceive it at the time, they were the ones He was alluding to as "thieves and robbers" who shunned the "door" and climbed over the wall at another place. They were thieves and robbers because they were usurping the prerogatives of God's true Shepherd, using stealth and violence to exploit and dominate His sheep. The main point here, however, is that they were not entering the fold through the "door," that is, in the legitimate way—in a word, they acted from self-will rather than submit to the will of God.

"But," Jesus went on, "he that entereth in by the door is the shepherd of the sheep" (verse 2). This, like the foregoing verse, is a general statement of fact. Just as it is normal for a thief to avoid the guarded door, it is normal for a legitimate shepherd to use it.

In light of all that follows, there can be no doubt that our Lord was even in the first section, portraying Himself as the true "Shepherd of the sheep." Unlike the Pharisees and elders, who wielded the shepherd's staff as a club to further their own ambitions, His sole desire and intent was to fulfill the will of God. "Wherefore when he cometh into the world, he saith . . . Lo I am come to do thy will, O God" (Hebrews 10:5-7). As to its basic, underlying significance, "the door" represents God's will, whatever it may be, as opposed to "some other way." This "door" our Lord Himself had to pass through in order to become "the Door of the sheep" (verse 7), an act whereby He became the personification and embodiment of the will of God "by which will we have been sanctified through the offering of the body of Jesus Christ once for all" (Hebrews 10:10).

Had the Pharisees entered the "door" (in the sense of submitting themselves to God), they would have recognized Christ as the Door through whom believing sinners may pass into the Messianic "fold"— but, "ignorant of God's righteousness, and seeking to establish their own, they did not subject themselves to the righteousness of God" (Romans 10:3). Then as now—and always—the "door" stood for the course of God's appointment.

Even Christ Jesus Himself, incarnate, had to pass through that

---

"door" to become the Door through whom we enter into everlasting
life and immortality. His passing through that *"door"* was precisely
the meaning of His temptation in the wilderness, on the pinnacle of
the temple, and on the *"exceeding high mountain"* (cf. Matthew 4:1-
11). The devil was trying to prevail upon Him to ignore the
"determinate counsel" of God (cf. Acts 2:23), to seize the shepherd's
staff without first enduring privation, dishonor, and death to redeem
the sheep. God was preparing Christ in the crucible of discipline for
His vicarious ministry (cf. Hebrews 5:8). But Christ's triumph over
every temptation to evade the Cross was His way of saying, *"not my
will, but thine, be done."* It vouched for His determination to lay
down His life for the *"sheep,"* thus making it morally possible for a
just God to lavish mercy on penitent sinners. This truth is basic to
all that follows, spelling out in concrete terms the moral grounds of
Jesus' Messianic claims.

But all of these concepts were to be explained by Jesus in the second section of the allegory.

Seven characteristics of the true shepherd. The Savior points
out (in verses 3–5) seven situations which are characteristic of
a shepherd's relations with his flock, all of which, being equally
characteristic of His relations with the Church of God, serve to
confirm the genuineness of His Messiahship.

1. Alluding to Himself as the true shepherd, Jesus says, *"to
    him the porter openeth"* (verse 3). The porter, or doorkeeper,
    was an undershepherd who served as a night watchman
    over the fold while the regular shepherds were asleep. He
    was responsible for the sheep until the other shepherds
    arose in the morning. The point here is that he would never
    think of admitting anyone except a legitimate shepherd.
    From a strictly historical point of view, it would seem that
    in this case the porter represents John the Baptist, who was
    ordained of God to introduce Jesus Christ to Israel as the
    promised Messiah. John certainly served in that capacity,
    as he demonstrated abundantly by his accomplishments.
    The *"sheep,"* including many of John's own disciples,
    "heard him speak, and they followed Jesus" (John 1:37).

That alone should have convinced the Pharisees of our Lord's Messiahship.

2. *The sheep "hear his voice"* (verse 3). That is, they *hearken* to his voice; they not only hear, but obey it. So it was with God's elect in Israel when Christ appeared: hitherto they had been "straying like sheep;" now they "returned to the Shepherd and Guardian of [their] souls" (I Peter 2:25, RV). Some—like Andrew, Peter, James, and John—forsook their boats and nets; some, like Matthew, forsook their lucrative customs tables; and a few others, like Paul, "counted all things but loss for the excellency of the knowledge of Christ" (Philippians 3:8).

3. *He "calleth his own sheep by name"* (verse 3). He calls the sheep personally and vocally, one by one, each by its name. Naming and recognizing sheep was a common practice in the ancient East, and it still is today. It would be difficult to locate a better Scriptural illustration of personal election and the effectual call, or one having so many analogies in the record of our Lord's own ministry. It recalls the Savior's first words . . .

   • to Peter, "Thou art Simon the son of John: thou shalt be called Cephas";
   • to Nathanael, "Behold, an Israelite indeed, in whom is no guile";
   • to the little publican at Jericho, "Zacchaeus, make haste, and come down"; or
   • to Paul, "Saul, Saul, why persecutest thou me?"

   It reminds a Christian of the intensely personal character of his *own* experience when he first heard Jesus calling him, as it were, by name.

4. *He "leadeth them out"* (verse 3)—that is, he leads his *own* sheep out of the *common* enclosure to the "green pastures and "still waters" of the open countryside (cf. Psalms 23:2). This action being a normal, daily procedure in the life of a human shepherd and his flock, its mention in a parable illustrative of Jesus' ministry is (in view of what actually took place) almost certainly intended as an allusion to the outcalling of the Church. Jesus' first disciples had belonged

to the Jewish fold, but in time, He led them out of Judaism
and formed them into one great spiritual flock that knows
no racial bounds. A tremendous undertaking, it was effected
by providential developments which Jewish believers were
naturally slow to understand. Some—probably most of
them—demurred when they first saw the great transition
taking shape, but in time, they would be convinced by the
verdict of history, as they saw the Great Shepherd "putting
forth all his own" (verse 4).

5. *He goes before them, as an example.* Next, Jesus says of the
true shepherd that, "When he hath put forth all his own,
he goeth before them" (verse 4). He "puts them forth" in
the sense of bringing them out; he does not *drive* them, but
leads them—going "before them" to clear the way for their
pursuit. So it is with Jesus,

> the Leader and perfect example of our faith, who,
> for the joy that lay before him, endured the cross,
> heedless of its shame, and now has taken his
> seat at the right hand of the throne of God (cf.
> Hebrews 12:2, TCNT).

He went before His own—through judgment, death, and
Hades—to open for them "a new and living way" into the
heavenly Kingdom (cf. Hebrews 10:20).

6. *His "sheep follow him"* (verse 4); they not only hear, but
heed, that is, they do his bidding. Thus most (if not all) of
the apostles—and after them, millions of faithful martyrs—
followed their great Exemplar through "the valley of the
shadow of death" (cf. Psalms 23:4). The willingness to do
so, if need be, is implicit in every Christian's profession.
Subjectively, in his spiritual experience, every real believer
does participate in the death and resurrection of the Lord.
As the Apostle Paul says:

> Know ye not that so many of us as were bap-
> tized into Jesus Christ were baptized into his
> death? Therefore we are buried with him by

> baptism into death: that like as Christ was
> raised up from the dead by the glory of the Fa-
> ther, even so we also should walk in newness
> of life (cf. Romans 6:3–4).

This "baptism into death" makes it possible for each of us to confess with Paul

> I am crucified with Christ: nevertheless I live;
> yet not I, but Christ liveth in me: and the life
> which I now live in the flesh I live by the faith
> of the Son of God, who loved me, and gave
> himself for me (Galatians 2:20).

7. *His sheep "know his voice"* (verse 4). They recognize his voice intuitively—that is *why* they follow him—further proof that he is a true shepherd indeed. Likewise, the fact that the hearts of God's elect respond to the Gospel proves that Jesus is the Shepherd of whom the Gospel testifies.

The validity of this circumstantial evidence of Jesus' Messiahship is further confirmed by the fact that it cannot be predicated of anyone else. As for actual sheep, we are told that "a stranger they will not follow, but will flee from him: for they know not the voice of strangers" (verse 5), and this statement is equally true of God's elect. Strange voices may momentarily confuse an ill-instructed saint, but we have "an anointing from the Holy One" that keeps us from continuing in serious error (cf. I John 2:20).

"This parable spake Jesus unto them: but they understood not what things they were which he spake unto them" (verse 6). The Master's similitude was all but transparent, yet the Pharisees were utterly blinded with prejudice to the point that they really did not recognize either Him or themselves in the allegorical mirror. As far as they could see, His illustration, however true to familiar facts of pastoral life, was altogether pointless. Doubtless this reaction was as Jesus had expected. But in describing a situation His critics could not contest, He had laid the groundwork for its elaboration and elucidation in an inescapably convincing way.

Part II "The true Shepherd is the Door" *and*
"Three promises to those who enter through the Door."
(verses 7–10)

The true Shepherd is the Door. In order to accurately interpret this entire discourse, one must realize that the second section is both an explanation *and* an expansion of the first—not merely the one or the other. This fact is true from the very start.

Because the Pharisees had not understood His preliminary remarks (verses 1–5), Jesus continued, "Verily, verily, I say unto you, *I am* the door of the sheep" (verse 7, italics added). To begin with, He had called Himself the Shepherd who *enters through* the "door" into the sheepfold (verse 2), offering that as proof of His Messiahship. Here, while keeping the meaning implied by His preliminary reference to the door as the way of God's appointment, He went on to identify Himself as the Door—the only way by which the sheep may enter into the privileges of salvation and eternal life. Only He, the Personal Embodiment of the Gospel, can make it morally possible for repentant sinners to pass through Him, the Door—by faith through His good offices—into the Kingdom of God, because He alone has fulfilled the will of God on our behalf. He had to pass through the door of God's appointment, before *becoming* the Door appointed of God for us.

In this capacity He was—and is—unique, though there have always been pretenders intent on arrogating His offices to themselves. Every religious dignitary ever presuming to hold the power of life and death over other people's souls is one of the false shepherds Jesus alluded to as "thieves and robbers" (verse 1). The Pharisees in His audience had just presumed thusly when they excommunicated the formerly blind man who defended Jesus after He had restored his sight. Of course, they were much too enamored of themselves to suspect that such derogatory language could have been aimed at *them*.

Now the Master fitted the shoe to the foot so snugly that even *they* could no longer miss His meaning: "All that came before me are thieves and robbers: but the sheep did not hear them" (verse 8). Now, this statement must be construed in close connection with its immediate context: *"I am the door.* All that came before me [i.e., in *that* capacity, posing as the Door] are thieves and robbers . . ." The use of the verb *are* in the present tense shows Jesus was speaking specifically of contemporary opponents, not merely, in a general way, of the impostors of former times. The Pharisees and their confederates were "thieves and robbers," because they usurped the prerogatives of Christ, exploiting the gullibility of their fellow men, thus lording it over God's heritage by stealth and violence.

But the "sheep" did not hearken to them. The believing remnant in Israel, like the man who had just been converted after receiving his sight, had been moved by neither the wiles nor the frowns of Jesus' enemies.

Three promises to those who enter through the Door. The next verse, a classic expression of Gospel truth, enumerates three principal benefits accruing to those who follow our Lord and depend on His good offices. Jesus says most emphatically:

> I [that is, *I, and no one else*] am the door; by me if any man [or, literally, *anyone*] enter in, he shall be saved, and shall go in and go out, and shall find pasture (verse 9).

This statement contemplates the believer as a sheep, that is, anyone who is disposed to enter the fold of God through Christ the Door. It promises three things: salvation as deliverance, as freedom, and as sustenance:

1. *Salvation as deliverance: The sheep "shall be saved."*
   We know from countless Scriptures that salvation, in its broadest sense, embraces both the negative and positive benefits of Christ's redemptive ministry: both deliverance from sin and death *and* the enjoyment of eternal life and

blessedness. Here, emphasis is obviously on deliverance, with the rest of the verse stressing the positive aspects of our Christian heritage.

2. *Salvation as freedom: The sheep will be liberated to "go in and go out."* Here, a reader who thinks only in English encounters one of those apparent contradictions resulting from a too-literal translation of one language into another. On the face of it, this expression appears to say that the believer will "go in and go out" of God's fold (and that, through Christ, who is its Door!), whereas it is actually a Hebrew idiom meaning, as we might say, "to have the run of the place."

This idea is beautifully illustrated in Numbers, where Moses pleads with God to appoint someone to succeed him as the leader of Israel:

> Let the LORD, the God of the spirits of all flesh,
> set a man over the congregation, which may go
> out before them, and which may lead them out
> and which may bring them in; that the congre-
> gation of the LORD be not as sheep which have
> no shepherd (Numbers 27:16–17).

Yes, the language of Moses' petition not only illustrates the Hebrew usage, which was carried over into the Greek of our text, but also portrays the same pastoral background. And it is remarkable that God responded by appointing Joshua as Moses' successor—a man whose Hebrew name was the same as that of the Lord Jesus (*Jesus* being the Greek form of *Joshua*) and who was an outstanding type of Christ, the true Shepherd of the Israel of God.

In a word, our gracious Lord not only saves His sheep from every ill, but also "gives us the run" of His Kingdom. This is to say, as He did on another occasion, "If therefore the Son shall make you free, ye shall be free indeed" (John 8:36).

3. *Salvation as sustenance: The sheep will "find pasture."* Jesus promised that besides being saved and blessed with

all the privileges of the fold, every one of His "sheep" will "find pasture." That provision in all events, means ample life-sustaining food, which is altogether as vital to the soul as to the body. In effect, it means Christ Himself—for, to use His own words, "the bread of God is he which cometh down from heaven, and giveth life unto the world" (John 6:33). Or, as He says again, "I am the bread of life: he that comes to me shall never hunger; and he that believeth on me shall never thirst" (John 6:35).

This sustenance is what was hopefully depicted by the manna in the wilderness and by all the sacrificial feasts that were observed by the ancient Jews, and it is what we now confess with the symbolic bread of the Lord's Supper. Jesus Himself speaks with finality on this subject when He says:

> He that eateth my flesh and drinketh my blood hath eternal life: and I will raise him up at the last day. For my flesh is meat indeed [*true meat*, meaning, "real food"], and my blood is drink indeed [*true drink*, that is, "real drink"]. He that eateth my flesh and drinketh my blood abideth in me, and I in him. As the living Father hath sent me, and I live because of the Father; so he that eateth me, he also shall live because of me. This is the bread which came down out of heaven: not as the fathers ate, and died; he that eateth this bread shall live for ever (John 6:54-58).

It should be needless to say that this is a *spiritual reality* which can be experienced only by faith. The Jews who ate the manna died; so did those who partook of the Levitical feasts; so do modern sacramentalists. But those who truly "feast" on Christ, by faith, "shall live forever." This truth, in substance, is what Jesus means when He goes on to say:

> It is the spirit that giveth life; the flesh profiteth nothing: the words that I have spoken to you

are spirit, and are life (John 6:63).

Thus, the Savior's chief concern was for the safety and welfare of the "sheep"; however, that was not at all true of the false shepherds of Israel.

"The thief cometh not," He chided them, "but that he may steal, and kill, and destroy: I came that they may have life, and may have it abundantly" (verse 10). His motives and theirs were as different as grace and greed, love and hate, mercy and murder. *They* were out to aggrandize themselves at the expense of their fellow men—religiously but relentlessly—by any means whatever, with no regard for anyone's well-being but their own. *He* came to spend Himself on our behalf, to die our death that we might share His life and receive an "abundant entrance" into the heavenly Kingdom:

- *Truly* He, and He alone, can say: "I am the resurrection, and the life: he that believeth on me, though he die, yet shall he live; and whosoever liveth and believeth on me shall never die" (John 11: 25–26) . . .
- *just as* He, and only He, can say: "I am the way and the truth, and the life: no one cometh unto the Father, but by me" (John 14:6) . . .
- *because* He, and He alone, has—through obedience unto death—transformed the forbidding gates of justice into a triumphal arch of redeeming grace!

Part III: "Shepherd vs. hireling, when the wolf comes" *or* **"The Good Shepherd lays down His life for His sheep."** (verses 11–18)

In the third section of this allegory, the Savior reiterates the same basic truths we have found in the former two, but now uses several new figures of speech and adds some luminous sidelights. He again inveighs against the imposture of the Pharisees, in this instance likening them to a hireling who flees before "the wolf." However, His dominant theme deals with the significance of His approaching death.

"I," He says (meaning, *I, and I alone*) "am the good shepherd" (verse 11). Here the Greek word translated *good* actually warrants the rendering *par excellence*. In other words, it might have been translated, "I am the Shepherd Par Excellence" or "I am the true, the genuine, the ideal Shepherd of whom the holy prophets testified." Then, in confirmation of so bold a claim, He goes on to cite the ultimate proof: "the good shepherd layeth down his life for the sheep (verse 11). This statement might be construed as a general statement of fact, i.e., that any good shepherd would give his life for his sheep. But here our Lord particularizes the maxim by applying it to Himself.

The willingness to die for the sheep is the critical factor marking the difference between a true shepherd and a mere hireling, for Jesus says:

> He that is a hireling, and not a shepherd, whose own the sheep are not, beholdeth the wolf coming, and leaveth the sheep, and fleeth, and the wolf snatcheth them, and scattereth them: he fleeth because he is a hireling, and careth not for the sheep (verse 12–13).

Thus, it is the "wolf test" that shows up the difference between the owner of the sheep, who loves them for their own sake, and an opportunist who tends them at his own convenience for personal profit. This statement, also, is a general truth— but here it undoubtedly narrows down to a radical contrast between Jesus and the current rulers of the Jews. In this way, the wolf, universally acknowledged as a mortal enemy of sheep, apparently represents death. *Death* was the door through which the Savior had to pass to save His own sheep and the door which the hireling, or false shepherds, shunned by "climbing up some other way." However different the emphases of its several parts, this discourse retains its basic unity throughout.

Unity is reflected again in the next sentence. It reiterates the intimacy of the shepherd-sheep relationship to illustrate the subjective spiritual rapport between Christ and each of His followers (cf. verses 3–4). Jesus repeats:

> I am the good shepherd; and I know mine own
> and mine own know me, even as the Father
> knoweth me, and I know the Father; and I lay
> down my life for the sheep (verses 14–15).

This is a tremendous assertion, one only our Lord Himself could make, and one we scarcely *could* receive from the lips of anyone else!

Even as, as *truly* as, God the Father knows the Son, and God the Son knows the Father, the Lord Jesus Christ knows us and we know Him. Thus, a profound, intuitive, and reciprocal relationship underlies our communion with Christ and with one another—the same kind of vital, subjective intimacy as prevails among the members of the Godhead (though, of course, at a much lower level and of far less intensity). To Jesus, this holy fellowship is so implicit with mutual understanding, confidence, and responsibility that the very mention of it moved Him to reaffirm His resolution to lay down His life for the sheep. But why did Jesus divulge this sacred information to His inveterate foes, who, as He well knew, were already plotting to kill Him?

First, it certainly served notice that all their opposition would be in vain. Already, in spite of all His critics' efforts to discredit Him, He had a host of devoted followers who "knew" Him much too well to be turned from the faith. But this was just the beginning; He would soon have more, not only among the Jews but also throughout the nations of the world. As He told them:

> And other sheep I have, which are not of this
> fold: them also I must bring, and they shall hear
> my voice; and they shall become one flock, one
> shepherd (verse 16).

So the Savior's enemies were foredoomed to disappointment: despite their treacherous machinations, God would overrule their opposition and turn it to good account. He would call out His elect from among the Gentiles as well as the Jews. And having set aside the Old Theocracy, He would eventually bring all believers together into a single fold—the Church, the body and bride of Christ. This sanguine prediction cut the Pharisees down to size, for—granted that they were free to pursue their pernicious course—it reminded them that God would so rule and overrule as to accomplish His own designs, against all odds.

Also, it showed His enemies that Jesus never for a moment thought of Himself as a mere religious reformer or as the founder of a new Jewish sect, but that He was, from the very outset, keenly aware of the universal and timeless relevance of His mission in the world. He would have His enemies *know* that they were not dealing simply with a helpless, defeated Jewish martyr, but with the omnipotent Son of God—therefore that His approaching death would be His voluntary sacrifice offered in obedience to God, not a reluctant capitulation to His murderers. For that reason He explained to them:

> Therefore doth my Father love me, because I lay down my life, that I may take it again. No one taketh it away from me, but I lay it down of myself. I have power to lay it down, and I have power to take it again. This commandment received I from my Father (verses 17–18).

Thus, it was God's will for His Son to come into the world as a man, and to submit to death at the hands of men, to redeem mankind from death. That, the Father's commandment to lay down His life, was the door through which the Savior had to pass before he could become the Door for us.

His death was not a martyrdom; it was done voluntarily. It was not a suicide, for His enemies brought it about. It was an act of complete, unqualified obedience that made it morally possible for a just God to be gracious to penitent sinners; "on this account," it satisfied the Father's approving love.

This personification of Eternal Majesty in shepherd's garb

would have reproved, humbled, and converted the Pharisees had they only believed their ears.

At least one Pharisee (the apostle Paul), on hearing the same report this side of Calvary, did believe it—so much so that he spent the rest of his life proclaiming it as "the power of God unto salvation" (Romans 1:16).

Part IV: Jesus' summation "Unbelievers are not My sheep"
and **"Unbelievers can never destroy My sheep."**
(verses 25–30)

The foregoing portions of this discourse evidently were delivered during the final hours of Jesus' visit in Jerusalem at and after the Feast of Tabernacles in the last autumn before His crucifixion. That would have been in October, probably the latter part, after which He returned to Galilee for several weeks.

In late December, He made a brief visit to Jerusalem during the observance of the Feast of Dedication. At this time He summed up the fateful implications of His pastoral discourse.

During Jesus' absence from Jerusalem, there had been a quite heated controversy among the Jews as a result of His recent remarks on the Shepherd of the sheep. But no minds had changed; instead, all parties were clinging still more tenaciously to their several opinions (cf. verses 19-21). Upon the Savior's return, His opponents, obviously disturbed by both the size and enthusiasm of His following, cornered Him and demanded a showdown. They murmured, "How long doest thou hold us in suspense? If thou art the Christ, tell us plainly" (verse 24).

Jesus, knowing that they were not requesting information, but setting a trap, replied:

> I told you, and ye believed not: the works that I do in my Father's name, these bear witness of me. *But ye believe not, because ye are not of my sheep* (verses 25–26, *italics added*).

The believing remnant's cordial response to His message was indeed an impressive confirmation of His Messiahship. And since it is characteristic of inveterate reprobates to oppose the truth, even the opposition of His critics tended to *support* the truth they *denied*. Jesus had pointed out the same, in even plainer words, on a previous occasion: "He that is of God heareth the words of God: for this cause ye hear them not, because ye are not of God" (John 8:47). Thus our Lord held that both the assent of the "sheep" and the dissent of the "goats" served to corroborate His claims.

Even as He stood in the shadow of the cross, resigned to the death His adversaries planned for Him, He would put them straight about one thing: they could never destroy the precious sheep for whom He was about to die. *That* was what had His enemies disturbed: the impact of His burgeoning following. *That* was what they were determined to nip in the bud. As for Himself, He was willing to obey the Father's commandment by letting them take His life, but He would have them know that His appointment with the wolf (*death*) would frustrate their own designs.

Their opposition might—would—intimidate many of His followers, but nothing would subvert the faith of His elect. This guarantee He went on to spell out in unmistakable terms, which I interpret, based on the Scriptures, as follows:

When Jesus stated . . .	He was, in effect, declaring . . .
"My sheep hear my voice"	Nothing can prevent a prodigious response to the Gospel after I have met and conquered death.
"I know them"	Nothing can prevent my sheep from being owned and honored as "children of the promise" in the true "Israel of God," for I recognize them as such.

The Moral Grounds of Jesus' Messianic Claims

"they follow me"	Nothing can prevent their perseverance in the trying days that lie ahead.
"I give unto them eternal life"	My sheep can never be wiped out by torture, fire, or sword.
"they shall never perish" [Since this clause uses Greek middle voice, it may thus be rendered, literally, *They shall never destroy themselves.*]	My sheep can never forfeit their salvation through personal apostasy.
"and no one shall snatch them out of my hand."	My sheep shall never be destroyed by any external foe.

This guarantee means that His sheep are absolutely secure and indestructible, both from within and from without, for as Jesus said:

> My Father, who hath given them to me [meaning, *has given me once and for all as a permanent gift*] is greater than all; and no one is able to snatch them out of the Father's hand [for] I and the Father are one [that is, *in character, purpose, and ability to keep these promises*] (verses 27-30).

All these predictions were to become recorded history, and the promise still stands with the record. The true Shepherd met the wolf head-on, with a shout of triumph on His lips. At the Father's command, He laid down His life; and He took it up again. Now He can say "I died, and behold I am alive for evermore" (Revelation 1:18, RV.). He also says, "Because I live, ye shall live also" (John 14:19). To us, this spells the triumph of life and the doom of death. The Shepherd is alive again, the wolf is dying, and the sheep are safe!

21

A Hortatory Parable

THE GOOD SAMARITAN

Love's Answer to the Law

Primary text: Luke 10:25-37

Our Lord spoke this parable to a Jewish lawyer—somewhere in the vicinity of Jerusalem—on returning from Galilee for the Feast of Dedication, during the latter part of December in the third year of His public ministry.

Introduction. The discriminating reader will hardly need to be told that this lovely story is both a parable and an allegory. As a parable, it answered the lawyer's question regarding who is one's neighbor, revealing one must *be* a neighbor instead of *selecting* his neighbors, if he is to carry out the spirit of the Law. But as an allegory, it portrays our Lord Himself as the Personification of the Law's ideal, exhibiting perfect love in the prosecution of His redemptive ministry on our behalf. It is therefore fitting that in our evaluation of this passage we should, first, consider its local application and, then, its more extensive relevance to the Savior's historical mission in the world. Nor can it subtly be objected that the second, larger interpretation reads too much into a parable which, admittedly, was addressed to a local need, for we know that the Author of this illustration was capable of blending two distinct lessons and, accomplishing a dual purpose with a single illustration.

Background. To discover the application of this parable on the spot, let us begin with a preliminary glance at the events which led up to, and furnished the occasion for, its utterance. The context indicates it was spoken somewhere in the environs of Jerusalem, as our Lord and His disciples were returning from a preaching mission in Galilee (cf. Luke 10:17, 38). As Jesus was reminding His disciples of their peculiar blessedness as heirs of the grace of God (cf. verses 23–24), "a certain lawyer" who had overheard these words was piqued because he and his fellow Jews were apparently excluded from the Master's benediction. Seething with resentment at what he considered a personal affront, yet obviously disturbed by a twinge of real anxiety, the offended legalist rose to defend himself.

"And behold, a certain lawyer stood up, and tempted him, saying, Master what shall I do to inherit eternal life?" (verse 25). Most likely, this man was mentally measuring himself against Jesus' disciples, as if to say, *"If they are worthy of this rabbi's benediction, why not I?"* But, in the way he posed his question, he stressed the *what*: *What* had the disciples done, more than he, to deserve more blessedness than he? *What* more must he do, than he had already done, to earn eternal life?

Examination and local application. This questioner was not a civil lawyer, or barrister, but a recognized authority on the Hebrew Scriptures, an expert on Mosaic Law, otherwise known as a doctor or scribe. Although it certainly would seem from his associations that he was scarcely in sympathy with Jesus, it does not appear that he was, this time, trying to ensnare our Lord or jeopardize His life, as some of His other critics did from time to time.

At any rate, the language of the text does not necessarily imply anything more than his intention to test out a teacher who reserved His benediction for His personal followers. One who based his hope upon his Jewish pedigree, construing the Law accordingly, he saw Jesus' revolutionary doctrine as a vexatious heresy that should be discredited when possible— and to that extent, at least, he assumed the role of an adversary. This classification is not to say, however, he was insincere, for although a dedicated legalist, his question did betray a note of genuine concern. *"Teacher,"* he asked, in effect, *"by doing what may I inherit this 'eternal life' you talk about?"*

Who knows but that he really wanted an answer that would quiet the misgivings of a troubled heart? The sympathetic tenor of our Lord's reply at least suggests this latter situation may have been the case.

Although the lawyer's word for *inherit* simply means "to receive by lot," in actual usage, it was often made to imply the acquisition of something as a *legal* right. He was by nature and training just the kind of person to insist on that construction. He thought he must *do* something to inherit eternal life. And, he phrased his question in a way that would sound out Jesus' attitude toward the Law, thus challenging Him to reconcile His teaching with that of Moses on this point. And so, although Jesus doubtless knew that He was being lured into a contest on His opponent's own home ground, our Lord seized this new opportunity and made good use of it.

"What is written in the law," He answered; "how readest thou?" (verse 26). Knowing that the Law finds its fulfillment in the Gospel, He was glad to have Moses on the witness stand and was content for the lawyer to act as Moses' interpreter. Did not this lawyer, as did every other Pharisee, have a tiny copy of Deuteronomy 6:5, a passage he recited twice every day, in the phylactery that dangled from his forehead? That text was the answer Jesus had asked for. He knew it by heart. He was able, if he would, to verify the Gospel for himself. Why shouldn't this doctor of the Law confess that the Law itself conditions eternal life on love, perfect love, that love which is personified in Christ alone and realized by no one else except through union with Him? Such a maneuver would reverse the situation, putting the lawyer on trial instead of Jesus, testing both the lawyer's competence and his sincerity—but mainly, challenging his consistency.

As for His competence, the lawyer passed our Lord's test with flying colors: like the theologian he was, he answered by appealing to the Scriptures.

In fact, he replied with the words of Moses:

Thou shalt love the Lord thy God with all thy
heart, and with all thy soul, and with all thy
strength, and with all thy mind; and thy neighbor as thyself" [thus combining Deuteronomy
6:5 with Leviticus 19:18 to show only perfect love
for God and for one's neighbor can realize the
aspirations of the Law].

So far, so good—but as for his consistency, it remained to be
seen whether he treasured this golden knowledge in his heart
or only in his head.

Hence, on the principle that "not the hearers of the law are
just before God, but the doers of the law shall be justified"
(Romans 3:13), Jesus agreed: "Thou hast answered right; this
do, and thou shalt live" (verse 28)—qualifing a concession with
an indictment of the lawyer's own lovelessness. Jesus knew
that even as the lawyer extolled the love the Law requires, he
shared his colleagues' contempt for local sinners and his
nation's hatred of the Gentile world at large.

Now the lawyer, all too aware of this glaring inconsistency,
betrayed his embarrassment by trying to defend himself.

"But he, willing [or, *wishing*] to justify himself, said unto
Jesus (verse 29), And who is my neighbour?" This question
was a tacit admission of some degree of uneasiness on the
lawyer's part. Hitherto he had chosen his "neighbours" to suit
himself, deciding who was worthy or unworthy of his love;
now, in the presence of one to whom his conscience was an
open book, he could no longer delude himself. He tried, but
even his question, fraught as it was with desperation, showed
that he had reached and exhausted his last resort. As a man of
outward piety, he evidently assumed that his love for God was
incontestable, but there was no denying that he scorned the
rank and file of his fellow men—the Gentiles in general, the
Samaritans in particular, and even his wayward brethren
among the Jews. Heretofore he had squared his conscience with
the Law, evidently, by insisting that only those who deserved
his affection were neighbors indeed. And that was apparently
the artifice he had in mind when he tried to deflect the Savior's

searching gaze by raising the flimsy technicality, "And who is my neighbour?"

At this point Jesus, taking up the challenge the lawyer posed with his evasive question, answered with the story of the Good Samaritan. So far as it affected the lawyer, this parable was meant to illustrate the truth about true neighborship and its bearing on one's profession of salvation. Though to him it could hardly have been an elaborate analogy of Christ's redemptive ministry as it is to us, he must at least have perceived that it pictured Jesus as the ideal neighbor envisaged by the Law.

Strange as it may seem, some modern writers question this interpretation, finding in this story no personal allusions at all to either Christ or His examiner. Such questioning is, to my mind, to gloss over a veritable cluster of personal allusions in the context, which virtually compel us to search for an intensely personal interpretation. Three personal allusions are apparent from the contextual approach, and a fourth may be seen in the conclusion of the parable:

One: As we have already seen, the lawyer's object was personal: to test out a controversial "Rabbi" who, contrary to conventional taboos, fraternized with publicans and sinners, who recognized them and befriended them as neighbors.

Two: Although his ostensible purpose was to elicit Jesus' views about acquiring eternal life—his question, into which he expressly put himself, was far more personal than philosophical. He demanded of Jesus, addressing Him personally "Master, what shall *I* do to inherit eternal life?

Three: Moreover, after the lawyer, at Jesus' insistence, had cited the Law to show the vital relation of perfect love to eternal life, our Lord applied the legal precept specifically to the lawyer: "this do," He said, "and *thou* shalt live" (verse 28). And the lawyer took this admonition personally, for he immediately undertook to "justify himself."

Jesus' answer in the parable he told was a personal defense on His part and a personal lesson for the lawyer.

Accordingly, the whole drift of the parable tends to fulfill that expectation. Instead of being desirable neighbors, the general run of men are hapless sinners—like a nameless wretch who has been stripped, wounded, and left half dead (cf. verse 30). What an opportunity for some aspiring devotee of the Law, some priest or Levite (organs of their *lawyers*), to exemplify the love the Law demands by showing compassion to a fellow human being in a moment of distress! But no, the priest and the Levite (and this typical lawyer) were "passing by on the other side" (cf. verses 31–32). Wonder of wonders, though, a despised Samaritan—one who cherished Israel's Law, but was disowned by her lawyers,

> . . . came where he was: and when he saw him, he had compassion on him, and went to him, and bound up his wounds, pouring in oil and wine, and set him on his own beast, and brought him to an inn, and took care of him. And on the morrow when he departed, he took out two pence, and gave them to the host, and said unto him, take care of him; and whatever thou spendest more, when I come again, I will repay thee (verses 33-35).

These verses conclude the story. But to drive his lesson home, Jesus asked the lawyer a personal question that called for a personal reply: "which now of these three, thinkest *thou*, was neighbor unto him that fell among thieves?" (Verse 36.)

To this question, the lawyer was candid enough to answer, "He that shewed mercy on him" (verse 37) . . . but he was still too bigoted to dignify the word *Samaritan* with his Jewish lips. However, he admitted that (in this case, at least) the Judaism of which he was a part had failed to show the love the Law required, whereas another man, an unmentionable Samaritan, had done so.

Now *who*, by any manner of thinking, could that "good Samaritan" be, if not our Lord Himself? *He* was the one who was defending Himself against the lawyer's testing, and this parable was His defense. Here Jesus presents the fourth and final personal allusion in the conclusion:

Four: The Savior dismissed His questioner with a word of personal advice: "Go, and do *thou* likewise" (verse 37), which is to say, *"Stop acting like the priest and the Levite, and follow the example of the good Samaritan."* (In this case *Go* means "Come," for one must *come* to Christ by faith before he can possibly follow Him in practice.) This advice again implies the lawyer's *personal* involvement in the imagery of the parable.

So much for the local application; now let us consider the broader implications of this versatile illustration.

Extended significance. This parable corresponds so closely with known facts, both historical and experiential, that it is almost impossible to attribute the resultant analogy to sheer coincidence. Since this story depicts divine/human relations as they are described throughout the Scriptures, we are—considering its authorship—bound to conclude that it was *meant* to be what it obviously *is*—which is to say, it is an allegorical representation of rudimentary Gospel truth.

"A certain man went down from Jerusalem to Jericho, and fell among thieves" (verse 30). This language suggests no clue about the nationality of the unfortunate victim, nor does it provide so much as a hint as to whether he was a Jew or a Gentile. In both our English version and original Greek, a generic term is used, which simply characterizes the *man* as a human being—a typical member of the human race. In this context, it naturally reminds us of Adam and our involvement in his predicament. Accordingly, the story begins with a calamity: the man *"went down* from Jerusalem, and *fell* among thieves." What a graphic allusion to our racial fall! Consider these aspects of the story:

- Jerusalem, the holy city, is suggestive of our original state of innocence in Eden.
- Jericho, the city of the curse, is equally suggestive of our

subsequent depravity.

• The thieves, or robbers, represent the malignant agencies of Satan. Just as the robbers "stripped [their victim] of his raiment, and wounded him, and departed, leaving him half dead" (verse 30), Satan also has despoiled the human family, bestrewing the roadsides of history with successive generations of ghastly casualties, lives forever wasting in the shadow of death.

But the story continues:

"And by chance [or, more precisely, *by coincidence*] there came down a certain priest that way" (verse 31). Now, this statement evidently alludes to the *Law,* since it was the priests who administered the legal code. The Law found the Chosen People in mortal need, and after reigning for hundreds of years, passed away without saving, in and of itself, a single soul from death. The Law not only "passed by on the other side," but eventually took the other side—for, one famous Jew confesses, "the commandment, which was ordained to life" was "found to be unto death" (Romans 7:10).

"And likewise a Levite, when he was come at the place, came and looked on him, and passed by on the other side" (verse 32). This event, also, dramatizes the incompatibility of law and grace, but with special emphasis on *the futility of legal works.* Under the Mosaic order in which the priests officiated, Levites did most of the actual work. Assuming, as we must, that Jesus intended some such distinction, this is certainly the likeliest one that meets the eye. Moreover, the same meaning is undeniably confirmed by the teaching of our Lord's apostles later on. Though it was apparent that the letter of the *moral code* invoked unmitigated wrath upon those who broke it, the Jews by and large deluded themselves that they could balance the scales of justice by heeding the *ceremonial code.* Forgetful that Levitical rites were valid only as expressions of faith in the provisions of God's redeeming grace, they placed their trust in the rites themselves—rather than repent of sin and claim the sovereign mercy to which their ceremonies testified. That act, like later sacramental perversions of nominal Christianity, was an attempt to bribe the Holy One of Israel with "filthy rags" (cf. Isaiah 64:6). Such misguided piety has never availed with God. As He chided the Jews of Isaiah's day:

> Unto what purpose is the multitude of your sacrifices unto me? . . . I am full of the burnt-offerings of rams, and the fat of fed beasts; and I delight not in the blood of bullocks, or of lambs, or of he goats . . . Bring no more vain oblations; incense is an abomination unto me; the new moons and sabbaths, the calling of assemblies, I cannot away with it; it is iniquity, even the solemn meeting (Isaiah 1:11, 13).

Some seven centuries later, the Apostle Paul also denounced the worthlessness of legal observances apart from faith in Christ. "But," he declared, "that no man is justified by the law in the sight of God, it is evident: for, the just shall live by faith" (Galatians 3:11). And Paul's declaration is just as true today: the exertions of Levites, whatever their modern names, are as ineffectual now as in olden times.

The Law is still a "ministration of condemnation," and its ministers are still engaged in a "ministration of death" (II Corinthians 3:7, 9). It would appear this is the reason we are told that *both* the priest and the Levite "passed by on the other side."

"But a certain Samaritan, as he journeyed, came where he was: and when he saw him, he had compassion on him" (verse 33). This was our Lord's answer to those critics who had derided Him as a "Samaritan." Although they had meant that epithet as a gross insult, He now adopted it and adorned it with benign significance. Did they employ this loathsome name to stigmatize Him as an object of contempt? Then He would accept it, thus enduring the "contradiction of sinners against himself" to "redeem us from the curse of the law" by "being made a curse for us" (Hebrews 12:3; Galatians 3:13). What a marvelous exhibition of His condescending love, that He could take the calumny of His critics and turn it into a triumphant prophecy of reconciliation! He, our Good

Samaritan, came to us where we were, became one of us, saw
our plight, and—as a man among men—took compassion on
our souls.

The rest of the story reads almost like a passage from the
Book of Isaiah. The Samaritan, we are told, "went to him, and
bound up his wounds, pouring in oil and wine" (verse 34). Or,
as the prophet exclaimed when he foresaw our Savior in the
selfsame role:

> Surely he hath borne our griefs, and carried our
> sorrows: . . . wounded for our transgressions, he
> was bruised for our iniquities: the chastisement
> of our peace was upon him; and with his stripes
> we are healed (Isaiah 53:4–5).

Thus was *our* Good Samaritan to translate His compassion into
"oils and wine": the ointment of grace and the blood of His
cross.

Nor only so. The parable goes on to say that the Samaritan
"set him [the wounded man] on his own beast [or, literally, *set
him on his own property*], and brought him to an inn, and took
care of him" (verse 34). Likewise, although everything belongs
to Christ by right of creation, He relinquished it all to succor
us in our distress. He,

> . . . being in the form of God, thought it not
> robbery to be equal with God: but made himself
> of no reputation [or, literally, *emptied Himself*],
> and took upon him the form of a servant, and
> was made in the likeness of men: and being
> found in fashion as a man, he humbled himself,
> and became obedient unto death, even the
> death of the cross (Philippians 2:6-8).

Thus, "in bringing many sons unto glory" (cf. Hebrews 2:10),
Christ laid aside the outer garments of deity and took upon
Himself the tatters of a human slave. As we are told in another
place, "though he was rich, yet for [our] sakes he became poor,

that [we] through his poverty might be [or, rather, *become*] rich" (II Corinthians 8:9). Of course, this *becoming rich* entails, on our part, the completion of our sanctification. Meanwhile, He sees to it that we are cared for in the *inn*—that is, it would appear, the *Church*—where we enjoy the comfort and spiritual support of the Christian ministry.

So far, our interpretation of this parable is confirmed by the well-known facts of history and personal experience. The rest is equally consistent with Bible prophecy. The story concludes:

> And on the morrow when he [the Samaritan] departed, he took out two pence, and gave them to the host, and said unto him, Take care of him; and whatsoever thou spendest more, when I come again, I will repay thee (verse 35).

Payment upon departure is precisely what *our* Good Neighbor has done for us. Having finished the work of our redemption, He is now away on other business—His priestly ministry of intercession—for a while, but, just like the Samaritan in the parable, He will soon return.

In the meantime, those who serve Him are amply rewarded for their faithfulness: "two pence," or double pay for each day's work, together with the promise of more, still more, upon His reappearing. Our work may or may not entail a good deal of overtime, for it is not ours to know the day or the hour of the Second Advent. But we do know this:

> God is not unrighteous to forget [our] work and labour of love, which [we] have shewed toward his name, in that [we] have ministered to the saints, and do minister (Hebrews 6:10).

22

THE IMPORTUNATE FRIEND

The Discipline of Prayer

Primary text: Luke 11:5-8.

Our Lord addressed this parable to His disciples—probably on the way from Jerusalem to Perea—after the Feast of Dedication, late in December of the third year of His public ministry.

Introduction. The Lord Jesus, in His preaching and teaching, never told a story simply to entertain His audience. Instead, every parable He uttered served some definite purpose—to emphasize a point of doctrine, to illustrate an argument, to encourage the disciples with the revelation of secret truths, to warn His enemies with veiled reproofs. And, His parables are usually interwoven with the record of His teaching ministry to the point that the illustration and its narrative history are complementary and more or less interdependent. Hence, when viewed together, the context usually furnishes a key to the illustration, which in turns illuminates its narrative passage. This interrelationship and its reciprocal effects may be observed throughout the Gospels—but nowhere more distinctly than here in Luke's report of Jesus' story about the importunate friend.

Background. Here, first of all, we find our Lord's disciples in the grip of amazement as He absorbs Himself in prayer. They are so greatly impressed by the majestic spontaneity of His devotions that one of them, speaking for all the rest, entreats Him, "Lord, teach us to pray" (verse 1). In response to this request, the Master gives them what is now commonly known as "The Lord's Prayer," as an example to guide them in their own petitions. But, aware that their real difficulty lies much deeper than in the mere choice of words, He goes farther to dramatize their real problem and its solution with a thought-provoking parable.

Although it is not expressly mentioned in the record, we know what that problem is, for we, too, have had to wrestle with it from time to time. How often do we ask ourselves: *Why pray, when we have no tangible proof or palpable assurance that we are being heard?* We try so hard to pray aright, but no answer seems to come. *Why should we pray again, and hope again, at the risk of being disappointed again?*

We all, no doubt, feel such misgivings now and then. Not that we should—but Alas! we do. Yet, though our frailty must grieve Him, Jesus understands. We may be sure this parable, like the rest of the Bible, was "written aforetime . . . for our learning, that we through patience and comfort of the Scriptures might have hope" (Romans 15:4).

Examination and interpretation. This homely illustration is so similar to our own experience that it is in some respects almost allegorical. A man awakens a neighboring friend at midnight to borrow three loaves of bread. He does not ask or expect such an untimely favor strictly on his own account, nor would he think of doing so: he needs the bread for the entertainment of another friend, who, being on a journey, has stopped by for the night. Having no provisions of his own to set before his unexpected guest, he is facing an emergency and appealing for help. At first his neighbor is immovable, indignant at what he considers an utterly unreasonable request:

> *"Go on," he complains, in effect. "Don't annoy me at this unearthly hour! I've already barred my door,*

tucked in my children, and gone to bed. Would you
have me rouse the little ones and put them to sleep
again? It's midnight, man! Go home, and let me get
my rest!" [This rendition based on verse 7.]

It isn't that he wishes to seem unneighborly; he simply feels
that any other course is out of the question now. Nevertheless,
he finally does get up and give his insistent friend the bread,
for like it or not, there is no other way to stop his friend from
knocking on his door.

That is the story. Now what is Jesus' point? Does He mean
to say that God is like the reluctant neighbor who wants to be
left alone, and that we must extort His favor by wearing Him
down with our begging until He relents against His will?

Assuredly not!

The context shows, as we shall soon see, that God delights
in hearing our petitions and granting our legitimate requests.
The churlish fellow in the parable may, indeed, exemplify our
mistaken conception of God when, in our doubting minds, it
seems to us that He is saying, "Go on! Don't annoy Me." We
pray, and when no answer comes, we feel that God has locked
us out and left us in the midnight all alone.

We *feel* that way, and Jesus knows how prone we are to
think it *is* that way. Because of this common human frailty, He
has given us this parable, to show us that:

• we should not allow ourselves to be dismayed because of sheer
  appearances; and
• God is not a fair-weather friend who mocks our pleas in times
  of need and helps us only at his own convenience; but
• He is a loving Father who always has our interests at heart;
  moreover, He longs to grant us "every good and perfect gift"
  (cf. James 1:17).

These points undoubtedly constitute the primary lesson in our
Lord's illustration, for He goes on to say:

If a son shall ask bread of any of you that is a
father, will he give him a stone? or if he ask a
fish, will he for a fish give him a serpent? or if

> he shall ask an egg, will he offer him a scorpion?
> If ye then, being evil, know how to give good
> gifts unto your children: how much more shall
> your heavenly Father give the Holy Spirit to them
> that ask him? (verses 11-13).

The Savior is insisting that God wants to give us not only as much as we ask, but immeasurably more. This being the case, He would encourage us to keep on asking until we get exactly what we want. His argument, briefly, is this:

> If even a fair-weather friend will grant a grudg-
> ing favor to a neighbor who keeps on asking it,
> much more will our Heavenly Father supply His
> children's needs when we appeal to Him for help!

But if the foregoing interpretative statement is true, why doesn't God *immediately* give us everything we ask of Him? Why, if He delights in blessing us, do most of us have to plead so long before an answer comes?

Doubtless, many of us find such questions in our minds from time to time. Not all of us, though—at least, not as often as in bygone days. We have learned from long experience that prayer itself must discipline our hearts until we yearn for only what is right and best, and that God will give us what we ask when we have tarried in the school of prayer until mastering the art of asking as we should. We have learned to keep on praying, not to persuade God to change His mind, but to exercise our consciences in His presence until our minds are brought into agreement with His. As we commune with Him from day to day and year to year, we gradually find ourselves thinking His thoughts and sharing His desires until, at last, when we tell Him our wants, we are asking only for what He wants us to have.

How grateful we should be that He refrains from humoring our childish longings until we have cultivated a preference for better things! that He does not respond to our faulty praying until His gracious reticence has constrained us to pray more

The Discipline of Prayer

prudently!

Only then do we see that His apparent reluctance to honor our petitions in the past was actually His fatherly forbearance toward petulant children still too immature to ask aright. While we were waiting for Him to answer our prayers, He was waiting for us to come to Him with nobler desires. And so it will be, henceforth, until our wills merge into His. As we pass, through continuing prayer, to ever-nobler aspirations, we shall discover that His momentary nays are truly intended to school us for the enjoyment of His eventual yeas:

- If He withholds the stone we mistake for bread, it is to refine our taste until we want a better fare.
- If He ignores our hankering for pretty scorpions, it is that He may teach us to ask for eggs.
- If He denies us a serpent, it is that He may feed us with fish instead.

In these concepts we understand the meaning of the Savior's exhortation, when He says:

> Keep on asking, and the gift will be given you; keep on seeking, and you will find; keep on knocking, and the door will open to you. For everyone who keeps on asking, receives; and the one who keeps on seeking, finds; and to the one who keeps on knocking, the door will open (verses 9–10, CBW).

We learn to pray effectually by keeping on praying!

Prayer is an art mastered only by constant practice. It is somewhat like learning to swim or read or sing: we can never develop such abilities except by cultivating and exercising them. We learn to pray by praying, and prayer itself prepares us for the appropriation and enjoyment of its benefits.

All things considered, this message means that there are no unanswered prayers. If God's nays condition us for the reception of His yeas, that conditioning itself is "earnest money" toward the eventual "contract payment,"—a grant which could never be enjoyed without such preparation. If a mole asked for heaven and get its request, it would not be able to see the ivory palaces and golden streets. And likewise, if an ignorant beggar were awarded an honorary college degree, he would only be embarrassed by his inability to read his diploma and shoulder its implicit responsibilities. Unless and until we have passed through the school of prayer, we shall, when God puts answers at our fingertips, be unable to grasp and enjoy the blessings for which we asked.

Thus, our importunity gives God an opportunity to do for us, "exceeding abundantly above all that we ask or think" (Ephesians 3:20). Not that God is moved by "vain repetitions" performed as perfunctory chores, but that He always rewards the earnestness of those who take Him at His word. Most of the prayers we recite at dawn and noon are mere rehearsals of those we really pray after dark. It is usually at "midnight" that our chastened spirits reach up to heaven and seize the prize!

23

THE FOOLISH RICH MAN

The Self-Defeating Folly of Covetousness

Primary text: Luke 12:16-21.

Our Lord Jesus spoke this parable to an unidentified petitioner—on the way from Jerusalem to Perea—near the end of the third year of His public ministry.

Introduction and background. At this point in His career, even though the Jewish authorities were turning against Him on every hand, the Savior's fame was attracting common people as never before. According to Luke's account, "myriads" [or, literally, *thousands*] of people were in His audience—"insomuch that they trode one upon another" (verse 1, cf. Greek). Despite the presence of this surging multitude, Jesus, knowing that His time was short, directed His attention principally to His personal followers, to prepare them for the trials of the rugged days that lay ahead. While in the midst of an extended review of His former teachings, He was interrupted by an impetuous favor-seeker in the crowd, whereupon, He digressed from His discourse to tend to that situation with the parable we are now considering.

"And," says the record, "one of the company said unto him, Master, speak to my brother, that he divide the inheritance with me" (verse 13).

Now to us, the intrusion of such an untimely request on

---

such a solemn occasion may seem as inappropriate as if an American citizen were to break in on the President's State of the Union Address to ask for an autograph. But, in fairness to Jesus' petitioner, it must be conceded that his interruption was scarcely at variance with the customs of his day, for many of the rabbis welcomed any question that afforded them a chance to inject their influence into secular affairs.

This man was blamable on another, far more serious score— that being his preoccupation with a relatively trivial matter when he should have been absorbed in Jesus' discussion of vital spiritual truths. The Savior was dealing with tremendously important subjects, all relating, directly or indirectly, to the Kingdom of God: subjects such as the perils of Pharisaism, the threat of persecution, the constancy of providential oversight, the momentous results of confessing or denying the faith, and the unforgivable sin against the Holy Ghost. But, despite the urgency of these transcendent issues, this beggarly upstart's only thought was to turn this distinguished "Rabbi's" prestige to his own selfish advantage!

Nor did he, alas, represent an exceptional case. Would to God it were so, but anyone of ordinary discernment knows better.

Religion has always been used by worldlings to enhance their temporal interests, and this man was not the first nor the last to look upon Christ as a spiritual means toward natural ends. How else can we explain the bulging coffers, pompous titles, the hierarchical powers and the privileges of today's ecclesiastical establishment? (Not to mention the greed of sects and cults in the pagan world!) How else can we account for the widespread exploitation of church membership solely as a means of securing business contacts and social preferments?

As much as we might wish this were an isolated instance of inordinate desire for earthly aggrandizement, that simply was not the case. It was instead a fairly normal example of an almost universal practice, not only in the world at large but also among professing Christians, even ministers. That Jesus, also, viewed it as such is clear from His extensive treatment of the subject, here and elsewhere, in studied words addressed to friends and foes alike. Our Lord knew the insidious nature of human greed: how slow we are to detect it in ourselves . . . how prone we are to justify and dignify it as a virtue . . . to call it "thrift" or "prudence" or "foresight," instead of recognizing it as the vice it really is! Clothed with the outer garments of success and respectability, it is often admired and exalted among us on almost every hand. The minds and hearts of countless people who would never think of being dishonest, unchaste, or intemperate are vitiated by this subtler sin—a sin all the worse for harboring secret covetousness rather than flaunting open shame.

Clearly, Jesus' aggrieved petitioner was a person of this stripe, for He answered him curtly, "Man, who made me a judge or a divider over you?" (verse 14). This reply in no way meant our Lord was incompetent or unable to serve that magisterial capacity, had He wished to do so, but that He had an infinitely higher mission in the world. Still, although He never allowed Himself to be drawn into purely civil or political wrangles, He did take advantage of this occasion to put His finger on the underlying cause of many, if not most, of our social ills. From Jesus' point of view, whether or not His petitioner's grievance was valid was of little consequence compared to the spiritual poverty it betrayed. Just or not, it showed that he was utterly injudicious and profane.

For all that we know, this petitioner may have been peeved because his brother, as a matter of primogeniture, had received a double portion of the family estate (cf. Deuteronomy 21:15-17)—or he may indeed have been the victim of an unbrotherly fraud. In any event, a man who esteemed material wealth more highly than the Gospel, being more concerned about his earthly fortunes than his spiritual welfare, was devoid of any sense of values worthy of the name. Granted that he may have been entitled to a share of a disputed patrimony and that he had a perfect right to press a claim before the proper authorities, it was nevertheless irrational of him to disturb the Master about such a relatively trivial matter while being offered the riches of grace and the gift of eternal life. He was committing the folly of putting first things last, of esteeming a mere transitory *living* more highly than the gift of everlasting *life.*

This petitioner's besetting sin was a consuming desire for natural things—it was why he yearned for more of the family inheritance. No petty matter, this, so far as he was concerned. It was far more important to him to get ahead in this world than to hear the rest of a disquisition on the one to come. Not that he was an irreligious man. He was, we may suppose, an ordinary Jew. Moreover, he acknowledged Jesus as "Master" and was willing to trust Him as an arbitrator. But so long as a few shekels were at stake, nothing else really mattered very much. His attitude was what alarmed the Savior—that such a worldly view should be shown by an otherwise intelligent son of Abraham without any qualms whatever.

But it did not surprise Him. He "needed not that any should testify of man: for he knew what was in man" (John 2:25). In fact, knowing human nature as He did, He then turned to the surrounding throngs to sound a general warning. "Take heed, and beware of covetousness," He warned them: "for a man's life consisteth not in the abundance of the things which he possesseth" (verse 15). The key words in this utterance are *life* and *covetousness.* Because we value life so greatly, it is very understandable that we be concerned about its sustention and enrichment, but we do err in supposing this enrichment to be contingent upon the abundance of our earthly possessions. Covetousness, an inordinate desire to have more and more of this world's goods, stems from an erroneous assumption that *life* is measured by the multiplicity of earthly baubles, carnal supports. Thinking so, we misconceive life's nature, for it is one thing to *live,* and quite another merely to have a *living.* True, one's *living* is affected by the measure of his temporal prosperity, but *life* is given and sustained by God, who may extend or recall it at will, regardless of our variable fortunes in the world.

This view neither overlooks nor minimizes the importance of our actual natural needs. It simply emphasizes the fact that life itself is not maintained or enhanced by the possession of superfluous wealth; therefore, an obsession for more than we actually need is in fact irrational and vain. Indeed, as far as our natural state is concerned, we must eat to live; even so, a rich man who has more than enough to eat is no more *alive* than a poor man who has barely enough.

Obviously, then, "life is more than meat, and the body is more than raiment" (verse 23). Our Lord reminds us that we cannot add even one *cubit* (about 18 inches) to our stature by simply wishing to be taller (cf. verse 25)—or, in effect, one *day* to our lifespan by increasing our surplus of natural things. Moreover, we are assured that God, who feeds the ravens (cf. verse 24) and clothes the lilies (cf. verse 27), will make ample provision for His children (cf. verses 24, 28, 31).

How foolish, then, to yearn for more than He supplies! All such anxiety spends itself for nought. Even worse, it is self-defeating behavior, for all the time and effort we spend amassing excessive riches might better be invested in "bags which wax not old, a treasure in the heavens that faileth not" (verse 33). Covetousness tends to thwart the true purpose of life, which is not to *get*, but to *give*, and by selfless giving, to realize the ideal fulfillment for which we were made. Far from an asset to our personal welfare, covetousness is a malignant disease that blights and withers the selfish soul.

This truth is just what we find depicted in the following parable: the ironic undoing of a prosperous "fool."

Examination and interpretation. Actually, the epithet Jesus used is not so harsh as it appears in our common version. It is, rather, pathetic: "You poor, stupid, senseless fellow."

Our Lord was not portraying a vicious infidel, nor was He necessarily warning against the future punishment of the damned. His theme was not salvation or damnation, heaven or hell, but the self-defeating folly of covetousness in *any* case. He brought no charge against the rich farmer except that he had acted foolishly by wasting his life in an effort to surfeit it with natural surpluses. As far as the record shows, the man in this parable may have been a Pharisee, a publican, a disciple, even a heathen. There was nothing wrong with his being a successful farmer. It wasn't amiss for him to store his produce well. His folly, like that of Jesus' avaricious petitioner, was that, though made in the image and likeness of God, he took a bestial view of life. He thought like a dog or a hog—or, at best, like a squirrel—making provision only for the flesh, "to fulfil the lusts thereof" (Romans 13:14).

After all, what is said about the foolish rich man that cannot be said of most of us? He was a hard-working, thrifty, farsighted person who planned larger barns for bigger crops, for the very same reasons that most of us stretch every nerve and muscle to invest as much as we can in real estate, stocks and bonds, annuities, and Social Security. He simply wanted to lay up a nest-egg and retire, as millions of Americans, including thousands of Christians, are doing today. What was so wrong, or so foolish, about that?

Nothing that would bar him from membership in most modern churches. He was a typical business man. Based on one's point of view, he might be termed either ambitious or selfish, discreet or self-centered, persistent or self-willed. All these qualities made him an outstanding "go-getter," or, as Jesus would say, an extremely "covetous" person. Not that he openly defrauded his fellow men; presumably he was an ostensibly honest man; *he simply wanted more than his actual needs*—for that is what *covetousness* means in this context.

No, manwise, this farmer could not be charged with any heinous offense. Godwise, however, he was faithless—a greedy, grasping wretch, exploiting his stewardship instead of administering it as a sacred trust. His fault, an outgrowth of consummate selfishness, is graphically demonstrated in his soliloquy with "his soul," which is here synonymous with "himself." He consulted himself instead of God, his repetitious first-person pronouns betraying an egocentric attitude utterly devoid of any sense of responsibility toward either God or his fellow men:

> What shall *I* do, because *I* have no room where to bestow my fruits? . . . This will *I* do: *I* will pull down my barns, and build greater; and there will *I* bestow my fruits and *my* goods.

The Self-Defeating Folly of Covetousness

> And I will say to My soul, Soul, *thou* hast much
> goods laid up for many years; take *thine* ease,
> eat, drink, and be merry (verses 17-19, *italics
> added*).

His plans for self included all that he had or ever hoped to
have; like apostate Lucifer, he boasted of his self-sufficiency
by saying "I will" instead of praying "thy will be done" (cf.
Isaiah 14:13–14; Matthew 26:42). His folly was the delusion
that he himself could sustain himself with earthly goods.

> But God said unto him, Thou fool, this night
> shall thy soul be required of thee: then whose
> shall those things be, which thou hast provided?
> (verse 20).

As one author has aptly aphorized, "man *proposes*, but God
disposes."[3] So it is here, as always. The foolish farmer proposed
to nourish his soul for many years, but found, alas, that all his
provisions were inadequate to tide him over another night.

He had made a good living, but wasted his life—not in
slothfulness or crime or open shame, but by putting first things
last.

"So is he that layeth up treasure for himself, and is not rich
toward God" (verse 21). Or, to summarize the teaching of this
parable in a more hopeful vein by viewing the same truth from
its positive side, we have the Savior's exhortation: "But rather
seek ye the kingdom of God; and all these things shall be added
unto you" (verse 31).

---

[3] Thomas á Kempis (1380–1471), *Imitation of Christ*, Book 1, Chapter
19.

24

THE BARREN FIG TREE

The Goodness and Severity of God

Primary text: Luke 13:6-9.

Our Lord spoke this parable to certain news-bearers in His audience—on the way from Jerusalem to Perea—at about the end of the third year of His public ministry.

Introduction. Unless we are willing to assume this parable has no connection whatever with its context, we must conclude that it contemplates the Jewish nation as Jesus saw it at the time He spoke. Nor is there any valid reason for questioning either its contextual position in the Bible or its relevance to the then-existing situation. It is thoroughly germane to its setting in the narrative; it would be virtually incomprehensible apart from it. And subsequent history has confirmed its prophetic allusion to the abrogation of the Jewish Theocracy.

Furthermore, this application is borne out by a number of lateral passages:

* It harmonizes perfectly with Jesus' acted parable when, a few months later during Passion Week, He was to curse an unfruitful fig tree—a fig tree which, as a consequence, immediately "dried up from the roots" (cf. Mark 11:12-14, 20-22)—thus foreshadowing the imminent fate of apostate Jewry.

- It corresponds precisely with the teaching of several of Jesus' other parables—such as, for example, "The Wicked Husbandmen" (cf. Matthew 21: 33-46).
- It anticipates the explicit warnings of His Olivet Discourse (cf. Luke 21:6, 20-24).
- It depicts God's temporary abandonment of Jewry exactly as Paul describes it (cf. Romans 9—11).

Certainly, this parable, as do all the rest, embodies a spiritual lesson of universal significance, but as with the others, we must identify this one's primary theme before we can deduce its deeper spiritual meaning.

Background. First, then, let us glance at its background in the record. This parable was spoken about three months before the Crucifixion, while our Lord was en route from Jerusalem to Perea.

Painfully aware that He had already been rejected in all but an official way, He was greatly exercised with forebodings of the critical conflict that lay ahead. Taking the worst for granted, He had begun instructing His disciples concerning their future role while awaiting His second coming (cf. Luke 12:35-48). Then He had foretold of His death and the ensuing controversy that would attend the preaching of the Gospel (cf. Luke 12:49-53). Then, despite these foregone conclusions, He had turned to the people in a desperate effort to shake their unbelief and alert them to the inevitability of judgment unless they should even yet repent (cf. Luke 12:58–59).

There was no excuse for their spiritual stupidity. They could "discern the face of the sky and the earth" to predict the weather. Why, then, did they not discern the ominous issues of their times? (Cf. Luke 12:54-56.) Or failing in that, why did they not allow the sheer light of conscience to guide them in recognizing the Savior's Messiahship? (Cf. Luke 12:57.) One thing was sure: they were going to have to turn to Him with no further delay or else face the fearful consequences. They were headed for judgment, and Moses, whom they trusted, would testify against them (cf. John 5:45). Their only hope of deliverance lay in Christ. If they rejected Him, they would not escape without "paying the very last mite."

His audience seems to have concurred most heartily with this pronouncement on at least one point: terrible retribution awaits the sinner. But it's plain enough they didn't regard this as a threat to *themselves*. Yes, sinners should, and would, be overtaken by swift, irremediable judgment. As for *themselves*, they little dreamed of suffering such a fate. *They* were tithe-paying Jews, not lawless criminals! Surely, they thought, this "rabbi" must be referring to hapless outsiders, such as the band of Galilean seditionists whom Pilate had recently slain as they were offering their sacrifices in the temple court; or eighteen workmen who had been crushed to death by a collapsing tower at the Pool of Siloam—workmen Pilate had hired with money from the sacred treasury. However, Jesus answered them:

> Suppose ye that these Galileans were sinners above all the Galileans, because they suffered such things? I tell you, Nay: but, except ye repent, ye shall all likewise perish. Or those eighteen, upon whom the tower in Siloam fell, and slew them, think ye that they were sinners above all men that dwell in Jerusalem? I tell you, Nay: but, except ye repent, ye shall all likewise perish (verses 1-5).

By so saying, our Lord justified neither the seditious Galileans nor the unscrupulous workmen—nor did He say whether or not their deaths had resulted from providential punishment. Those issues, for His immediate purpose, were beside the point. Those people had perished as members of the same sinful race to which the overconfident Jews in His audience belonged. Neither their guilt nor its penalty was at all exceptional. He was saying, in effect:

> What then? are you better than they? No, in no wise: for we have before proved both Jews and Gentiles, that they are all under sin . . . for all have sinned, and [still do] come short of the glory

of God (Romans 3:9, 23).

His reminder was true of them both personally and nationally, and we may be sure that He was appealing to them on both of these scores. *National* guilt and its impending punishment were immediately in view, but without subtracting a whit from their *personal* liability to the retributive justice of which their national plight was but a collective accompaniment. As sinners, guilty as all the rest, they were confronted with two alternatives: they must either repent or perish.

It was against this background Jesus began to relate His parable . . .

Examination and interpretation. "A certain man used to have a fig tree which had been planted in his vineyard . . ." (verse 6, RV). The "Song of the Vineyard" in the fifth chapter of Isaiah— though its imagery is not altogether the same as that occurring here—provides some invaluable clues to the meaning of this illustration. There we are told that "the vineyard of the LORD of hosts, is the house of Israel, and the men of Judah his pleasant plant . . ." According to that passage, the *vineyard,* as "the house of Israel," represents the special sphere of divine favor; its *owner,* "the Lord of hosts," is God; and the *fig tree,* which in this case is "his pleasant plant," stands for "the men of Judah" in particular, as distinguished from other Israelites.

And if these distinctions should seem unduly discriminate, it is enough to point out that they are verified by the known facts of history. Fortunately for us, they cut several Gordian knots of Biblical interpretation. Otherwise, if Israel in general is represented by both the vineyard and the fig tree, how are we to account for their implicit discreteness in the parable? But if the fig tree represents the men of Judah, as distinguished not only from the Gentiles but also from the Ten Tribes of the Dispersion, it is easy to see both the historical and theological accuracy of the parable. It was, in fact, the men of Judah who at that time enjoyed the privileges of the house of Israel; it was they, not the Israelites in general, whose rejection of Christ was about to precipitate the destruction of their land and city. This fig tree was not necessarily a young one, as some interpreters surmise; it was one which had been planted previously, at an unspecified time.

"A certain man used to have a fig tree which had been planted in his vineyard; and he came seeking fruit on it, and did not find any" (verse 6, RV). The original verb translated *came* indicates that the owner of the vineyard came at a single, specific time; likewise, the form of the verb *did* (not) *find* refers to that same particular time. This specific time can refer only to the First Advent of Christ. Although, God had looked for fruit in Israel in the times of Moses, of the judges, and of the kings and prophets, these occasions are not contemplated here. Here, He is said to have come at the fruiting season proper, so to speak, when, above all other times, He had a right to expect an abundant yield. He looked in vain, "looked for judgment, but behold oppression; for righteousness, but behold a cry" (Isaiah 5:7).

Then the owner said to his vine-dresser, "Lo, for three years I come seeking fruit on this fig tree, and I do not find any . . ." (verse 7, RV). Here the single, specific coming in search of fruit is shown to have comprised a period of three years. Such is the meaning of the language, and that is precisely what God, the vineyard owner, had done during the earthly ministry of Christ. For three years He had demanded Jewry (the men of Judah) to bring forth the fruits of repentance and faith, but as a nation, they had responded with "nothing but leaves" (cf. Mark 11:13)—meaning, the pretentious externals of soulless legalism. With this obvious meaning of three years mentioned so specifically, it is hard to understand why any responsible expositor should hesitate to say so. Is it, after all, too great a burden on scholarship to believe that the Lord Jesus was able to describe a historical fact exactly as history now records it?

There is, however, one thing in the story that history does not record. We are told that when the owner of the vineyard despaired of finding fruit on the fig tree, he told the vine-dresser to "cut it out" of the vineyard at once (verse 7, RV). That event means that God was minded to let Jesus (since, evidently, the *vine-dresser* represents Jesus, the "wellbeloved" in Isaiah's song) disinherit Jewry summarily without any further delay, if He chose to do so. This addition is not a gratuitous flourish, but a significant stroke, in the imagery of the parable—much like the time when God, greatly incensed at Israel's faithlessness, had said to Moses, "Now therefore let me alone, that my wrath may wax hot against them, that I may consume them: and I will make of thee a great nation" (Exodus 32:10). Such was God's attitude toward Jewry now. As the Owner of the vineyard, God was saying, "Why cumbereth it the ground?"—or, in so many words, "*Why allow an unproductive tree to make the ground it occupies unproductive?*" (Cf. verse 7.) Jewry was barren, but not only barren, it was abusing a privileged position which might have been put to better use by a better tree.

As did Moses of old, the vine-dresser then asked the lord of the vineyard to give his charge yet another opportunity:

> Spare it this year also, until I may dig around it
> and apply manure: perhaps it may bear fruit in
> the near future, and if not thou shalt cut it down
> (verses 8–9, RV).

The language is complicated with some untranslatable idioms, but this rendering, I think, keeps the intended sense.

For three years, the Lord had been pleading with the Jews to repent and believe the Gospel. A good many individuals among them, mostly of the lower classes, had done so; but the nation at large, and especially the ruling clique, had rebuffed His message with stolid indifference or, worse, with outright contempt. Now, God was ready to take the Kingdom from them and give it "to a nation bringing forth the fruits thereof" (cf. Matthew 21:43). But, according to this parable, the Son besought Him to give them one more year to reconsider their perilous course. He questioned neither the justice of God's decree nor the inevitability of its execution—in the absence of a national repentance. He only asked for one more year of grace. Then, He agreed, if the "fig tree" was still unfruitful after being digged and manured for another year, it should indeed be given up as a hopeless liability.

How, in Christ's remaining months on earth, He "digged" about the Jewish nation's conscience and used every means at His command to elicit faith repentance and faith! All to no avail—for instead of figs, it brought forth gory thorns. How, even after His death, the apostles, pointing back to Calvary and the open tomb, continued to plead:

> Repent ye therefore, and be converted, that your sins may be blotted out, when the times of refreshing shall come from the presence of the Lord; and he shall send Jesus Christ, which before was preached unto you: whom the heaven must receive until the times of restitution of all things which God hath spoken by the mouth of all his holy prophets since the world began (Acts 3:19-21).

Again, no better response. Jewry sinned away its remaining days of grace. Paul made a desperate effort to revive the dying "tree," but eventually he gave up the task, turning to Gentiles (cf. Acts 28:25-28). Then came Titus with his merciless legions. The land was ravished. The city was burned. Those few "men of Judah" who survived the bloody siege were dragged in chains to the ends of the earth.

The lesson of this parable may well be summarized with the words of Paul, when he saw God's patience being spurned and the fate of the impenitent Jews taking shape:

> Behold therefore the goodness and severity of God—

It is a lesson we all need to learn by taking heed to Jewry's plight, lest, failing that, we too should have to learn it by bitter experience. Now, as then, it holds forth only two alternatives:

> —on those who fall, severity; but toward us, goodness, if we continue in His goodness: otherwise we also shall be cut off (cf. Romans 11:22).

The Goodness and Severity of God

25

An Admonitory Parable

THE AMBITIOUS
WEDDING GUESTS

The Moral Implications of
Bad Manners

Primary text: Luke 14:7-11.

*Our Lord spoke this parable to certain lawyers and
Pharisees—in the home of a prominent Pharisee, in
Perea—about three months before the Crucifixion.*

Background. When He told this parable, the Master was being
entertained at a Sabbath dinner in the home of a well-to-do
Pharisee, along with a number of local Jewish dignitaries, who
had been invited so they might scrutinize His conduct and, if
possible, impeach His Messianic claims (cf. verse 1). These other
guests had been "watching" the distinguished "Rabbi" who
claimed to be Israel's King. Now He, in turn, was "marking"
them (verse 7)—those proud, aspiring ecclesiastics who liked
to think of themselves as children of the kingdom (cf. Matthew
8:12), but whom He knew to be veritable strangers to the true
Israel of God.

The atmosphere was tense. It could have become explosive.
How would the King react to the inquisition of His examiners?
How would He counter the strategy of these scheming cavilers
determined to discredit Him in any way they could?

210

He began by healing a dropsical man who evidently had been planted on the scene to provoke a work of mercy on the Sabbath, in violation of rabbinical taboos (cf. verses 2-4). He then justified that action with an argument that left His critics speechless (cf. verses 5–6) and turned the searchlight on them. Using a parable as a rhetorical mirror, He confronted them with the sorry spectacle they had unwittingly made of themselves.

Having noticed each of the ambitious guests making a studied effort to maneuver himself into a place of special distinction at the table (cf. verse 7), Jesus simply described what He had just seen, using the imagery from an Oriental wedding feast to reprove their misbehavior.

Not that His object was merely to excel in a battle of wits. Neither then nor at any other time did He allow Himself to be drawn into an exchange of mere personal recriminations, returning blow for blow just to win an argument. In fact, He never digressed from His appointed mission to censure trivial inconsistencies or to amuse His audience. Christ invariably confined Himself to proclaiming some vital spiritual truth— or, as in the present case, to exposing some serious fault. Here He used a commonplace situation to dramatize the hypocrisy of His opponents, thereby compelling them to take the witness stand against themselves.

Examination and interpretation. On the very scene which had been designed to embarrass Him, He turned the foils of His critics' trap into a boomerang by using a parable that was so transparently applicable to what was taking place that just to be there to hear it was to feel oneself involved in its censure. No one could possibly miss the point.

This representative group of Jewish aristocrats were guilty, each and all, not only of an ugly breach of etiquette, but of conduct that betrayed a spirit utterly incompatible with the Messianic hope they feigned to hold so dear. So, although this parable certainly affords some needful lessons of a personal nature for the individual, it is clear from the larger considerations of the context that it deals primarily with the ethical demands of the promised Kingdom.

Still, since any social group is composed of individuals, its collective deportment is, at its roots, intensely personal. For this reason, not even so slight a matter as rudimentary etiquette may be regarded as insignificant. Most people usually veer to one of two extremes regarding social manners and proprieties, some taking a facetious or scornful view of such amenities, while others go overboard to observe them with meticulous care. But Jesus, in keeping with His characteristic moderation, took a middle course. Frowning on the squeamish austerity of the scribes and Pharisees, still He stressed the need for ethical integrity in human conduct, insisting that one should do the proper thing—not to conform to the prevailing fancies of the social set, but because it is *right*.

Thus He gave us the underlying motivation of practical Christianity: unselfish zeal to treat others right—and, if need be, *more* than right—not to escape the frown or win the smile of supercilious critics, but because it becomes the heirs of grace to be gracious. Moreover, our consideration for the dignity and well-being of our fellow men reflects an attitude indicative of our own personal character.

Those wretched men who saw their meanness portrayed in the Savior's parable had violated a canon of polite society, thereby unwittingly exposing the carnal pride, conceit, and selfishness that characterized their lives—in spite of all their hypocritical pretensions to the contrary. As Jesus spoke, they could no longer escape the glare of open embarrassment, for they were mutually conscious that each of them had coveted the highest seat. Nor does the parabolic mirror look much better now than then! By and large, the ancient scene is as modern as our own society—or should we say, as our dining rooms? or even, as our churches? Which of us has not beheld, in our own churches . . .

- ambitious preachers vying for the highest pulpits?
- deacons competing for the highest places on the board?
- singers scrambling for the highest perches in the choir?
- rival families contending for the highest offices in the church?

Why else are our churches cluttered with the wreckage of severed friendships, broken hearts, and shattered nerves? There may be scores of answers that at first seem plausible enough. But by far the most of this tragic confusion stems from a perennial struggle for the "highest seats." And what a ruthless contest that can be, and often is! All too frequently, it is a battle royal that regards no rules and bars no holds, no weapons, no blows. It is quite appalling to see what depths of shame are plumbed, what ignoble devices are resorted to, and what treacherous means are used when envious saints begin to rough up one another in the name of the Lord! It is, strangely enough, the relative "innocent" who suffers most of the initial casualties, for the *immediate* advantage almost always belongs to the unscrupulous person who brandishes weapons a better man would never stoop to use.

Nor is this situation something new. The Scriptures abound with instances in which we see "servants upon horses, and princes walking as servants upon the earth" (Ecclesiastes 10:7):

- When Abel was threatened by Cain, he fell easy victim to his brother's wrath because—as an honorable man of peace—he could ill afford to ward off blow with blow.
- Isaac, when mocked by Ishmael, was himself too noble to retaliate with mockery.
- Moses endured the insolence of Korah, Dathan, Abiram, and On when—but for his incomparable meekness—he might have silenced them summarily with the sword.
- David's tender care for Absalom, his treacherous son, put him completely at the youthful rebel's mercy and cost him his throne.

Thus were Godly men restrained by their virtues; but their enemies, free to molest them with impunity. Similar examples are easily multiplied. Consider . . .

- Judas, who took advantage of his Master's love;
- Ananias and Sapphira, who used deceit to exploit the confidence of their fellow saints; and
- Diotrephes, who oppressed his brethren to make himself preeminent.

Down through the ages, such remorseless people have stopped at nothing in their relentless scramble for the "highest seats."

It might be asked: *Why does Providence seem silent while such unscrupulous opportunists victimize their meeker peers?* But that question can readily be answered with other ones:

- Where are the Cains, the Ishmaels, the Korahs, and the Absaloms now?
- Where are Judas, Ananias, and Diotrephes today?
- Where, on the other hand, are those long-suffering souls of whom they took advantage?

In each such case, initial perplexity is eventually resolved by the verdict of history. Sooner or later, the moral machinery of cosmic justice "puts down the mighty from their seats, and exalts them of low degree" (Luke 1:52). So Haman flourishes until he gets a scaffold built for Mordecai: then he hangs while Mordecai goes free! This universal and inexorable principle is so unerring that a perceptive poet warned, long centuries ago:

> Though the mills of God grind slowly,
> Aft they grind exceeding small.
> *Oracula Sibyllina*, viii:14 [4]

The arrogant fellow who wangles his way into the highest place is eventually compelled to yield it to some humbler but nobler guest. At last, the Lord of Providence looks down and says, "Give this man place" (verse 9). A red-faced status-seeker is degraded, and a worthier but less aggressive saint is bidden to

---

[4] *Bartlett's Familiar Quotations* attributes this quotation to George Herbert (*Jacula Prudentum*, pub. 1651) and Friedrich von Logau (*Retribution* in *Poetic Aphorisms*, pub. 1654, trans. by Henry Wadsworth Longfellow). One may find this quotation in various forms and attributed to various authors because of its frequent repetition in Western literature. The general sentiment of divine retribution being "slow but sure" goes back at least as far as the Greek dramatist Euripedes (c.484–406 B.C.), though of course, he was referring to beliefs about the Greek gods. (Cf. *Bartlett's*, 69:2, 244:38, and 247:15).

"go up higher" to a seat of honor he has never sought (cf. verse 10).

Essential teaching. "For whosoever exalteth himself shall be abased; but he that humbleth himself shall be exalted" (verse 11). Thus the Master concluded His story. Let us see if we can distinguish the specific message Christ intended this parable to convey to the listening Jewish leaders on the scene (not to forget that the lesson is equally applicable to us today):

- It was concerned primarily, not with the rude behavior of the Pharisees, but rather with the moral condition that caused them to misbehave.
- It dealt not so much with the ugly conduct of the dinner guests as with what their misconduct revealed about their unfitness for an incalculably greater feast.
- It deprecated not merely a local breach of etiquette, but the national depravity of Jewry as a whole.
- It weighed that generation in the balances and found it wanting in the elementary qualifications for citizenship in the Kingdom of God.

In the Sermon on the Mount, our Lord Jesus had defined the requisites for entrance into His Kingdom; here He warned the Jews that they were altogether ineligible.

The Messianic promises belong to those who are:	**but the Jewish leaders were:**
• poor in spirit	• self-sufficient
• mourn	• impenitent
• are meek	• arrogant
• hunger and thirst after righteousness	• already righteous in their own conceit
• are merciful	• ruthless
• pure in heart	• hypocritical
• peacemakers	• faultfinders
• persecuted for righteousness' sake	• the persecutors of the righteous.

As aspiring Theocrats, the Jews had completely disqualified

themselves. Descendants of Abraham they were, but they were not the true "children of the promise" (Romans 9:6-8). They would have to be "born again" before they could even *see* the Kingdom, much less *enter* it (cf. John 3:3, 5).

Such was the message couched in the original utterance of this parable, and it is just as true and needful now as then. It may be bitter in the belly, but it's sweet in the mouth—for "God resisteth the proud," but "giveth grace to the humblest" (I Peter 5:5).

26

THE GREAT SUPPER

The Perilous Folly of Overconfidence

Primary text: Luke 14:15-24
Cf. Matthew 22:1-4.

Our Lord spoke this parable to certain lawyers and Pharisees—in the home of a prominent Pharisee, in Perea—about three months before the Crucifixion.

Introduction. This parable has a good deal in common with "The Marriage of the King's Son" (p. 328; cf. Matthew 22:1-4), where substantially the same story is adapted (with certain variations) to illustrate a somewhat different situation. Here, it depicts the polite indifference of official Jewry toward the Savior's Kingdom message, but there, it pictures His eventual rejection by the ruling clique. In both cases, it foreshadows the subsequent extension of the Gospel to the world at large.

Presently, during the course of His Perean ministry, the Lord would deliver a series of seven related parables in defense of His reception of believing publicans and sinners. This one, though it antedates those seven, anticipates them in a more or less introductory way. Its interpretation must be determined largely by its chronological setting, that being a time when Jewry's unbelief had not reached its fateful climax. Although Jewish leaders made much ado about their pretended zeal for the Messianic Kingdom, they were actually more concerned

217

about their temporal affairs (much more so, no doubt, than they themselves were aware). Therefore, although they had not yet committed themselves to open rebellion, they were inwardly disposed to take that final step.

At first, they sought to conceal that ominous tendency by resorting to excuses. In time, however, such temporizing was to lead (as it all too often does) to an eventual crisis when a definite, irrevocable decision would have to be made. Already they were on the road to ruin, and Jesus, in the passage before us, warned them of the suicidal nature of their stubborn course.

Background. Behind everything else, both on the local scene and in the minds of Jesus and His audience, loomed colorful associations of an Oriental feast (part of which scene we have already examined in the foregoing parable, "The Ambitious Wedding Guests").

To recap: Jesus was sitting as guest of honor at a banquet in the home of a prosperous Pharisee, surrounded by the leading personalities of the area. They were "watching" Him, and He was "marking" them (cf. verses 1, 7). Several events already had taken place:

- On that Sabbath day, Jesus had healed a dropsical man in defiance of their critical scrutiny (cf. verses 3–4).
- He had defended His work of mercy with an argument that left them speechless: *Would not they themselves rescue an ox from a pit on the Sabbath?* (Cf. verses 5–6.)
- He had rebuked them for vying with one another for the most honorable places at the table (cf. verses 7-11).
- He had told His host it would be far better, rather than to entertain affluent friends and relatives (ones expected to return his favors), to make a feast for "the poor, the maimed, the lame, the blind," that he might be "recompensed at the resurrection of the just" (verses 12-14).

At this point, the record says, "And when one of them that sat at meat with him heard these things, he said unto him, Blessed is he that shall eat bread in the kingdom of God" (verse 15).

Was the man trying to change the subject in order to relieve the embarrassment of his host? to head off any further chiding of the entire company? to impress Jesus with his own piety? Or, did such motives combine to prompt his exclamation? At any rate, it seems that his allusion to the *festive* nature of the promised Kingdom elicited Jesus' reply. Therefore, this event throws a good deal of light on the forthcoming parable.

It is clear from all that follows that, while Jesus did not dissent from the sentiment which had just been expressed, He regarded it as merely a pious platitude on such a speaker's lips. The sanctimonious guest was just another worldling who was always ready to use religion to further his temporal aims. Just as Balaam of old, if he must die, he would fain "die the death of the righteous"—but to him the "hope of Israel" was only a vague, idealistic afterthought, in all respects secondary to his carnal ambitions. Doubtless he was familiar with the Biblical prophecy which likened the coming Kingdom to a "feast of fat things, a feast of wines on the lees" (cf. Isaiah 25:6). Unheedful of the Kingdom's ethical requirements, he fondly assumed that *he,* as a privileged Jew, was destined to inherit its felicity automatically!

He was, however, to be abruptly disabused of that conceit by the Savior's ensuing remarks. Indeed, the Kingdom of God would be a spiritual banquet for those who entered it. But the Pharisees, at the same time they were paying lip service to God, were actually excluding themselves from His royal feast. That fact was the unmistakable meaning of the forthcoming parable.

Examination and interpretation. Addressed directly to that talkative guest (he being representative of the other ruling Jews), the parable pictured them as being so absorbed in their earthly pursuits that they were disdainful of the Kingdom they pretended to cherish so much. Yes, they prized the prospect of feasting on the "fat things" of God at some distant day, but for the moment they were preoccupied with tastier viands of their own. Exploiting the present, they relegated the Kingdom to the future.

"Blessed is he" their spokesman had said, "that *shall* eat bread in the kingdom of God." Jesus insisted on the relevance of the Kingdom to the time at hand, having the parabolic host say, "Come; for all things are *now* ready" (verse 17, *italics added*). God had already prepared the "great supper" prefigured by the various "feasts of the LORD" in Levitical times and heralded by the prophets of succeeding centuries. It was now "at hand." Those who had been bidden for so long were now being given their final invitation. Notwithstanding their affected zeal for God, they were snubbing His unwanted bounty.

In a word, they were engrossed with other, more important affairs; so "they all with one consent began to make excuse" (verse 18). The excuses mentioned here are not exhaustive, but merely typical:

1a. One man had bought a tract of land, and he was eager to inspect it without delay (cf. verse 18).

2a. Another had purchased five yoke of oxen; he was in a hurry to try them out (cf. verse 19).

3a. Another, who had just got married, felt it was simply out of the question for him to be away from home for any cause (cf. verse 21).

Broadly speaking, their excuses represented the commercial, occupational, and social interests of life—all of which are quite legitimate in themselves. They were not mere pretexts, as we are sometimes told, but matters of real, *inordinate* concern, so much so that they held far more attraction than an ordinary feast.

Therein lay the recusants' unpardonable fault—not in their involvement in the customary activities of the workaday world, but in their contempt for an *extraordinary* privilege—as if it, too, were a common thing. Having been given ample notice that a banquet was being prepared for them, they should not have made conflicting plans—nor would they have done so, except for their low regard for their host and the table he set.

We shall not find the basic interpretation of this part of the parable by speculating about the nature of the various excuses, as is often done, although those occurring in this passage do, indeed, reflect the dominant characteristics of those men who offered them:

1b. The man of means imagined he was driven by necessity.

"I *must needs* go and see my newly acquired land," he said.
2b. The workman simply acted on his own discretion, seeing
no reason why he should even defend his right to do so.
"I go," he explained, "to prove my newly purchased oxen."
3b. As for the family man, his overweening preoccupation with
the responsibilities and pleasures of domestic life left him
quite helpless—or so he thought—to take any other course.
"I have married a wife," he said, "and therefore I cannot
come."
Thus were typical excuses cloaked in the guise of necessity,
prudence, and duty: *I must, I go, I cannot.*

But in the last analysis, the point is that all these excuses
were essentially alike—unwarranted, unjustifiable, foolish—
because they betrayed a woefully incorrect estimate of true
values. The real interpretation is echoed in Jesus' subsequent
comments on the conditions requisite to discipleship:

> If any man come to me, and hate not his father,
> and mother, and wife, and children, and breth-
> ren, and sisters, yea, and his own life also, he
> cannot by my disciple (verse 25).

It was because of these and similar earthly ties that Pharisees
deemed themselves excusable. Far from stopping to evaluate
the relative merits of such considerations, our Lord insisted
that *no excuse* can avert the terrible consequences of unbelief.
His invitation had to be given precedence over every other
interest—else its proffered blessings would be forfeited.

Christ Himself is the *servant* in the parable. And as such,
He evidently discussed Jewry's evasive tactics with God the
Father (the *host* in the parable) in His daily prayers. Being fully
conscious of the Father's will, Jesus had already been calling
"the poor, and the maimed, and the halt, and the blind"—that
is, the publicans and sinners—to the Kingdom feast (cf. verses
21–22). After His final rejection, crucifixion, and resurrection,
He would send forth His apostles to bring in the Gentiles also
(cf. verse 23).

"For," He concluded, as if He were emerging personally

from the imagery of the parable, "I say unto you, That none of those men which were bidden shall taste of my supper" (verse 24). It was idle for a Pharisee to speak of "eating bread in the kingdom of God." They all might as well give up the delusion that they would partake of that feast; by *excusing* themselves now, they were *excluding* themselves forever.

However, the conclusion of this parable can hardly mean (as is sometimes said) that an angry God commanded His house to be filled with heathen so there would be no room remaining for the Jews even if they should repent! It *is* true that

- God was indignant at Jewry's rejection of His gracious invitation;
- it was His intention to evangelize the Gentiles quickly during the present Age of Grace; and
- those who reject His invitation will never be saved.

But in light of all the rest of the Scriptures, we may be sure that those who fail of salvation will have only *themselves* to blame. It is not that God has withdrawn the invitation, but that they have rendered themselves incapable of accepting it.

Yet despite the self-reprobation of such willful disbelievers, the festive halls of grace will even so be filled with guests—for God, foreknowing Jewry's default, has chosen a people from among all nations to ensure that the divine desideratum shall be satisfied. His rich provisions must, of necessity, be offered, bestowed, and duly received—even if this means that other festive guests must be "compelled" to "come in" (cf. verse 23).

Here again, there is need for a word of caution, lest we read the wrong kind of compulsion into the language of the naked text. God never *forces* an unwilling person to accept salvation, but He constrains as many as will to receive it of their own accord. He does this, not through coercion, but through divine persuasion and enablement. The idea of drafting confessors by the sword, by the imposition of baptism, by means of spurious evangelistic methods—or by any other devious measure—is contrary to the moral constitution of both God and men. It is obnoxious to the spirit of the Gospel. The evangelist's task is to prevail upon impotent, undeserving sinners to believe that the invitation is truly bona fide, overcoming their misgivings, not the freedom of their wills: whereupon, if they do not resist the truth, the Holy Spirit prevails upon them then to accept forgiveness and eternal life of their own accord.

As for humanity in general, this parable warns that those who spurn "the goodness of God" are thereby treasuring up "unto themselves wrath against the day of wrath" (Romans 2:4–5).

Such a course, not necessarily fatal at the start, eventually leads to a state of impersuasibility and, hence, to an impasse which, morally speaking, "ties God's hands" and leaves the unbeliever to his doom.

The unbelief that damns is usually more a gradual descent than a sudden jump. Even so, in the end it issues in inexorable commitment, as the result of a volitional attitude that has slowly crystallized until it is rigid, inflexible, and unalterably fixed. Once so inconclusive, it eventuates in irretrievable finality. Meanwhile, however, the road to that dreadful fate is ordinarily paved with plausible excuses.

27

THE TOWER-BUILDER &
THE WARRIOR-KING

The Rationale of Self-Renunciation

Primary text: Luke 14:28-33.

Jesus spoke this parable to the multitudes, including a sizeable party of Galilean zealots— somewhere in Perea—during the third month (January) before His crucifixion.

Introduction and contextual background. This passage, as one might gather from the double title we have given it, actually embraces two distinct illustrations. However, since they set forth complementary aspects of the same lesson, it is, for all practical purposes, best to treat them together. Admittedly there is some question as to how this twofold illustration should be classified. As a warning against the risk of taking discipleship too lightly, it is *admonitory*. As a defense of our Lord's exacting requirements, it is *apologetic*. In any event, as an explanation of His call for complete self-renunciation, it is, unquestionably, *expository*.

Of one thing we may be sure from the start: it definitely is not, as some suppose, a depiction of how we must "pay on the barrelhead" to *buy* salvation from a tight-fisted God! Neither is it (granted that discipleship and salvation are not identical) a

---

demand on the disciple to count his resources and pay his own way. Besides being unable to do so, "What soldier ever serveth at his own charges?" (Cf. I Corinthians 9:7, ASV.)

What, then, did Jesus mean by "counting the cost?" To whom did He refer? A look at the foregoing context will, as usual, help us to get our bearings and find the right answers.

Despite the determined opposition of Jewry, as represented by the ruling classes at Jerusalem, the last few months of our Lord's career saw His popularity spiraling to an unprecedented high in the outlying regions of Perea. Vast multitudes, mostly composed of impetuous Galilean zealots, thronged about Him, evidently on the verge of volunteering for discipleship (cf. verse 25) . . . or so they thought.

Long weary of their Roman oppressors, not particularly fond of their own national leaders, Galileans were dreaming of a God-sent revolution and a better day. Having heard—and misunderstood—the Master's Kingdom message, they were ready to cast their lot with Him, in hope of sharing in the new order they thought He was about to set up. Meanwhile, the Savior, having "steadfastly set his face to go to Jerusalem" (cf. Luke 9:51), was sore at heart, burdened with premonitions of the cross awaiting Him there.

Our Lord knew that He would have to suffer on the cross before entering His glory (cf. Luke 24:26). He also knew that whoever followed Him "must through much tribulation enter into the kingdom of God" (cf. Acts 14:22). He understood that whoever became His disciple in a truly significant way would have to share the same unstinted devotion and singleness of heart that moved the Savior Himself to do the will of God— without counting the cost. As far as His personal mission was concerned, "paying the price without counting the cost" was exactly what He did: He "endured the cross with no regard for its shame" (Hebrews 12:2, CBW). Now, He called upon His followers to do the same (though not necessarily on the cross).

He did *not* tell His Galilean friends to count the cost of salvation to see if they had sufficient means with which to pay the price—as if salvation were for sale, or could be *bought*, at any price. Nor did He tell them to weigh their resources against

the cost of discipleship—as if any man could *entitle* himself to
such a calling. He urged them, rather, to take a pauper's oath,
so to speak: to relinquish everything they had and to depend
altogether on Him whose "strength is made perfect in our weakness" (cf. II Corinthians 12:9). He did not demand personal
assets, but complete self-renunciation, so that His disciples
might be used to exhibit the all-sufficiency of God. As He had
already insisted,

> If any man come to me, and hate not his father,
> and mother, and wife, and children, and breth-
> ren, and sisters, yea, and his own life also, he
> cannot be my disciple (verses 26–27).

Although this language must certainly be taken rhetorically, it
is, nevertheless, a most serious admonition. Christ, above all
others, teaches and inspires us to *love* our fellowmen—to love
not only our friends, but even our enemies—and none other is
quite so devoted to his loved ones as a consecrated Christian.

But when a loyal disciple has to choose between Christ and
a possession, a loved one, or even his own life, he really has no
choice at all. *Anything,* no matter how dear, that challenges the
preeminence of Christ in a Christian's heart must then occupy
the position of a detestable idol. However much a disciple may
cherish that object, whatever it is worth to him personally, he
will renounce it when it rivals his devotion to his Lord.

In a sense, such loyalty does entail a tremendous *cost,* if
one considers it such, but that is not the feeling of those who
actually forsake all else to follow Christ. They feel, instead, as
Paul did when he said:

> Howbeit what things were gain to me, these I
> have counted loss for Christ. Yea verily, and I
> count all things to be loss for the excellency of
> the knowledge of Christ Jesus my Lord: for
> whom I have suffered the loss of all things, and
> do count them but refuse, that I may gain Christ
> ... (Philippians 3:7–8, ASV).

Note that the author of these words, who outdid all his peers in denying himself for Jesus' sake, never bothered to count the *cost* of his commitment, rather considered only the *gain* accruing from the losses he sustained.

As for what it means to "hate" one's "loved ones" out of loyalty to Christ, Paul left us a classic example. "I could wish that myself were accursed from Christ for my brethren, my kinsmen according to the flesh" (Romans 9:3), he did confide under oath—yet as he wrote the words, he was submitting to Jewish ostracism rather than compromise his allegiance to Christ. That is how a true disciple "counts" and "hates."

Whatever "cost" that course may entail—if one insists on that kind of reckoning—that is *not* the subject of the following parable! Our Lord never dignified a fallacy in an effort to elicit a better response than He could win with the simple truth, nor is this case an exception to that rule. True, personal surrender and obedience are implicit in the initial act of faith, and every believer should carry out that resolution ever afterward. But we may be sure that this parable was not meant to extort our fidelity by conveying an impression that salvation depends upon mere human perseverance rather than the faithfulness of God.

Nor was it meant to teach, contrary to all the rest of the Scriptures, that we disciples must rely on our own resources to discharge the duties of our calling. Far from inculcating a spirit of self-reliance, the Master proposed, instead, to explain why He demands complete self-renunciation from those who follow Him.

Examination and interpretation. So, did these temperamental Galileans think of becoming His disciples? Then they should consider well the course He meant to pursue. He was going to "build a tower" and "wage a war." A sea of blood and tears lay between Him and His goal.

He was a King indeed, but He must build His Kingdom from start to finish, not merely seize and reform the existing order. An enemy would oppose His building program, just as Sanballat had harassed the forces of Nehemiah as they struggled to restore the walls of Jerusalem. Therefore, He would be in need of dedicated workmen free to use the trowel, willing to wield the sword (cf. Nehemiah 4:7-18). He Himself would lay the foundation of His royal house, but in the providence of God, He would need recruits to carry the work to completion, men who—notwithstanding their personal inadequacies—were free of all encumbrances, willing to be used as instruments of God, and unconditionally loyal to Him.

Thus, Christ Himself was counting the cost and assessing His assets—not, indeed, with a view to the prosecution of His own mission, which He had already resolved to fulfill at all events—but to make sure that He would have the necessary resources in terms of faithful warrior-builders. That, He told His impulsive friends, was why they must renounce all their worldly interests if they were to follow Him. It was as if He had said:

> *Why are My requirements so exacting? I will tell you. I am like a man building a magnificent mansion with parapets soaring upward to the sky. I am a thoroughly competent architect, having all the resources of heaven at My command; even so, My plans call for dependable workmen. Now, I have carefully considered what it will take, in the face of enemy opposition, to bring My Kingdom to completion; and there is no substitute for the kind of discipleship the situation demands.*

Or, as Christ delivered the message:

> For which of you, desiring to build a tower, does not first sit down and count up the expense, whether he has what is necessary for its completion; lest, perchance, after he has laid its foundation and is not able to finish it, all who look on begin to jeer him, saying, This man began to build and was not able to finish? (Verses 28-30, revised.)

This paragraph was as much a soliloquy as an exposition—or, at least, it was a soliloquy before it *became* an exposition. It shows that Jesus was pondering the Great Commission a good while before He went to Calvary. If it indicates comparatively few real disciples exist, it also discloses the tremendous faith the Savior places in them.

His belief that His disciples would not fail him was why He could say on the night before His death:

> Verily, verily, I say unto you, He that believeth on me, the works that I do shall he do also; and greater works than these shall he do; because I go to my Father (John 14:12).

He knew that without the single-hearted loyalty He required, the foundation He laid at Calvary would have had no "tower" to rise above the skyline of the world. As things turned out, the time came when Gamaliel had to say:

> Refrain from these men, and let them alone: for if this counsel or work be of men, it will come to nought: but if it be of God, ye cannot overthrow it; lest haply ye be found even to fight against God (Acts 6:38–39).

And "to him," the record says, the Sanhedrin "agreed" (Acts 6:40)—thus, in the light of subsequent history, making Jewish officialdom a solemn witness to God's endorsement of Jesus' Messiahship and the Theocratic claims of the Christian Church.

Jesus goes directly on to the second illustration:

> ... what king, going forth to engage in war with another king, does not first sit down and consider whether he is able with ten thousand to meet one who comes against him with twenty thousand? And if not, while he is still a great way off he dispatches an envoy and asks terms of peace (verses 31–32, RV).

The Rationale of Self-Renunciation

That kind of forethought is what any king would do. Jesus, in considering the forces He would need to vanquish those of His enemy Satan, had been over all that ground. He knew that from the start, His followers would encounter tremendous odds, for they were a mere handful of "sheep" against all the merciless "wolves" of the Jewish hierarchy; a few thousand defenseless peasants, freedmen, and slaves against millions of Romans; a small minority against the teeming masses of a godless world.

For those reasons He must insist on disciples of sterling quality—men who could face and withstand the minions of the Sanhedrin, the wild beasts of Sphesus, the Caesars of Rome, and the more sophisticated, but nonetheless formidable, perils of modern times.

The Galileans could understand why it would be imperative for one building a palace, waging a war, or doing both at the same time to have a corps of thoroughly dedicated warrior-builders. Jesus gave this double-sided illustration to help them realize He was not just some political revolutionist, but that He was God's Messiah, intent on building a new Theocracy; He was God's anointed King, intent on waging war against His foes until "the kingdoms of this world" have "become the kingdoms of our Lord, and his Christ" (Revelation 11:15).

As such, and with such ends in view, He had to be extremely careful in selecting those who, under God, were to finish the work He began. "So therefore," He warned, "every one of you who does not bid farewell to all his worldly interests cannot be My disciple" (verse 33, revised).

This may be, and doubtless is, a lisping interpretation. But I sincerely believe that even if it stammers, it stammers out the truth. The Lord Jesus *never* put salvation up for sale. He *never* conditioned discipleship on self-sufficiency. He *did* insist that we must be emptied of *self* to be filled with the power of God, and that only such disciples are disciples indeed.

SECTION FIVE
INTEGRITY OF THE KINGDOM

"Back of everything lay
a conflict and an indictment.
The conflict raged between
Judaism as the Pharisees
interpreted it and the
Gospel as Jesus preached it.
The indictments hurled
against Jesus by the Pharisees
and scribes brought Him
to task because He made a
practice of showing kindness
to the 'untouchables'
of that day ..."

Preliminary Thoughts on the Apologetic Parables

Then drew near unto him all the publicans and sinners for to hear him. And the Pharisees and scribes murmured, saying, This man receiveth sinners, and eateth with them.—Luke 15:1–2.

The foregoing scripture introduces a series of seven parables delivered by the Lord Jesus during His major tour of Perea in February before His crucifixion. He had once before visited the trans-Jordan region, and He was to pass that way again on His final journey from Ephraim to Jerusalem. But this was by far His most lengthy itinerary in that area, as well as the most important—owing to the critical issues with which He dealt at that time.

Characteristics of apologetic parables. As we proceed with our examination of these seven, it will become apparent why we have grouped them together and designated them as *apologetic parables,* for although the first four are more closely connected than the final three, they were all spoken *in defense of the Savior's ministry.* Or—inasmuch as His ministry and His message were virtually indissociable—it would be equally fitting to say that this cluster of parables constitutes a comprehensive defense of the Gospel. Hence, as distinguished from vindicative parables, which were meant to *authenticate* His personal claims, these apologetic ones were intended to demonstrate the validity and authority of His teaching.

There is no difficulty whatever in perceiving the apologetic character of the first four of these stories, which were addressed to the Pharisees. However, since two of the latter three were spoken to the disciples, an indiscriminating reader is likely to overlook their bearing on the same general theme, unmindful that the disciples, also, needed to realize the integrity of the Master's doctrine.

Purpose of apologetic parables. Moreover, the dual purpose of these parables—to instruct believers and unbelievers alike— may be seen in the fact that all but, perhaps, the last one were heard by both classes. The first four were spoken to the Pharisees in the presence of the disciples; the fifth, to the disciples in the presence of the Pharisees; the sixth, to the Pharisees in the presence of the disciples; and only the last one, to the disciples alone (as far as the record shows). In all events, we must consider the series as a whole, and each parable in its proper sequence, if we wish to see their several details in their true perspective.

The charges against Jesus. Back of everything lay a conflict and an indictment. The conflict raged between Judaism as the Pharisees interpreted it and the Gospel as Jesus preached it. The indictments hurled against Jesus by the Pharisees and scribes brought Him to task because He made a practice of showing kindness to the "untouchables" of that day: i.e., the publicans and sinners. Just as the Jews in general regarded the Gentiles as "dogs," their religious leaders looked upon the wayward masses of their own nation with little less contempt.

Publicans, who hired themselves to their Roman overlords to gather exorbitant taxes from their fellow countrymen, were especially detested, and all open sinners were treated as moral lepers. No self-respecting rabbi would so much as read the Scriptures in the presence of such outcasts. The oath of one of these was disesteemed as a worthless gesture in court. They were not even allowed to sue for the recovery of lost property. Yet here was a popular "Rabbi" who actually encouraged their attentions; defying conventional taboos, He was known to treat these undesirables with courtesy and respect. The Pharisees were horrified. The scribes raised their eyebrows. And they all agreed among themselves that such a course of conduct was outrageous, unreasonable, and wrong.

But their real grievance was against the *message* that offered forgiveness, peace, and divine acceptance to the common horde. To their way of thinking, it was manifestly false: a spurious gospel that pampered stupidity, glossed over irresponsibility, and put a premium on willful disobedience, thus condoning immorality, engendering contempt for the Law, encouraging delusive hopes that could never be realized.

Or so our Lord sized up His critics' complaints, if we may judge by the way He answered them in the following parables.

Christ's defense. The first three of these illustrations—"The Lost Sheep," "The Lost Piece of Silver," and "The Lost Son"— defend the reasonableness of recovering the stupid, the irresponsible, and the willful, in that order. The fourth, "The Elder Brother," exposes the *un*reasonableness of resenting such a ministry of mercy. The fifth, "The Unjust Steward," defends the moral integrity of the Gospel. The sixth, "The Rich Man and Lazarus," shows how the Gospel remands all impenitent unbelievers to the retributive justice required by the Law. The seventh, "The Unprofitable Servant," emphasizes the fact that redeeming grace is the sinner's only hope.

Thus, together, these parables argue that the Gospel is not only reasonable, but profoundly ethical; not only feasible, but absolutely indispensable!

28

THE LOST SHEEP

The Reasonableness of Recovering the Stupid

Primary text: Luke 15:3-7
Cf. Matthew 18:12-14.

Jesus spoke this parable to the scribes and Pharisees in the presence of His disciples, including a number of converted publicans and sinners, somewhere in Perea—during the second month (February) before His crucifixion.

Spiritually, this passage alludes to our Lord in His role as the Good Shepherd. The parable depicts a typical Pharisee or scribe owning a hundred sheep. Jesus asks a searching question:

What man of you, having an hundred sheep, if he lose one of them, doth not leave the ninety and nine in the wilderness, and go after that which is lost, until he find it? (Cf. verse 4.)

He was saying, in effect:

Just as, by human standards, you think it reasonable to salvage one valuable animal, to Me it is not only

---

> *reasonable but imperative to save each and every lost*
> *man. You cannot understand My compassion for these*
> *sinners because you have none yourselves. In turn,*
> *that attitude betrays your perverse set of values. You*
> *recognize the worth of a domestic animal—a sheep,*
> *whose mutton and wool contribute to your carnal*
> *needs and comforts (your sumptuous tables, your*
> *splendid wardrobes)—but it seems preposterous to*
> *your callous hearts that I should value the soul of*
> *one erring man for its sake alone. It is, therefore,* you
> *who are unreasonable, and it is your lovelessness that*
> *makes you so.*

It might, of course, be replied there is no excuse for the sinner's stupidity, and therefore, he does not deserve such compassion. That is all too true; nor did Jesus deny it. But this objection takes no account of the magnanimous grace underlying God's whole redemptive program, apart from which we should all alike be doomed. Jesus replies by calling attention to a similar case in the natural realm: The same is true of a wayward sheep, which even a Pharisee would eagerly recover—regardless of its stupidity and undeservingness.

In the case of humans, an additional consideration—though by no means *obliging* God to save us—fully *justifies* Him in doing so: as possessors of His image, we are valued, if not for what we are, for what we are capable of becoming. Thus, our *potential* worth is enough to vouch that God's love for us, wretched as we are, is eminently rational and reasonable.

In this parable a sinner's plight is considered more as a result of sheer stupidity than of culpable perversity, for a sheep is far more doltish than deliberate. No other domestic animal is quite so dull-witted, prone to wander, and helpless to find its way back home. Its straying results from inadvertence, not design— a fact which, though it does not excuse the animal's folly, does tend to extenuate its accountability. Although there is a good deal more that might be said on this subject, suffice it to say that we are, by our nature, sufficiently sheeplike to be morally

The Reasonableness of Recovering the Stupid

reclaimable—not so utterly responsible as to be incapable of restoration by God's appointed means.

Despite a widespread misapprehension to the contrary, the Bible does not teach that Adam was created either righteous or unrighteous, but simply in a state of innocence. Unlike the case of the apostate angels, who placed themselves beyond the reach of righteous grace by sinning against unlimited light, the fall of man was sufficiently mitigated by ignorance to permit his redemption by evangelical means.

This divine analysis is implicit in that matchless Isaianic passage that says:

> All we *like sheep* have gone astray; we have turned every one to his own way; and the LORD hath laid on him [our blessed Savior] the iniquity of us all (Isaiah 53:6, *italics added*).

The nature of our lost condition admits of our reclamation. It does not necessitate our salvation in the sense of obligating God to bestow it, but—granted that He is willing—it allows Him to do so. In view of His unquestionable benevolence, this condition makes His redemptive efforts manifestly reasonable. Moreover, the manner in which He imparts His mercy is just as rational and ethical as His desire to do so:

- In a world governed by His decrees, all laws and agencies of the cosmic order cooperate to promote the welfare of those who are in His will.
- As for those who oppose Him, all the mechanism of the divine economy is organized to ferret out and penalize their sins, and finally, to expel them as undesirable aliens from the presence of the Lord.
- And that expulsion is what it means to be lost: to be like a sheep estranged from its proper environment, at odds with its surroundings, cut off from providential protection and support, and exposed to immediate hardship and eventual ruin—all as a result of stark *stupidity*.

"But God commendeth his love toward us in that *while we were yet sinners*, Christ died for us" (Romans 5:8, *italics added*).

Why did Christ die for us sinners? "That he might be just, and the justifier of him which believeth in Jesus" (Romans 3:26). "God was in Christ, reconciling the world unto himself" (II Corinthians 5:19). We were/are stupid, sinful, and utterly undeserving of such divine solicitude, but

> ... God, who is rich in mercy, for his great love wherewith he loved us, even when we were dead in sins, hath quickened us together with Christ (by grace are ye saved) and hath raised us up together, and made us sit together in heavenly places in Christ Jesus (Ephesians 2:4-6).

This idea, to the world, is foolishness, but to us who are saved, it is "the power of God, and the wisdom of God" (cf. I Corinthians 1:18-24). It was unreasonable to the merciless Pharisees only because they were too stupid to perceive the gracious logic of God's impartial love.

This parable also probed a touchy area of resentment which, though not expressly mentioned in the Pharisees' complaint, stood out like a swollen thumb:
- Why did this "Rabbi," go out of His way to patronize the mean and lowly, yet pay little or no attention to the nation's religious leaders?
- Why did He virtually ignore the rabbinical schools and the doctors of the Law and the venerated Sanhedrin?
- Why did He "turn a cold shoulder" to the ecclesiastical aristocracy of His day?

We may be sure that these affronts to the "ninety and nine" offended His critics as much as, or more than, His concern for the "one sheep!"

In these unspoken accusations, the Jewish leaders were blaming Him for a situation of their own making. Hadn't they, in protesting their self-sufficiency, placed themselves outside the scope of His special ministry? He had come "to seek and save that which was lost" (Luke 19:10)—*they* had disclaimed any need for such services on their behalf! The peers of Israel considered themselves secure in the legal fold, and it would have been futile to challenge that conceit while they were in their current frame of mind. So, on the principle that "They that are whole need not a physician; but they that are sick" (Luke 5:31), Jesus was ministering to those who recognized, who *felt*, their need of His good offices.

This parable closes (as do the two which immediately follow it) with a climactic stress on the meetness of *rejoicing* when the lost are reclaimed. To do so is to share God's attitude and, thus, show oneself to be in moral harmony with Him. This test found the Pharisees both wanting and self-condemned, for although they too would have celebrated the rescue of an errant animal, they were not only joyless, but actually bitter, when they saw "the lost sheep of the house of Israel" being saved.

They followed, in the realm of nature, the very practice they condemned in the realm of grace—thereby endorsing an earthly standard that convicted them before the court of heaven. It demonstrated that their objection to the Gospel rested not on principle, but on self-interest. They could sell or fleece or eat a sheep, but the only way they could exploit a sinner was to use him as a whipping boy.

This brief analysis sums up the primary teaching of the first apologetic parable and anticipates that of the following three. Elsewise, they differ materially only in their respective emphases, depicting the sinner's lost condition from various points of view.

29

THE LOST PIECE OF SILVER

The Reasonableness of
Recovering the Irresponsible

Primary text: Luke 15:8-10.

Jesus spoke this parable to the scribes and Pharisees in the presence of His disciples, including a number of converted publicans and sinners—somewhere in Perea—during the second month (February) before His crucifixion.

Still reasoning with the loveless Pharisees, our Lord went on to say:

> Either what woman having ten pieces of silver, if she lose one piece, doth not light a candle, and sweep diligently till she find it? And when she hath found it, she calleth her friends and her neighbors together, saying, Rejoice with me; for I have found the piece which was lost (verses 8–9).

It would appear that, as far as the scribes and the Pharisees were prepared to understand it, this parable simply reiterated the teaching of the preceding one by clothing the same truth with new imagery—at most underscoring the universality of

---

241

human concern for things that are lost.

They most likely understood it to mean, in effect, that:

*Just as any man among them would have sought and
rejoiced upon finding a wandering sheep, any woman
who had lost a piece of silver would have felt and acted
the same way, it being normal for any human being,
regardless of class or sex, to follow such a course.*

This basic lesson, it seems to me, was about as much as the
Master's critics could have gotten from His current illustrations
up to this point. No Pharisee would have chided a fellow man
for recovering a sheep or a woman for recovering a coin. Why
did they take offense at Jesus for reclaiming His lost property?

However, to the disciples who overheard these words—and
certainly to us who read them in light of the New Testament as
a whole—they were doubtless meant to illuminate several other
facets of the Gospel that a callous unbeliever could scarcely be
expected to appreciate. Whereas the parable of the lost sheep
undoubtedly alludes to Christ as the Seeker of wayward souls,
this one may be understood as picturing the ministry of the
Holy Spirit through the Church. It is thus construed by many
enlightened interpreters. According to this view—
• the *woman* is generally thought to represent the Church;
• the *candle* (more correctly, *lamp*), the Word of God; and
• the act of sweeping, various kinds of evangelistic activity
—all of which is at least plausible from hindsight, though it
should not be pressed as a dogmatic interpretation.

More to the point is the nature of the article the woman is
said to have lost—the piece of silver, or *drachma*. Unlike the
sheep, an animate creature possessing volitional freedom within
the bounds of limited intelligence, a piece of silver is altogether
lifeless, insensible, and irresponsible. In the former case, there
was volition with qualified accountability, but in the latter, no
volition or responsibility at all.

But how can one and the same lost person be represented
under figures so radically dissimilar? Can he at once be both
alive and without life, sentient and insentient, responsible and

irresponsible? Evidently, in some sense, yes!—and this variety of seemingly disparate attributes will be extended still further when we see the sinner described as a *son* in the next parable! Nor are these qualities actually contradictory when viewed as various facets of the fallen human personality. In his natural constitution, man certainly has a will of sorts. However, in view of the will's being contingent upon the checks and drives of his innate predisposition, it can hardly be said to make him utterly accountable.

As to his spiritual nature, the unregenerate man is equally as impotent and irresponsible as a piece of insensate silver. But when, under the quickening power of the Holy Spirit, he "comes to himself" (cf. verse 17), he is then invested with full, unfettered ability either to spurn or to yield submission to the overtures of grace. His will is completely free of all constraint except the necessity of exercising its freedom.

At this critical juncture—

- If he chooses to *resist* the Holy Spirit, he renders himself impersuasible, thus making it morally impossible for God to prevail upon him to repent of sin and believe the Gospel of his own accord—with the result that he is thenceforth self-confirmed in fateful unbelief.
- If he *acquiesces* in the liberating and enabling power of the Holy Spirit, he will, despite his ill deserts and impotence, soon find himself a willing captive of divine persuasion

—and ere long he will be singing:

> 'Tis done, the great transaction's done!
> I am my Lord's, and He is mine;
> He drew me, and I followed on,
> Charmed to confess the voice divine.

But this aspect of God's plan will be seen more clearly in the following parable, which was doubtless meant to round out the teaching of the former two.

The Reasonableness of Recovering the Irresponsible

30

THE LOST SON

The Reasonableness of Recovering the Willful

Primary text: Luke 15:11-24

Jesus spoke this parable to the scribes and Pharisees in the presence of His disciples, including a number of converted publicans and sinners—somewhere in Perea—during the second month (February) before His crucifixion.

Introduction and background. No one parable illustrates the whole plan of salvation. In few (if any) of the more elaborate ones do *all* the details have definite, demonstrable, doctrinal significance. But this one, more than any other, appears to pose an exception to that rule. It radiates so much basic spiritual truth pertaining to universal Christian experience that one may draw analogies from it to illustrate many different aspects of human redemption.

Various interpretations. Therefore, it has been variously interpreted in keeping with numerous points of view:

1a. It is perhaps most frequently construed as a depiction of our racial fall, with the prodigal son representing Adam, or of our personal conversion, with the son symbolizing a penitent sinner.

2a. It is often made to demonstrate the backslider's return to fellowship with God.

3a. No less plausibly, the larger parable—including the section on the Elder Brother—is often seen as a veiled prediction of Jewry's resentment at the conversion of the Gentiles.

I have no objection to these views as *partial applications.* It is by no means incredible that the omniscient Son of God was able to weave all these ideas into the fabric of a single illustration.

Serious interpretation. However, in view of its context, a serious interpretation of the parable must be germane to our Lord's compassion for the lost: The prodigal must be seen as representing the penitent publicans and sinners; the elder brother must be identified with the scribes and Pharisees; and these classes must be viewed as being representative of their corresponding types, the world over, in subsequent times. A full application of both details and overall framework of the parable lend themselves consistently and unfailingly to this approach and none other.

Problems with partial applications. All other schemes of interpretation are established upon plausible fragments—and are embarrassed by incongruities, if not outright contradictions, here or there. As the third in a series of seven related parables, this one must be considered in its connection with the rest. The principal character in the first one is the shepherd, and the leading object is the lost sheep. The principal character in the second is the woman, and the leading object is the lost coin. Here the outstanding character is a "certain man," the father of two sons, and the lesson is centered around the younger son. In the first we saw that the shepherd represents God the Son. In the second the woman is apparently the instrument of God, the Holy Spirit. Here, in the third, the man undoubtedly stands for God the Father. We are told that this man had two sons.

1b. This text immediately besets the racial, Adamic theory of interpretation with considerable difficulty, for if the younger son is taken to represent Adam, then whom does the elder son represent?

2b. Likewise, it cuts the ground from under the notion that the prodigal stands for a backslider—for as we shall presently see, the younger son had still to become a son indeed, and

the status of the elder will be left doubtful, to say the least.
3b. Nor is it altogether compatible with the view that the Jews
and the converted Gentiles are depicted here, inasmuch as
that would be to confuse natural and spiritual relationships.
But . . .

How the more serious interpretation fits. But if we begin
by considering the original filial relationship of both these sons,
elder and younger, as reflecting the creation of humanity at
large in the image and likeness of God, then there will be no
difficulty in seeing them as representative of the Pharisees and
repentant sinners, respectively.

Examination and interpretation. In this view, the elder brother
corresponds with legalistic religionists in general, and the
prodigal with sinners who have heard and obeyed the Gospel.
In what other sense can we understand God to be the father of
an *unregenerate* person? But that, in this sense, He is. Thus—
a. Adam is referred to as a "son of God" (cf. Luke 1:38);
b. The Apostle Paul agrees with a heathen poet that we are all
God's "offspring" (cf. Acts 17:28); and
c. James observes that all of us are "made after the similitude
of God" (cf. James 3:9).
Since all human beings were originally constituted for divine
"sonship," they are therefore *potential* sons of God, though no
one can actually realize that exalted privilege in a true and
abiding way except through a new spiritual birth.

Indeed, there are elements in the story which undoubtedly
reflect a universal fall and the common experience of those
who are brought to repentance. True, the prodigal fell *before* he
departed from home. That fall took place in his heart when,
having grown weary of paternal supervision, he decided to go
forth on his own. Moreover, his father, knowing this but being
unwilling to violate the personal freedom of his child, raised
not a hand to restrain him from his purpose.

All this accords precisely with our racial experience and
with God's invariable manner of dealing with fallen men. He
made us *free* that we might be capable of receiving His favor.
He vouches for our freedom, even when we misuse it, in order

to preserve our capacity for the reception of forgiveness after having been induced to repent. This is not a stopgap measure, but an abiding principle on the basis of which all of the elect will be brought to repentance in the course of time.

If the prodigal's father had used *forcible* means to curb his recreant son's perverse plans, he would have had a chafing rebel on his hands; he could never have prevailed on that son to choose a better course. Instead, he paid that youth's tuition in the bitter school of experience, financing his excursion to the "far country" in order to bring him to his senses, and to a *voluntary* change of mind and heart. The price was dear, but not too dear, for that accomplishment; and it was the father, not his son, who bore the cost. The Son "spent all"—but the father paid the bill. The son endured the famine, fed the swine, and hungered for the carob pods—but the father not only shared the anguish, but was also anguished by the loss of his wayward child.

Then, at last, the chastened prodigal "came to himself" (verse 17). This is the first high point in the story, the pivotal point around which all the rest revolves. Now the sinner was no longer like a stupid sheep, its will dominated by its natural instincts and appetites; He was no longer spiritually inert and irresponsible, like a soulless drachma; now, for the first time, all his higher faculties were alert and competent to face the issues of destiny. He was now free—free, and *compelled* to make an all-decisive choice. So it alwasys is with any rebel, when the Holy Spirit convicts him of sin, confronts him with the Gospel, unshackles his will, and enables him to make his inevitable response. Until that time, no one can really repent of sin and place his trust in Christ. As for anyone who refuses to do so, we are expressly told that

> . . . it is impossible for those who were made par-
> takers of the Holy Ghost, and have tasted the
> good word of God, and the powers of the world
> to come, if they shall fall away, to renew them
> again unto repentance (Hebrews 6:4-6).

Somewhere, sometime, somehow, the Holy Spirit thus brings every human being "to himself." If the disillusioned sinner does not misuse his then-emancipated will to "do despite unto the Spirit of grace" (cf. Hebrews 10:29), he soon finds himself resolving:

I *will* . . .

I will *arise* . . .

I will *go to my Father*" (cf. verse 18).

We must not surmise that the prodigal's decision was prompted by any virtue of his own—it was his father's: *what he knew* about his father's loving kindness engendered his new resolution and nourished it with hope. In this sense, his father drew him with—and he responded to—*sheer love*. In the absence of an impersuasible attitude, such love is truly irresistible!

Again, so it is with us. Jesus tells us in another place:

> For no man can come to me, except the Father which sent me draw him . . . It is written in the prophets, And they [that is, *the elect*] shall be all taught of God. Every man therefore that hath heard, and learned of the Father, cometh unto me (John 6:44–45).

God's drawing us to Him is what the psalmist meant when he exulted, "blessed is the man whom thou *choosest*, and *causest* to approach unto thee . . ." (Psalms 64:4). It is what the apostle meant when he explained, "For it is God which worketh in you both to will and do of his good pleasure" (Philippians 2:13).

Accordingly, if we do not deliberately harden our hearts against the Gospel, God grants us the gift of "repentance unto life" (cf. Acts 11:18) and opens to us the "door of faith" (cf. Acts 14:27), thereby inclining and enabling us to "believe through grace" (cf. Acts 18:27).

All these messages are implicit in the record of the prodigal's return:

- His *reason* was restored, enabling him to perceive the folly of his sinful condition: "How many hired servants of my father's have bread enough and to spare, and I perish with hunger" he groaned (verse 17).

- His *volitional powers* were liberated from the dominion of his fallen nature, and he was enabled to act freely, on his own, contrary to the predispositions of his natural heart: "I will arise and go to my father," he resolved (verse 18).
- His *heart* was moved with the spirit of genuine penitence: "Father," he confessed, "I have sinned against heaven, and before thee, and am no more worthy to be called thy son" (verses 18–19).
- His *former arrogance* gave place to abject humility: "Take me as one of thy hired servants," he implored (verse 19).

And then he, exhibiting faith in action, "arose, and came to his father (verse 20). But . . .

But he did not have to come all the way home alone, for "when he was yet a great way off, his father saw him, and had compassion, and ran, and fell on his neck, and kissed him" (verse 20). The story reaches its climax. We've already seen that there is joy "in heaven" when a sinner repents, joy "in the presence of the angels" (verses 7, 10). Here we learn *who* rejoices in heaven, in the presence of the angels: *God Himself!* No doubt the hosts of glory, both saints and angels, join in that gladsome celebration, but even so it is God Himself who rejoices most in the salvation of the lost.

This concept of God rejoicing is undoubtedly one of the most difficult things men are ever called upon to believe. In view of all the evidence, it is no great task to believe in the inspiration of the Scriptures, Biblical miracles, the virgin birth of Christ, and the resurrection of the dead.

But, knowing ourselves as we do, *how* can we be convinced that a holy God sincerely loves us and is eager to reclaim us as His own?. It is relatively *easy* to terrify the human conscience with thunderbolts from Sinai, to frighten sinners with lurid visions of fiery wrath, or to prevail upon the guilt-conscious masses to cringe at an altar, buy indulgences, do penance, pay tithes, or make almost any other response to naked fear.

Ah, but how *difficult* it is to console the human spirit with undoubting assurance that God is looking down in fatherly compassion from afar ... that He is doing everything within His power to draw us to Himself ... and that He yearns to embrace us with forgiving love and kiss away our tears!

Sonship. In spite of all our fearful misgivings, it is "the goodness of God" that "leads us to repentance" (cf. Romans 2:4), restores our filial heritage (cf. Romans 8:17), and robes us in "the glorious liberty of the children of God" (Romans 8:21). The prodigal son planned to close his confession with a single request, asking only to be given the place of a hired servant in his former home. After having been received so graciously—not as a slave, but as a son—he could not bring himself to mock such mercy with such an incongruous petition. God's paternal joy is the strongest possible guarantee of our final standing in His sight. We, therefore, do Him no honor by posing as slaves. To cringe is to doubt. We must receive the robe of *sonship* to justify His joy, and wear it well to magnify His grace.

For *sons* we are. He has been pleased to make us such now—not only provisionally by nature—but *eternally* through a new birth from above.

Grace and sonship. The prodigal began his confession just as he had planned, but his father abruptly broke it off when the question of *sonship* was raised. No, the erring son was not "worthy," but the father was gracious—and *grace,* of course, finds its occasion in its beneficiary's ill desert and neediness: There would be no need for grace if sonship were deserved.

"Bring forth the best robe," the father instructed, "and put it on him; and put a ring on his hand, and shoes on his feet" (verse 22).

All these—the robe, the ring, the shoes—were symbols of sonship: the robe of its standing, the ring of its prerogatives, and the shoes of its dignity. Such gifts were not bestowed upon a hired servant—only upon an heir. So it is with us, the sons of God. As regenerate believers, we stand before God our Father in heaven's best robe, the righteousness of Christ. We wear God's special favor like a ring set with gems of "exceeding great and precious promises" (cf. II Peter 1:4). Our feet are shod with holy boldness that puts us perfectly at ease in our Father's house.

A step further. We are often told it would be a mistake, at this point in the story, to construe the slaughter of the fatted calf as a depiction of the sacrifice of Christ, since it seems to be out of chronological order as far as the believer's personal experience is concerned. Is this not to read our own historical experience into the parable, overlooking its original reference, that is, to the converted publicans and sinners? From *their* point of view, the Savior's death *was* still in the future, and this portion of His illustration was prophetic of that event. They had repented and had been received as sons by virtue of the sacrifice which was shortly *to be made* at Calvary, after which they would feast upon the proceeds of that transaction. From *God's* point of view, the death of Christ is an eternal fact. From *our* point of view, it is a past accomplishment, but to the penitent sinners of that time, it was still in the offing. Moreover, as in the ancient peace offering (and also in our own Memorial Supper), the believer continues to feast on the Sacrifice *after* his initial act of faith.

Repentance precedes faith. This interpretation accords with universal Christian experience, in which "repentance toward God" always precedes "faith toward our Lord Jesus Christ" (cf. Acts 20:21). Granted repentance and faith are the negative and positive aspects of one and the same experience, still their order is irreversible. Just as the prodigal repented before he partook of the festive sacrifice; and just as the publicans and sinners had repented before their redemption was accomplished at the cross—so we must repent before we can repose our faith in Christ in a meaningful way.

The parable (or this section) closes with a reminder of our former condition and an intimation of the eternal blessedness of our new estate. The parabolic prodigal son's father justifies his festive arrangements with these significant words: "For this my son was dead, and is alive again; he was lost, and is found. Then they began to be merry" (verse 24).

This final verse recapitulates the essential points in the first three Apologetic parables, summing up those human factors involved in a personal conversion and underscoring the joy that follows the triumph of grace. The natural son had been as spiritually dead as an inanimate silver drachma, but now he was alive in every part of his personality. Though alive in the natural sense, he had been *lost*, like a stupid, lackadaisical sheep—now he was *found*, at home with his father, reinstated as a son. No wonder the father and all the household (well, nearly all of it, at least) were making merry. But that is not exactly what the record says. More precisely, "they began to be merry." They contemplated no end to the feast.

Nor do we! In the words of a popular chorus, "Every day with Jesus is sweeter than the day before!"

31

THE ELDER BROTHER

The *Un*reasonableness of Resenting the Gospel

Primary text: Luke 15:25-32.

Jesus spoke this parable to the scribes and Pharisees in the presence of His disciples, including a number of converted publicans and sinners—somewhere in Perea—during the second month (February) before His crucifixion.

Introduction. The closing section of Jesus' discourse on lost things is, in large measure, an additional story that borrows its characters from the former one. Still, it ties in with all three of the preceding illustrations, summarizing and pressing home their leading emphases.

It does precisely what modern preachers are expected to avoid, else be considered rude or even unethical: it applies its lesson to certain people in the audience. To be sure, the elder brother represented the scribes and Pharisees on the spot, ones whose murmuring had provoked this series of parables in the first place. Of course, further applications are admissible; the behavior of the elder brother has many parallels in subsequent history. After Christ, the Antitype of the fatted calf, was slain at Calvary, repentant sinners from far and wide in every land

253

and nation, did partake of the Gospel feast, while the legalistic Jews refused to join them. Ever since that time, both of these classes have appeared on the scene wherever the Christian message has been proclaimed. With the situation confronting us on almost every hand, we can scarcely err in associating it with the circumstances pictured in this passage. But we shall run into trouble whenever we attempt to press the details of the story to establish points not immediately relevant to its central theme.

Faulty interpretations. Much ingenuity has been misspent in futile attempts to prove or disprove that those represented by the elder brother are saved. That question, unessential to the primary purpose of the illustration, is left wide open here. The matter of personal salvation must necessarily be decided, in any particular case, by considerations expressly set forth elsewhere in the Scriptures. Salvation is simply not the point in question here, as far as the elder brother is concerned. He was ostensibly a son; at least, he regarded himself as such. His father insisted only that he deport himself accordingly.

Moreover, since he was the elder son, he was entitled to the rights of primogeniture, thus prefiguring the relation of Israel to Gentile Christianity. Now, although the entire parable envisages the local scene at that particular time, this portion of it appears to have anticipated the course of future events. No, the story of the elder brother does not address the question of his salvation, but it *does* afford some abiding lessons which are manifestly relevant today.

Application. Surely, from any point of view, it can be seen that the surly attitude of the elder brother reflected the churlish spirit of Jesus' critics who kept busy protesting His kindness to their wayward brethren. Judging from this parable, as well as the three preceding ones, our Lord regarded their pitiless bigotry with as much displeasure as (if not more than) He did the moral obliquity of the open sinners they despised. Although He deplored the stupidity, insensibility, and prodigality of the delinquent masses, He sought to awaken the consciences of their accusers to their own shortcomings, which—being of a *spiritual* nature—were more insidious, and less susceptible to correction, than the *carnal* weaknesses which they condemned in others. The publicans and sinners were hapless victims of their lusts; the abstemious Pharisees were *willful* hypocrites. They not only sinned against fellow men, but also dishonored God. The Savior was saying, in so many words:

> *In your stony, loveless unbelief, you really murmur against God—not only against the Son, but against the Father and the Holy Spirit as well:*
> - *I rescue a wandering sheep, and all heaven rejoices—but* you *complain!*
> - *The Holy Spirit recovers a lost drachma, and angels shout—but* you *are offended!*
> - *The Father restores a penitent prodigal, and everyone else is jubilant—but* you *sulk off from the festive hall to pout!*

The only way to grasp the force and solemnity of this imagery is to transfer the scene to the gates of heaven and view the elder brother as a petulant Pharisee, miffed at God for being gracious to a penitent sinner. God has let an erring one inside the gate; the Pharisee sees this event only as a "slap in the face" to his own status!

The prodigal, having been willing to take the place of a household servant, has been reinstated as a full-fledged son and heir. The elder brother, who insists on his filial rights while showing a most unfilial spirit, virtually disinherits himself by assuming the role of a slave:

- Grace being foreign to all this son's thoughts, he works to obligate his father and expects to collect his earnings "on the barrelhead."
- To his ears, all music is out of key unless it honors *him.*
- He is not only unmoved by his brother's repentance, but is angry with his father for forgiving the prodigal.
- While boasting he has never disobeyed parental commands, he spurns his father's beckoning to join the feast.
- Instead of rejoicing at his brother's restoration, he takes

delight in recalling that younger one's former sins.

- Instead of partaking of the fatted calf to celebrate the prodigal's return, he chides his father for not rewarding his own slavish service with so much as a baby kid.

All the words and actions of the elder brother betray his own besetting sin: the callous lovelessness of a self-righteous heart. Gladly would he have wined and dined his respectable friends while his wayward brother perished among unhallowed swine in a heathen land. Far from deploring that tragic turn of events, his sordid pleasure most likely would have been enhanced by reflecting on his brother's misery.

On first thought, his attitude may seem quite unbelievable. Yet, who has not seen all too much of such sadistic "piety," not only in the outside world, but even within the precincts of the "saints"?

The father's graciousness. Still—How gracious to one so ungracious!—the father in the parable replies for our Father in heaven: "Son [literally, *Child*], thou art ever with me, and all that I have is thine" (verse 31).

Regarding the elder brother's salvation. Even this text does not settle the question of the Pharisees' personal salvation. It simply assumes the possibility, subject to forthcoming proof, and leaves the matter there. So far as the elder brother was concerned, he could—if he would—even yet repent, join in the feast, and show himself to be a son and brother indeed. If a son in character as well as in name, it was only meet that he should share his father's joy. What he did from that time forth would show him up for what he really was.

In this way did Jesus, while defending the magnanimity of the Gospel against the onslaughts of its critics, leave the door of mercy ajar for them as well as for the rest of us.

32

THE UNJUST STEWARD

The Ethical Integrity of the Gospel

Primary text: Luke 16:1-9.

Our Lord spoke this parable to His disciples, in the presence of the scribes and Pharisees—somewhere in Perea—during the second month (February) before His crucifixion.

Introduction. The rich man in this story is more or less a part of the setting; the steward occupies the leading role. Accused of squandering his master's possessions, he is quite unable to defend himself. All that follows is indicative that his guilt is undeniable.

When ordered to render an account and notified that he is to be discharged, he is greatly shaken at the prospect of being left without a livelihood. Unfit for menial labor and too proud to depend on public charity, he resolves to make use of every opportunity he has, while still in office, to assure himself of the hospitality of his master's debtors afterwards. To this end he calls them together and, reviewing their several obligations, one by one, instructs each one to replace his original bill of indebtedness with another showing a considerably smaller sum. One who owes a hundred baths of oil is allowed to settle for only fifty; another is told to revise his debits downward from a hundred homers of wheat to eighty. Apparently all the rest are given discounts of similar proportions. Presumably, he thus wins for himself a place in their hearts and homes, and his farsightedness attracts the admiration of even his lord.

This story is not expressly called a parable. For all we know, it may be an account of an actual event (not at all unlikely). However that may be, it was certainly *not* intended to be taken allegorically, as if each detail in it had a counterpart in some analogous case. Such an interpretation would represent our Lord as if He were urging His disciples to imitate the rascality of an outright rogue!

No, in a case such as this, which confronts us with many exegetical difficulties right from the start, it is well to begin by taking notice of every circumstance that is indubitably clear. Now, we know this discourse was addressed to the Savior's disciples (cf. verse 1) and that its stated purpose was to advise the disciples to "make to themselves friends of the mammon of unrighteousness" (verse 9)—that is, to use their worldly wealth in a way that would assure them of having friends to greet them in the coming world. This much we can be sure of. May we not be equally confident that, though this illustration involves an unjust steward, our Lord had absolutely no thought of commending such an unjust practice to His followers, the stewards of His kingdom?

Obviously, then, the purpose of this story is to emphasize the importance of some one desirable quality that this steward displayed—along with, and in spite of—all his faults. Nor is that solitary virtue hard to discover: the record stresses and the context shows, that his wisdom, his prudence, took the form of forethought, disposing him to make good use of his opportunities to ensure his future welfare and security. In this respect, although he was sadly reprehensible in many others, he demonstrated more practical wisdom about earthly affairs than many professing Christians do with respect to heavenly things.

Why did our Lord bring up the subject of money (ill-gotten money, in fact) at this particular time? What does the use of "unrighteous mammon" have to do with making preparation for the future life? The answers to both of these questions lie in the immediate context; we must find them to understand either this passage or the following one ("The Rich Man and Lazarus).

Examination and interpretation. In the foregoing parables of Luke 15, our Lord addressed the scribes and Pharisees in the presence of the converted publicans and sinners. Here, in the presence of the Pharisees, He was speaking to His disciples— which group included a number of converted publicans. It is obvious that He was dealing with a problem that publicans, especially, were facing and could not ignore: the need to bring their financial practices into harmony with their Christian faith. Before their conversion, material gain had been their principal interest in life. As tax collectors, they had been "stewards" of Caesar, or the Roman Empire. Furthermore, since most of them were notorious for extorting excessive profits for themselves, all of them were fairly well-to-do, and some were rich. How would their new relationship with Jesus affect their business? What effect should their conversion have on how they spent the tainted wealth they had already accumulated?

One thing was clear. They could not be loyal disciples of the lowly Nazarene and retain their lucrative positions very long. If they were true to the lofty ethics of the Gospel, they would be soon accused of neglecting Caesar's interests and eventually deprived of their employment under him. Nor could they, as consistent Christians, keep using their current fortunes for purely selfish ends—for submitting to the lordship of Christ was to renounce all rival loyalties, to become His stewards, and thenceforth to administer all their holdings as a sacred trust. They had learned all men are by nature stewards, not proprietors, and conversion to Christ, far from annulling this principle, simply involves a change of masters, with as much allegiance due the new one as was ever given to the old. It was not a question of switching their loyalty from Caesar to Christ, but of turning from Mammon to Christ: money itself, not their Roman overlords, had until now reigned in their hearts as a sovereign idol. Since "No servant" could "serve two masters" (verse 13), to follow Jesus meant they would have to cast their "unrighteous mammon" at His feet.

They had been unrighteous stewards of an unrighteous lord. Now they must be righteous stewards of a righteous Lord.

Natural wealth, as much as they had formerly prized it, was now their least possession. If they proved unfaithful to so small a trust, how could they be entrusted with the "true riches" of the heavenly Kingdom? (Cf. verse 11.) If they could not be trusted with their Master's goods, how could He trust them with an inheritance of their own? (Cf. verse 12.) It was not a question of earning salvation with their money, but of using the Master's money in a way consistent with their profession. It was, in other words, a test of saving faith—in their case, the acid test. Like the rich young ruler, they were called upon to "sell all" they had and "distribute unto the poor" (cf. Luke 18:22): not as a means of salvation, but as evidence that they were already saved indeed. [The parable also shows us, in an incidental manner, that such faithful stewardship will win an abundant reward: Just as the farsighted steward had won a host of friends to show him hospitality after his dismissal, those who use their earthly assets to relieve the poor and propagate the Gospel will be greeted in heaven by the grateful saints they have helped on earth. But where the unjust steward in the story was motivated by the thought of reward, that is *not* the reason for doing Christian work—it is instead a sort of "bonus," a natural consequence in God's kingdom.]

The major point of the parable now becomes apparent: Jesus knew that the best way to prove the faith of the converted publicans was to challenge their loyalty at its most vulnerable point—their pocketbooks. Lest they fail this crucial test, He urged them to exercise the same foresight in regard to their spiritual interests as that by which they had distinguished themselves in temporal affairs.

Beforehand, when the stakes were infinitely lower, they had exhibited a single virtue among their many faults. Now, with the stakes so much higher, should they abandon that virtue? should they be less discreet?

Underneath its more apparent appeal for personal dedication, this parable presented a defense of the Gospel against the evil misrepresentation of its foes.

Christ would leave no room for His critics to charge, or for His disciples to think, that He condoned the vicious teaching of those who say, "Let us do evil, that good may come" (cf. Romans 3:8). His opponents must know, and His disciples must learn, that grace is righteous both in its administration and its results. In view of the provisions of the Gospel, He was doing right by saving penitent sinners; having been saved, they too must do right. The scribes and Pharisees stood self-condemned before the very Law in which they boasted, but the Gospel met the requirements of the Law in the believing publicans, thus exhibiting its integrity as a rebuke to its opponents.

However viewed, few lessons are more needful for the rest of us today.

33

THE RICH MAN AND LAZARUS

The Finality of the Gospel

Primary text: Luke 16:19-31.

Our Lord spoke this parable to the Pharisees in the presence of His disciples—somewhere in Perea—during the second month (February) before His crucifixion.

Introduction. The much-mooted question as to whether this is a parable or the account of an actual experience is immaterial to the problem of interpretation. For, if only a parable, it must nevertheless be taken as true to fact, for it is unthinkable that the Lord Jesus Christ would employ misleading similitudes. And even if it is authentic history, it is adapted to parabolic purposes, as no discerning reader will deny.

There is a double key to its correct interpretation: (a) the general drift of the larger context and (b) the closing statement about the necessity of heeding "Moses and the prophets" (cf. verses 29, 31). This latter point, in turn, connects it with the underlying argument of the other apologetic parables. We are bound to infer from this concluding statement that Lazarus is representative of those who *had* hearkened to Moses and the prophets; the rich man, of those who had refused to do so. Applying the parable to the local context, Lazarus represents

---

the penitent publicans; the rich man, the rigid Pharisees. (Of course, in the broader application, there are corresponding classes, to which this parable may be applied, in virtually all religious communities.)

It is obvious to begin with, then, that Jesus envisaged the whole scheme of redemption as implicit in the pre-Christian Scriptures and that His ensuing illustration anticipated all the moral grounds for the mediation of righteous grace which were yet to be provided by His redemptive ministry.

Background. To discover a satisfactory contextual perspective for the consideration of the story that follows, we must go back at least to the beginning of the Savior's current discourse (in the preceding chapter), where the principal point at issue in the minds of the Pharisees is presented:

Q. Is Christ's compassion for sinners consistent
    with the lofty ethics of the Law?

The parables of Luke 15 were meant to justify an affirmative answer by showing that, just as men in general feel concern for their natural possessions, God (as Father, Son, *and* Holy Spirit) yearns to reclaim wayward men. Thus far, the argument had been, in effect:

A. God is doing it; thus, it cannot be inconsistent
    with His holy Law.

Then, in the parable of the unjust steward, our Lord asserted and vindicated the ethical integrity of the Gospel by showing its results:

A. Those who are saved by grace must thereafter,
    in the nature of the case, transfer their loyalties
    to God without any reservations whatever. (In
    an incidental way, He also assured that such
    saints would be rewarded abundantly.)

The Pharisees who overheard "The Unjust Steward" were quite unconvinced: they did not believe that the Gospel could have the power to redeem and transform the avaricious publicans. Moreover, they were greatly offended and angry. Just as they correctly inferred, while Jesus was urging his disciples to turn to God from Mammon, He was also, indirectly, denouncing one of the secret sins of the scribes and Pharisees as well.

If they were to accept Jesus' condemnation of covetousness, they would incriminate themselves. As quick as they were to invoke the sanctions of the Law against open sinners (and equally slow to admit such transgressors might be saved), they must have realized they themselves were just as covetous, hence just as guilty in the sight of God, as the lawless rabble. Unwilling to change their ways, anger was the only response acceptable to them.

In the absence of any better defense, "they derided him" (cf. verse 14) [literally, *turned up their noses at him*], pretending indignation in an effort to dignify their shame. However, Jesus, testifying as an eyewitness, parried their jeers with a thrust to the soul:

> **A.** Ye are they which justify yourselves before men;
> but God knoweth your hearts (verse 15).

One adopts the world's standards to win the world's approval, and that invariably means to lower the standards ordained of God. As a rule, material wealth commands universal respect, and those who have it tend to assume it gives them a right to treat the poor with disrespect. The Pharisees, no exception to that "rule," considered their affluence a sign of divine approval, as God's recognition and reward for their moral superiority. Hence, their wealth became a way to impress others with their personal integrity. Thus, the more they prospered, the more they attracted the admiration of the carnal masses—even while in their hearts they cherished the very vices they feigned to loathe in others!

Such was the case as God beheld it, not to presume that they *themselves* perceived it so. As they may have asked:

> **Q.** Doesn't the Law offer the promise of temporal
> prosperity to those who honor it?

Jesus met this mode of reasoning with another shattering blow:

> **A.** The law and the prophets were until John: since
> that time the kingdom of God is preached, and
> every man presseth into it. And it is easier for
> heaven and earth to pass, than one tittle of the
> law to fail (verses 16–17).

The Pharisees had no right to consider their wealth a reward for keeping the Law. According to John the Baptist, they had utterly failed to practice the spirit of the ancient Covenant and, thus, had forfeited its promises. Their customary practice was to get around the Law while pretending to keep it. For example, they broke the Seventh Commandment by permitting divorce on insufficient grounds; Jesus, while granting forgiveness to *repentant* adulterers, insisted that

> Whosoever putteth away his wife, and marrieth another, committeth adultery: and whosoever marrieth her that is put away from her husband committeth adultery (verse 18).

And now, although the legal dispensation had terminated in human failure, the very ones who had dishonored the Law were trying to force their way into the Kingdom on the pretext that they had entitled themselves to enter it by keeping the Law's commandments. Nay, Jesus would have them know they were self-deceived: their claims were false and their "righteousness" was spurious—and only through the provisions of grace could they be saved, in keeping with the actual requirements of the Law which they had honored only with their mouths.

As violators of the very Law in which they boasted, they were trying to "press" their way into the Kingdom in defiance of the conditions prescribed by the Law. He would have them know that only by winning divine acceptance on the terms of righteous grace, as offered in the Gospel, could they enter in. To be saved, they had to repent of their sins and trust Christ for forgiveness, just as the publicans did. Public opinion had no jurisdiction in this matter. In the sight of God there was, morally, no distinction between a covetous Pharisee and an open sinner. All alike had broken God's holy Law; all alike would have to be saved by righteous grace if they were to be saved at all.

Thus, Jesus, not the Pharisees, was really contending for the righteousness envisaged by Moses. He altered not a "tittle" of the Law in showing mercy to the penitent, but His critics habitually mutilated its basic ethic in an effort to maintain their reputation for piety while ignoring or circumventing its real demands.

The foregoing paragraphs of background context serve to demonstrate what I believe to be Jesus' intentions with this parable, those being to show that:

- Temporal prosperity, far from being evidence of personal righteousness, may even indicate one has been unfaithful to his sacred responsibilities.
- Believers true to their calling are willing to suffer the loss of all temporal things for Jesus' sake.
- In any case, one's actual spiritual condition will be revealed and fitly rewarded in the coming world.
- One's response to the Gospel, even as it is contained in "Moses and the prophets," will make the difference.

Examination and interpretation. Now, let us look at the story itself, as well as we may, through the eyes of our Savior.

Here was the covetous but self-righteous Pharisee as Jesus saw him—
> There was a certain rich man, which was clothed
> in purple and fine linen, and fared sumptuously
> every day (verse 19) . . .

—and the penitent publican, who, when forgiven, left all to follow the Savior—
> And there was a certain beggar named Lazarus,
> which laid at his gate full of sores, and desiring
> to be fed with the crumbs which fell from the
> rich man's table (verses 20–21) . . .

—and the fate of each, revealing and rewarding accordingly:
> And it came to pass, that the beggar died, and
> was carried by angels into Abraham's bosom: the
> rich man also died, and was buried; and in hell
> he lift up his eyes, being in torment . . . (verses
> 22–23).

Meanings. It would be easy, and the temptation is strong, to elaborate on the *figurative* meaning of the descriptive details:

- to construe the rich man's purple as a symbol of self-will; his fine linen as self-righteousness; his sumptuous fare as self-complacency;
- to see in Lazarus' sores, hunger, and general misery (pitied even by dogs!) the afflictions of one who "loses his life" here to "find it" hereafter (cf. Luke 9:24).

Better that we concentrate on the main line of thought, lest we allow the drapery of the story to deflect our attention from its major emphases. The most important thing for us to see here is this:

- the issues that have run their course and crystallized in permanent character in the present life will be clarified by their results after death, which is to say—
- the spiritual status of confirmed believers and unbelievers will be clearly manifested by their contrasting fortunes in the other world—rather than on earth.

Here Jesus is not depicting the fate of millions of uncommitted infants and heathen who die without having heard and either accepted or rejected, the Gospel. He is, instead, portraying the future lots of two particular classes: the "Pharisees," who have heard and rejected the truth, and the "publicans," who heard and heeded it. Surely, anyone of ordinary discernment must be able to perceive these distinctions.

Terminology. Also we need to understand and differentiate the names used to designate various areas in the unseen realm beyond the grave:

1. The word rendered *hell* in our common version is *Hades* in the original Greek, the same as *Sheol* in the Hebrew Old Testament—a general term for the invisible spirit world in which the souls of the dead were kept in waiting until the death and resurrection of Christ, and in which the wicked dead are still awaiting the Last Judgment. At the time this passage was uttered, Sheol/Hades included a region known as *Abraham's bosom* (or *Paradise*), as well as *Gehenna* (or the place of torment)—not to mention *Tartarus* (or "bottomless pit")—and we know not how many other areas it included then or still includes today (cf. II Peter 2:4; Revelation 20:1).

The Finality of the Gospel

2. Until Christ's death and subsequent resurrection, the Old Dispensation saints were detained in Abraham's bosom, but they accompanied Him to heaven when He arose from the dead (cf. Ephesians 4:8). And it is clear from a number of related Scriptures that, from that time onward, Paradise has been no longer in the underworld, but in the heavens (cf. II Corinthians 12:4).

The place of torment is still in Hades; and all confirmed unbelievers who die—after they have heard and rejected the Gospel—will be detained there until the Last Judgment; then they will be consigned to "everlasting destruction" in the "lake of fire" (cf. II Thessalonians 1:9; Revelation 20:15).

3. Our parable is concerned with only these two places: the paradisiacal abode of confirmed believers and the infernal abode of incorrigible unbelievers. It has nothing whatever to say about the destiny of those who have never yet heard or accepted or rejected the Gospel; therefore, it discloses nothing concerning the lot of the uncommitted dead.

4. Whereas the rich man in this story represents an inveterate unbeliever, he is said to have gone directly to the place of torment at the time of his death. Since Lazarus stands for an Old Dispensation believer, we read he was immediately conveyed to "Abraham's bosom."

From this point onward, the respective lots of the righteous and the wicked, in general—and of the penitent publicans and the unbelieving Pharisees, in particular—are depicted with exquisite metaphorical imagery that spells out tranquil peace on one hand, misery on the other, and finality on both.

Because Jesus was addressing the Pharisees, He dwelt at length on their future condition as reflected in the experience of the rich man, barely touching on the case of Lazarus, to bring out the contrast between the two. There are, in fact, but two brief notices about what happens to the beggar after his death: that he is carried by angels to Abraham's bosom and that he is comforted. In keeping with the foregoing parable, he has "friends to greet him in the other world" and enjoys serene repose in the "everlasting habitations" of the blessed (cf. verse 9)—the promised reward of those penitent publicans who would turn from Mammon to God.

The rich man, however, finds no such friends to welcome him, and no such peaceful habitation for his soul. He can see "Abraham afar off, and Lazarus in his bosom" (verse 23), but he himself is isolated from them in a fiery flame (verse 24). In distress he calls for help, but calls in vain. *Now,* relying on the ancient Covenant he so wantonly dishonored in better days, he cries in desperation:

Q. Father Abraham, have mercy on me, and send Lazarus, that he may dip the tip of his finger in water, and cool my tongue (verse 24).

Now he would gladly welcome relief, however slight, from the former beggar's hand.

A. Abraham, while he acknowledges their natural relationship, reminds him of the impassable gulf that lies between his uncircumcised soul and the spirits of those who are "Israelites indeed."

Though a racial son of Abraham, the rich man renounced the "hope of Israel" for the "good things" of Mammon. Alienating himself from the "children of promise," he has forfeited the blessings of eternal life. Lazarus, however, has sacrificed earthly advantages for heavenly gain. So goes the story of "Dives," the unbelieving Pharisee, and Lazarus the penitent publican.

Clearly this parable (if it is a parable) does not concern itself altogether with the eternal state, for the rich man is said to have had "five brethren" still on earth at the time.

Now, His belated concern for his brethren is hardly, as is sometimes supposed, a sudden upsurge of missionary zeal, but rather a covert effort to defend his own impenitence.

As if to hint that he himself was not duly warned, he then entreats Abraham to

Q. send Lazarus back from the dead to warn his brethren, lest they also may be plunged into torment.

But Abraham, dismissing the rich man's implicit protest with a blunt rejoinder, answers:

A. They have Moses and the prophets; let them hear

them (verse 29)—which is to say, *You did have sufficient light, and so have they; for anyone who has the Scriptures has enough light to be saved, if he will only heed what they say.*

"Nay, father Abraham," the rich man replied; "but

Q. if one went unto them from the dead, they will repent" (verse 30)

—again implying that he himself would have repented under more propitious circumstances. In other words, God is at fault; not he, but God, has been guilty of criminal negligence. Let his brethren now be given some overawing "sign," some kind of convincing spectacle, that he himself, alas, has been denied. This time Abraham replies with curt finality:

A. If they hear not Moses and the prophets, neither will they be persuaded though one rose from the dead (verse 31).

This ending clinches the identification of the rich man with the Pharisees and brings us to the climax of their predicament. Their fatal sin was that of willful impersuasibility. They could not believe the truth, because they would not accept it: *that,* and that alone, accounted for their reprobation.

Despite the testimony of God the Father, John the Baptist, Jesus' mighty works, and their own sacred Scriptures (cf. John 5:36-39), they were still demanding,

Q. What sign shewest thou then, that we may see, and believe thee? (John 6:30).

to which our Lord, like Abraham, replied:

A. There is one that accuseth you, even Moses, in whom ye trust. For had ye believed Moses, ye would have believed me: for he wrote of me. But if ye believe not his writings, how shall ye believe my words? (John 5:45-47).

The Old Testament and salvation. If it should be objected that the saving message of grace is not found in Moses and the prophets, it is sufficient to reply that we have the testimony of Abraham, as well as that of Christ Himself, to the contrary! Moreover, Paul affirms of the Old Testament Scriptures that they "are able to make thee wise unto salvation through faith which is in Christ Jesus" (II Timothy the 3:15).

The Law was, indeed, "a ministration of condemnation," but it did reveal an adequate means of justification. Every death which it exacted, on the sacrificial altar, for sin prepictured the believer's redemption through the death of Christ. Such is the all-pervading message of the Old Testament as well as the New, the only important difference being their dissimilar emphases:

- The Old Testament stresses the demands of righteousness, while anticipating their satisfaction at Calvary.
- The New Testament underscores the freeness of salvation, while insisting that it has been brought about by righteous means for righteous ends.

The foregoing couplet, wherever the accent falls, is the Gospel of Christ: the truth that makes us free from condemnation (cf. John 8:32): the "word of truth" whereby we are begotten unto eternal life (cf. James 1:18; I Peter 1:23).

A universal principle. This justifying, life-giving truth must be received by faith, not by senses—not by a "sign"—for "faith cometh by hearing, and hearing by the word of God" (Romans 10:17). This principle is universal and unexceptionable. It is as true of deceased infants and unevangelized heathen as it is of responsible adults in enlightened Christian lands.

> Except a man [literally, *anyone—any human being, regardless of age, sex, or class*] be born again, he cannot see the kingdom of God (John 3:3).

The only way any human being can be saved is to receive a new spiritual birth which results from his having heard and believed the Gospel. This principle signifies that...

- no one has a genuine opportunity to be *saved* until he *hears* the Gospel;
- no one can be *condemned* for rejecting the Gospel until he *has heard* it; and, therefore,
- everyone *must hear* it—somewhere, sometime, somehow— before his final destiny is fixed for either weal or woe (cf. I Peter 3:18, 4:6).

The Finality of the Gospel

Both the Pharisees and the publicans had heard the Gospel. So, why were the publicans saved, and the Pharisees left in unbelief? Both classes were undeserving, sinful, impotent—incapable of either repentance or faith apart from divine intervention and enablement. Did God freely grant these graces to the publicans but withhold them from the Pharisees?

By no means—or at least, not arbitrarily. He exhausted the resources of divine persuasion in an utterly impartial effort to save them all. The publicans, who offered no resistance, were drawn into the portals of grace of their own accord. But the Pharisees who had made themselves impersuasible by deliberately meeting proffered mercy with contempt—thus had reprobated themselves, contrary to the will of God.

And so the story goes until this day. Wherever faith and unbelief confront each other and reap their diverse rewards, this parable is reenacted in actual experience.

34

THE UNPROFITABLE SERVANT

The Indispensability of the Gospel

Primary text: Luke 17:7-10.

Jesus spoke this parable to His disciples—somewhere in Perea—during the second month (February) before His crucifixion.

Introduction. This illustration, if taken out of context, is fertile soil for fanciful speculation. Anyone familiar with its treatment in commentaries can hardly doubt it has suffered overmuch from the gratuitous flourishes of all-too-hasty pens. This is not to suggest that any of our expositors would willfully trifle with the Word of God, but that some of them simply *write* faster than they *think*. In fact, the besetting sin of many a brilliant author is the substitution of rhetoric for painstaking research and reflection. This passage calls for far more diligence and insight than superficial eloquence.

Like most of the Savior's parables, this one ties in with many lateral truths more or less incidental to its principal thrust. Unless we are careful to relate it to Jesus' general line of argument at the time, we are apt to busy ourselves with generalities and miss the main point. But if we take time to trace the continuity of the Master's dominant theme, in this series of parables (as well as the accompanying narrative), we may then interpret this last one in its connection with the rest.

Thus, and only thus, will this passage make perfect sense and involve no jarring incongruities with certain others that hold forth the prospect of special rewards for faithful service.

Background. The Lord Jesus, now approaching the end of His major itinerary in Perea, was concluding a course of teaching built around a series of seven illustrations, the first four of which were closely knit together, and the final three connected only by their tangential relations to the rest:

1. After the Pharisees had objected to His gracious reception of penitent sinners, He had defended His ministry of mercy by presenting the parables of "The Lost Sheep," "The Lost Piece of Silver," "The Lost Son," and "The Elder Brother."

2. To emphasize the moral aims and demands of the Gospel, He had used the parable of "The Unjust Steward" to show the converted publicans that they must now surrender themselves and all their worldly belongings to God.

3. In answer to the critical jeers of the covetous Pharisees, He had told the story of "The Rich Man and Lazarus," to warn them of the terrible retribution which, according to both the Law and the Gospel, was awaiting them in the coming world.

4. Turning to the disciples, He launched into the discussion of offenses, leading up to the present parable.

Purpose. Looking toward the future even as the jibes of the Pharisees still rang in His disciples' ears, the Master warned (in verse 1): "It is impossible but that offenses will come: but woe unto him, through whom they come!" The false shepherds of Israel were already busy doing their best to discredit the faith and undermine the confidence of the newly converted publicans. Jesus knew that from then on, every conceivable snare would be contrived in an effort to trip up His followers, just as history now bears witness. He also knew that there would be times when conscientious Christians would revolt at the failures of their erring brethren and be minded, Phariseelike, to thrust them from the fold instead of encouraging them to mend their ways.

Therefore, He admonished them, "Take heed to yourselves" (verse 3)—as much as to say, *"Be careful lest you, also, cast a stumblingblock before My little ones."* To prevent that very thing, He urged his followers to take the initiative in bringing about the restoration of a wayward saint, forgiving any brother of any trespass as often as he would repent.

This double-barrelled challenge moved the bewildered apostles to plead, "Increase our faith" (verse 5). Confronted by the dual threats of seduction or persecution from without and intolerance from within, clearly they were overwhelmed with feelings of inadequacy. So much was at stake, in either case, that they were loath to grapple with such issues without a good deal more spiritual wisdom and vigor than they were conscious of possessing at the time. Their request itself bore witness to a modicum of faith—but not enough, they felt, to ensure their faithfulness under such demanding circumstances as they were told to expect. So they yearned, and asked, for more: *Add to us faith,* they implored.

Whereupon, Jesus agreed with the reasoning behind their petition, but proceeded to correct an unwarranted assumption. They were right in assuming spiritual strength sufficient for their needs must spring from faith, but they must learn any degree of genuine faith is capable of unlimited expansion—it needs not increase but development through constant use. They must learn why, if their faith was only comparable to a tiny mustard seed (and the language Jesus used implied that it was), why that tiny amount would be quite ample to sustain them in all eventualities. As the ensuing parable would show, their faith would grow and flourish under testing, with every new challenge eliciting the spiritual vigor by which it should be met, by which alone it could be met. No, they would not be pampered with a sort of magical faith which would, in effect, dissipate all their difficulties in advance and, thus, leave no occasion for real faith at all. No, the quality of their faith would improve with use, from trial to trial, from crisis to crisis, from victory to victory:

- They asked for *additional* faith with which to meet additional requirements.

- They were told the faith they had would prove adequate if they would exercise it faithfully.

But—this is the burden of the following parable—the disciples must never think for a moment that their faith, no matter how disciplined and fruitful, would put God under obligation to them, because faith itself is a gift of God, a part of the salvation it appropriates (cf. Ephesians 2:8–9). In other words, God never *owes* man anything.

Examination and interpretation. Now the Master was not merely defending the Gospel. Attributing even our faith to the grace of God, he was insisting that the Gospel is our only hope and that to be saved at all is to be totally and eternally indebted to Him as our Sovereign Lord. However reciprocal love may be, and however much the Lord may be pleased to bless us simply because He loves us, thanksgiving is a one-way street. Hence, Jesus went on to say:

> But which of you, having a servant plowing or feeding cattle, will say unto him by and by, when he is come from the field, Go and sit down to meat? And will not rather say unto him, Make ready wherewith I may sup, and gird thyself, and serve me, till I have eaten and drunken; and afterward thou shalt eat and drink? Doth he thank that servant because he did the things that were commanded him? I trow not (verses 7-9).

In several ways this parable summarizes the leading lessons of the preceding six. A redeemed believer is the property of his gracious Redeemer; henceforth, the sole purpose of his life is to do his new Master's will. No longer a "servant of sin," he is a "servant of righteousness" (Romans 6:17–18), a bondman of Christ. An undeserving sinner saved by grace apart from any works or merits of his own, he is eternally obligated to serve his Savior; he can never do enough to repay that debt, much less to entitle himself to extra rewards. Thus it was with the forgiven publicans, thus with the apostles, and so it is with us. That view was foreign to the minds of the conceited Pharisees, who cherished the delusion that their servile works entitled them not only to salvation but to temporal honor and material wealth as well.

Both the Pharisees and the converted publicans occupied the place of servants, but their motives were as different as night and day:

The Pharisee served in order to:	The converted publican served in order to:
ingratiate himself with God.	pay a debt of gratitude for grace received.
obligate God to him.	own his obligation to his Master.

Jesus, accordingly, meant this parable to teach the apostles they should outdo the Pharisees themselves in rendering diligent service, but for a very different reason—not to earn salvation or earthly rewards, but as an expression of their gratitude for God's free gifts. After having done their perfunctory chores, the Pharisees expected to "go at once and sit down to meat" (verse 7)—that is, to receive their "good things" here and now. Forgiven sinners were to count it a privilege to endure the "evil things" of the present world until "the night cometh, when no man can work" (cf. John 9:4).

That subsequent history has borne out this interpretation is common knowledge to all of us. Professional religionists of every hue and stripe have enjoyed their various preferments and lived out their days as privileged pensioners while Christ's disciples toiled and suffered at their seemingly thankless tasks until their dying hours. Often there was, for them, no letup, no vacation; no retirement, compensation, or commendation—only ceaseless labor, endless persecution, and at last a dungeon, a fiery stake, or a headsman's block. And, except for all the variations incident to changing times, so it is until this day.

Times change, but Dives still reclines in purple splendor at his sumptuous board while Lazarus shares his crumbs and sores with sympathetic dogs outside the gate.

"So likewise ye, when ye have done all those things which are commanded you, say, We are unprofitable servants: we have done that which was our duty to do" (verse 10). None of us ever does all that we should—but even if we did, we would not put God in our debt. The most anyone can do for Christ is nothing more than his duty.

Our toils and sacrifices, although far from useless, always leave us debtors to the Lord. Yet—since they constrain us to go on "from faith to faith" (cf. Romans 1:17), with each new trial gaining us "more grace" (cf. James 4:6)—they do promote our apprehension of "that for which [we are] apprehended of Christ Jesus" (Philippians 3:12).

Despite our ill deserts, despite the inadequacy of even our best performance, the record here assures us that after all the interests of the Master have been served, we too shall "eat and drink" (verse 8). Eventually, not to pay a debt but as a gift of pure grace, our Master will "make [us] sit down to meat, and will come forth and serve [us]" (cf. Luke 12:37).

Conclusion. Thus, according to the teaching of the apologetic parables, the Gospel is not only reasonable and valid, but also absolutely indispensable—the only way a just God can lavish mercy and blessing on undeserving sinners who are helpless to save themselves.

SECTION SIX
MORE KINGDOM VALUES

We doubt because our thinking is so myopic that we fail to see God weaving out His answers in the tapestry of history. He is not running a single province, but a universal empire. ... He is dealing with all mankind, and with all of us substantially alike, at the same time.

35

An Inspirational Parable

THE UNJUST JUDGE

Keeping Faith with God
in Times of Adversity

Primary text: Luke 18:1-8.

Jesus spoke this parable to His disciples, somewhere between Ephraim and Perea—on His last journey to Jerusalem, somewhat less than a month before His crucifixion.

Introduction. Whether we can plumb the depth or survey the breadth of the teaching couched in this parable, there is no doubt about its fundamental purpose. The first and final verses, taken together, clearly show that it urges constant prayer as a means of keeping faith with God in troubled times. Nor is there question about the identification of its characters. The *unjust judge* represents an erroneous conception of God. The *widow* represents the elect: not only the Jewish remnant, but also the whole household of faith—as well as the individual believer, regardless of his dispensational associations. In the first place, the Jewish remnant is obviously in view:

Reign of Antichrist. In the foregoing chapter we find Jesus discussing the shape of things at the end of this age, when Jewish believers are going to be severely tested during the cruel reign of Antichrist. The Savior declares that His followers will

---

then be in a position similar to that of Noah among the wicked antediluvians or of Lot before the destruction of Sodom. He warns that anyone who forsakes the faith to save his life will do so at the risk of certain death. In those dreadful days, there will be such tribulation as the saints have never encountered before. It will seem as if God has utterly abandoned them to their enemies. They must, therefore, pray unceasingly, lest their faith should fail and they should be disloyal to their Lord.

Pertinence. Although we live in a different dispensational setting, the same admonitions are just as pertinent now—not any less applicable to the Church today than they will be to the Jewish remnant during the Great Tribulation—nor a whit less urgent. True, times change, but the basic issues are the same in all ages. Already "there are many antichrists" (I John 2:18), and already the "mystery of iniquity" is at work (cf. II Thessalonians 2:7). Even now our profession is being tested by many fiery trials. We, too, must pray without ceasing if we are to be among the overcomers who inherit the Kingdom.

The habit of praying—an individual matter. Again, this is, at all events, an individual matter. We are all individuals by birth, and we remain so ever afterward. Thus we live, thus we commit our souls, thus we endure the trials of our faith, and thus we shall stand before the judgment bar of God—and these concepts tell us that each one of us "ought always to pray, and not to faint" (verse 1). To that statement, every pious soul will readily agree—perhaps too readily. That is the trouble: we are prone to laud the habit of praying, without really practicing it. We talk about it, we do a good deal of formal praying from time to time, but we scarcely ever really pray until we find ourselves in trouble. Then we pray—for a while at least. But the trials that cause us to pray may have an opposite effect if they continue overlong—as, sooner or later, they usually do. As they multiply, intensify, and prolong themselves—despite our praying—we may sometimes wonder whether God does hear us, after all.

Tests of faith. Our faith is sorely tested in such ordeals, especially when we know that we are suffering wrongfully—when, being ever so innocent, we are unjustly accused, slandered, stigmatized or when, being at a disadvantage, we are exploited, oppressed, and abused.

It simply isn't right, we murmur. *If a righteous God is mindful of us, why doesn't He rebuke our adversaries, protect our interests, and vindicate us before the world?* If even our complaint receives no answer—Well!—unless our faith has been disciplined and matured by a life of incessant prayer, we are likely to "faint"— to despair of praying any more at all. Just such a state of mind is what the current parable was intended to prevent.

It is not concerned with generalities, but with one problem in particular: how to keep faith with God when it seems He has forgotten and deserted us—or, worse, when it seems He is an unjust judge, allowing the wicked to oppress the righteous with impunity.

Examination and interpretation. How like the helpless widow do we then find ourselves in the cruel gauntlet of this callous, unsympathetic world! Abandoned, defenseless, exploited, with no one to plead our cause! Still, even a widow such as the one in our parable has one recourse: she can persist in unrelenting prayer. If even an unjust judge will finally give in and grant her petition lest she wear him out with her entreaties, surely we may trust that our loving Heavenly Father will vindicate and relieve His children in due time. Ah, that is the question: How long until "due time"? Why doesn't He respond to our pleading now—right now?

Wheels within wheels. Although we find our answer in the first chapter of Ezekiel, few of us seem to take this passage very seriously. In fact, it is common to hear people joke about the "wheels within the wheels," to make sport of those who dare to take this text without a grain of salt. Nevertheless it is here, among the whirling wheels of Providence, we find the solution to many of life's enigmas, such as why God waits so long to answer some prayers. Rewriting the prophet's language in modern terms, it seems to say that

> ... *the moral mechanism of the universe is a vast complex of interacting principles and potencies, like*

> *the meshwork of an imponderable transmission in which all sorts of gears, poised at every conceivable angle, operating in all directions, are synchronized in a way to ensure that God's overriding purposes will be worked out—here today, there tomorrow, and everywhere eventually. In Ezekiel's imagery, then, the various laws and agencies of God's government are so many wheels—outer and inner counter-wheels— that make up a cosmic "chariot," adjusting itself to all contingencies, surmounting all obstacles, always going straight forward toward its goal. Often opposed but never stopped, it may seem off-schedule, but is never actually late—notwithstanding the paradoxes and enigmas of life (cf. Ezekiel 1).*

God "accomplishes all things according to the counsel of his will" (Ephesians 1:11, RSV), and "none can stay his hand" (Daniel 4:35). So, let us keep on praying; the "Judge of all the earth" will grant us our petitions in due time!

Our limited vision of God's universe. We doubt because our thinking is so myopic that we fail to see God weaving out His answers in the tapestry of history. He is not running a single province, but a universal empire. In fact, He is dealing with all mankind, and with all of us substantially alike, at the same time.

1a. While He seemed to be lax in delivering the Israelites, He was giving Pharaoh all the time he needed to repent.

2a. While He detained the Chosen People in the "waste and howling wilderness," He was deferring the judgment of the Canaanites until the cup of their iniquity was full.

3a. God not only of Jews but also of Gentiles, in allowing Jews to persecute the early Christian Church, He used their opposition to scatter the sparks of truth beyond their own borders throughout the heathen world.

4a. Likewise, He turned every fiery stake of pagan Rome into a pulpit and made her wrath an instrument of grace.

So it is today and will be tomorrow, until we all have received sufficient light and opportunity to be saved, sanctified, and glorified. The wheels of Providence whirr in their unalterable course; the mills of God grind out their inexorable grist.

1b. Pharaoh finally drowns, and Israel sings the song of Moses and the Lamb.

2b. The Canaanites finally flee, and Joshua's victorious armies seize possession of the Promised Land.

3b. Jerusalem, the Jewish capital, finally falls before the Romans, and the early disciples escape to peace and safety in distant Pella.

4b. Rome is finally baptized by the blood of her martyrs.

We are children in God's universe. As for ourselves, we may be sure that "the stars in their courses" will fight our foes until each and every curse is turned into a blessing (cf. Judges 5:20; Deuteronomy 24:5). The "vision is yet for an appointed time, but at the end it shall speak, and not lie: though it tarry, wait for it; because it will surely come, it will not tarry" (Habakkuk 2:3). Meanwhile, "the just shall live by his faith" (Habakkuk 2:4.; cf. Romans 3:17; Galatians 3:11; Hebrews 10:38).

"Nevertheless, when the Son of Man cometh, will He find this kind of faith on the earth?" (Verse 8, RV.) If so, it will be among those who have dared to keep on praying after prayer seemed in vain.

We must "endure, as seeing him who is invisible" (Hebrews 11:27), "against hope believing in hopes" (Romans 4:18).

Assured that God is mindful of His promises and faithful to His Word, then, "let us not be weary in well doing: for in due season we shall reap, if we faint not" (Galatians 6:9). These verses summarize, I believe, substantially what our Savior meant this parable to say.

36

THE PHARISEE AND THE PUBLICAN

The Truth About Justification

Primary text: Luke 18:9-14.

Our Lord spoke this parable to certain unnamed but self-righteous Jews—probably within the borders of Perea—on His final journey to Jerusalem, during the last month (March) before His crucifixion.

Introduction. It is not of little significance that *He*—our blessed Savior—spoke this parable, for what we find here is a far cry from the customary preachments of conventional religionists. The Pharisee in this story is the kind of person a good many pulpiteers insist we all should be! In most other settings, he would be considered a model saint. The situation as we find it shows Jesus saw things differently. Here, as in other instances, He draws an indelible contrast between Christianity and mere religion—exposing a sanctimonious priest as a consummate hypocrite and, in defiance of popular standards, reserving His benediction for a penitent renegade.

Nor may this characterization of the Pharisee be softened by explaining it as an exceptional case—nothing unusual about it, it reflects the tenor of the Master's teaching from first to last. Though He never failed to censure wickedness of any kind, there is nothing in the record to indicate He actually castigated an ordinary sinner—only the pretentious clerics, mainly the Pharisees. He freely pardoned several adulteresses, heaped mercy on penitent publicans and other social outcasts, and saved a notorious thief in His dying hour. But He made no effort to conceal His disgust for the vested clergy of His day.

"Ye do err," He chided the sophisticated Sadducees, "not knowing the scriptures, nor the power of God! (Cf. Matthew 22:29.) Their erudition was, to Him, a thin disguise for willful ignorance. In His sight, the Herodians were wicked (Matthew 22:18; the scribes and Pharisees, were "hypocrites . . . blind guides . . . fools . . . like unto whited sepulchres, which indeed appear beautiful outward, but are within full of dead men's bones, and all uncleanness" (Matthew 23:13-27).

Against this backdrop, we easily see why Jesus spoke this parable to "certain which trusted in themselves that they were righteous, and despised others" (verse 9). Though it is not said that He addressed the Pharisees directly on this occasion, the context leaves little doubt that they were prominent in His audience. Still, the language of the record is broad enough to include all those of a similar stripe, possibly some of our Lord's own disciples—for, alas! the ancient Pharisees have always had numerous bedfellows, like them in all points short of owning the fact.

Such a person is characterized by two inseparable attitudes: conceit and contempt. He is self-convinced that he himself is a righteous one and looks down on everyone else—feels assured of his personal acceptance with God by virtue of his integrity, but sets all other men at nought because of their ill deserts. Pharisaism builds its castle from a quarry-hole in somebody else's yard, exalts itself by disparaging others, glorifies itself at another's expense. Worst of all, a Pharisee's delusions of grandeur usually reach their height and plumb their nether depth religiously.

Examination and interpretation. Our Lord chose the temple, at the hour of prayer, as the setting for His depiction of these contrasting types of worshipers.

"Two men," He said, "went up into the temple to pray; the one a Pharisee, and the other a publican" (verse 10). One a paragon of virtue in the public eye, one a common symbol of obliquity, they had one thing in common that day: They had come to pray.

The Pharisee's prayer. Few things bare the soul as does the way one prays. The Pharisee, striking a sanctimonious stance, prays—not just *with* himself, as our popular version has it, but *to* himself. No, he doesn't address himself as God—but he does eulogize himself in the Divine Presence! Standing before the August Majesty of heaven and earth, he punctuates every breath with a self-conscious *I*:

> God, I thank thee, that I am not as other men are, extortioners, unjust, adulterers, or even as this publican. I fast twice in the week, I give tithes of all that I possess . . . (verses 11–12).

Here Jesus, as if this were enough to exhaust His patience, leaves the Pharisee pulling his beads. But who has not heard such prayers extended, on and on, with additional *I*'s? Let's look at the Pharisee's prayer more closely:

1. He congratulates himself on being *morally superior* to the remainder of mankind—as represented, on the scene, by the disconsolate publican.
2. As for himself, he is not an extortioner, an unjust person, or an adulterer, he reasons; therefore, as compared with ordinary people, he is above reproach.
3. Besides, he actually has an excess of legal righteousness—more than the Law requires (or so he thinks).
   a. Not only does he fast on the annual Day of Atonement as commanded by Moses, but also fasts twice every week of his own free choice (cf. verse 12).
   b. Not only does he tithe crops and cattle, in accordance with Levitical regulations, but goes still further and gives a tenth of *all* his increase, not even excepting such things as mint, anise, and cumin (cf. verse 12).

With all these "works of supererogation" to his credit, who could doubt that his moral assets were as excessive as other people's liabilities?

Certainly not the conscience-stricken publican on the scene.

The publican's prayer. Standing "afar off " lest his proximity be offensive to his betters, the publican prays, also—but in a very different manner:

1. He frankly confesses to all the charges the Pharisee has made.
2. Instead of assuming a pious posture, he beats—and keeps on beating—his breast as a token of abject contrition.
3. Rather than looking heavenward to offer a defense, he fixes his hopeful gaze toward the bloody mercy seat beyond the veil and begs for pardon on the ground that a sacrificial substitute has died on his behalf (cf. verse 13).
4. He petitions, "God be merciful to me a sinner" (verse 13). This statement might be translated more correctly as "God be merciful to *the* sinner." As the Pharisee thinks himself *the* most righteous of men, the publican thinks himself *the* vilest of the vile.
5. Even so, his prayer reveals more spiritual discernment than any unregenerate Pharisee ever had: he sees his need for the grace of God; he perceives the only means whereby a helpless sinner can be forgiven righteously.
6. Standing between a sacrificial altar and a judgment throne, he trusts the blood from the altar to turn the judgment bar into a throne of grace.

That was as far as any believing Jew could go then. Except for our clearer apprehension of antitypes, we can go no farther now.

Justification. Some respectable scholars will not allow that this publican could have been conscious of the elementary Gospel truth that is admittedly reflected in the language of his request. However, this position, in view of our Lord's own comment to the contrary, ignores the basic teaching of the parable. That the central theme of this parable is *justification* is shown by Jesus' concluding words: "I tell you, this man went down to his house justified rather than the other" (verse 14). But *justification* is an empty academic term in the absence of conscious dependence on the provisions of redeeming grace. The teaching couched in this parable is so specific it served a definite purpose on the local scene at the time of its deliverance, yet so general it has provided abiding lessons for succeeding generations.

Whatever may have been its immediate purpose, it certainly illustrates the reason for God's rejection of national Jewry and the extension of His mercy to believers among the Gentiles. No one who is familiar with subsequent history should fail to see the resemblance between (a) the Pharisee who boasted of his legal righteousness and the whole of unbelieving Jewry— and (b) the publican, who sought and found divine forgiveness by relying on the merits of sacrificial blood, and the penitent heathen.

The Apostle Paul also saw this contrast on the mission field, asking—"What shall we say then?"—and, replying to his own question, answered—"That the Gentiles, which followed not after righteousness, have attained to righteousness, even the righteousness which is of faith. But Israel, which followed after the law of righteousness, hath not attained to the law of righteousness. "Wherefore?" [or, *Why did Israel fail?*] "Because they sought it not by faith, but as it were by the works of the law (Romans 9:30–32).

True righteousness vs. a self-righteous attitude. Neither this parable nor any other Scriptural text disparages the worth of genuine righteousness, but the entire Bible consistently warns against the worthlessness of *pious conceit.*

• The Pharisee who thought himself so good was actually no better than anyone else; yet, unaware of his real condition, he felt no need for God's justifying grace.
• The publican, convinced of his guilt, had no recourse but to throw himself upon the mercy of the Lord.

All of which portrays the spiritual moods of impenitent Jews and believing Gentiles during the present age.

A warning for all, not only Jews. Jews have not consciously forsaken the way of righteousness—but the righteousness they seek to attain is altogether illusory. As the Apostle Paul said:

> I bear them record that they have a zeal of God, but not according to knowledge. For they being ignorant of God's righteousness, and going about to establish their own righteousness, have not submitted themselves to the righteousness of God [meaning, *"the righteousness of God as it is revealed in the Gospel"*] (Romans 10:2–3).

This condition is by no means confined to the Jews. Wherever religious but unbelieving men parade their piety and rely upon their own dead works while penitent sinners are being saved by grace, this parable is being fulfilled in current history. The Scriptures say that hell will teem with disillusioned people who pinned their hopes on goodness they never had, and heaven will abound with forgiven sinners who enjoy peace with God despite their ill deserts.

"For," Christ reminds us with a closing comment, "every one that exalteth himself shall be abased; but he that humbleth himself shall be exalted" (verse 14; cf. Luke 14:11).

37

THE LABORERS IN THE VINEYARD

The Relationship Between Salvation and Rewards

Primary text: Matthew 20:1-16.

Jesus spoke this parable to His disciples—probably within the borders of Perea—on His final journey to Jerusalem, about two weeks before His crucifixion.

Introduction and background. This text is generally regarded as unusually problematic; after due consideration, I believe its difficulties more apparent than real. To begin with, a good deal of debris can be cleared away by giving due heed to two simple, universally recognized guidelines of Scriptural interpretation.

Two "rules" of Biblical interpretation—
1. Debatable passages of Scripture must be understood in keeping with those which speak out more clearly on the same subjects.
2. It is not the normal function of parables to present new doctrine, but to illustrate truths revealed elsewhere.

—and where they lead us—
a. Accordingly, regardless of any perceived obscure elements in a particular illustration, we must conclude that there can be nothing in it that contradicts any authentic teaching of

the Bible.
b. Therefore, a correct interpretation of this parable must square with what the Scriptures teach elsewhere about free grace and personal rewards.

Contextual background. And yet, if we consider this parable candidly in its context, we must see that (a) it *does* in some sense bear directly on the question of salvation, and (b) it *does* suggest that all of God's children will eventually receive an identical reward of some kind. Nor are we at liberty to gloss over these facts just because they appear to be out of kilter with the general rule. As elsewhere and always, here it is best to recognize *all* the facts, then "prove the things that differ" (cf. Philippians 1:10), in other words, to distinguish them. On this principle, I propose to show that the true teaching of this parable is not inconsistent with, but complementary to, all the Bible affirms on the points in question. The solution, it seems to me, is found in the varying connotations of the terms used, their meanings determined by contextual considerations.

Different meanings of the term salvation. In Biblical usage the term *salvation* performs a rather wide variety of services, to wit:

1. *Salvation* often denotes physical or national deliverance—usually, however, with the additional idea of positive benefaction, not merely the provision of a means of escape.
2. These levels of meaning are carried over—immeasurably enhanced—in *salvation* as a spiritual experience, with its positive aspects tending more and more to outweigh the negative ones (but the position of the emphasis varies with the case).
3. Sometimes, *salvation* means deliverance from sin or death or hell—or all these things together—viewed as a past, present, or future accomplishment.
4. Then, at times, *salvation* is used in a broad, general sense as including all the factors and processes involved not merely nor necessarily in sheer deliverance from the penalty of sin, but in the outworking and enjoyment of the potentialities of saving grace—grace freely bestowed and received, apart

---

The Relationship Between Salvation and Rewards

from any consideration of meritorious works.

This last, I propose to show, is undoubtedly the connotation of *eternal life, the kingdom of God,* and *salvation,* as these terms are used in the contextual setting of this parable.

Local background. It would be much to our advantage if we could somehow project ourselves into the scene of the Savior's labors, sense the problems and expectations of His hearers, and evaluate His teachings in the light of the various needs and aspirations to which they were addressed. True, all other issues converge around the question of the soul's eternal destiny, but it is a mistake to construe everything Jesus said as if meant to define the rigid boundary between salvation and damnation. He did that on some occasions—and the line He drew was often sharp and clear. But, already having pointed out the indispensability of repentance, faith, and regeneration, Jesus then devoted quite a large measure of His attention to the subsequent realization of the latent capabilities of redeeming grace—a process frequently encompassed by the general term *salvation,* since it is the *outgrowth* of the initial experience of conversion. The work of grace embraces all the potentialities that issue in its eventual consummation, just as an acorn is pregnant with the oak it produces.

Jesus is viewing salvation, not in its *inception* (which is brought about by God with no effort on the subject's part), but in its *cumulative development,* as resultant obedience crystallizes in Christian character. Although He assures us that our works will be amply rewarded, He insists that, in the last analysis, this is not so much a matter of "earning legal wages" as of "receiving dividends accruing from a capital gift." Although this principle holds good in the case of rewards in general, that is not immediately in view in this particular parable, for it contemplates the acquisition of a single composite prize (as we shall see). The decisive clue to its interpretation lies in an antecedent train of thought, beginning with Jesus' parting words to the rich young ruler:

> If thou wilt be perfect, the Master told him, "go and sell that thou has, and give to the poor, and

thou shalt have treasure in heaven . . . (Matthew 19:21).

The pivotal terms in this utterance are *perfect* and *treasure in heaven*; both terms contemplate salvation as the full realization of eternal life; both terms include all the benefits of salvation, henceforth and forever. All things considered, one can scarcely assume that this exemplary young Jew was asking Jesus to draw a hard and fast line of demarcation between salvation and damnation. Much likelier, his object was to find out how he might attain to moral perfection and thus achieve the ideal embodied in such concepts as eternal life and the kingdom of heaven. He had already called Jesus "good," which (assuming he had enough discrimination to understand the implications of his language) amounted to a confession of faith in the Savior's deity—for, as our Lord was quick to remind him, only God is absolutely good. On the assumption that the young man believed in Jesus' Messianic claims, I hold, the Master exhorted him, in so many words, to "press toward the mark for the prize of the high calling of God" (cf. Philippians 3:14) by obeying the will of God as it is revealed in the Law. Surely, it would be in defiance of all Scripture to propose that Jesus suggested that a sinner can save himself by keeping the Law. He was, instead, declaring that one who is already a justified saint must "work out [his] own salvation" (cf. Philippians 2:12–13) by obeying the known will of God. Only in this sense of the word does the *penny* in the ensuing parable depict salvation.

Consequently, we are not told that the zealous young man dashed off in unbelief to a reprobate's doom, but that "he went away sorrowful" (cf. Matthew 19:22) because of his reluctance to sacrifice temporal advantages in the interest of his spiritual aspirations. It was not that he denied the claims of Christ, but that, like most of us, he balked at giving Him priority over his own affairs. Else, if we construe his attachment to his worldly possessions as proof of fateful unbelief, we shall be compelled on that principle to write off the vast majority of professing Christians as deluded hypocrites. *That,* I prefer to believe, would be a rash mistake. No, it is one thing to have received

The Relationship Between Salvation and Rewards

salvation in its germinal bud and quite another to realize all the potentialities of spiritual growth and enrichment inherent in the hope of our calling. The latter conception, it seems to me, is contemplated in the teaching of this parable: Rather than our feeble efforts entitling us to compensation, the privilege of service—with its concomitant blessedness—is, in the main, its own reward.

At the moment, it remained for our Lord's disciples to learn that this is so. Although he had just heard Jesus declare that salvation is a miraculous work of sovereign grace (cf. Matthew 19:26), Peter (doubtless speaking, as usual, for all the rest of the apostles) interjected. "Behold we have forsaken all, and followed thee; what shall we have therefore?" (Cf. Matthew 19:27.)

In Peter's mind, the all-availing grace of God still lay in eclipse behind a deserving *we*. He felt that he and his fellow apostles—in contrast with the selfish young ruler—were justly entitled to some compensation for the sacrifices they had made. Peter was slow to perceive that

- there can be no better reward for serving Jesus than simply the privilege of doing so;
- Christ Himself is God's best gift to those who follow Him;
- only in Him and through Him may we realize the *summum bonum* of salvation, the ideal felicity of the Kingdom, and the consummate blessedness of eternal life.

The situation might be viewed metaphorically as if a newly wedded wife were to say to her husband, *"Now that I have forsaken all others to marry you, how much do you propose to pay me for cooking your meals?"* Of course, no devoted wife would think of doing that, for she would find her chief delight in her husband himself. In the same spirit, the apostles should have counted it all joy to have and to follow Jesus at any cost. Peter's question showed their underlying motives were not altogether different from those of the rich young ruler.

In either case, it was a question of *having* or *not having*. Rather than be a *have-not*, the disillusioned youth declined an invitation to follow Jesus. Peter was, at least partly, following the Savior to become a *have*—and Peter was not alone in this respect. James and John are known to have sought the highest honors in the promised Kingdom (cf. verses 20 ff.), and the rest of the apostles frequently quarreled among themselves about who should be "the greatest" (cf. Mark 9:34). Unworthy motives threatened to nullify the value of their sacrifices. Like Baruch, Jeremiah's fretful scribe, the disciples stood in need of the admonition "Seekest thou great things for thyself? seek them not" (Jeremiah 45:5). Not to worry; such a warning would be forthcoming presently (cf. verses 22-28).

But first, the Savior assured them that, yes, they would be rewarded with the privilege of reigning with Him in the glory of His Kingdom, adding that not only they but all other saints as well would receive "an hundred fold" for all the losses they should suffer in their zeal for Him. This reward would be given in addition to their inheritance of eternal life as a sovereign grant (cf. Matthew 19:28-30).

These thoughts, leading as they do to the current parable, serve as weather vanes to indicate the prevailing winds of its interpretation. Jesus was thinking not only in temporal, but also in eschatological terms—thinking not only of principles in operation here and now, but also of their culmination after "the regeneration," in the world to come (cf. Matthew 19:28). Note the care with which He distinguishes between rewards, as such, and the gift of eternal life (cf. Matthew 19:29).

Against this backdrop, the basic clue to understanding the parable lies in the solemn apothegm with which the Lord Jesus cautioned His apostles against the danger of complacency and overconfidence: "But many that are first shall be last, and the last shall be first" (Matthew 19:30). Here the terms *first* and *last* are employed in both a temporal and a relative sense.

To the apostles, this aphorism meant they could not take their original preeminence for granted, as if precedence in the Master's service entitled them to some preferential treatment, regardless of their future conduct. They would have to humble themselves to be exalted, serve in order to excel, and content themselves with being last to eventually be first. Many who had followed Jesus from the outset would regard their calling as a means of personal aggrandizement instead of discharging

The Relationship Between Salvation and Rewards

it as a sacred trust, and would allow gross motives to degrade their ministry. But there would be humbler souls of nobler mind who would use their offices well, "purchasing to themselves a good degree" (cf. I Timothy 3:13). This warning is not a novel element in Jesus' message; in one form or other, it pervades His teaching from start to finish. But perhaps nowhere else as here does it bear such a trenchant edge.

Examination and interpretation. Someone has ventured the opinion that this parable is made up largely of contrasts rather than strict analogies. It is difficult to reconcile that notion with the Savior's opening statement that the Kingdom of Heaven is *like* the situation He proceeds to describe. From this wording, it appears His story, however idealistic in nature, was meant to suggest the actual state of affairs in the realm of religious experience from first to last.

Nature of the "day." There is no good reason for limiting the *day* mentioned in this parable to any particular epoch in history, nor will the other circumstances of the story allow us to do so. The *day* is simply an incidental feature, an item in the setting of an illustration designed to dramatize the operation of certain timeless principles and their ultimate results. Nor can the day be equated with the whole of history, for all the characters on the scene are represented as contemporaries; nor for any specific dispensation or generation alone, since that would render it irrelevant to all the rest. No, it contemplates, evidently, *any* and *every* period in which believers serve the Lord—and thus depicts God's manner of dealing with the saints of all times. To the apostles, it meant the Apostolic Era; to each succeeding generation, its own span of life; to all, a season of probation followed by a final reckoning.

Motives of the workers. The thrust of this parable seems to be both historical and eschatological. Obviously, then, its basic interpretation does not hinge on the date of the day, but rather on a more prominent and altogether perspicuous feature of the story: the motives of the various laborers, as reflected by the conditions under which these agreed to go to work. The first ones are hired at dawn, presumably at about 6 o'clock.

These are joined by three other groups, at about 9 A.M., 12 noon, and 3 P.M., respectively. The last are recruited at about 5 P.M.

The first group work on a strictly contractual basis, each man for "a penny a day" (verse 2). The middle groups consent to the promise of "whatsoever is right" (verses 5–6). But those employed at the "eleventh hour" consider the invitation itself a gracious favor, and asking no questions, they go to work with no stipulations at all. The words *and whatsoever is right, that shall ye receive,* present in verse 7 of the *Authorized* or *King James* Bible, are definitely absent in the authentic text.

The foregoing paragraph supplies all the information strictly essential to the principal lesson in view. Reference to the intermediate groups appears more or less incidental. The decisive factors stand out in the contrast between the spirit of the first group, who work for a specified wage, and that of the last, who prize the opportunity to serve with no guaranteed wage whatever. It is as if the first group have demanded, *"What shall we have therefore?"*—but the last group have counted it an honor to serve at all. As to the relationship between length of service and compensation, there is indeed a comparison by way of contrast, with God's estimation of value clashing with that of men: *The worth of service is not defined by its duration, but by its motivation. In God's eyes, one hour of devotion outweighs a dozen of selfish toil.* To apprehend this truth is to dispense with every *semblance* of inequity in the illustration.

Our Lord was not describing the situation as it should be, but as it actually was—and still is. Most Christians do insist, as Peter did, on some guarantee of ample compensation for their sacrifices. So, not in approbation, but in condescension to their spiritual immaturity, the Lord assures them that they will receive "whatsoever is right" at the end of the day (verse 4). But there are some—a few—who, conscious of their ill deserts and limitations, want nothing else so much as to serve on any terms whatever. Although hosts of professional time-servers hang a price-tag on their ministry—unwilling to preach Gospel, sing in the choir, play the organ, or even sweep the church without commensurate pay, there are nobler saints who will, if need be, tax themselves to "buy" such opportunities (cf.

The Relationship Between Salvation and Rewards

Ephesians 5:16). Some Christian "servants" capitalize on their advantages, but others serve despite their disadvantages.

But, as in the parable, there are going to be some surprises when "evening" comes. For one thing, the last will be paid off first; for another, they will all in the long run be paid alike—"every man a penny" (verses 9–10).

It is quite amazing to find some eminent commentators explaining these arrangements on the supposition that this householder is a humorist who takes delight in bewildering his laborers with whimsical tricks. Away with such nonsense! This is Holy Scripture! The Lord Jesus Christ is speaking! His story takes its form because that form depicts the case *as it is*. The *householder* is God, not a trickster who amuses himself by playing with the moral sensibilities of servants, but a righteous Sovereign under obligation to Himself—and only to Himself—to treat His servants right. Thus, on the principle that grace *must* be administered righteously, we must conclude that it is only just of God to recompense the labors of the faithful first, though He is pleased that, in the long run, all shall fare alike.

Order in which rewards are given. Undoubtedly one of the distinctive features of the parable is the order in which these laborers receive their otherwise equal reward. It is this factor alone that makes the difference between the *first* and the *last*: they each get a penny, but some receive it sooner than the rest. From a temporal standpoint, there is a judicial distinction made in the distribution of impartial beneficence here. Although the first group of laborers complain that the last are "made equal" to themselves, the latter actually enjoy precedence over the former in their experiential realization of the same reward.

Distinguishing between rewards. This parable shows, among other things, that the transaction contemplated here must not be confused with the allotment of personal rewards, to every man according to his works, at the Lord's return (cf. I Corinthians 3:11-15; II Corinthians 5:10). In *that* instance, it appears, all believers will receive their rewards more or less simultaneously; moreover, no two persons will necessarily fare exactly alike. True, in the current case, the last receive their "penny" before the first; yet in the end there is no disparity at all. The distinction lies in the difference between the particular and the general. Unlike specific rewards for one's several deeds, the *penny* must represent total realization of one's salvation, considered in its broadest sense—not in its *inception,* which is effected gratuitously by God on His own initiative, but in its *consummation,* which is "worked out" in personal experience through divinely enabled cooperation with God (Philippians 2:12). It is the believer's appropriation of all the benefits and privileges of his potential calling and, hence, of eternal life— the realization of his personal fulfillment as a son and heir of God.

In this view, thus and only thus, the ethical harmony of our parable stands out in bold relief with no shadow of divine caprice to mar the scene. Only thus, the impartial grant of the uniform penny to all alike, though to some before the rest, is fully justified.

How? But *how,* it may be asked, does such compensation take place? Since the realization of our heavenly destiny will be an endless process—continuing forever, never reaching completion—how can it be said that *any* of us will receive the whole penny except in an ideal way?

Nature of our destiny. Many of us err in our judgment about eternal destiny by assuming that death (or translation) will somehow, like an old-fashioned clutch, jerk us into a state of consummate perfection. In either case, our transition from glory to glory will come about more nearly after the fashion of a fluid drive. Our souls shall pass from this life into the next just as we are; *then* we shall pursue the conquest of our personal fulfillment, from whatever state we're in when we get there. And though, admittedly, our reception of the penny will be a relative matter, depending on our ability to make good use of it, the Savior's parable leaves no doubt that the meek will be first to inherit heaven as well as the earth.

Personal rewards and "the whole penny." Although our personal rewards are not in view in this passage, we know from other Scriptures they will contribute to the realization of the whole penny of which they are part. Subjectively, they are our inborn capacities for the appropriation and appreciation of the riches of glory, which—though available to all of us alike—are actually enjoyed by "every man according to his eating," so to speak (cf. Exodus 12:4). Like a gourmet's special aptitudes, our spiritual tastes are cultivated beforehand in the school of practical experience.

A person may be saved, glorified, and given access to all the treasures of heaven, in that sense being in full possession of his penny, and still be poor in comparison with other saints with maturer spiritual sensibilities—just as infant, child, youth, and man may hear the *same* music or view the same work of art without deriving *equal* pleasure from the experience. Based on the same principle, the *last* will get their penny *first*, in the sense of being able to enjoy it sooner.

Although the "wage" is actually a *gift*, the manner of its disposition is a divine necessity. The moral government of the universe ensures and expedites the promotion of those whose dispositions are most amenable and responsive to the grace of God.

38

An Admonitory Parable

THE POUNDS

The Practical Challenge of the Gospel

Primary text: Luke 19:11-27.

Our Lord spoke this parable to a mixed multitude—
at Jericho—a week before His crucifixion.

Introduction and background. This parable may be understood
by simply examining it in light of its *local* and *historical* setting.
It is largely allegorical, using a bit of familiar local history to
illustrate the impending course of Christ's career and its effect
on the fortunes of His followers and enemies.

Local setting. Behind the imagery lies an episode in the
political life of Archelaus, whose royal palace (which he had
built and occupied some thirty years earlier) stood at Jericho,
perhaps within sight of Jesus' audience as He spoke. Even
though his kingdom had been bequeathed to Archelaus by his
father, Herod the Great, that action had been contested by his
younger brother, Antipas, and opposed by certain influential
Jews. Archelaus had been compelled to go to Rome to defend
his claims before Augustus Caesar. Having been appointed
ethnarch, he heaped rewards upon his friends and punishment
on his foes. Now, as the throngs at Jericho listened to another
claimant to another throne, they must have been aware that
Jesus was using lingering memories of Archelaus' experience
to illustrate His own procedures in the critical days that lay

ahead. The analogy was easy to draw, as easy to discern, and superbly adapted to the simultaneous instruction of believers and their sympathetic but uncommitted countrymen.

Relevance to Jesus' main objectives. This parable was told at the home of Zacchaeus, on Thursday before Jesus' entry into Jerusalem. He spoke to a surging throng of largely Galileans and Pereans (many on their way to Jerusalem for the feast of Passover) who had been accompanying Him and His disciples. The story line of this parable was ideally suited to serve three main purposes Jesus evidently had in mind.

1. *To remind His disciples that the Messianic Kingdom would be deferred indefinitely, pending His second advent*—Jesus knew the festive throngs were buoyant with hope that He would take advantage of the coming feast days to proclaim His Messiahship and mount His throne. In an allusion to the prior conversion of Zacchaeus, He explained that His immediate mission was to seek and to save the lost (cf. verse 103), and that He would have to redeem His subjects from their sins before they could be exalted in His Kingdom.

2. *To impress them with the urgency of practical faithfulness on their part in the meantime*—Our Lord conveyed this message using the newly converted publican's resolution to devote his wealth, from that time forward, to righteous purposes (cf. verse 8).

3. *To warn the irresolute masses that a terrible fate would overtake His enemies at His return*—The inclusion of this element in the parable was evoked by the caviling of those who resented His compassion for sinners (cf. verse 7).

We are told that "as they heard these things," the Master went on to instruct them with His parable, "because he was nigh to Jerusalem, and because they thought that the kingdom of God should immediately appear (verse 11). It was "therefore," the record says, Jesus told them the story of "a certain nobleman" who "went into a far country to receive a kingdom for himself, and to return" (verse 12).

Jesus' message for the locals. Jesus knew it was needful for His followers to be informed of the unexpected turn of events they were about to witness at Jerusalem during Passion Week—

lest they mistake His death as an ordinary martyrdom, rather than recognize it as the focal part of God's predeterminate plan for their redemption. He wanted them to know that, although His triumphal entry into Jerusalem would constitute a bona fide offer of Himself as Israel's King, His rejection by official Jewry would by no means defeat, but would further, God's redemptive purposes. Although he would be crucified by His enemies, He would not remain in the grave, but would rise, ascend to heaven, and tarry in that "far country" until the time arrived for His enthronement as David's heir on Millennial earth. In the meanwhile, His servants must be given ample opportunity to prove their qualifications for nobler service in His Kingdom after His return, and His foes must be warned of the dreadful fate awaiting them if they persisted in unbelief.

Examination and interpretation. There should be no difficulty identifying characters or recognizing events in this illustration.

a. The *nobleman* is the Lord *Jesus* Himself.

b. His *ten servants* (verse 13; original text, *ten of His servants*) represent devoted *disciples* entrusted with the Christian ministry in the interim between the risen Lord's ascension and His Second Advent. Notice, not *twelve* of His servants, as if indicative of His apostles only, but *ten*, a symbolic number certainly comprising, if not all believers, all those who are endowed with special gifts.

c. His *citizens* (verse 14) are, or were first of all, the *Jews,* as fellow members of the Theocratic nation, but in a larger sense this term embraces the whole Adamic race with which the Savior has identified Himself both by His virgin birth and His vicarious death.

d. Of course, the *enemies* mentioned at the end of the story (verse 27) are wicked people, whether Jews or Gentiles, who have willfully rejected Jesus' lordship over their lives.

Two groups, the *servants* and the *enemies,* are prominent in the opening and closing sections of this parable. At the beginning, each servant is given a pound and told to put it to profitable commercial use. At the end, he is rewarded according to his faithfulness (measured by his accomplishment). At the start, the nobleman's enemies do their utmost in opposition to his assumption of royal authority. At the end, their treachery is punished with death.

Although it would be a mistake to minimize either of these parallel developments, much more attention (at least two-thirds of the text) is given over to the nobleman's reckoning with his servants. Still, one must keep *all* the elements of the story in view, especially those of a preliminary nature, to grasp the full significance of the rest.

Two important features. In this connection, two matters call for particular consideration: (a) the symbolical meaning of the *pounds* and (b) the typical significance of the conduct of the nobleman's *enemies.* For our present purposes, it is better to examine these items in converse order.

Crimes of the enemies. One is immediately reminded of the way in which the Jewish priests and officers answered Pilate's pleas on behalf of Jesus, with their bloodthirsty chorus: "Away with him, away with him . . . We have no king but Caesar" (John 19:6, 15). That was their way of saying, "We will not have this man to reign over us" (verse 14). But their opposition did not by any means exhaust itself in bringing about the Savior's death. Ere long, even after being confronted with "infallible proofs" of His resurrection (cf. Acts 1:3), they *continued* their resistance: flogging and imprisoning both Peter and John, threatening and molesting the Christian community, stoning Stephen, instigating the decapitation of James, and driving Paul into the jaws of martyrdom. Such crimes were not exceptional, but typical, attempts to silence His witnesses. All were aimed at One beyond their reach.

Nor has such opposition been confined to apostate Jewry. The Jews have been succeeded—and exceeded—in their cruel role by countless Christ-hating pagans, ruthless inquisitors, and anti-Christian philosophers, educators, employers—even relatives—throughout the Gentile world.

Symbolic meaning of the pounds. In such a milieu servants of Christ must hazard the investment of their *pounds.* What pounds? The Greek *mina,* the monetary unit indicated in the text, is a weight of silver variously estimated to be worth from about $12 to $30, depending on the fluctuation of values both in ancient and modern times. For purposes of interpretation, this means little or nothing other than that the pound, or *mina*, represented a modest endowment. It was obviously not the nobleman's object to make his servants rich while he was away, but to test their qualifications for the assumption of much greater responsibilities after his return.

Amply demonstrated in actual experience, the concept is that Jesus is making trial of His servants during the present age with a view toward allotting our privileges in the coming Kingdom in proportion to the measure of our faithfulness here and now. I am unable to extract any special significance from the circumstance that all the servants in this parable are given *equal* amounts, for that would necessitate the introduction of a notion which is patently contrary to Gospel fact. It cannot be maintained that the pound represents salvation, for salvation cannot be multiplied by five or ten times by some servants or taken from one servant and given to another, as are the pounds in the parable. Nor, for practically the same reasons, can it be construed as one's calling, as if our several callings were all alike, which they are not. Nor to our charismatic gifts, which are known to differ, quite radically at times. All things duly considered, the pound evidently represents one's opportunity and equipment for service, irrespective of variable factors and circumstances in different cases. Only this view meets all the requirements of the parable without doing violence either to reason or some other area of Biblical truth.

The rendering of accounts. The main lesson for believers is bound up in what takes place when the nobleman returns as king and calls upon his servants to render their accounts. Only three cases are described, but these are evidently typical of the rest. The first servant, not boasting of his achievement, reports his lord's investment has yielded a tenfold return, whereupon, the king commends him for his diligence and rewards him with ten cities, one for each additional pound he has acquired. The second servant, with a gain of five pounds, receives five cities in recognition of the corresponding degree of his faithfulness.

Not so with the third, who scarcely deserves to be called a

"servant" at all. Lest he be required to make up any losses sustained in trading, he has kept his trust money hoarded in a handkerchief. Worse, he excuses his indolence by imputing ungracious motives to his lord (verse 21). Indignant at this calumnious charge, the king converts it into an indictment against the man who uttered it. If this "wicked servant" thought his master unduly exacting, he should have made all the greater effort to win his approval and avoid his wrath. If he doubted his own ability to succeed in profitable business ventures, he might at least have let out the trust money on interest. Thus, even when judged by his own excuse, this man is found to be utterly at fault and therefore undeserving of any trust at all. What he has is taken from him and given to the servant who has shown himself most likely to make the best use of it.

Such are the dealings of the nobleman with his servants once he has received full title to his kingdom and returned to begin his reign.

Main points and application. The general application of these principles to Christ and Christians is obvious, corresponding as it does with all that we are told in the rest of the Bible about the mysteries of the Kingdom and the Judgment of Rewards, both which subjects are too extensive for elaborate treatment here. Nevertheless, there are several salient features in this portion of the illustration which should at least be pointed out.

1. *Purpose of the endowment.* The nobleman's purpose in endowing his servants and assigning them their tasks is the same as the reason given for the eventual reckoning, or namely, "that he might know how much every man had gained by trading" (verse 15). It is not his principal aim to profit by their trading, but to determine and develop their several capabilities for an incalculably greater mission. Now, consider our Lord's like purpose in our own assignments during the present age. Using the world as a proving ground, He is screening His followers, so to speak, before making the permanent appointments that will really count. Granting whatever elements of truth one may read in the poet's lines, "God has no hands but our hands . . . no feet

but our feet," one fact remains: God uses us not so much because He needs our service as because we need to be used—if we show ourselves usable, He may lavish us with nobler opportunities of service in the coming world.

2. *Nature of the endowment.* All three servants mentioned in connection with the final reckoning, even the "wicked" one, acknowledge that the money they hold in trust is actually the property of their lord. Each of them, when addressing him, say "thy pound" (verses 16, 18, 20); the lord, also says "my money" (verse 23). To us this means we should regard our endowment for service, not as an inherent ability or right, but as a gracious privilege implemented by divine enablement. "For it is God which worketh in [us] both to will and to do of his good pleasures (Philippians 2:12–13). When we, by His grace, "work out [our] own salvation," He "is not unrighteous to forget [our] work and labour of love" (Hebrews 6:10). Indeed, He commends our efforts and rewards our deeds. The nature of grace requires that all its favors, though undeserved, be righteously meted to us— not that God would be unrighteous to withhold His grace altogether did he so desire—but that, once having offered it, He is obliged to carry out His sovereign commitment on behalf of those who take Him at His word. On our part, there is certainly no merit in making the most of the gift; although, in the nature of the case, it is positively wicked *not* to do so (cf. verse 22).

3. *Nature of the reward.* The sweeping magnitude of grace is depicted in the remarkable disparity between the servants' tasks and their rewards. In each and every proportionately equal case, faithfulness in "very little" (verse 17) is rewarded with immeasurably more than anyone should expect—a city for every pound gained! Thus does grace reward its own accomplishments "exceeding abundantly above all that we ask or think, according to the power that worketh in us (Ephesians 3:20). Thus we see that our future rewards will not be determined by our respective abilities, but by our relative fidelity.

4. *Nature of wickedness in not using the endowment.* The

wicked servant's "napkin" (handkerchief)—or, rather, the use he makes of it—points up a telltale weak spot in his character. Whatever other faults he has, he is evidently lazy; instead of using his handkerchief to wipe away honest sweat, he uses it as a substitute for toil. Truth be known, it's likely that much of our own delinquency stems from downright laziness, though most of us would be as slow to admit it, and as quick to excuse ourselves, as the man who used his "sweat cloth" to keep out of work. But sloth is not the only, even the principal, cause of one's unfaithfulness. Oftener than not, it is a symptom of some more serious fault. This servant's wickedness consists in his unbelief: not the kind of unbelief that comes from enmity, nor that which results in enmity—for the man in question is in no sense an enemy of the nobleman. No, this wickedness is evident in an otherwise loyal servant's distrust of a master whom he does not understand. The nobleman takes this servant's plaintive excuse at face value; so must we. Yes, the servant is entirely mistaken, but he actually looks upon his lord as a grasping tyrant and has been sincerely afraid to run the risk of business failures that might lay him liable for whatever loss it might incur. He *should* have considered the risk of facing his master with no profits to report—but the parable presents the case as it *is*, not as it *should* be. Indeed, what validates this interpretation is its correspondence with self-evident facts: There are too many fearful Christians like the doltish fellow in the parable. Such legalistic saints, with their distorted conception of God, are virtually incapacitated by a pseudoreverence that amounts to cowardice. Yet they are Christians; they are believers despite their misgivings. In a sense they are servants; in no sense are they enemies. Although they stand to lose their rewards, they will by no means lose their souls.

This parable has another lesson for such timid saints, as well as for the rest of us. The king, assuming that the fearful servant is sincere in his delusions, still insists that he should at least have deposited his trust money with a dependable banker, enabling a more competent person to put it to profitable use. Certainly, if this has any analogy in Christian experience, does it not suggest that those who cannot or will not devote themselves entirely to the service of the Lord should invest their means in the ministry of those who do? It seems we must accept this conclusion or else write off this portion of the parable as irrelevant to us.

5. *Inverse ratio of reward to penalty.* The unfaithful servant is deprived of his unused pound; it is given to the servant who has shown himself most profitable. Some of the king's attendants remonstrate, in so many words, *"Lord, why give this poor fellow's money to one who already has ten times as much?"* (Cf. verse 25.) The king ignores this protest except to explain that "unto every one which hath shall be given; and from him that hath not, even that which he hath shall be taken away from him" (verse 26). Here, Jesus seems to assume the role of the king in the parable. The king's words are His words. He would have us know that unless we use our endowments, we shall lose them, whereas whoever makes the most of his gifts will be given even more—which is another way of saying, as our Lord taught elsewhere, that one must lose his life in order to save it (cf. Luke 9:24). Even so, although the unfaithful servant "shall suffer loss" in his rewards, "he himself shall be saved; yet so as by fire" (I Corinthians 3:15). We are reminded once more of the inverse ratio between the rewards of achievement and the penalties of loss in the moral order.

6. *The fate of enemies.* "But," Jesus has the king continue, "those mine enemies, which would not that I should reign over them, bring hither, and slay them before me" (verse 27). In the case of unbelieving Jewry, this prophetic element was partially fulfilled in the destruction of Jerusalem by Titus a few years afterward. It will be completely fulfilled when along with the rest of an impenitent world, they are "punished with everlasting destruction from the presence of the Lord" at the final Judgment of the Great White Throne (cf II Thessalonians 1:9; Revelation 20:11-15).

39

THE TWO SONS

The Messiah's Vindication of His Authority

Primary text: Matthew 21:28-32.

Our Lord spoke this parable to the chief priests, scribes, and elders—in the temple at Jerusalem—most likely on Tuesday morning of Passion Week.

Introduction and background. Like most of Jesus' parables, this one, complete in itself, still leans heavily on the narrative and the local historical scene. Some three and one-half years earlier, John the Baptist had introduced Jesus Christ to Israel as God's Messiah. In keeping with that role, since that time Jesus had been preaching, teaching, and healing the Jews.

Instead of acknowledgment from the leaders of the nation, He had encountered suspicion and opposition, practically from the beginning of His public career. Their initial skepticism and moderate resistance had developed into active animosity, though until now, they had been unable to contrive a pretext quite convincing enough to arraign Him in open court. Now, a crisis had arrived which promised them the opportunity they had awaited! They were firmly resolved to put Him to a final, all-conclusive test. On Sunday of the final week of His public ministry (later to be called "Palm Sunday"), the Savior made

His triumphal entry into Jerusalem to the acclamation of a large throng of sympathetic pilgrims come to observe the feast of Passover. This overt demonstration of our Lord's popularity infuriated the priests and elders, and they were quick to voice their displeasure. On Monday, their resentment seethed to its climax when He expelled the moneychangers to whom they had sold lucrative concessions in the temple court. So now, on Tuesday morning, determined to bring about a showdown, they challenged Jesus to justify His recent actions by producing proof of His authority. Because He had never been ordained or even recognized as a prophet by the official hierarchy, and because of His open defiance of the ruling clique, they interrupted Him as He was teaching, to demand: "By what authority doest thou these things? and who gave thee this authority?" (verse 23).

Evidently, their purpose was to ensnare Him in His speech, however He might reply, and thus expose Him as an impostor before the multitude. They reasoned that because He had no credentials from any official Jewish source, He would have to either (a) assert His personal deity or (b) admit that He had no legitimate authority at all—thus laying Himself open to one or the other of two charges: (a) blasphemy or (b) insubordination to the Theocratic Covenant. As they had it calculated, He would have to discredit and incriminate Himself before a disillusioned populace, which would then condemn Him as a false messiah— or at least unfrock Him as a would-be prophet unable to authenticate His claims. But they were letting themselves in for an embarrassing surprise, for Jesus answered them with a question of his own:

> I also will ask you one thing, which if ye tell me,
> I in likewise will tell you by what authority I do
> these things. The baptism of John, whence was
> it, from heaven, or of men?" (verses 24–25).

Boomerang! their inquisition had been turned back on them, confronting them with an unexpected dilemma. Since John had publicly certified Jesus as the promised Christ, the situation was apparent to everyone: Our Lord's credentials could be no less valid than the testimony of the venerated Baptist himself. And that famous forerunner of Christ also had ministered with no blessing from Jewish officialdom. It was patent: either John had received his commission directly from God or his mission was a farce; he himself, no more than an enterprising pretender. If he were sent by God, his testimony was unquestionably a divine authentication of Jesus' claims. If the Savior's critics should acknowledge John's authority, such a concession would be tantamount to recognizing that of Jesus also. Nor were those wily opportunists unaware that this was so. At this point, they consulted one another, reasoning thus:

> If we shall say, From heaven; he will say unto us, Why did ye not believe him [that is, believe John the Baptist, when he proclaimed that Jesus is the Christ]?
> But if we shall say, Of men; we fear the people, for all hold John as a prophet (verses 25– 26).

The priests and elders were caught in the toils of their own trap. They could not appease the throng by endorsing John without acknowledging that his testimony concerning Jesus' Messiahship was valid. And they could not repudiate John without incensing the people's wrath against themselves. The only safe answer they could come up with was "We cannot tell" (verse 27), or literally, "We do not know" which really meant, in effect, We do not choose to say what we think about the legitimacy of John's ministry.

Oh, they knew well enough how they regarded John, and they must have known Jesus recognized their evasive answer as a deliberate falsehood. But having failed to discredit His authority, they would belittle it by refusing Him a respectful reply. Nevertheless, they had already seen their strategy turned against them. Jesus, taking advantage of their embarrassment, retorted: "Neither tell I you by what authority I do these things" (verse 27). Why did the Lord answer them so?

Not because He was reluctant to assert His claims—in an

Matthew 21:28–32   Vindicative appropriate way, at the proper time—but that He deemed it more appropriate at the moment to thwart the cunning of His enemies by exposing the unbelief motivating their conspiracy. Since His Messianic claims were well known, it was obvious their initial question was altogether forensic (which is to say, *argumentative, rhetorical*). Moreover, He had won His case: His opponents had admitted that they were not prepared to pass judgment on John the Baptist's credentials, and that answer amounted to a confession of their incompetence to judge John's testimony concerning his Lord's Messiahship.

Such was the net result of the contest thus far, but now the Savior went on to chide His critics for the impenitence that underlay their perfidy. In so many words, He challenged them:

> *Now, let Me ask your opinion about a similar case. A man had two children, and approaching the first one, he said, "Child, go work today in my vineyard." And the child, answering, said, "I will not," but later, having reconsidered and changed his mind, he went.*
>
> *And, approaching the other child, the father said the same thing. And the second child, answering, said, "As for me, I will go, sir," but he did not go.*
>
> *Now, which of these two children really did the will of his father?* (Verses 28-31, revised.)

Local application. The parable was such an apt caricature of the situation as described in the narrative that no one in Jesus' audience could have missed His point. His critics were bound to have known that they were being depicted by one of the children in this striking similitude, nor could they have doubted that they were represented by the second son. This we must keep in mind if we are to arrive at a correct interpretation. The story affords some abiding lessons for succeeding generations, as we shall see a bit later. But we *must* look for its immediate, local application in connection with the train of incidents that called it forth in the first place.

Considering that the events occurred within the precincts of Jewry during the ministries of John the Baptist and our Lord, we easily see its symbolic representations in the eyes of His audience: The *certain man* or *father* represented God, as viewed in His covenant-relationship with Israel at the time. The *first son* [literally, *first child*, though the accompanying pronouns in the original show that both children were males] stood in the parabolic role of those delinquent children of the Covenant, such as publicans, harlots, and other open sinners among the Jews, who had carelessly ignored and flagrantly violated the laws of God. The *second son* depicted the unbelieving element among the more respectable classes who professed to keep the Law, especially the abstemious but hypocritical professionals in the priesthood and the Sanhedrin. The *vineyard*, of course, was the Messianic Kingdom which was then being offered to the Jewish nation.

Application of terms. Now, when the time had come for the vineyard to be occupied and dressed by the children of the kingdom, God, through John the Baptist, had urged the people—both those who were outwardly unfaithful, and the so-called faithful who were inwardly wayward—to repent and bring forth fruit consistent with their national calling. At first, the carnal masses had shrugged off John's entreaties with curt reluctance. "We will not" or "We do not want to" had been their initial attitudinal response. But in the course of time, vast numbers of these sinners had reconsidered, changed their minds, and rallied to the Savior's call. Meanwhile, the more respectable classes, who professed such zeal for the Law and the Messianic hope, belied their affected piety by spurning both God's official messenger and His royal Son. This "current events lesson"—and their role in it—was what the Savior was trying so hard to get His critics to see. Holding up the two parabolic sons before their minds, He asked:

> What think ye? . . . Whether of them twain did the will of his father?
> In so many words, He was saying: *Now, in your opinion, which of these two children really obeyed his father, the reluctant son who later changed his mind and went to work, or the one who glibly*

> *pledged his obedience but did not obey?*

And of course, they had to answer, "The first" (verse 31).

Whereupon, the Master, without any further ado, proceeded to identify the second son with his examiners:

> Verily I say unto you, That the publicans and the harlots go into the kingdom of God before you. For John came unto you in the way of righteousness, and ye believed him not: but the publicans and the harlots believed him: and ye, when ye had seen it, repented not afterward, that ye might believe him (verses 31–32).

The priests and elders had considered themselves veritable paragons of religious integrity, but when the testing time had arrived, they had failed. They resented John for demanding what they had already pledged themselves to do! In spurning his appeal for genuine righteousness, they exposed their own hypocrisy, for had they been sincere in their profession, they would have welcomed his message and gladly welcomed the Righteous One to whom he testified.

By their profession they had always said, "We go, sir," but in actual practice, they "went not" at all. If for no other reason, the spectacle of open sinners' turning to God should have melted their hearts. Nor could they excuse their unbelief on the ground of honest incredulity, for they were *unwilling* to repent so that they might believe a message that called for real submission to the will of God. The only reason they *could not* believe was that they *would not*. Hence, it was their deliberate refusal to obey the Gospel—an infinitely worse offense than the carnal sins which they condemned in others—that kept them from being saved.

So much for the teaching of this parable in its local setting. Now we consider its abiding lesson for succeeding generations.

Extended application. Although it was originally directed to a particular group some nineteen centuries ago, this little story

illustrates a practical admonition applicable to almost any time
or place. It holds forth the penitence of erstwhile irreligious
profligates as a standing rebuke to religious hypocrites, whose
actual attitudes and practiced deeds betray the insincerity of
their superficial piety. This, the principal point of emphasis,
needs to be stressed today as much as ever before. *But . . .*

Faulty inferences. But as we do so, we must be careful to
avoid unwarranted conclusions based on faulty inferences that
have no real support in the sacred text:

1. We must not infer that Jesus meant to minimize or gloss
   over the lawlessness of ones who flout genuine proprieties
   of society. He deplored the shamelessness of the publicans
   and harlots. Never in any of His teaching did He excuse or
   condone *any* kind of immorality. Instead, He constantly
   warned against the fleshly sins that tarnish the soul; He
   urged transgressors to turn from their folly to the path of
   righteousness. The ancient world reeked with unspeakable
   debauchery, and the Jewish nation was by no means free
   from the corruption and promiscuity plaguing its heathen
   neighbors. We may be sure that the holy Son of God was
   deeply grieved at the wantonness of these times, and we
   have no right whatever to interpret anything He said as if
   meant to defend or minimize the rampant wickedness of
   rebellious people.

2. Neither can we justly construe this parable as having been
   intended to discredit legitimate institutions or those who
   observe them. No one showed greater esteem for the Law,
   the temple, or *genuine* acts of piety than did our blessed
   Lord. He repeatedly gave His personal sanction to all the
   divine ordinations of the dispensation under which He
   lived. He taught all those under the Mosaic Covenant to
   examine their conduct by its provisions—and He did so
   Himself. He was no disillusioned iconoclast who delighted
   in debunking the revered ideals or wholesome customs of
   honest worshipers; rather, He delighted in every gesture
   of sincere devotion to God. He had been circumcised on
   the eighth day of his temporal life and dedicated on the
   fortieth. At the age of twelve, He had attended the Paschal

Feast and visited the temple like any other godly Israelite. At thirty, at His own insistence, He had been baptized by John. He often attended worship services in the synagogues, and as an obedient Jew, He consistently adhered to the spirit of the Law. He honored wholesome mores and conventions of His time, and we may be sure that He would do the same if He were here in the flesh on a similar mission today.

There is no condonation either here or elsewhere in the Scriptures for those who shirk their God-given duties. All Christians ought to be baptized. All of us ought to belong to some good Gospel church. All of us ought to pursue a holy life and attend our worship services, ought to observe the ordinances and support the ministry of the Word. It would be inexcusable to wrest this parable in any manner calculated to turn it into a pretext for the neglect of such responsibilities.

3. This parable does not imply that all those who professed their zeal for the Law back in Bible times were insincere. Nor was that, in fact, the case, else Simeon, Anna, John the Baptist, and all other such Jewish believers were guilty of hypocrisy! No, there were then, as now, vast numbers of irreproachable saints who made a conscientious effort to perform the many duties connected with their profession, and our Lord did not allude to such persons as these when He exposed the empty sanctimony of His unbelieving foes.

Appropriate interpretation. This passage does teach that, no matter what sinners have done, they may be saved if only they are willing to repent. At the same time, it warns against the sterile self-righteousness of nominal religionists who "say, and do not" (cf. Matthew 23:3). It *implies* the first, while *pressing* the latter, of these points.

It was a well-known fact that numerous social outcasts had, despite their ugly past, received forgiveness and restoration under the preaching of John. Also obvious, from their hatred of Jesus, was that most of the leading Jews were, despite their pious pretensions, still unregenerate. Christ's own application of this parable makes it clear His object was to use the example of penitent sinners to induce their complacent leaders, also, to submit to the terms of grace. His words implied it was not too late for even His bitterest foes to enter the Kingdom if only they would believe. The implication was, just as the publicans and harlots had gone in before them, they also might even yet go in.

Sin is sin, whatever be its symptoms, and all sin, short of deliberate *contumacy* (willful contempt), is forgivable under the right conditions (cf Matthew 12:32). The same God who saves the unrighteous can save the self-righteous, too, *if* they repent. But should they meet God's gracious patience with contempt, they make the impartation of saving faith impossible, thereby sealing their doom, as this parable so aptly dramatizes.

40

THE WICKED HUSBANDMEN

The Case Against Apostate Jewry

Primary text: Matthew 21:33-44
Cf. Mark 12:1-12; Luke 20:9-19.

Our Lord spoke this parable to the chief priests, the scribes, and the elders—in the temple at Jerusalem-probably on Tuesday morning of Passion Week.

Introduction and background. Essentially allegorical, this text presents a pictorial review of Israel's history up to its rejection of Christ (cf. verses 33-38), together with a preview of the tragic days of retribution soon coming (cf. verses 39-44). According to Matthew, the parable was addressed to the "chief priests and elders;" Mark adds "and the scribes;" Luke tells us that it was spoken to "the people." Judging from all reports, we may safely surmise it was directed to the leaders of national Jewry within the hearing of the multitude. In Matthew, it stands in close connection with an extensive discourse; therefore, this account provides the best background for its interpretation.

On the Sunday before, our Lord had made His triumphal entry into Jerusalem only to be disowned by the ruling Jews. Monday, He had pronounced a curse on an unfruitful fig tree, thus setting forth a parabolic portrayal of unbelieving Jewry's imminent ruin, and had cleansed the temple in protest against its desecration by moneychangers and the avaricious priests

---

321

who sponsored them. Then, on being challenged by the priests and elders to vindicate His actions by producing proof of His authority, He had replied with the parable of the two sons. As we have seen, that parable exposed for the listening crowd the hypocrisy of His critics, who had persistently defied the will of God despite their affected zeal for the Law. For this cause He had warned them that the publicans and harlots would go into the Kingdom of God ahead of them (cf. verse 31).

Examination and interpretation. Not content with so mild a rebuke, Jesus went on to specify their crimes and to describe the terrible day of reckoning that awaited them. "Hear another parable," He said, as He began a similar story—one much more elaborate and dramatic in its details. Creating an illustration of His own, He nevertheless drew His imagery from Isaiah's well-known "Song of the Vine," in which Jehovah had said:

> Now I will sing of my wellbeloved a song of my beloved touching his vineyard. My wellbeloved hath a vineyard in a very fruitful hill: and he fenced it, and gathered out the stones thereof, and planted it with the choicest vine, and built a tower in the midst of it, and also made a winepress therein: and he looked that it should bring forth grapes, and it brought forth wild grapes.
> And now, O inhabitants of Judah, judge, I pray you, betwixt me and my vineyard. What could have been done more to my vineyard, that I have not done in it? wherefore, when I looked that it should bring forth grapes, brought it forth wild grapes? And now go to; I will tell you what I will do to my vineyard: I will take away the hedge thereof, and it shall be eaten up; and break down the wall thereof, and it shall not be pruned, nor digged; but there shall come up briers and thorns: I will also command the clouds that they rain no rain upon it. For the vineyard of the LORD of hosts is the house of Israel, and the men of

---

Judah his pleasant plant: and he looked for judgment, but behold oppression; for righteousness,
but behold a cry (Isaiah 5:1-7).

Now, the Jewish audience, being familiar with this ancient
prophecy and its explicit reference to themselves, could hardly
have failed to apprehend the meaning of its figurative terms
or the way in which Jesus used them now:
Undoubtedly ...
• the *householder* represents God;
• the *vineyards*, the house of Israel;
• the *husbandmen*, the priests and elders;
• the *servants*, first the prophets and later the disciples of Christ;
• the *householder's son*, the Lord Jesus Himself;
and quite likely ...
• the *stones* represent the original heathen inhabitants of
  Palestine;
• the *hedge*, the one Law;
• the *winepress*, the Levitical sacrificial system; and
• the *tower*, the Theocratic government.
It was easy enough for the Master's audience to understand
the historical portion of this analogy:

Historical review. God (*the householder*) had planted Israel (*the
vineyard*) in the Promised Land (*the very fruitful hill*), expelled
the native Canaanites (*the stones*), fenced in the Chosen People
with the moral safeguards of the Law (*the hedge*), provided for
their spiritual welfare through the proceeds of the sacrificial
altar (*the winepress*), and established the Theocracy (*the tower*)
to oversee and promote their national interests. Then, as to the
outward manifestation of His presence, He had withdrawn
Himself "into a far country," and thereafter had entrusted the
care of His vineyard to the priests and elders (*the husbandmen*)
as the recognized spiritual guardians of the nation. Then at
last, when time drew near for the promised Messiah to appear
and begin His reign of righteousness on earth (*the time of fruit*),
God sent the prophets (*his servants*) to call for the firstfruits of
obedience.

> I have sent unto you all my servants the
> prophets, rising up early and sending them,
> saying, Return ye now every man from his evil
> way, and amend your doings (Jeremiah 35:15).

However, instead of rendering a faithful account of themselves,
"the husbandmen took his servants, and beat one, and killed
another, and stoned another" (verse 35)—even as Stephen in
his dying hour would remind them with a damning question,
"Which of the prophets have not your fathers persecuted?"
(Acts 7:52). Yet, God, amazingly long-suffering in the face of
these provocations, "sent other servants more than the first,"
evidently referring to John the Baptist and the Savior's own
disciples, "and they did unto them likewise" (verse 36). Then,
in the language of the parable:

> . . . last of all he sent unto them his son, saying,
> They will reverence my son. But when the
> husbandmen saw the son, they said among
> themselves, This is the heir; come, let us kill him,
> and let us seize on his inheritance (verses 37–
> 38).

We can hardly fail to notice how well the latter part of this
passage—including the current scene—merges into history,
thus bringing the record of the husbandmen's perfidy right up
to date for Jesus' audience.

Moreover, the parable brings to light hidden motivations
and, hence, terrible culpability of those wicked men who were
ultimately responsible for the Savior's death. Although they
were convinced that He was the rightful heir of the Davidic
Covenant and was God's Messiah, as He claimed to be, they
nevertheless plotted His death—to usurp for themselves the
power and glory that belonged to Him alone. Of them it could
scarcely be said, as of their less perceptive colleagues, that "they
knew him not" (cf. Acts 13:27) or that, indeed, they erred
"through ignorance" (cf. Acts 3:17), but only that they had "no
cloke for their sin" (John 9:41; 15:22). Like other husbandmen

of later times, even now, they stopped at nothing in their effort to entrench themselves as "lords over God's heritage" so that they might have all the produce of the vineyard for themselves.

Prophetic preview. As the parable begins to take on the form of a prophecy, we read that "they [*the husbandmen*] caught him [*the householder's son*] and cast him out of the vineyard, and slew him" (verse 39)—a graphic forecast of our Lord's arrest, His repudiation before an alien tribunal, and His execution "without the camp" (cf. Hebrews 13:13). Already, several weeks earlier, the Sanhedrin had convened in an emergency session and determined to put Him to death (cf. John 11:47, 53). Now they were being told *how* their infamous plan would be carried out. But they would not be allowed to comfort themselves with the delusion that they were acting in good faith, but would, instead, be forced to pass judgment against themselves.

"When the lord therefore of the vineyard cometh," Jesus demanded, "what will he do unto these husbandmen?" (verse 40). And then, having posed this searching question, He paused for a reply.

Even in no higher court than the human conscience there could be but a single verdict. So, reluctantly, they answered, "He will miserably destroy those wicked men, and will let out his vineyard to other husbandmen, which shall render him the fruits in their seasons" (verse 41). Thus they foretold their own fate with remarkable precision, for in less than forty years those evil men were to come to an evil end. Their tenure of office would cease. Their city would be reduced to bloody rubble; their nation would be decimated by the sword—and those who survived would be enslaved and scattered to the ends of the earth. All this has been fulfilled, just as Jesus knew it would be. Yet there is a sense in which *it did not have to be that way*. God did not cause it; He only suffered it to happen. Knowing this to be the case, Jesus was warning, but also pleading, when He replied:

> Did ye never read in the scriptures, The stone which the builders rejected, the same is become the head of the corner: this is the Lord's doing,

it is marvelous in our eyes (verse 42)?

The Jews were familiar with that passage from Psalm 118; they even believed it referred to the Messiah. But this was indeed "the Lord's doing," for *they* had other plans! Wittingly or not, they were opposing God. Nevertheless, and although our Lord admittedly expected to be slain, He also knew that He was to be the head of a new Theocracy; so, turning to those wicked "husbandmen" who had "rejected the counsel of God against themselves" (cf. Luke 7:30), He added, "The kingdom of God shall be taken from you, and given to a nation bringing forth the fruits thereof" (verse 43).

Nor was it very long until this sentence was carried out. The nation's doom was sealed a little later on that very day when, on the Savior's departure from the temple, He declared: "Behold, your house is left unto you desolate" (cf. Matthew 23:38). Scarcely a generation would pass before the abandoned temple lay in ruin. Meanwhile, however, other "husbandmen" were tilling the "fruitful hill"; and after nearly two thousand years, the Church of Jesus Christ is flourishing where Jewry failed.

Alas! this is not to say that the whole of Christendom is keeping faith with God. It, too, has blood on its hands—much blood, much more than Jewry ever had. What is worse, it too, is stumbling where Jewry fell. While bearing the name of Christ, thousands of professing *Christians* regard the Jesus Christ of the Gospels as a rock of offense—a roadblock in the path of intellectual progress, academic freedom, and the realization of their carnal dreams. Today, as of old, the official custodians of the vineyard are confronted with a solemn issue and a fateful choice. May not this be the reason for the *supposedly misplaced* metaphor in the Master's closing words?

> And whosoever shall fall on this stone shall be broken: but on whomsoever it shall fall, it will grind him to powder (verse 44).

In view of nominal Christianity today, this warning seems to be well placed in the record, as it comes immediately after an allusion to our era. We face the dreadful possibility of being broken on the Stone of Stumbling, for the Scriptures plainly teach that apostate Christendom, along with heathendom, will eventually be crushed and ground to powder when the Lord of the Vineyard calls for another day of reckoning (cf. Daniel 2; Revelation 17–18).

Against this background, surely we should ponder another of Jesus' sayings, which, although spoken elsewhere, is equally pertinent here: "Blessed is he, whosoever shall not be offended in me" (Matthew 11:6).

41

THE MARRIAGE OF THE KING'S SON

The Fearful Penalty of Spurning the Grace of God

Primary text: Matthew 22:1-14
Cf. Luke 14:15-24.

Our Lord spoke this parable to the chief priests and elders—in the temple at Jerusalem—most likely on Tuesday morning of Passion Week.

Introduction and background. One cannot help noticing the similarity between this parable and that of the Great Supper (cf. Luke 14:15-24), though they are distinctly different in some of their leading features. Both involve an invitation to a feast, but with considerable variations in their accompanying details.

There . . .	*Here . . .*
A splendid supper was given by a man to entertain certain select acquaintances.	A banquet is spread by a king in celebration of the betrothal of his son.
Those invited politely excused themselves.	Some decline the invitation, some ignore it, and the rest abuse and slay the servants sent to summon them.

There . . .	*Here . . .*
Jewry's unbelief was depicted in its incipient stage.	Their unbelief is portrayed in its horrible finality.

Both parables foreshadow the passage of the Kingdom from natural, national Israel to the true "Israel of God"—that is, all regenerate believers without respect to their racial descent—though this parable alone includes the episode about the ill-clad guest.

This parable was spoken to the chief priests and elders while they were still furious with resentment at the foregoing story, "The Wicked Husbandmen." They were, in fact, chafing for an opportunity to do away with Jesus as quickly as possible, by any means, and at almost any cost. Their unbelief, no longer passive or indifferent, had now grown into virulent hatred that knew no bounds. This change of attitude prompted the Savior to answer them (verse 1) with the dreadful warnings in this parable, a graphic preview of the terrible retribution awaiting His murderers. Standing in the shadow of the cross, taking His death for granted, the rejected King sketched the march of history very much as it would later be recorded in the book of Acts, followed by the death throes of Jewish nationalism and the diffusion of Christianity throughout the pagan world, and on up to the proceedings of an awesome judgment at the end of the age.

Examination and interpretation. "The kingdom of heaven," Jesus said, "is like unto a certain king, which made a marriage for his son" (verse 2).

This *king* is, of course, God the Father, and his *son* is the Lord Jesus Christ. The *marriage* is actually a marriage feast, in this case not the banquet that celebrates the consummation of the nuptial rites, but the preliminary festivities associated with public announcement of the betrothal. Jews were thoroughly familiar with the customs underlying this imagery and were equally aware of their prefiguration of God's relations with His elect. As recorded in the Old Testament, God had called

Himself the husband of Israel; but then He had put away the natural wife because of her unfaithfulness to him (cf. Hosea 1–2). In the New Testament, God in Christ, claims the *church* or *spiritual Israel,* as His bride, betrothed in preparation for the eventual vows of the Marriage of the Lamb (cf. Revelation 19:7).

A many-sided truth is this concept, and no earthly analogy does full justice to the spiritual reality. But when all pertinent Scriptures are considered together, they obviously contemplate a time when the imperfect types will be fully realized in the perfect union of Christ and His Church. We are, individually, betrothed to Christ when we, through personal faith, accept the Gospel invitation, which is His "proposal," so to speak. When the marriage is consummated, all believers as members of a single body, will be the heavenly bride (cf. Ephesians 1:22–23; 4:4; 5:30, 32; Revelation 21:2–9; 22:17).

The Jews had been invited, long before the event, to attend the feast—to participate in this glorious privilege. But at the time appointed, God, in the language of the parable, "sent forth his servants to call them that were bidden to the wedding: and they would not come" (verse 3). Customarily in the ancient East, a person awaited a second bidding before attending such a feast. The first invitation had been extended through the prophets; more recently, a second one had been pressed by John the Baptist and Jesus' own disciples, only to be declined. This imagery is the only allusion to *antecedent* history in this parable; all that follows was entirely prophetic at the time of its utterance. As we are told:

> Again he sent forth other servants, saying, Tell them which are bidden, Behold, I have prepared my dinner: my oxen and fatlings are killed, and all things are ready: come unto the marriage (verse 4).

This text clearly anticipated the early days of Christianity—from Pentecost until the destruction of Jerusalem in 70 A.D.

The slaughter of "oxen and fatlings" need not indicate more than customary procedure in preparing a feast, but it may very well—in such an apposite context—allude to the redemptive death of Christ, which was prefigured by animal sacrifices the proceeds of which provided food for the Levitical feasts.

The *other servants* were the apostles and fellow disciples who, on the Day of Pentecost and afterward, appealed to the Jews to reconsider their fateful choice, to acknowledge Jesus as their Messiah even then. Their characteristic message was, undoubtedly, substantially the same as that of Peter urging his fellow countrymen to claim and feast upon the merits of the Sacrifice which they themselves unwittingly had slain.

> Repent, therefore and return, that your sins may be wiped away, in order that times of revival may come from the presence of the Lord; and that He may send Jesus, the Christ appointed for you, whom heaven must receive until the period of restoration of all things, about which God spoke by the mouth of His holy prophets from ancient times (Acts 3:19-21, NASB).

The tone of this appeal pervades the book of Acts, ceasing only after Paul's last plea to the Jews in the Roman capital fell on deaf ears (cf. Acts 28).

There were, of course, some notable exceptions, including all of the original converts, many priests, and Paul himself. But by and large, when the invitation of grace was renewed to Israel,

> . . . they made light of it, and went their ways, one to his farm, another to his merchandise. And the remnant took his servants, and entreated them spitefully, and slew them (verses 5–6).

At first, the rank and file of the apostate nation did their best to shrug off the Gospel and to ignore those who proclaimed it, engrossing themselves, as was their usual practice, with purely temporal concerns. But in time, their rulers—the Sadducees in particular—launched a relentless drive to harass and, finally, to wipe out all of the risen Savior's followers. Peter and John were flogged and imprisoned. Stephen was stoned. James was beheaded. And Paul was hounded from pillar to post as if he had been a wanted criminal, until at last he was driven into the clutches of Nero and eventual martyrdom at Rome.

The story continues . . .

> But when the king heard thereof, he was wroth: and he sent forth his armies, and destroyed those murderers, and burned up their city (verse 7).

Although God, in His infinite wisdom, suffered unbelieving Jewry to afflict His servants, He was not apathetic about her merciless course. After allowing her to seed the virgin soil of Christendom with her victims' blood, He marshaled ruthless military legions of Vespasian and Titus to requite her cruelty with fiery wrath. There is perhaps no better commentary on this portion of our parable than Josephus' account of that ghastly siege, in which he reports the intrigues, betrayals, and internecine struggles within the beleaguered city; the gruesome crimes of her panic-stricken hordes as they connive and wrangle among themselves for crumbs and gold; and the final collapse before the relentless Roman juggernaut—the shattered gates, the gory streets, the flaming houses, and the shambles where the temple once stood but stands no more. No wonder Jesus wept when He foresaw the tears that were to publish Israel's anguish at the Wailing Wall!

But even all this gruesome history does not complete the scene envisaged by the parable. The king had somewhat more in view than the destruction of his foes.

> Then saith he to his servants, the wedding is ready, but they which were bidden were not worthy. Go ye therefore into the highways, and as many as ye shall find, bid to the marriage (verses 8–9).

Again, as in the "The Great Supper," there is a foreshadowing of the exclusion of those who were Israelites only after the flesh, accompanied by the extension of the Gospel to the Gentiles. The Jews had proved unworthy of the proffered invitation— not because of their moral poverty (which is common to all mankind), but because of their self-righteous contempt for God's best efforts to save them despite their moral bankruptcy (as He later lavished mercy on so many equally undeserving pagans). As one of our popular hymns so aptly says, "All the fitness He requireth is to feel your need of Him." The Jews disqualified themselves as heirs of grace by clinging to their illusion of self-sufficiency, while many of the vilest outcasts of heathendom, nothing to commend them but their conscious neediness, were brought into the portals of the nuptial feast.

The parable proper concludes,

> So those servants went out into the highways, and gathered together all as many as they found, both bad and good: and the wedding was furnished with guests (verse 10).

This ending clearly refers to an ingathering from among all nations, right up to the return of Christ—at which time the "wedding hall" will be "filled with guests" (RV).

It is not so clear what is meant by the phrase *both good and bad*. Is this an idiomatic way of saying "people in general"? or does it imply a distinction between those who are worthy and those who are unworthy to attend the feast? According to the consensus of all Scriptures, no one is worthy of salvation in the sense of being *morally fit*, apart from the provisions of grace. The meaning, perhaps, is "both pagan Gentiles and previously uncommitted Jews of the Dispersion" or, as some scholars have suggested, "both sinful heathen and their fellow pagans who have at least made an effort to obey their natural light." Of these two views, the first would seem to be the likelier, for it is more in keeping with the facts of life and history as we know them. At any rate, the point is that people of all kinds and classes are to be enlisted through the preaching of the Gospel until the festive chamber of the Kingdom is full of guests.

The Fearful Penalty of Spurning the Grace of God

Since we all "come short of the glory of God" (Romans 3:23), it is obviously a mistake to identify the *bad* with the ill-clad guest who appears in the sequel of this story.

So far, our parable has addressed Jewry's rejection of the Kingdom and the subsequent extension of the Gospel to the world at large. From this point onward, it contemplates the fortunes of saints at the end of this age.

"And," we read, "when the king came in to see the guests, he saw there a man which had not on a wedding garment" (verse 11). At this juncture, the ingathering will be complete and the time will have come for the Kingdom feast (or, the "marriage supper of the Lamb," as it is called in Revelation 19:9) to begin its course. The question here is not whether the guests are *saved*, but whether, though justified by grace, they are sufficiently *sanctified* to share in our Lord's Millennial reign, with no further discipline required before their glorification. Though not the generally accepted view (the one popularized by commentators still laboring under the yoke of hidebound ecclesiasticism), this is the view maintained by all the rest of Jesus' prophetic parables, as we shall see.

If it were the case that Jesus' brief excursus on the ill-clad guest stood alone, without the additional light afforded by the rest of His teaching on the same subject, we might be pardoned for accepting the traditional interpretation (which contains a good deal of truth amply supported in other connections)—but, the case being as it is, that interpretation ignores the analogy between this parable and several later ones which employ similar imagery to describe the fates of disobedient saints.

Here, all guests occupy the position of genuine believers, but one of them—who doubtless represents a considerable class—is nevertheless ineligible to share the feast, because he does not have on the requisite "wedding garment." What, then, does the *wedding garment* represent?

The answer is found in the Revelation, where we are told that those who participate in the Marriage Supper of the Lamb are "clothed with fine linen," which are "the righteous deeds of the saints" (Revelation 19:8, RV). From this Scripture, it is evident that the wedding garment in question does not stand for *justification*, the imputed righteousness of Christ which belongs to all believers alike, but to the personal conduct of the saints which reflects the measure of their *sanctification*. Hence, the king in the parable says nothing to indicate that the man without a wedding garment is not a bona fide guest, but only censures him for presuming to enter the royal banquet hall in improper attire.

"And he saith unto him, Friend, how camest thou in hither not having a wedding garment?" (verse 12). The man had been invited and had accepted the invitation, but had not prepared himself for the enjoyment of his special privileges; "he was speechless" (verse 12), not because he was a gatecrasher, but because he was morally *en deshabille*—improperly dressed for such an august occasion.

He represents an unfaithful believer who, having neglected to "work out [his] own salvation" during the present life, is unprepared to reign with Christ at His return and must be perfected through further discipline before he can be glorified (cf. Romans 8:17; Hebrews 12:5-11). Such a person, according to Paul, "shall suffer loss: but he himself shall be saved; yet so as by fire" (I Corinthians 3:15). Having failed in self-discipline, he now must be "chastened of the Lord, that he may not "be condemned with the world" (I Corinthians 11:32). Having been unwilling to suffer for Christ's sake, he will not be permitted to "reign with him," for—although he has been unfaithful to God—God will still be faithful to him. God cannot "prove false" to His own commitments (cf. II Timothy 2:12–13, CBW).

The king's sentence against the ill-clad guest accords with this interpretation: "Bind him hand and foot, and take him away, and cast him into outer darkness; there shall be weeping and gnashing of teeth" (verse 13). This was not the sentence that would have been meted out for a capital offense—that is, the penalty of death—but one that called only for expulsion from the feast and the infliction of corrective discipline: the very same treatment Jesus warned His own apostles to expect if they should prove unfaithful to their trust (cf. Luke 12:42-48).

The Fearful Penalty of Spurning the Grace of God

"For," our Lord concludes in verse 14, "many are called, but few are chosen" (literally, *many are invited ones but few are chosen-out ones*—KSW, which probably means, "few are *choice ones*"). Now, this proverbial saying is not a rigid theological formula with fixed connotations; no, it must be construed in keeping with its context.

Here it seems to sum up the teaching of the whole parable, not merely the closing section—and subsequent history leaves no doubt that this is so.

* The Jews, as an entire nation, were first to be invited to the Kingdom feast, but most of them passed up their golden opportunity.
* Then the invitation was extended to the world at large, and vast multitudes have gladly accepted it.
* Alas, however, there are many who receive the *grace* of God without assuming its concomitant *responsibilities*, and thus do not prepare to reign with Christ at His coming.

Of those who have been invited, many will be excluded on account of unbelief; others because of temporary unfitness; and comparatively few will actually share in our Lord's Millennial glory (these few being the "overcomers" of Revelation 2–3).

SECTION SEVEN
KEEPING WATCH ON
THE KINGDOM

"It is just as important to be ready for the uncertain hour of death as it is to be ready for Christ's appearing. In both cases, the end results are the same. ... Whether we, as individual believers, are to be overtaken by death or by the Rapture, the urgency is the same as if we knew we were destined to be here, alive, when Christ descends in glory to the earth! 'Watch ye therefore ...' "

Preliminary Thoughts on the
Vigilance Parables

Most, if not all, of our Lord's parables illustrate one or more aspects of Kingdom truth; directly or indirectly, they all look forward to His second advent and the establishment of His Kingdom on the earth. They are all, therefore, anticipatory to some degree. But seven parables are devoted almost entirely to instructions, warnings, and promises about the imminence of Christ's return. These Vigilance Parables, although each has its own emphasis, all insist on the tremendous importance of personal watchfulness and readiness. The parable of . . .

- "The Fig Tree" sets forth certain definite signs of our Lord's return to the earth.
- "The Absent Householder and His Porter" urges vigilance on the part of Christian ministers.
- "The Watchful Servants" promises special blessedness to those who are faithful until Christ's appearing.
- "The Householder and the Thief" stresses the imminence of Christ's return.
- "The Steward and his Fellow Servants" portrays the laxity and chastisement of those who assume that Christ's return will be delayed.
- "The Ten Virgins" warns against the folly of presuming that His return may *not* be delayed.
- "The Talents" emphasizes the practical nature of Christian vigilance.

All but one of these parables appear in various accounts of the Lord's valedictory address on the Mount of Olives, the evening after His final departure from the temple during Passion Week—and all but two are found in Matthew's report of that remarkable sermon. Only Mark tells "The Absent Householder and His Porter" in his record of the Olivet Discourse; "The Watchful Servants" is found only in Luke, where it is related in connection with an earlier utterance of several of these same illustrations. Though "The Watchful Servants" does not appear in any version of the Olivet Discourse, it *is* closely associated with the parables which do and clearly reflects the same point of view. Establishing this connection is important because our interpretation of the Vigilance Parables must harmonize with the overall viewpoint of the passages in which they occur.

Aside from its allusion to the Jerusalem's destruction by Titus in A.D. 70, the Olivet Discourse does not contemplate the present age as such. Rather, it envisages the time when God will resume His special dealings with Israel during Daniel's seventieth week—that is, a "week" of years foretold by the prophet Daniel (cf. Daniel 9:27), or a period of about seven years starting with Christ's descent from heaven into the *air* (cf. I Thessalonians 4:13-18) and ending with His descent to *earth* (cf. II Thessalonians 1:7-10). Thus, it is obvious that these prophecies were addressed to the Judeo-Christian point of view, assuming the intervention of this present age but viewing the end-time as if there were not any such interim between the sixty-ninth and seventieth "weeks" of Daniel's prophecy.

Failure to perceive this vital truth has been a cause of much needless confusion—not only with respect to the Vigilance Parables, but also with regard to prophecies bearing on the *time* of our Lord's return. From the Judeo-Christian point of view (the view adopted in the Olivet Discourse), the return of Christ is expected to occur within the compass of that seven years, in keeping with Daniel's prophecy. True, the *day* and the *hour* are unknown (cf. Mark 13:32), for though it is revealed that the seven-year period is to be shortened (cf. Matthew 24:22), no one but God the Father knows by *how much* it will be curtailed. Believers alive on earth at that time will see predicted signs surrounding them on every hand and will certainly know that "their redemption draweth nigh," that "the kingdom of

Preliminary Thoughts on the Vigilance Parables

God is nigh at hand" (cf. Luke 21:25-31). So far as our Lord's descent into the air to rapture His waiting saints is concerned, there is *no sign* to pinpoint the date of His return. After that takes place and Daniel's Seventieth Week begins its course, the only remaining question will be: By how much will the final seven-year period be shortened?

The foregoing text explains an *apparent* inconsistency which is often read into the Vigilance Parables by some expositors who would apply them directly to our current era. According to *their* view, Jesus (a) alerts us with numerous signs that He will soon return; (b) encourages us to believe that His coming is "near, even at the door" (Matthew 24:33); (c) then insists that it may or may not be deferred indefinitely! Whereas, in actuality, these parables refer primarily to the post-Rapture era, and the *indefiniteness* they ascribe to the time of Christ's return is restricted to somewhat less than a span of seven years!

Not that they have no present value for us. Except for the temporal limitations involved in their primary reference to Daniel's Seventieth Week, they are applicable in principle to all generations. It is just as important for one to be ready for the uncertain hour of death as it is to be ready for Christ's appearing. In both cases, the end results are the same. There will be relatively few surviving when Jesus comes, compared with the teeming myriads who, meanwhile, will have gone to meet Him beyond the grave.

In general, whatever our dispensational lot and whether we are to live until Jesus comes or to depart this life before, these parables underscore the urgency of proper vigilance and preparedness. They warn us that we should assume neither the deferment nor the immediacy of our appointment with the Lord, lest we might, on one hand, become complacent—or, on the other, be ill-prepared to persevere until the time arrives. They teach us to regard that appointment, whatever form it may take, as a certain, inevitable, imminent event, and thus, to translate our expectancy into practical obedience.

Finally, let it be noted that these parables were not intended to annul or dilute the Gospel of the Grace of God, as if a true believer's eternal destiny were conditioned on the degree of his vigilance. They lend no support to the belief that salvation depends on works, nor do they touch directly on the ultimate question as to who is going to heaven or to hell. Those ideas have been read into them by modern proponents of medieval eschatology—but, happily, the facts are clearly against it.

Consider:

1. All these parables were addressed to believers—six of them to Peter, James, John, and Andrew (cf. Mark 13:3) and one to a larger company of disciples (cf. Luke 12:22).

2. They all expressly contemplate real Christians—*servants*, *stewards*, or *virgins*, although some of these are shown to be unfaithful, foolish, slothful, even (relatively speaking) wicked.

And why not? Do not most modern Christians fall into one or the other of these deplorable categories?

As to our eternal destiny, we are saved by pure grace—but only those who are fully sanctified will enjoy the blessedness of Christ's Millennial glory. The rest of us will receive further discipline until our sanctification is complete. This essential teaching of the Vigilance Parables is abundantly borne out by the general consensus of relevant scriptures.

Preliminary Thoughts on the Vigilance Parables

42

THE FIG TREE

Harbingers of Christ's Return

Primary text: Matthew 24:32-34
Cf. Mark 13:28-30; Luke 21:29-32

Our Lord spoke this parable to Peter, James, John, and Andrew—on the Mount of Olives—probably on Tuesday evening of Passion Week.

Introduction. Every careful Bible student knows that, just as the rose stands for England, the shamrock for Ireland, the thistle for Scotland, and the pomegranate for Spain, the fig tree is the emblem of the Jewish nation. In Jeremiah 24, the dispersed Jews who should never return to Palestine were called "bad figs" and those who were destined to return were called "good figs." We are told in the Gospel of Luke that our Lord likened Jewry to a fruitless fig tree which was then being given a final opportunity to yield fruit (cf. Luke 13:6-9). A short while later, on Monday of Passion Week, He put a curse on an unfruitful fig tree, thereby setting forth an acted parable to show that the Jewish nation would be disowned as a witness for God during the present age (cf. Matthew 21:17-19).

Here, in anticipation of the end-time, He foretold a day when the "fig tree" would revive and "put forth leaves" again. Nor only so; for this, according to Luke, will also be true of

---

343

"all the trees" (cf. Luke 21:29)—or, the other leading nations of Biblical lands. Now, as an alert Bible student knows, all this prophecy is being fulfilled right before our eyes, as not only Israel but also Italy, Egypt, Syria, Arabia, and Persia recover their former prominence in world affairs. To be appreciated, this development must be viewed in its historical setting—or *settings* in both ancient and modern times.

Examination and interpretation. Circa 587 B.C., after several centuries of declension, the Jewish monarchy was suspended by the sudden destruction of Jerusalem and the deportation of the Jews to Babylon. The subsequent rule of Nebuchadnezzar began the "times of the Gentiles" (cf. Luke 21:24). From then until A.D. 1948, Jews had no durable autonomous government under a ruler of their own choosing. They had a momentary but abortive political revival under the Maccabees. Then they submitted themselves, reluctantly, to those Idumean Herods appointed by Rome; and then to a long succession of Roman governors. After that, their land was ruled by the Turks for some 1,200 years. But only in the last two centuries has their national "fig tree" shown any signs of flourishing again.

With hindsight, we trace the beginning of Israel's modern awakening to A.D. 1896, when a Zionist movement germinated under the inspiration and leadership of Dr. Theodore Herzl. The first Zionist congress convened in August 1897, in Basles, Switzerland. From that time onward, wistful Jews all over the world began to turn their eyes toward Palestine and dream of settling in their ancient homeland once again. That yearning, strangely enough, was greatly encouraged by the outcome of the World War I, from which Jews alone emerged as clear-cut beneficiaries. Nor can we doubt this restoration of a homeland was effected by providential arrangement.

That great struggle, WWI, which ultimately gave the Jews a new lease on Palestine, began on August 4, 1914—the 9th day of Ab on Israel's calendar, a day known as *Tisha B'ab.* Jews observe this day, year in and year out, with mourning and fasting. Why? On this date in 587 B.C. their *first* temple was pillaged and burned by the Chaldeans. On that event's anniversary, in

A.D. 70, their *second* temple was destroyed by Titus and his Roman legions! Then, on *Tisha B'ab* in 1914, while thousands of pious Jews all over the world were pouring out their hearts before God for the "peace of Jerusalem," another fire was kindled—one destined to clear the way for the retrieval of Israel's losses under Nebuchadnezzar and Titus. The hand of God is conspicuous in ensuing events.

A few months after the outbreak of war, the British found themselves facing a critical shortage of conventional explosives. A Jewish chemist, Dr. Chaim Weizmann, came to the rescue with a new chemical substitute that remedied the emergency. Then, in lieu of accepting financial payment for his product, Dr. Weizmann requested that the British Government lend its influence to the furtherance of the Zionist cause. Britain was not to forget that obligation. On November 2, 1917, the British Government issued the Balfour Declaration, assuring Zionists of England's determination to help the Jews recover Palestine as "a national home for the Jewish people."

Scarcely more than a month later, a British army wrested the Holy Land from the Turks. The first shock struck the Turks when Britain, using confiscated Standard Oil Company equipment, began pumping water from the Nile River to supply her armies in the southern deserts of Palestine. Now there was a popular superstition of long standing among the Turks that if the waters of the Nile ever flowed into Palestine, that event would signal the end of Turkish rule there. Such an occurrence had always seemed highly unlikely, of course, so when the Turks discovered it was actually happening, they took the worst for granted as a matter of fate. Still another bit of superstition, doubtless mingled with justifiable awe, contributed to their eventual capitulation to the invading British troops.

On hearing that General Allenby was about to besiege Jerusalem, they misunderstood the famous general's name as *Allah Bey,* meaning in their language, "the prophet of God."

When General "Allah Bey" arrived, the Turks surrendered without so much as firing a shot!

That day, December 9, 1917, was the 24th day of the ninth month on the Jewish calendar—the day the Lord had forecast as the starting point of Israel's future blessing. He had said to His wayward people,

> Consider now from this day and upward, from the four and twentieth day of the ninth month, even from the day that the foundation of the LORD's temple was laid, consider it . . . from this day will I bless you (Haggai 2:18–19).

Now, this may be mere coincidence (and I do not press it), but however one interprets this prophecy, its ultimate fulfillment was obviously not realized during Bible times. But Israel, in spite of all her setbacks and sorrows, *has* been "blessed" in modern times.[5] Since the 24th day of her ninth month in 1917, her resurgence as a nation has been phenomenal. Consider:

- In the peace conference that followed WWI, the Allies gave England a mandate over Palestine, facilitating the British plan for bringing about the repatriation of the Jews.
- By 1921 a homeward exodus of Jewish people had begun, and it has constantly mounted from year to year until the present hour.
- On April 23, 1948, more than twenty-five centuries after the collapse of the ancient monarchy, another sovereign Jewish state was formally established in the Holy Land.
- On May 11, 1949, the new Israeli Government became a full-fledged member of the United Nations.
- It has since been recognized by most of the leading nations of the world, including Moslem Turkey and Iran.

These triumphs have not been accomplished without a great deal of suffering abroad and persistent opposition on the part of Arab nations throughout the Middle East. But the "fig tree" *is* putting forth new leaves, and nothing on earth can stop it!

---

[5] For much of the foregoing information about modern Jewish history, I am indebted to L. Sale-Harrison's excellent volume, *The Remarkable Jew*, as well as to a number of standard works.

Persecution in foreign lands only drives more forlorn Jews to Palestine. As for local harassment by the Arabs, there can be no doubt that sooner or later "Isaac" will once again survive the mocking of "Esau."

God has spoken, and His Word will prevail. His promise to Israel stands: "I will take you from among the heathen, and will gather you out of all countries, and will bring you into your own lands" (Ezekiel 36:24).

Meanwhile, the political center of gravity is shifting back in the direction of Bible lands, where "all the trees" are taking on new life:

- Once again, in their midst, the crucial "fig tree" occupies the most significant place as far as the future is concerned.
- Once again, the Biblical standpoint is being reestablished in history.
- Once again, Israel is situated at the "navel" of the earth (cf. Ezekiel 38:12), surrounded by her ancient foes.

As her national aspirations have become more vigorous, her former enemies have challenged her from every side and will continue to do so, despite all attempts at peaceful negotiations. In the course of time, the ensuing conflict will draw all nations to Armageddon for the bloody showdown that will terminate this age and usher in the Millennial reign of Christ.

The return of Israel to Palestine and her revival as a nation and as a political power indicate that God is about to resume relations with His ancient people. Prophecy which relates to the earth centers around the Jewish nation; therefore, inasmuch as the Lord is to come for us before the Davidic Kingdom is restored to Israel, every step she gains should strengthen our conviction that the day of our redemption "draweth nigh."

How nigh?

A responsible answer to this question hinges on the meaning of a single statement as determined and qualified by its context. Our Lord declared: "This generation shall not pass, till all these things be fulfilled" (verse 34). Coming at the end of the Olivet Discourse and in immediate juxtaposition with a graphic description of the Second Advent, this passage, addressed by Christ to His disciples, would naturally seem to adopt the standpoint of the saints who are to be on earth at the time of His return—and . . .

- the expression *all these things* refers to the apocalyptic events of the Great Tribulation
- *this generation* evidently refers to the life span of those who witness *all these things.*

It seems to me that this is the most natural interpretation and the one encumbered with fewest difficulties. If correct, it means that, although no one knows the "day and hour" of the Lord's return (cf. verse 36), the generation that lives long enough to see God resume His dealings with Israel will also witness the Second Advent. This sign—like all other signs referred to in the Olivet Discourse—will reach complete fulfillment during Daniel's Seventieth Week, after the rapture of God's faithful saints. But also like the other signs, it will come about as the culmination of a previous trend. So, with the "fig tree" already putting forth its first precocious buds before our very eyes, who can doubt that we may live to see the King "in his beauty," without ever tasting death!

43

THE ABSENT HOUSEHOLDER AND HIS PORTER

A Call for Vigilance on the Part of Christian Ministers

Primary text: Mark 13:34-37

Our Lord spoke this parable to Peter, James, John, and Andrew—on the Mount of Olives—probably on Tuesday evening of Passion Week.

Introduction and background. This parable is found only in Mark, where it appears in the Olivet Discourse. Although it shares similarities with "The Wicked Husbandmen," in which also "a certain-householder . . . went into a far country" (cf. Matthew 21:33 ff), these two stories are otherwise distinct. "The Wicked Husbandmen" had to do with Jewry's rejection of Jesus at His First Advent, whereas this one pertains to His return to the earth at the end of the Great Tribulation. This one has a good deal in common with "The Talents" (cf. Matthew 25:14-30), which contemplates the same time period; moreover, these latter two have strikingly similar introductions—but other than those items, their lesson and emphasis are different. In this parable, the opening words, "For the Son of man is . . ." (verse 34), were supplied by translators, but the words undoubtedly facilitate the rendering of the sense embodied in the original

---

text. The connection in which this parable occurs provides a clue to its leading theme, coming as it does right after "The Fig Tree."

Jesus had just reiterated the principal point of the former illustration with an assertion that, from the standpoint of those living on earth during Daniel's Seventieth Week, His coming will be "nigh, even at the door" (verse 29). He had even gone so far as to say that "this generation"—that is, the one that witnesses the phenomenal signs of the end-time—"shall not pass, till all these things be done" (verse 30). Immediately He added, "But of that day and hour knoweth no man, no, not the angels which are in heaven, neither the Son, but the Father" (verse 32). He promised His return within that generation, but insisted that nothing more than this had been revealed even to Himself.

Such a qualified timetable is manifestly inapplicable to the current age, but from the standpoint of the Tribulation saints, it makes perfect sense. They will know from the signs foretold by Christ that His coming is very near; they will know from Daniel's prophecy that it will take place within seven years; but having no way to determine how much "those days" will be "shortened," in keeping with Jesus' promise to that effect (cf. verse 20), they will be at a loss to so much as guess at the crucial "day and hour." Hence, it will behoove them, as it now behooves us, to maintain an attitude of constant expectancy. If we apply this parable primarily to Daniel's Seventieth Week, it is obvious there was no discrepancy in Jesus' declaration that He will come during that "generation," while, in the same breath, admitting that only the Father knows the exact day and hour.

Examination and interpretation. Some may object that—since Jesus addressed these words to His apostles—it is inconsistent to apply them to a future generation so remote from Apostolic times. Such objection, however, overlooks the fact that Jesus obviously considered the apostles as representative of Jewish believers right up to the end-time, although as individuals, they were to live out their careers during the present "interim

---

Mark 13:34–37   *Vigilance*

of mystery." Else for such an objection to be consistent, it would have to hold that the apostles will still be personally alive on earth to witness all the future events foretold in this discourse, whereas we know they departed this life long centuries ago.

However we may apply this parable, whether primarily to believers of the end-time or secondarily to ourselves, the fact that it was addressed to the apostles, not to a mixed audience, seems to narrow down its principal reference to apostolic men. Accordingly, as we shall see, the *porter* evidently represents the Christian minister, whose business is, among other things, to keep the Lord's people alert to the imminence of His return.

It was probably on Tuesday evening of Passion Week that Jesus—His approaching death, resurrection, and ascension looming before His mind—admonished four of His leading apostles:

> Be constantly taking heed, be constantly on watch, for you do not know when it is the strategic season. It is as a man gone off to another country, having left his house, and having given his slaves the authority, to each his work; and to the doorkeeper he gave orders to be constantly alert and watching (verses 35-37, ASV).

Because no one but the Father knows "the strategic season," whether the hour of death or of Christ's return, believers—especially ministers—should *therefore* be continually on the watch. Our crucified and risen Lord, Master of the "household of faith," has gone abroad. On leaving His "house," having entrusted to His servants the keys of privilege and authority (cf. Matthew 16:19; 18:18) and appointed to each his particular task, He has commanded His upper-servants to keep the whole house in readiness to receive Him back at any moment.

Here the structure of the original text is rather unusual, with a series of more or less incidental allusions leading up to the principal assertion. The Master is abroad, "away from his people"—having (a) left the house, (b) authorized His servants to manage His estate, and (c) assigned to each one his special duties ... All these participial phrases are preliminary. The main verb follows in the clause "and [He] commanded the porter that he should watch"—this is the focal statement. All the *servants*, all believers, are entrusted with the privileges and responsibilities of the house, to each in keeping with his own personal calling. However, the *porter*, the Christian apostle or minister, is charged also with keeping the whole household alert.

According to Dr. Marvin R. Vincent, this imagery reflects the manner in which the temple was guarded by night in New Testament times.

> The apostles are thus compared with the door-keepers ... and the night season is in keeping with this figure. In the temple, during the night, the captain of the temple made his rounds, and the guards had to rise at his approach and salute him in a particular manner. Any guard found asleep on duty was beaten, or his garments were set on fire. [That custom, as Dr. Vincent suggests, probably underlies our Lord's language when He says in another place, "Blessed is he that watcheth and keepeth his garments" (Revelation 16:15).] The preparations for the morning service required all to be early astir. The superintending priest might knock at the door at any moment. The Rabbis use almost the very same words in which Scripture describes the unexpected coming of the Master. "Sometimes he came at the cock crowing, sometimes a little earlier, sometimes a little later. He came and knocked and they opened to him."[6]

At any rate, Jesus is indeed Lord of the temple (cf. Malachi

---

[6] Vincent, Marvin R. *Word Studies in the New Testament*, Vol. I, pp. 224, 225; New York: Charles Scribner's Sons, 1906.

3:1), "head over all things to the church" (Ephesians 1:22), Master of the "household of God" (Ephesians 2:19)—and His ministers do not stand at the door for nought. Or do they?

It is a deplorable but notorious fact that, although one of a Christian minister's main responsibilities to his members is to inculcate the spirit and practice of vigilance, Christ's Second Coming is scarcely—if ever—mentioned in some pulpits. In many of the rest, it is tacitly relegated to the class of secondary truths. Some preachers deliberately shun this doctrine in an attempt to dissociate themselves from others who abuse it (it is, unfortunately, true that many irresponsible sensationalists do pervert it to ignoble ends). However that may be, our Lord's injunction still cries out from the record! And we are less than faithful porters if we fail to take it seriously—nor may we at all excuse ourselves based on the supposition that the time is inopportune, as if the parable's future reference robbed it of its present relevance!

Whether we, as individual believers, are to be overtaken by death or by the Rapture, the urgency is the same as if we *knew* we were destined to be here, alive, when Christ descends in glory to the earth! "Watch ye therefore . . ."—in any case, Christ's words are equally pertinent.

Wherefore? Because we, as porters, are charged with that responsibility and because we "know not when the master of the house cometh, at even, or at midnight, or at cock crowing, or in the morning."

One thing we do know is that our appointment with the Lord will take place suddenly and—unless we are watching—unexpectedly. However alert we may be, it will involve an element of unexpectedness—just as, however predictable and slow death may be, it still arrives with a shock of surprise. As for the "trump of God," who can doubt that it will startle us even more with its momentous blast? God grant that we may not be sleeping in that day!

Although the burden of this parable falls on the Christian minister, it is not a whit less relevant to the saints in general, for Jesus concluded: "And what I say unto *you* I say unto *all*, Watch." The minister must keep not only himself vigilant, but also the other members of God's household. As the porter, the minister is entrusted with keeping all believers alert to their responsibilities. *That* is the only difference, and that message, I believe, is the primary focus of this parable.

44

The Third Vigilance Parable

THE WATCHFUL SERVANTS

The Rewards of Vigilance

Primary text: Luke 12:35-38

Jesus spoke this parable to His disciples—on the way from Jerusalem to Perea—about three months before the Crucifixion. It is treated here for reasons which are given in the following exposition.

Introduction. Although this text combines several leading ideas found in some of the other Vigilance Parables, it is in no wise merely an amalgam of the rest, for it culminates in a unique revelation of its own: that our Lord Himself is going to *serve,* or minister to, His faithful subjects during the Kingdom Age! (Cf. verse 37.) Not a formal, elaborately developed parable, this one is, rather a more or less casual illustration—beginning with an admonition that injects the disciples into its imagery and ending with a promise which identifies the Lord Himself as its leading character. Hence, it is actually what may well be called a *prophetic allegory.*

This is the only Vigilance Parable that does not appear in some account of the Olivet Discourse. According to Luke, who alone records it, the Savior delivered it while en route from Jerusalem to Perea several months before His passion. There can be no doubt, however, that it belongs to this particular group of illustrations, for (aside from a connection with earlier versions of both "The Householder and the Thief," and "The Steward and His Fellow Servants") its *context* and its *content* require this classification, and its *audience* supports the same.

The context is largely a recapitulation of the Sermon on the Mount, extolling the moral glory and desirability of the Kingdom. Jesus represents the Kingdom as a *treasure* to be sought at all odds (cf. verses 31, 33–34) and assures believers that it is the Father's "good pleasure" to give us that prize (cf. verse 32). Then, identifying the promised Kingdom with the King at His return, it warns disciples to prepare themselves to share the exaltation of the Lord (cf. verses 33–34).

Content. This parable represents the *prize,* the blessedness of the Kingdom, as a marriage feast where Christ will gird Himself and minister to those *servants,* believers who have been faithful to Him (cf. verse 37). Thus, this parable points up the real issues underlying all the Vigilance Parables, showing that they do not envisage the salvation or damnation of sinners, but set forth the conditions on which acknowledged believers will either be granted or denied the privileges of the Kingdom at Christ's return.

Audience. It was addressed to, and contemplates, believers alone, mainly those of the end-time, but depicts the operation of certain principles equally relevant in the meantime.

Examination and interpretation. Actually, the basic issues in this and all the other Vigilance Parables have to do with the matter of *personal sanctification,* the degree of which in this case is indicated by the practical results of the believer's attitude concerning Christ's return. Although we are saved, justified completely, when we first place our faith in Christ, the Bible teaches that we must be fully sanctified before we can receive and enjoy our ultimate inheritance. This status, not brought about arbitrarily, as if by fiat or magic, is wrought in us by the Holy Spirit as we learn to submit and respond to wholesome discipline. It is the work of God, but one which benefits only in proportion to our yieldedness; progress in sanctification is measured by the extent of our obedience.

From this truth, it follows that the work of sanctification is completed sooner in some of us than in the rest, depending on our tractability, and, therefore, that some of us will be ready for glorification before the rest. Normally,

> . . . we all, with unveiled face beholding as in a mirror the glory of the Lord, are transformed into the same image from glory to glory, even as from the Lord the Spirit (II Corinthians 3:18, ASV).

Q. But what of some wayward saints who shirk their duties, fawn before the world, and shun divine correction, to evade the cost of Christian sacrifice?

A. Like Paul, we may be confident "of this very thing, that he which hath begun a good work in [us] will perform it until the day of Jesus Christ" (Philippians 1:6).

In other words, *He* (God, through the Holy Spirit) will keep on dealing with us—not merely until death, but if need be until our Lord's return! The sooner we "humble" ourselves "under the mighty hand of God," the sooner we shall be prepared for Him to "exalt" us (cf. I Peter 5:6). Neither here nor elsewhere does our Lord ever teach that imperfect saints will be damned, rather that *only* those who have been faithful will be sufficiently sanctified to reign with Him at His coming. *Only* the watchful saints will be admitted to the Kingdom feast; the rest, as we shall see in our examination of the last three Vigilance Parables, will have to be perfected through remedial discipline before being finally glorified. This doctrine gains further support in the Apostolic Scriptures. For example, Paul declares the Lord "shall also confirm you unto the end, that ye may be blameless in the day of our Lord Jesus Christ" (I Corinthians 1:8). Farther on, Paul makes it clear this work of confirmations can and should be brought about through self-discipline:

> For if we would judge ourselves, we should not be judged. But, when we are judged, we are chas-

The Rewards of Vigilance

tened of the Lord, that we should not be condemned with the world (I Corinthians 11:31–32).

We must either examine ourselves and mend our ways or else
be disciplined, or "child-trained," by the Lord until we become
what we were reckoned to be from the start. Our sanctification
must realize all that was imputed to us when we were justified
at the point of faith. And this invariably entails some measure
of suffering. There is no other way to be refined and perfected.

If we shun the fires of trial now, we must endure them later
on. We are "heirs of God, and joint heirs of Christ; *if so be* that
we suffer with him, that we may be glorified together (Romans
8:17). It is one thing to be *saved,* and another to *reign.* Paul says:

Scripture:	*Interpretive comment:*
For if we died with him, we shall also live with him	... *that* is salvation
If we endure, we shall also reign with him	... and *that* is sanctification
If we shall deny him, he also will deny us	... and *that* is to miss the Kingdom feast, but
If we are faithless [more correctly, *unfaithful*] he abideth faithful, for he cannot deny himself ...... (II Timothy 2:11-13, ASV)	... *that* means our *ultimate* perfection is assured!

Thus, the Apostle held that all real believers are kept secure
because of the faithfulness of God, but that only those who
suffer (in the sense of enduring needful discipline) will be ready
to reign with Jesus when He comes. This is, likewise, evidently
the meaning of the risen Savior's promise to the Laodicean
church: "He that overcometh, I will give him to sit down
with me in my throne, as I also overcame, and sat down
with my Father in his throne" (Revelation 3:21, ASV).

Our parable applies this truth primarily to the end-time saints; but foregoing passages from the Epistles and the Revelation show that it applies to us as well.

In the parable, the master of the house, is away from home attending the celebration of a wedding; his servants are at home awaiting his return (cf. verse 36). The disciples were told to assume the role of such servants—to be "like unto men that wait for their lord" (verses 35–36). Their attitude was to be watchfulness; they were to express it in keeping themselves girded for service, their lamps aglow with expectation until their master's return.

A wedding lies in the background of this parable—whose wedding, we are not told here. Going by a number of related passages, however, I deem this one, also, to contemplate the Marriage of the Lamb. Such an interpretation accords with the sequence of events in Bible prophecy.

- The Marriage of the Lamb will take place in heaven while the Great Tribulation is finishing its course in the world below (cf. Revelation 19:7).
- The Marriage Supper of the Lamb, or the "Kingdom feast," corresponding with the Millennial reign of Christ, will follow afterwards (cf. Revelation 9:9).

Hence, as we have seen, the primary lesson of this parable is for the Tribulation saints, however much it applies in principle to the rest of us. In either case, the Savior urges His followers to keep themselves in readiness to welcome and serve Him immediately when He comes (cf. verse 36). There must be no need for belated preparations or afterthoughts. Only those who are ready to greet Him immediately will be prepared to enjoy the feast He is to spread. Jesus put it this way:

> Blessed are those servants, whom the lord when he cometh shall find watching: verily I say unto you, that he shall gird himself, and make them sit down to meat, and will come forth and serve them (verse 37).

Here the allegory virtually merges into a statement of fact.

The Rewards of Vigilance

And what an astonishing fact! The Son of God is going to serve His servants! The King of Glory is going to gird Himself with loving condescension and lavish all the resources of heaven on His loyal subjects. And even if less loyal saints are excluded for the moment, it is only that their temporary loss may school them for their belated exaltation in the course of time!

Our Lord concluded this parable with a sidelight on the value of the very *indefiniteness* that veils the time of His return. Note how the reference shifts from the parabolic "lord" to Christ Himself: "And if he [that is, our Lord Himself] shall come in the second watch, or come in the third watch, and find them so, blessed are those servants" (verse 38). That the parabolic servants did not know just when their master would return served to *intensify* their ordeal but to *enhance* their reward. So it is with all of us who await the coming of Christ: there is a tremendous disciplinary value in the prolonged suspense we must endure; it is through such schooling that we are fitted for the enjoyment of the feast.

This added note throws a good deal of light on the relative time of the "strategic season," which is, otherwise, veiled in mystery.

In implying that the "master of the house" was to return either in the second or third watch, not in the first or the fourth, our Lord leaves us to infer that He will return neither as soon as some impatient souls suppose—nor as late as many careless saints may think. This is such an important matter that two of the remaining Vigilance Parables were given to warn against both of these extremes:

- "The Steward and His Fellow Servants" shows the folly of assuming that the Lord will delay His coming.
- "The Ten Virgins" shows the folly of assuming that He must return right away.

But we have already learned enough to know what our proper attitude ought to be—patience sustained by joyous expectancy and sanctified by practical obedience.

45

THE HOUSEHOLDER
AND THE THIEF

The Imminence of Christ's Return

Primary text: Luke 12:39–40
Cf. Matthew 24:42-44

Jesus spoke this parable on two different occasions: first to His disciples in general—on the way from Jerusalem to Perea—about three months before the Crucifixion; later to Peter, James, John, and Andrew—on the Mount of Olives—probably on Tuesday evening of Passion Week.

Introduction and background. Although this parable occurs in Matthew's account of the Olivet Discourse (which provides an ideal background for its interpretation), its connection with the other Vigilance Parables is more apparent in Luke's report, from which, therefore, we have selected our text. The opening *And* may better be rendered *But* (as the word *is* translated in Matthew's version, cf. Matthew 24:43); it begins a qualifying "footnote" on the foregoing parable. That is, this parable is explanatory of the closing statement in the former one.

• *There*, Jesus had divulged the relative time of His second coming, indicating, or at least implying, it will be neither as soon nor as late as extremists on either hand suppose—

---

not during the first or fourth "watches," but during the
second or third (cf. Luke 12:38).
• *Here,* by distinguishing the characteristics of the various
watches, He cautions the disciples against the futility of
trying to identify the "strategic season."
To paraphrase His language:

> *But be sure of this, that if the householder had known
> what manner of hour the thief would come, he would
> have kept watch and not left his house to be broken
> into. And, as for you, be getting ready; for the Son of
> man is coming at an hour you do not suppose.*

The key phrase in this passage is *what manner of hour,* referring
to the nature of the time when the Lord will return. Since it
will be indistinguishable from the general tone of the end-time,
it will be, from the believer's point of view, imminent all the
while, from first to last. For different reasons, this concept is
equally true right now. From our point of view, the Rapture is
imminent. To acknowledge this fact does not necessarily mean
that the Lord is coming for us immediately, but that, so far as
we know, He may come at any moment. We should constantly
be looking for Him. There is no known reason that He may *not*
come today.

Thus, the imminence of His coming—whether now in the
air, or later to the earth—is what this parable stresses more
than anything else—although its primary reference definitely
contemplates the latter event. Our "unknowingness" is not an
accident, but a deliberate plan to hasten our sanctification. God
withholds the knowledge of the crucial day and hour, so that
the consequent suspense will discipline our souls and prepare
us for the realization of our ultimate inheritance. Accordingly,
the Apostle John lays down the general principle that "every
man that hath this hope in him purifieth himself, even as he
[our Lord Himself] is pure" (I John 3:3). This idea dominates
our Lord's exhortation to the Tribulation saints when He says,
"Be ye therefore ready also: for the Son of man cometh at an
hour when ye think not" (verse 40).

Examination and interpretation. God's urging us toward our sanctification is brought out in our parable by the presentation of a contrasting case. Actually, the *householder* represents an unfaithful disciple who suffers loss because he does not watch continually—as if the coming of the thief were imminent all the time. We are led to infer that . . .

- the careless householder was *expecting* the thief (cf. verse 39)—that is, a *certain* thief—to strike and
- he would have watched had he known at "what manner of hour" the thief would come; but that
- because of uncertainty about the *timing* of the burglary, he did not go to the trouble to watch at all.

That course of action, Christ insists, is both contrary to reason and certain to incur disaster. The element of uncertainty, rather than encouraging laxity, should have moved the householder to watch around the clock. Accordingly, in driving this lesson home, the Master urged His disciples, in so many words: "As for yourselves, be getting ready, for the very reason that you have no way of knowing just when your Lord will come" (cf. verse 40). Since the indefiniteness of the mysterious "day and hour" serves to make Christ's return an imminent possibility, it ought to heighten the believer's sense of expectancy.

There can be no doubt that the *thief* represents the Lord Jesus Christ at His coming. On first thought, it may seem quite strange that our Lord should liken Himself to a common thief! But it only goes to show, once more, that it is of the nature of a parable to illustrate a single point at a time. Here, the point is that our Lord's return will be thieflike in only one particular respect: He will come suddenly, unexpectedly, without a moment's notice (and that is the *full* extent of the suggested similarity).

Again, we have convincing evidence that these Vigilance Parables apply primarily to the saints of the end-time and only secondarily to the rest of us.

Terminology. Bible prophecy envisages two different but closely related epochs in connection with the Second Advent:
- *the day of Christ* comprises the Rapture, the Judgment of

Rewards, and the Marriage of the Lamb;
- *the day of the Lord* comprises the Lord's subsequent descent to earth, the Judgment of the Nations, and the Millennial Reign.

According to the Scriptures,
- the *day of Christ* should not (normally will not) overtake the waiting saints "as a thief" (cf. I Thessalonians 5:4); but
- the *day of the Lord* will certainly come upon both unfaithful believers and the unbelieving world "as a thief in the night" (cf. I Thessalonians 5:2–3; II Peter 3:10; Revelation 3:3).

As to *day of Christ*, this term is peculiar to Paul. Aside from frequent allusions to *the day* or *that day*, he employs the full term, *the day of Christ* or *the day of Jesus Christ* or *the day of the Lord Jesus* six times—invariably to designate the preliminary descent of Christ into the air to rapture the perfected saints of pre-Tribulation times. The term *day of Christ* is used once more in the *Authorized (King James)* text, but incorrectly (cf. II Thessalonians 2:2); translation of that scripture in the best manuscripts reads *day of the Lord*. In I Thessalonians 5, where *day of Christ* is simply called *the day*, it is sharply contrasted with *the day of the Lord*. There it is said that the *day of the Lord* will bring sudden, inevitable destruction on disbelievers (cf. verses 2–3), but we are told that *that day* should not overtake us "as a thief" (verse 4). Indeed, according to verse 13 of the preceding chapter, the *day of the Lord* will not overtake us at all if we are true to our calling, for we already shall have been in heaven for something like seven years when the day of the Lord begins its dreadful course in the world below. The whole of I Thessalonians 5:1-11 ought by all means to be reviewed in this connection.

As we have previously observed, it is primarily the *day of the Lord* that is envisaged in this and all the other Vigilance Parables.
- In I Thessalonians 5:2, Paul says, "For ye know perfectly that the day of the Lord so cometh as a thief in the night."
- In II Peter 3:10, we find practically the same words: "But the day of the Lord will come as a thief in the night."
- In Revelation 16:15, pertaining to the Tribulation saints and

their involvement in the *day of the Lord,* the risen Savior says,

> Behold, I come as a thief [that is, *as suddenly and unexpectedly as a thief would come*]. Blessed is he that watcheth, and keepeth his garments, lest he walk naked, and they see his shame.

This passage from Revelation refers to the same time period, voices the same admonition, promises the same reward, and warns of the same corrective discipline as do the Vigilance Parables. It is not concerned with salvation or damnation as ultimate alternatives in human destiny, but, rather, with the diverse lots of faithful or unfaithful saints. The faithful will be rewarded, as we have learned, with privileges of the Kingdom; and the unfaithful will be chastened with nakedness and shame—the figure here being drawn from the Jewish custom of setting a temple-guard's garments on fire when he was found asleep on duty. An erring temple-guard was never slain for his dereliction, but simply lost his clothing to the flames, being exposed to humiliation and disgrace (at most, he might receive a flogging).

The Scriptures nowhere teach that delinquent believers are lost—can be lost again after once being saved. As we shall see in the next three parables, they may be—

1. severely scourged, some with few and others with many stripes (cf. Luke 12:46-48);
2. forbidden to enter the Marriage Supper of the Lamb (cf. Matthew 25:10-12);
3. even cast into outer darkness (cf. Matthew 25:30)

—but all of these potentialities must be construed in keeping with Paul's declaration, "If any man's work shall be burned, he shall suffer loss: but he himself shalt be saved; yet so as by fire" (I Corinthians 3:15). The operation of this principle is not restricted to any specific dispensation (nor indeeed is any other essential feature of God's redemptive program). It is a serious error to construe Jesus' Kingdom teaching as a repudiation of the Gospel of the Grace of God.

One other allusion to our Lord's return "as a thief" occurs in His letter to the Sardis church, where He warns:

> If therefore thou shalt not watch, I will come on thee as a thief, and thou shalt not know what hour [or, *manner of hour*] I will come upon thee (Revelation 3:3).

This admonition, admittedly, is addressed to the saints of the present age, but rightly understood, it harmonizes perfectly with the thesis that Jesus will come "as a thief" at the *day of the Lord,* though not necessarily so at the *day of Christ.*

Nevertheless, it is a solemn warning that unfaithful saints will not be caught up in the Rapture, but will be left here in a troubled world for further discipline until Christ's final descent to the earth some seven years later. To this it may be objected that—

- Paul makes no such distinctions in his classical passages on the Rapture, such as I Corinthians 15:5-57 and I Thessalonians 4:13-18;
- Paul declares, without any qualification whatever, that "the dead in Christ shall rise first: then we which are alive and remain shall be caught up together with them in the clouds, to meet the Lord in the air" (I Thessalonians 4:16–17); and
- he goes on to explain that "God hath not appointed us to wrath [that is, the Day of Wrath, or the Great Tribulation], but to obtain salvation [that is, from the Great Tribulation] by our Lord Jesus Christ" (I Thessalonians 5:9).

These familiar arguments are plausible enough when their proof texts are considered alone, apart from other Scriptures that touch on the same subject. But are we at liberty to detach two or three general statements about the Rapture from the warp and woof of Bible prophecy, unheedful of intermeshing threads which spell out further details?

We vigorously, and not without just cause, object to this sort of reasoning when those who oppose our views use it! For example, some scholars argue from the following Scripture that our Lord prophesied a single, general resurrection, with both the righteous and the wicked rising in the selfsame hour:

> Marvel not at this for the hour is coming, in
> which all that are in the graves shall hear his
> [Christ's] voice, and shall come forth; they that
> have done good, unto the resurrection of life; and
> they that have done evil, unto the resurrection
> of damnation (John 5:28–29).

Admittedly, this text, if construed alone, apart from numerous related passages that supply additional details, seems to teach not only a general resurrection but also salvation by works— but, construed in the light of the rest of the Scriptures, it is in perfect harmony with the general scope of Bible prophecy and the Gospel of Grace.

The same is true of Paul's general statements concerning the Rapture. They set forth the normal Christian hope, of which the apostle was speaking at the time. But many other passages, even in Paul's writings, but especially in the teaching of Jesus, indicate that wayward Christians will temporarily come short of their proper inheritance, miss their rewards, and lose their crowns.

- It is very true that "God hath not *appointed* us to wrath, but to obtain salvation [from the Day of Wrath] by our Lord Jesus Christ,"
- *but* also true is that He suffers disobedient saints to expose themselves to tribulation along with unbelievers (cf. Luke 12:46) and hypocrites (cf. Matthew 24:51),
- *with* this difference: their affliction will be disciplinary and temporary, whereas that of the wicked will be punitive and destined to issue in eternal death.

This is unquestionably implied in Jesus' special promise to the faithful Philadelphia saints.

> Because thou hast kept the word of my patience,
> I also will keep thee from the hour of tempta-
> tion [that is, the Great Tribulation], which shall
> come upon all the world, to try them that dwell

upon the earth (Revelation 3:10).

Precious promise, this! But . . .

> Q.Are we at liberty to assume that all real believ-
> ers have "kept the word of [His] patience"? If
> not, what is to be the lot of those who have failed
> to do so?

Our Lord, as we have seen, gives one reply:

> A.If therefore thou shalt not watch, I will come on
> thee as a thief, and thou shalt not know what
> hour I will come upon thee (Revelation 3:3).

These last two passages sum up the warnings and promises of
the Apocalyptic letters, and the warning here sums up the
Savior's teaching in "The Householder and the Thief."

46

THE STEWARD AND HIS FELLOW SERVANTS

The Folly of Assuming Christ's Return Will Be Delayed

Primary text: Luke 12:41-48
Cf. Matthew 24:45-51

Jesus spoke this parable on two different occasions: first, to Peter, in the presence of the other disciples— on the way from Jerusalem to Perea—about three months before the Crucifixion; and, later, to Peter, James, John, and Andrew—on the Mount of Olives— probably on Tuesday evening of Passion Week.

Introduction. To begin with, it may be well to say a word about the title I have given this parable, since it reflects important considerations affecting the question of interpretation. As to its usual titles, neither "The Faithful and Wise Steward" nor "The Unfaithful Steward," is wholly adequate—each is only partially applicable, ignoring the part of the story suggested by the other. Besides which, both of these latter titles ignore the "fellow servants" mentioned at the end of the story. This parable presents two hypothetical cases—what happens when a steward is faithful, but also what would happen if the same steward proved unfaithful—then it closes with a "footnote"

369

on the relative responsibility of a servant who knows his master's will and that of an ill-informed fellowservant. Thus, it seems more accurate to call this little anecdote "The Steward and His Fellow Servants."

Again, it seems preferable to use Luke's more complete text; Matthew's report omits the part on the relative responsibility of different servants. Moreover, because these sacred writers reported the parable as delivered on two different occasions, there are minor variations. In both accounts the fundamental lesson is identical: it is a graphic warning against the grievous consequences of assuming that Christ's return will be delayed.

Audience. In Luke, the parable is addressed to Peter; in Matthew, to Peter, James, John, and Andrew. In either case, the choice of audience forbids us to apply the point of this parable to the unregenerate, since the genuine nature of the apostles' faith cannot be questioned. In fact what elicited our Lord's first use of this illustration was Peter's conviction that he and his fellow apostles were so unalterably devoted to their Master that any defection on their part was virtually unthinkable! Yes, already his spirit swelled with that self-confidence which would shortly move him to boast:

> ... though all men be offended because of thee, yet I will never be offended ... Though I should die with thee, yet I will not deny thee (Matthew 26:33-35).

It irked him to hear any suggestion to the contrary. He wanted to know

> *Why had Jesus felt it necessary to tell them—His very own apostles, men who had forsaken all else to follow Him—about a careless householder who had allowed his dwelling to be burglarized? Did Christ imagine for a moment that they stood in need of such a warning? or was He alerting them to a common danger threatening some of their weaker brethren?*
> *So—referring, perhaps, to the entire exhortation*

> on watchfulness, but particularly to the parable of
> the householder and the thief—Peter protested, "Lord,
> speakest thou this parable unto us, or even to
> all?" (verse 41).

To this, our Lord replied with still another parable, the sense
of which was to say:

> What I have been teaching applies, in the nature of
> the case, to all of My followers; but right now, I am
> speaking especially to you. You apostles are stewards,
> and your superior endowments entail exceptional re-
> sponsibilities. Now, if you prove faithful, you will be
> rewarded with special privileges in My Kingdom; but
> if not, your chastisement will be correspondingly se-
> vere. Meanwhile, you may be sure that your fellow
> saints will be dealt with equitably, each according to
> his light.

That is the gist of our Lord's reply, but let us look a bit more
closely at the details.

Examination and interpretation. The first three verses of the
parable proper portray, in the form of a rhetorical question,
the apostle in terms of what he *ought* to be:

> Who then is the steward who is trustworthy, the
> prudent one, whom the master will appoint over
> his corps of household servants to be giving
> them their portion of food? (verse 42, KSW).

From this text, it is clear that the apostle has been appointed
as a steward, or house-manager, over his fellowservants who
make up the Master's following. It is his special duty to make
timely provision for the spiritual nourishment of all the rest—
to be, in large measure, responsible for the edification of his
fellow saints. Hence, apostles should be especially heedful of
Jesus' warnings, not relegate them to their less enlightened

brethren (or, as Peter put it, "even to all"). This course alone would prove them to be "prudent ones"—not only men of faith, but faithful men. If they followed such a course, they might be assured of being appointed over all their Master's estate at His return (cf. verses 43–44).

I am reminded of a former occasion when Peter had won a similar promise from the Lord. "Behold, we have forsaken all, and followed thee; what shall we have therefore?" he had pleaded. And Jesus had replied:

> Verily I say unto you, that ye which have fol-
> lowed me, in the regeneration when the Son of
> man shall sit in the throne of his glory, ye also
> shall sit upon twelve thrones, judging the twelve
> tribes of Israel (Matthew 19:27–28).

So, promotion in the Kingdom—not salvation, but *promotion*—is conditioned on personal faithfulness.

Here Jesus, in the second section of His parable (verses 45–46), goes on to warn against the dreadful possibility that even the staunchest of believers might grow weary of waiting, relax his vigilance, become complacent, and fall into gross carnality. The steward had a glorious prize within his reach, but there was a terrible alternative which should by no means be ignored. The promise of blessing was conditional:

> But and if that [same] servant say in his heart,
> My Lord delayeth his coming; and shall begin
> to beat the menservants and maidens, and to eat
> and drink, and to be drunken; the Lord of that
> servant will come in a day when he looketh not
> for him, and at an hour when he is not aware,
> and will cut him in sunder [or, *severely scourge
> him* (KSW)], and will appoint him his portion
> with the unbelievers [or, the *unfaithful*] (verses
> 45–46).

This language is worded in a way that applies, more or less, to every responsible Christian. There can be no doubt that it held forth a fearful warning to the apostles on the spot. Like the rest of the Olivet Discourse, certainly it contemplates the saints of the end-time. Intervening history has amply demonstrated its relevance to the present age as well. Who can know how negligent some, if not all, of the apostles might have become had they not been thus forewarned? Else we must assume that Jesus had no cause to warn them in the first place. We are told that, during the Tribulation era, "because iniquity shall abound, the love of many shall wax cold" (Matthew 24:12). Meanwhile, who has not been shocked at the tendency of many religious leaders to make themselves "lords over God's heritage" (cf. I Peter 5:3.)—at their regimenting, oppressing, and exploiting their fellowservants instead of ministering to their needs? To all such, their appointment with the Lord—whether at death or the Rapture or His final descent to the earth—will entail a startling, inescapable confrontation with His chastening rod— for we are told that they will be "severely scourged" along with "the unfaithful" (verse 46) and "the hypocrites" (cf. Matthew 24:51).

This interpretation does not imply that unfaithful believers will lose their souls. True, they will share the temporal tribulation of the unsaved world—but the same experience that will be hopeless retribution for the ungodly will, for believers, be a sanctifying discipline to prepare them for exaltation by and by.

This brings us to the end of the parable as it appears in Matthew's account of the Olivet Discourse, but Luke's report of its earlier utterance adds a luminous postscript—a comment on the relation between a servant's *light* and his concomitant *responsibility.*

> And that servant, which knew his lord's will, and prepared not himself, neither did according to his will, shall be beaten with many stripes" (verse 47). [Here we see, for one thing, that to be "cut in sunder" means to be "beaten with many

stripes," from which it is obvious that Jesus used the harsher expression in a *figurative* sense.]

From this point on, the parable is transparently allegorical. *That servant* is an enlightened Christian, particularly a Tribulation saint; and *his lord* is, of course, the Lord Jesus Christ. On the principle that one's accountability is commensurate with his spiritual enlightenment, Jesus says that if such an enlightened servant should lapse into complacency and disobedience, it will take more chastisement to correct him than if he had not been so well-informed (cf. verse 47, above). In keeping with the same principle, Jesus went on to say, "But he that knew not, and did commit things worthy of stripes, shall be beaten with few stripes" (verse 48).

Let us beware of any suggestion that Jesus was alluding to the gradations in the future punishment of the *damned*. He may have done so in other connections,[7] but here He was definitely and unquestionably describing various degrees of chastisement (not punishment) that unfaithful saints must endure before they can be ready for the enjoyment of their ultimate inheritance. It will be in direct proportion to their personal advantages, for the Master goes on to say:

> To whomsoever much has been given, from him much will be required; and to whom much has been entrusted, of him more will be demanded (verse 48, RFW).

This is not the language of sovereign elective grace, which meets its own conditions instead of demanding personal deserts. This is the voice of a Father pleading with His erring

---

[7] Such as when He declared that it will be "more tolerable for the people of Sodom in the day of judgment than for those of Capernaum" (cf. Matthew 11:24)—though even this passage must not be restricted to the question of future punishment.

---

children to respect and, thus, avoid the sting of His chastening rod.

Although this parable abounds with needful instruction on lateral themes, it is basically a warning against a state of mind and heart which, consciously or unconsciously, complains:

> Where is the promise of his coming? for since the fathers fell asleep, all things continue as they were from the beginning of creation" (II Peter 3:3–4).

Can it be a mere coincidence that it is Peter, to whom Jesus first addressed this parable, who later corroborated the Master's warning with the foregoing allusion to early scoffers? Or must we not, rather, believe that the Savior's lesson lingered like a sleepless sentry in Peter's heart, safeguarding the integrity of his ministry against all odds even as it still admonishes the rest of us to stay alert and true to our profession, thus assuring ourselves of a nobler stewardship instead of a flogging?

The Folly of Assuming Christ's Return Will Be Delayed

47

The Sixth Vigilance Parable

THE TEN VIRGINS

The Folly of Trying
to Date Our Lord's Return

Primary text: Matthew 25:1-13

*Our Lord spoke this parable to Peter, James, John,
and Andrew—on the Mount of Olives—probably on
Tuesday evening of Passion Week.*

Introduction. Few of our Lord's parables have been so often
preached—and *mis*preached—as has this one. From Patristic
times onward, ingenious writers (with the *best* of intentions,
no doubt!) have used this text to prove much that is otherwise
unassailable but is utterly irrelevant here, and to prop up all
kinds of traditional notions and personal whims, many of
which are highly questionable—some unquestionably in error!

In all fairness, I must point out that this situation has most
likely resulted from the rich associations in the language of
this parable. The text abounds with terms that are pregnant
with peculiar significance in *other* connections, but which they
do not necessarily possess when occurring in the appurtenances
and embellishments of a parable. This acknowledgment may
explain, if not justify, some of the extravagant "interpretations"
of unskilled Bible students.

Even so, it does not permit a responsible expositor to give

his fancies precedence over facts.

Just the facts. Before we go farther, let's take a thoughtful look at a few decisive facts:

1. First of all, it should be kept in mind that we are dealing with a parable, by its nature meant to illustrate one specific main point—not with a comprehensive doctrinal statement that purports to detail with definitive precision a complex system of theology. The same might be said of virtually all parables, although admittedly some are allegorical—and are, therefore, illustrative of a number of closely related truths—while most focus the total effect of their imagery on a single, predominant lesson.

    The difference is found by listening for internal harmony or the lack of it. When the features of a parable harmonize readily with a set of known facts, they were obviously meant to do so, and they must be construed accordingly; but when no correspondence exists and they lend themselves only to the development of a single theme, we must evaluate them based on their support for the primary point of emphasis. This parable definitely belongs to the latter class. It is not allegorical; its terms are indigenous to the story, chosen to shape and sharpen its total effect, not theological symbols designed to convey the same significance they exhibit in other connections. Any exegetical effort which fails to take this distinction into account is foredoomed to confusion.

2. It is important to note the epoch Jesus was contemplating when He delivered this parable. Granted that the story of the ten virgins, like all the rest of Christ's parables, abounds with needful instruction for the saints of all ages, the fact remains that it refers primarily to the end-time, between the Rapture and our Lord's descent to the earth. That is the period envisaged throughout Matthew 24. Here, in the very next chapter, the same discourse continues without any break, maintaining the same dispensational point of view.

    "Then," says the Master—meaning, at the same time alluded to in "The Steward and His Fellow Servants" (at the end of the previous chapter). "Then shall the kingdom

---

The Folly of Trying to Date Our Lord's Return

of heaven be likened unto ten virgins . . ." (verse 1). This language leaves no doubt that the ensuing parable applies primarily to the end of the age and secondarily to the present dispensation. Of course, we need to ascertain its primary interpretation before we can deduce its secondary lessons for ourselves.

3. We should note well and give all due consideration to the fact that this parable expressly contemplates the Kingdom of Heaven. Jesus said, "Then shall the kingdom of heaven be likened unto ten virgins . . ."

- He is not speaking to the lost about the salvation or damnation of the soul.
- He is not discussing heaven and hell as such.
- He is not alluding to the issues of the Last Judgment.
- He is instructing believers, disciples whose salvation is assumed—and the question is whether they are going to be ready, to be *fit*, for admission to the Kingdom feast (the Marriage Supper of the Lamb) when He returns to reign in glory on Millennial earth.

As mentioned several times before but none too often, this (and every other) parable must be construed in keeping with the axiomatic assumptions of the Gospel. Trusting the inspired apostles as Christ's interpreters, we must concede that their subsequent epistles rule out any notion that He ever meant to teach that salvation or grace or the gift of the Holy Spirit can be earned and lost and bought again—or that any true believer can be damned because of his or her inadvertent delinquency.

In short, any interpretation *here* that contradicts the plan of salvation as it was preached by Jesus and explained by His apostles is bound to be erroneous—worse by far than the stupid but venial negligence of the foolish virgins, for it would damn us *all!*

4. The foregoing explorations leave a single decisive fact to be determined: What is the main lesson that the combined imagery of this story is meant to illustrate and emphasize? And to this, all things considered, it must be replied: Our Lord's chief object was to dramatize the folly of assuming

that His return may *not* be delayed.

As we have seen, the servant in the foregoing parable made just the opposite mistake when he decided, "My lord delayeth his coming" (cf. Matthew 24:48). Because of *that* assumption, he lapsed into complacency and disgraceful misconduct—a dreadful possibility . . . but it's also possible for a true believer to go to the other extreme, to fondle the unwarranted notion that Christ's return is undeferable— and, as a result of *this* assumption, to neglect to prepare himself for the duties and rigors of further waiting. Our Lord's concluding admonition shows us this parable was meant to check this latter tendency.

"Watch therefore," He added, by way of summation, "for ye know neither the day nor the hour wherein the Son of man cometh" (verse 13). This warning has a double thrust: not only does it mean, "Do not assume that there *will* be a delay," but also, "Do not assume there will be *no* delay." And, bear in mind, this warning was spoken to Christians—some of the staunchest Christians who have ever lived! It is not recorded for the instruction of the world at large, but for the saints.

Examination and interpretation. Now, keeping in mind the foregoing observations, we may go on to see how the details of the story contribute to its central theme. It would appear that the *number* of the virgins has no special significance other than its sheer appropriateness to the situation, since it was a custom among the Jews for at least ten persons to participate in public functions. Nor is it necessary to suppose that their division into equal groups of five is meant to indicate those precise proportions in the interpretation. Of course, calling the bridesmaids "virgins" suggests they all were pure, undefiled— which, if at all significant, can only mean that these *virgins* represent genuine believers. Their *lamps,* an essential part of their official paraphernalia, symbolize the believer's state of readiness for Christ's return.

The significant difference. In the first verse, we are told that all of the virgins "went forth to meet the bridegroom" (several reputable manuscripts add "and the bride" [8]). Clearly, all those represented by these virgins are, regardless of their different states of readiness, sincere believers, longing for the coming of the Lord. The only difference between these groups of virgins is not—some are righteous and the others wicked—but simply that five are wise and the others foolish. Assuming that all the virgins represent sincere believers, this astute characterization provides sufficient grounds for receiving some and rejecting others as festive guests, but no ground at all for glorifying some and *damning* the rest!

The nature of the difference. Then we are told that ". . . the foolish, when they took their lamps, took no oil with them: but the wise took oil in their vessels with their lamps" (verses 3–4, ASV). In short:

- The wisdom of the wise consists in their foresightedness: aware that they do not and cannot know exactly when the bridegroom will appear, they make suitable preparations for a possible delay.
- The folly of the foolish consists in their presumption that the bridegroom will come right away, for which cause they make no provision for a prolonged wait.
- It is not merely the possession of oil, but of *extra* oil, that shows the wisdom of the wise.
- It is not the lack of any oil, but of any *extra* oil, that bares the folly of the foolish.

The point is, there will be some Christians who, heedless of Jesus' repeated insistence that no one but God knows the day and hour of the Second Advent, will assume it is immediately

---

[8] As for the disputed phrase, "and the bride," it is at least consistent with the order of events revealed in related passages, which indicate that the Marriage of the Lamb will take place in heaven, whereas the Marriage Supper will follow shortly after, on earth (cf. Revelation 19:7-9; Psalms 45). Thus, notwithstanding some respectable interpreters to the contrary, this parable does reflect the usual Jewish procedure of that time. The nuptial ceremony did take place in the home of the bridegroom; and the feast, in the home of the bride.

---

in the offing and therefore will fail to prepare themselves for their prolonged responsibilities in the event of a delay.

The delay and the sleep. The next thing we are shown is that, for most believers at least, there will be a delay.

"While the bridegroom tarried," the story continues, "they all slumbered and slept" (verse 5). They nod momentarily and then begin to sleep—*all* of them, the wise and the foolish alike. Nor is there any intimation in the record that their drowsiness is considered reprehensible. It is simply mentioned as evidence of a normal human frailty. We all sleep; being human, we can scarcely do otherwise. Still, just as these virgins were, we are waiting for the Bridegroom even when we nod off. We are not required to forego the necessary pursuits of life to watch the sky, but we are admonished to maintain a watchful attitude in all circumstances.

According to all the evidence, although the foolish virgins did sleep along with the wise ones, their fault did not lie in their going to sleep, but in their want of forethought *before* they fell asleep. This imagery certainly suggests an application to those of us who are overtaken by the "sleep" of death while we are waiting (even though the parable *primarily* anticipates the end-time).

The coming of the Bridegroom, and folly exposed. In this parable, the bridegroom comes at midnight. "And at midnight there was a cry made, Behold, the bridegroom cometh; go ye out to meet him" (verse 6). However, according to Christ's own remarks in this very passage, this "plot development" must not be taken as a concrete clue to the time of His return. As in "The Watchful Servants," it suggests the *relative* time of His appearing as being *not so soon* and *not so late* as certain extremists suppose. It generally positions the time when the saints will be judged as to their fitness for the Kingdom, but that is all—it leaves the *actual* day and hour as indefinite as ever.

We do know it will be a time of anxious self-examination, as the text indicates: "Then all those virgins got up and put their own lamps in order" (verse 7, ANT). Each virgin freshens her lamp by trimming its wick and replenishing it with oil. At this juncture the *foolish* virgins are embarrassed by the first exposure of their folly: they have, alas, neglected to bring with them any *extra* oil, because they presumed it unnecessary. In a belated effort to make up for their oversight, they say to the wise, "Give us of your oil; for our lamps are going out" (verse 8, ASV).

The oil. The oil of *readiness* is so intensely personal in its nature that it is virtually nontransferable. Knowledge can be imparted by the learned to the unlearned, but not so wisdom to the stupid. It is even foolish for the foolish virgins to make such a request, and the wise virgins are much too wise to think of trying to grant it.

Thus viewed, the *oil* makes a significant and satisfactory contribution to the basic lesson of this parable, but any attempt to explain the *oil* as a symbol of the Holy Spirit—or saving grace—or faith—distorts the consistency of the illustration and does violence to some vital Gospel truth. The foolish virgins do not say, as in our popular version, "our lamps are *gone* out," but, as in all reliable revisions, "our lamps are *going* out." They have had oil in their lamps, but now it is well-nigh exhausted, and they have brought no *extra* oil for such an emergency. Their lamps are *going* out because their oil is *running* out—proving what the oil does *not* symbolize, for neither the Holy Spirit— nor saving grace—nor faith—is diminishable. But if the *oil* simply represents provision resulting from forethought, it is easy to see how the meager provision of shortsightedness is quickly spent.

Now we read the wise virgins' answer: "Not so; lest there be not enough for us and you: but go ye rather to them that sell, and buy for yourselves" (verse 9). This is not a curt, but a tactful, refusal; it is based on reason, not callous indifference. How could those who were wise enough to prepare for such an emergency be foolish enough to part with such a precious advantage—even if they *could*? As one discerning interpreter has said, "No man can have more of this provision than will supply his own wants." [9] *"Not so,"* the answer here, dismisses

---

[9] Alford, Henry. *Alford's Greek Testament.* 4 vols. Chicago: Moody Press, 1958.

---

the foolish virgins' request as a moral impossibility.

How, then, are we to understand the wise virgins' advice, "go ye rather to them that sell, and buy for yourselves"? It is obvious that the Holy Spirit cannot be *bought*, for Simon the Sorcerer tried to do that and got a curse instead (cf. Acts 8:9-24). Nor can saving grace, else "grace is no more grace" (Romans 11:6). And if, as we have said, the *oil* of readiness, or *oil of wisdom* is nontransferable, how can it be sold or bought?

The answer is, of course, that although wisdom cannot be handed from man to man, it can be, and often is, dispensed by God to men. James says, "If any of you lack wisdom, let him ask of God, that giveth to all men liberally, and upbraideth not; and it shall be given him" (James 1:5). And though James says nothing of "buying" it, we do find that figure used in Proverbs, where Solomon likewise exhorts: "Buy the truth and sell it not; also wisdom, and instruction, and understanding" (Proverbs 23:23). The wise virgins simply tell the foolish ones they will have to get their oil at its normal source, meaning one must "buy" wisdom from God by taking His Word at face value and acting accordingly. God tells us to watch *because* we do not know the day or the hour of Christ's return. To believe this is to regard His coming as an imminent but undated event; to act on it is to store "extra oil" to assure us of His approval whenever He comes! The next verse shows that, although it isn't too late for the foolish virgins to "buy" more oil, they do suffer an immediate loss of no small proportion as a result of their tardiness:

> And while they went away to buy, the bride-groom came; and they that were ready went in with him to the marriage feast: and the door was shut (verse 10, ASV).

Clearly implied is that they do secure the oil they seek—but while they are buying it, they miss the opportunity to use it *on the current occasion*. When the bridegroom comes, only those who are ready accompany him to the feast, the others finding themselves shut out when they finally return.

The Folly of Trying to Date Our Lord's Return

> "Afterward came also the other virgins, saying, Lord, Lord, open to us. But he answered and said, Verily I say unto you, I know you not" (verse 12).

This verse implies a good deal more than it actually says—but considerably *less* than some interpreters read into it:

- It recognizes the foolish bridesmaids as virgins who revere their lord, expect his coming, and long to be with him at the nuptial feast, *but*
- it shows that he is unwilling to recognize them as qualified bridesmaids, because they have not prepared themselves for the enjoyment of that special privilege.

They represent real Christians who look and yearn for the Lord's return, but who—by having neglected their extended responsibilities—have forfeited the right to reign with Him upon the earth. The meaning of the words, *I know you not,* as they are used here, is: "I do not recognize or acknowledge you as eligible bridesmaids."

Now, that definition explains, and is explained by, our Lord's concluding admonition: "Watch therefore, for ye know neither the day nor the hour wherein the Son of man cometh" (verse 13). To presume that Christ must come immediately is, far from a mark of exceptional spirituality, a mental effort to evade the duty of watching any longer. And that mistake is, in its practical effects, as costly as assuming that His return *will* be delayed. So, as do all the other Vigilance Parables, this one teaches that our Lord's return is to be regarded as imminent but dateless. Both possibilities—He may come *today,* and He may tarry until *tomorrow*—should intensify our determination to keep ourselves in constant readiness. To insist on a deadline is to shun the course of duty at the risk of being barred from the Kingdom feast.

Wisdom, therefore, bids us gird our zeal with forethought, patience, and fidelity.

48

THE TALENTS

The Practical Aspects
of Christian Vigilance

Primary text: Matthew 25:14-30
Cf. Luke 19:11-27

*Our Lord spoke this parable to Peter, James, John,
and Andrew—on the Mount of Olives—probably on
Tuesday evening of Passion Week.*

Introduction. This parable spells out the *kind* of vigilance our
Lord demands of His followers:
*   It is not sheer orthodoxy, no matter how exuberant with
    expectancy, nor mere enthusiasm, however discreet.
*   It is *work:* faith in action, zeal in practice, obedience to a
    trust.
"For the kingdom of heaven is as a man traveling into a far
country, who called his own servants, and delivered unto them
his goods" (verse 14). Note again that the Kingdom of Heaven—
not salvation as such—is the Master's theme, for although that
term is not in the original text here, the connecting *For* informs
us that the subject of the preceding parable (the kingdom of
heaven) is still under consideration.

However, this time there is a radical change of imagery,
which features the master/slave relationship; all the details of

the story draw their significance from that circumstance.

Examination and interpretation. Here a wealthy slaveowner is about to set forth on a long journey to a foreign country. Before he leaves, he summons his bondservants and divides among them a large sum of money, endowing each of them with a sizable trust to be administered on his behalf until his return. Thus far, the events call for very little interpretation. Ignoring the obnoxious connotations of *human* slavery, the story presents a transparent analogy of the practical relationship between Christ (the *wealthy slaveowner*) and those to Him he is their Lord (the *bondservants*).

1. He is, in the strictest possible sense, our *Owner,* by virtue of both God's creation and Christ's redemption.
2. As Jesus, the Son of Man, He *has* literally gone away to "a far country."
3. And He has, in fact, entrusted His "goods" to us until He returns.

According to some expositors, interpretation of this parable hinges largely on the nature of the goods mentioned here. On this question there is a considerable variety of opinions. Some hold that the *talents* represent strictly material wealth, which should be used to further spiritual aims. Others consider the talents symbols of a Christian's spiritual *resources* (such as the provisions of the Gospel) or of our personal *endowments* (which enable us to minister the riches of grace).

But why make such distinctions, seeing that we ourselves and all that we have belong to the Lord? that our total assets— personal, spiritual, and material alike—are a sacred trust, the sole purpose of which is to bring about the realization of Jesus' lordship over all the world?

Grasping this conception is critical to understanding the absoluteness—the all-comprehensiveness—of the master/slave relationship which pervades the teaching of this passage from start to finish.

It is quite remarkable how accurately this parable depicts the condition of various Christians and their providential lots— without explaining or defending the inequities of nature or attributing our diversities to ourselves. It simply represents us as we are, showing how equitably our tasks are allotted in keeping with our several capacities and how graciously they are rewarded regardless of our unequal accomplishments. The story implies the slaveowner is intimately acquainted with all his servants and makes it clear that his dealings with them are guided by his personal estimate of each man's qualifications and limitations.

Thus, "unto one he gave *five* talents, to another *two*, and to another *one*; to every man according to his several ability" (verse 15, *italics added*). This arrangement, far from betraying partiality, exhibits exquisite benignity on every hand.

How good of the master to entrust *each* servant with *all* the money he could safely handle! How thoughtful to overburden none of them!

Reckoning the value of a talent to be about $1,000, the first servant is considered able to make good use of five thousand dollars; the second, two thousand; the third, one thousand. Each of them is given *exactly* the amount he needs, to be assured of a successful stewardship. What magnanimity! What confidence! What discretion!

If this reflects the nature of Jesus' lordship over us, if it shows what it means to be His slaves, then truly His yoke *is* easy and His burden *is* light! Anybody who *will* can render acceptable service to such a Master, for in the words of Paul, "if there be first a willing mind, it is accepted according to that a man hath, not according to that he hath not" (II Corinthians 8:12).

But: Just as our endowments correspond with our *ability*, they likewise indicate the measure of our *responsibility*—not only its limitations, but also its extent. In other words, if our talents are limited to what we can use, then it follows that we can and should make *full* use of whatever talents we have.

Here I must pause to justify, or rather qualify, my use of the pronoun *we*, for the record seems to restrict the teaching of this parable to the apostles, or at least to those who cast their lot with Jesus before His departure to the "far country." After the slaveowner has distributed the talents among his servants,

the narrative adds, "and straightway [he] took his journey"
(verse 15)—which, if we press it, seems to identify the *servants*
with those who followed Jesus before His ascension.

Actually, as we have noted several times, all the Vigilance
Parables were spoken to the apostles as representatives of the
saints of the end-time. And that is the standpoint from which
a strict interpretation must be sought—but, here as elsewhere
in this series, a *secondary* application to believers in general is
certainty allowable. Therefore, the main thing to keep in mind
is that Jesus was contemplating His "own servants" (cf. verse
14)—that is, *genuine Christians,* not unsaved sinners, hypocrites,
or religious apostates.

Getting back to the story, most authorities hold that the word
straightway doesn't refer to the *slaveowner's* haste in beginning
his journey, but to the promptness with which his *servants* put
their talents to work. And *work* is the right word here! We are
told that the man who had five talents "wrought with them,
and made a profit of five other talents" and "likewise he that
had received two, he also gained a profit of two other talents"
(verses 16–17, revised).

Yes, while these two servants are waiting for their master's
return, they translate vigilance into work; work, into a profit;
and profit, into a convincing trophy of their faithfulness. Theirs
is the kind of *profitable* watching our Master expects of us. It
can be done because it requires nothing beyond our known
ability, requires only what we are definitely able to do. Therefore, the only way for us to fail is to deliberately disobey, as
did the third servant in the parable.

"But he that had received one [talent] went and digged in
the earth, and hid his lord's money" (verse 18). Why does he
so do? Not because he *cannot* put it to good use, as his fellow
servants have done with theirs, for it has been given him in
recognition of his ability to do so. Nor is it because he doesn't
expect his master to return, for that, as we shall presently see,
he does. Then, *why?* A little later he will answer for himself,
but this we know already: he *could* have used it profitably if he
would have.

Meanwhile, we read that, "After a long time the lord of those servants cometh, and reckoneth with them" (verse 19). The master away, each servant is free to conduct himself as he wishes; but after an indeterminate season of waiting, each must face a settlement of his account. So it is with us. Our Master does not compel us to discharge our appointed trusts, but in the course of time, however long (a little shorter day by day), we, too, must give a strict account of our stewardship.

The remainder of the parable has to do with the results of that accounting, which fall into two categories: *admission to* or *exclusion from* the Kingdom, with attention being given largely to the latter case. The object is not to illustrate various degrees of reward (which we know from other scriptures to be quite numerous), but to show that faithfulness as a rule of life will be approved and blessed, whereas habitual unfaithfulness will be visited not only with exclusion from the Kingdom feast, but also with the bitter discipline of remorse and tears.

This message is brought to light as our Lord proceeds with His story.

The first and second servants make the same report, receive the same commendation, and are given the same reward. Each of them reports that he has doubled his money by trading, and in each case the master replies with the same benediction:

> Well done, thou good and faithful servant: thou hast been faithful over a few things, I will make thee ruler over many things: enter into the joy of thy lord (verses 21, 23).

Although one servant begins with five talents and the other with two, there is, relatively speaking, no difference in their initial assets, since each of them has all the money he can use. Therefore, there is no moral difference in their accomplishments as reckoned in the light of all these facts. Their master's eyes are on them, not on their unequal assets and earnings; seeing no difference in their faithfulness, he makes no difference in the apportionment of their rewards. To him, the value of their

profits lies not in their quantities, but in their proportions—
the evidence of their fidelity to him. Their accomplishment is
one that cannot be reckoned in terms of shekels and pounds: it
is the practical evidence of their loyalty. Nor is their service
rewarded merely with shekels and pounds; indeed, the master
gives them something incomparably better—the privilege of
sharing his own felicity as lord of the estate. "Excellent! Well
done!" he commends them. Then he extols them as "good and
faithful servants" and promises to promote them from few to
many opportunities.

But their exaltation reaches its climax when he grants them
the privilege of entering his *joy* (cf. verses 21, 23). This part of
the story is virtually allegorical of a faithful saint's experience
as portrayed in numerous prophecies. It would be wonderful,
indeed, *just* to be honored with our Lord's "Well done," if there
were nothing more in store for us; still more so to be esteemed
of Him as "good and faithful servants," and to be shown the
prospect of a larger, more satisfying stewardship! But, wonder
of wonders! we are also to be "heirs of God, and joint-heirs
with Christ; if so be that we suffer with him, that we also may
be glorified together" (Romans 8:17). As the "overcomers" in
the Revelation sing, our gracious Master has "made us unto
our God kings and priests: and we shall reign on the earth"
(Revelation 5:10). *Reigning with him* is what is meant by the
promise that we shall "share His joy," for He Himself goes on
to say, in another place:

> To him that overcometh will I grant to sit with
> me in my throne, even as I also overcame, and
> am set down with my Father in his throne" (Rev-
> elation 3:21).

It is customary, at this point, to emphasize that Christ doesn't
require us to be *successful*, but assures us of His benediction on
the ground of *faithfulness* alone. In one sense that statement is
true, but for all the comfort it affords, it leaves much to be
said. By implying one can be faithful *without* being successful,
it allows a half-truth entirely too much latitude. To be faithful

in our Lord's sight, we must often *fail* in the eyes of men, but we are never so truly successful as when we experience such *defeats*! Faithfulness *is* success—only *un*faithfulness is failure. Those who obtain, by whatever means, our Lord's approval need not the dubious comforts of a consolation prize.

The story concludes with a rather elaborate account of the third servant's encounter with his indignant master. This, it would appear, is the climactic point both of the current parable and of the vigilance series as a whole. *Here* is the nearest approach to universality (since most of us likely are "one-talent saints," not to say we all *act* the same way). All basic issues crystallize into concrete expression here. All former warnings here find fulfillment in this servant's chastisement.

We shudder at his description: *wicked, slothful, unprofitable*— literally, *useless*. However, we must take care to evaluate these critical epithets in their context. Remember, they refer to one of the owner's "own servants" (cf. verse 14), one who takes a serious view of his master's return (cf. verse 25) and who to the end acknowledges him as Lord (cf. verse 24). He is not wicked in the sense of being willfully rebellious or dissolute, only in the sense of shirking his responsibility. At worst it must be said that, whether or not he realizes it, he is disaffected. His disaffection makes him slothful; his slothfulness makes him unprofitable; therefore, he is useless. From this train of thought, it becomes obvious that all his other shortcomings stem from disaffection, but how may that trait be accounted for?

The answer is found in the sorry defense with which he seeks to justify himself before his master.

"Lord," he murmurs, "I came by experience to know thee, that thou art a harsh, exacting man, who reaps where he has not sown, and gathers where he has not threshed . . ." (verse 24, RV). Very little discernment is necessary to detect in these embittered words a spirit of smoldering resentment. This man blames God for his handicaps and limitations, regards his meager talent as evidence of divine discrimination! It seems to him that, in view of his relative disadvantages, his lord has tried to reap too much from too little sowing, to gather too much from too little threshing—in other words, to drive an unreasonable bargain. To put it as mildly as possible, he deeply resents having been given but a single talent, when some of his more fortunate fellows have flourished on two or five.

I'm not suggesting that such a person's state of mind may not be complicated by other disturbing factors, besides sheer disaffection. The malcontented servant in the parable goes on to say, "and I was afraid, and went and hid thy talent in the earth" (verse 25). It becomes clear, however, from the tenor of his master's reply, that to some degree this man is feigning his fear in an effort to gloss over his reluctance to obey. His real reason for burying his talent crops out in what he says when he returns it: ". . . lo, there thou hast that is thine" (verse 25). He frankly acknowledges the talent as his master's property, and he has gone to considerable pains to ensure its safety. But he seems utterly oblivious of the fact that he himself is also part and parcel of his master's estate and that, therefore, he is and has been morally obligated to make his time and energy yield a profit on his master's behalf. Unlike the saints who "first gave their own selves to the Lord" (II Corinthians 8:5), he represents a Christian who surrenders everything except *himself* to Christ. (If it should be objected that no real Christian is capable of such dishonesty, I must retort that this man was far more honest than are many professing Christians who, not content with *burying* their talents, think nothing of running through with them!)

The owner's reply to his disgruntled servant must be read in the main as a rhetorical question, if we are to follow its logic:

> Thou mean-spirited and shiftless servant, didst thou come by experience to know that I am such an one as to reap where I have not sowed, and to gather where I have not threshed? Then, in that case, thou oughtest to have deposited my money with the bankers, so that at my coming I might have gotten it back with interest (verses 26–27, *freely revised*).

This passage shows that in the owner's judgment this servant owes his inaction to something more than fear. Had he really feared his master's wrath over a business failure, he could have (doubtless *would* have) at least placed his money in the bank to earn interest. No, he has buried his talent for an entirely different reason—to register a silent but sullen protest against the fancied discrimination of his lord. Must he make out with only half, or a fifth, as much as his fellowservants? Then he will do the right and honorable thing, leave no stone unturned to keep his master's money safe, and return every penny of it—but return *nothing more*. By the conclusion of the story, in view of all the evidence, it has become apparent that—rather than being afraid to risk a business failure—this servant had no desire whatever to promote his master's interests. Far from dreading his master's displeasure, he actually underestimated his austerity.

Doubtless, the owner takes this view of the matter, as is clearly indicated by his disposition of the case. He decrees:

> Take therefore the talent from him, and give it unto him which hath ten talents . . . And cast ye the unprofitable servant into outer darkness: there [in the outer darkness] shall be weeping and gnashing of teeth (verses 28, 30).

Severity, yes, but had it been duly feared, it would never have been displayed. Nor is it a "terror to rightdoers" (Romans 13:3, RFW): The same decree that stripped the profitless servant of his talent assigned it to the fellowservant who had gained the most. The same master who thrust the profitless servant out to mourn his losses in the dark heaped glory and honor on his faithful colleagues.

"For," our Master explains, "unto every one that hath shall be given, and he shall have abundance: but from him that hath not shall be taken away even that which he hath" (verse 29). This familiar maxim is demonstrated constantly, all about us, in every area of nature and human affairs:

• The stronger animal flourishes while the runt scarcely holds its own.

- The rich man has the wherewithal to multiply his holdings, while the pauper is hardly able to replace his rags.
- The "haves" stand to gain; the "have-nots," to lose.

Paradoxically, this was precisely the manner of dealing that irked the disaffected servant—unfairness, or discrimination, as he saw it; yet his master—made no apology or concession, but proceeded to judge him on the very grounds he resented so much! Summing up the teaching of His parable, our Lord and Master, also, invoked that principle to explain and justify His dealings with us.

Must we conclude, then, that God is unjust and that Christ is a willing partner to divine discrimination? That is certainly the feeling, if not the reasoned conviction, of many embittered people who, resentful of their disadvantages, betray disdain for God by showing contempt for those who seem to be more fortunate.

This parable lends no support to such an attitude.

It does indeed take note of our diverse abilities, resources, and opportunities, but shows (a) that we should accept and make the best of our providential lots, and (b) that, despite our varied fortunes in the present life (which are transitory and impermanent), we may eventually share the glory of an ideal destiny by being faithful *where* and *as* we are. For the moment, we must content ourselves with the assurance that "the Judge of all the earth" is "doing right" (cf. Genesis 18:25) and that whatever we may lack, or seem to lack, today is merely a challenge meant to protect and further our future interests.

The problem arises from restricting oneself to a "worm's-eye view" of life. From the viewpoint of a worldling, who sees only the here and now, assuredly the entire world reeks with wanton discrimination and inequity. An enlightened Christian sees his present lot—*whatever* shape it takes—as a divinely designed steppingstone to eventual exaltation and felicity. The servant in the parable represents a Christian who adopts the worldling's point of view, thus allowing disillusionment and bitterness to rob him of his crown. Otherwise, he may be ever so sound in the faith and exemplary in his conduct, but as long as he keeps his talent buried, he defers the realization of the glorious destiny for which he was made.

The vigilance Jesus demands is not a matter of reciting creeds, constructing prophetic charts, or gazing at the sky, but of getting one's accounts in readiness for a better day.

SECTION EIGHT
KINGDOM JUSTICE

"Come, ye blessed of my Father ... This benediction owns the sheep as God's elect, brands them with divine approval, and beckons them into the royal fold. It enjoins the sheep to inherit the Kingdom and receive their Royal Shepherd's bounty. It is the language of sovereign grace, at once condescending and imperious, solicitous and compelling, gratuitous and obliging."

49

A Parabolic Prophecy

THE SHEEP AND THE GOATS

The Judgment of the Nations

Primary text: Matthew 25:31-46.

Jesus addressed this prophetic illustration to Peter, James, John, and Andrew, on the Mount of Olives— probably on Tuesday evening of Passion Week.

Introduction and background. Admittedly there is reason for questioning whether this passage should be included in a work on the parables. Taken as a whole, it certainly is not a parable but an explicit *prophecy*, notwithstanding its poetic qualities. It does *contain* a parable of a shepherd who "separates his sheep from the goats" (verses 32–33), which it proceeds to explain in concrete terms. And yet the explanation is so colored by its supporting imagery that, after well-nigh 2,000 years, most of us tend to visualize the pastoral scene more vividly than the judgment it portrays. Perhaps the best argument for treating this discourse as a parable is—no comprehensive exposition of the Savior's illustrations would be complete without it.

In the interest of sound interpretation, it should be noted to begin with that the scene depicted here evidently is not the same as that of the Last Judgment, described in Chapter 20 of the Apocalypse. This text concludes the Olivet Discourse, which pertains primarily to premillennial events, particularly to a period of seven years between our Lord's descent "in the air" (cf. I Thessalonians 4:16–17) and His actual return to earth (cf. II Thessalonians 1 and 2). Here He judges the Gentile nations still alive on earth at the end of the Great Tribulation; at the Last Judgment He will pass sentence on the dead, raised for that purpose after the Millennium (cf. Revelation 20:5, 12).

Chronologically, this passage resumes (and elaborates on) Jesus' remarks on the signs of the times recorded in Matthew 24:4–31; He had interrupted the continuity of His sermon to inject the Vigilance Parables. At the juncture where this hiatus occurs, we read that "Immediately after the tribulation of those days . . ." (Matthew 24:29):

> . . . then shall appear the sign of the Son of man in heaven: and then shall all the tribes of the earth [that is, of the Jews] mourn, and they shall see the Son of man coming in the clouds of heaven with power and great glory. And he shall send his angels with a great sound of a trumpet, and they shall gather together his elect [the Jewish remnant] from the four winds, from one end of heaven to the other (Matthew 24:30–31).

As do several Old Testament prophecies, this text envisages a regathering, judgment, and exaltation of the Jewish remnant at the end-time.

Now, at the close of His protracted discourse (after telling the Vigilance Parables), Jesus describes the attendant judgment of those Jews' contemporaries among the Gentiles. Upon Christ's return, there will be various different judgments, but no general, all-inclusive judgment:

- When He first comes in the air to rapture His faithful saints, they will be judged and rewarded according to their works.
- During and at the end of the ensuing seven years, Daniel's Seventieth Week, He will judge the Jewish nation.
- After His return to the earth, He will judge the Gentiles as predicted in the passage we are now considering.

Bear in mind that any accurate interpretation of this passage must harmonize with the prophecies in the Revelation.

Matthew 25:31–46   *Prophecy*

The Olivet Discourse covers precisely the same period as that described in Revelation 4–19—i.e., the last seven years of this age (the last two years of which are the Great Tribulation). The Church, as such, is not in view from Revelation 3:22 to 19:1, that section dealing exclusively with the end-time as seen from the *Jewish* point of view. At that time our Lord, as the promised Messiah, will, in the eyes of the world, be identified with and represented by His loyal remnant among the Jews. Hence, *they* are the ones to whom He alludes as "my brethren" (verse 40), the treatment of whom will reveal the attitude of various Gentiles toward Himself.

Finally, among these preliminary observations, it cannot be stated too emphatically that any valid interpretation of this passage must square with all that the rest of the Bible teaches about justification by faith.

> Now to him that worketh is the reward not reckoned of grace, but of debt. But to him that worketh not, but believeth on him that justifieth the ungodly, his faith is counted for righteousness (Romans 4:4–5).

The Spirit of Christ who inspired these words in the book of Romans does not contradict them here. The parabolic sheep are not righteous (verse 37) because of their good works, but because of the antecedent faith that issues in their good works. And this conclusion is required and substantiated by the whole consensus of the Scriptures.

A few words about wording:

1. The popular version of our passage is weakened by the omission of a small but important word in the opening verse, the conjunction *but*. Having just concluded several illustrations of His future reckoning with Judeo-Christian believers, our Lord now turns His attention to another kind of judgment. *"But,"* He says—thus alluding to something different from the situation described in the prior Vigilance Parables, which are concerned primarily with Jewish

saints—

> [But] when the Son of man shall come in his glory, and all the angels with him, then shall he sit on the throne of his glory: and before him shall be gathered all nations . . . (verses 31–32, ASV).

2. Again, the word *when* ought to be rendered *whenever,* as the ideal expression for suggesting the indefiniteness of the time of Christ's return, in keeping with one of the major emphases of the previous Vigilance Parables.

3. In that same Scripture, the use of Jesus' favorite title, "the Son of man," is appropriate in this connection, marking His descent to the earth as the time when He, as the second *Adam,* will repossess all that the "first man Adam" lost through disobedience (cf. I Corinthians 15:45-47). He came the first time in humiliation to bear and put away our sins, but He will "appear the second time without [or, *apart from*] sin unto salvation" (Hebrews 9:28). At His first coming, He bore an ignominious cross; at the second, He will sit upon a "glorious throne."

   As we see Him here, He is about to inaugurate His Millennial reign—the era of regeneration, the "time when all things shall be restored to their pristine glory" (Matthew 19:28, KSW).

4. Many theories have been advanced about the identity of the *nations* mentioned here. Happily, we find a "more sure word of prophecy" in the third chapter of Joel, which settles that question and several related points with unmistakable finality. There Jehovah had said,

> I will gather *all nations,* and will bring then down into the valley of Jehoshaphat; and I will execute *judgment* upon them there *for my people* and *for my heritage Israel,* whom they have scattered among the nations . . ." (Joel 3:2, ASV, *italics added*).

For the moment, it will be sufficient to note the portions of this statement which are italicized for special emphasis. All together, they bespeak a judgment of all nations in regard to their treatment of God's people, or heritage, specified to be Israel. This can hardly leave any doubt that

- the subjects of the judgment in question are the Gentile nations of the end-time and
- the point at issue has to do with their previous treatment of the Jews.

As far as it goes, this interpretation corresponds with our Lord's disclosure that the nations will be dealt with based on their practical attitude toward His brethren (cf. verse 40).

5. Unlike Joel, Jesus goes on to reveal that some Gentiles will be acquitted and commended. However, Joel gives us a good deal of additional information as to where and how this judgment is to be executed. It will take place, he says, in the Valley of Jehoshaphat, in connection with the final battles of the end-time.

Now, it is obvious that *Valley of Jehoshaphat*, although a definite geographical locality in Judea, had come to have a symbolical meaning among the Jews, as *Waterloo, Yorktown,* and *Normandy* have become bywords for victory or defeat (depending on one's point of view) in modern times. The name of *this* valley recalls the providential destruction of Israel's heathen enemies during the reign of Jehoshaphat (cf. II Chronicles 20). The name itself means "the valley where Jehovah judges."

Neither Joel's nor Christ's prophecy necessitates the idea that all the population of the world is to be assembled at a certain definite point in time and space, but that Palestine will be the *moral center* of the judgment scene and that the judgment itself will cover a considerable period of time.

6. However those issues may be, there can be no question about the results of this judgment. We are told Christ will separate the Gentiles "one from another, as the shepherd separateth the sheep from the goats; and he shall set the sheep on his right hand, but the goats on the left" (verses

32–33, ASV).

Here our popular version seems to say that Christ will separate the *nations,* but the construction of the original text clearly indicates the separation of the *individuals* among the various national groups. This judgment is to be an intensely *personal* matter, and the verdict in every case will reflect the results of *personal commitment* on an antecedent scene.

- The antecedent scene is on earth, in Palestine, during the closing days of the Great Tribulation. Antichrist is doing his utmost to destroy the Jewish remnant, who have steadfastly refused his mark, at the cost of almost unendurable political and economic reprisals. They are in desperate need of food, drink, and clothing, but are unable to buy such necessities as long as they refuse to renounce their faith, as long as they refuse to accept "the mark of the beast" (cf. Revelation 13:16–17). As a result of these privations, they are constantly exposed to sickness, imprisonment, and death. They are quite literally at the mercy of their Gentile neighbors, whose help can spell survival—whose neglect will leave them in mortal jeopardy.
- The issue is *Christ,* with whom the Jewish remnant are identified in the eyes of the world (as opposed to being identified with *Antichrist*). For any Gentile, to *relieve* or to *ignore* their needs is to commit himself, one way or the other. That decision, in the fateful showdown, will be determined by one's faith or unbelief.
- The Gentile who believes in Christ will minister to His suffering brethren; one who does *not* will stand aloof and let them perish.

7. The last statement in item 6 demonstrates the fundamental consideration in the background of this passage, and it is, for a number of reasons, vital we grasp its full significance. Besides revealing issues in this judgment and clarifying the relationships among its participants, it also exemplifies the basic harmony between this passage and the Apostolic Epistles with respect to the relationship of faith and works. Here,

- as in Romans 2:1-10, good works are viewed as *evidence* of justifying faith "which worketh by love" (Galatians 5:6), and the absence of works is viewed as *evidence* of an unregenerate heart. In neither case, nor anywhere else in the Scriptures, is salvation *conditioned on* works, as such.
- as elsewhere, the sheep are those who, simply because they *are* sheep manifest a sheeplike attitude toward God's appointed shepherd; and the goats are those who, because they *are* goats, fail to do so. "Ye believe not," our Lord once told His critics, "because ye are not of my sheep" (John 10:26).
- going a step further, He shows that His Gentile foes do not exhibit the fruits of faith, because they are not of His sheep, whereas it may be said of believing Gentiles, as of their ancient predecessors among the Jews, "My sheep hear my voice, and I know them, and they follow me" (John 10:27).

In this case the "other sheep" who "are not of this fold" but belong to the selfsame flock are not God's elect among the *heathen* but among the *Jews* (cf. John 10:16, ASV).

8. This treatment presents a parallel example of the sense in which Jesus refers to the Jewish remnant as His "brethren." It is not uncommon for reputable Bible scholars to insist, on the basis of Matthew 12:48-50, that the *brethren* referred to here are believers in general. To say that is to confuse a *general* truth with a *particular* one. It is true that in a larger sense all believers are Jesus' brethren, as all of us are His sheep. *But,* just as this passage contemplates only *believing* Gentiles as "sheep," so it views only the Jewish *remnant* as their Messiah's "brethren."

9. And that is the way He now designates Himself, using His Messianic title, "the King."

Examination and interpretation. "Then," He continues in verse 34. "Then shall the King say unto them on his right hand, Come, ye blessed of my Father, inherit the kingdom prepared for you from the foundation of the world (verse 34).

"Then . . ." This word marks a definite time, a pivotal point in history, notwithstanding that it leaves the day and hour undated. Calvary is past. So is the long "interim of mystery." Now Christ has descended from heaven to earth. "All Israel," those who are "Israelites indeed," have recognized and owned Him as their Messiah. The *Lamb* who redeemed His subjects "out of every kindred, and tongue, and people, and nation" has returned as a *Lion* to reign (cf. Revelation 5:5–6, 9). Now, for the first time, He speaks officially as God's anointed King. And His first decree is a royal invitation to believing Gentiles.

"Come, ye blessed of my Father," He entreats them—or, as His actual language may be rendered—*"Come, ye who, having been blessed of My Father, are still in a state of blessedness."*

This benediction owns the *sheep* as God's elect, brands them with divine approval, and beckons them into the royal fold. It enjoins the sheep to inherit the Kingdom and receive their Royal Shepherd's bounty. It is the language of sovereign grace, at once condescending and imperious, solicitous and compelling, gratuitous and obliging. Regardless of all the eloquent deeds that certify their faith, the sheep have not earned their way into the Kingdom, but are to inherit it as an unconditional grant. This conclusion is strengthened by the fact that the Kingdom was "made sure" for the sheep from "the foundation of the world," implying that all creation, all the processes of history, and God's redemptive program were designed to ensure their participation in the *joy* of their Lord. By God's own admission, this welcome would be impossible except "by grace . . . through faith" (cf. Ephesians 2:8).

> . . . it is of faith, that it may be according to grace; to the end that the promise may be sure to all the seed; not to that only which is of the law, but to that also which is of the faith of Abraham, who is father of us all . . . (Romans 4:16).

Yet the faith that makes believing Gentiles "heirs of the world" along with believing Jews (cf. Romans 4:13) would be a sham apart from its resultant "labour of love" (Hebrews 6:10; cf. James

2:14-26). It is on this wise that the King, identifying Himself with the Jewish remnant of the Tribulation era, explains His reason for His favor on their Gentile friends:

> For I was hungry, and ye gave me to eat; I was thirsty, and ye gave me to drink; I was a stranger, and ye took me in; naked, and ye clothed me; I was sick, and ye visited me; I was in prison, and ye came unto me verses 35–36, ASV).

In hazarding their own lives and fortunes to relieve the King's brethren, they were ministering to the King Himself. What they did for them, they did for Him, because they believed in Him. It was not a question of Semitism or anti-Semitism, but one of choosing *Christ* instead of *Antichrist*. *That* is why the sheep are called "the righteous" (verse 37)—not that they are sinless, but that they are justified believers. Here as elsewhere and always, the hope of life and immortality rests on one and the same unchanging principle: "The just shall live by faith" (Romans 1:17).

> Then shall the righteous answer him, saying, Lord, when saw we thee hungry, and fed thee? or athirst, and gave thee drink? And when saw we thee a stranger, and took thee in? or naked, and clothed thee? And when saw we thee sick, or in prison, and came unto thee? (Verses 37-39, ASV.)

If it seems strange for believers to voice such misgivings, we need only consider the situation from their own point of view to understand the *way* they express themselves. They have never even seen the King until now; therefore they have never ministered to Him *personally*. This is what they mean by their diffident reply, as the King Himself construes it: hence, His reassuring explanation—

> Verily I say unto you, Inasmuch as [better, *inso-*

far as] ye did it unto one of these my brethren,
even these least, ye did it unto me (verse 40,
ASV).

This is a touching, but by no means novel, conception of our
Lord's identification with His people. "In all their affliction, he
was afflicted" (Isaiah 63:9). Likewise, when the risen Savior
expostulated with the first archenemy of the early Church, His
plea was, "Saul, Saul, why persecutest thou *me*?" (Acts 9:4).

The closing part of this passage deals with the King's judicial
verdict against the "goats."
      "Then," the record continues, "shall he say also unto them
on the left hand, Depart from me, ye cursed, into the eternal
fire which is prepared for the devil and his angels" (verse 41,
ASV).
      To this point, all the special circumstances of this judgment
stand in contrast with those of the last great assize described
in the Apocalypse, but here, in view of our Lord's allusion to
the ultimate doom of the wicked nations, this one appears to
impinge on the proceedings of the latter, which deals exclusively with eternal issues. I am convinced, however, this is true
only insofar as the *one* anticipates the *other*, with the sentence
here to be executed *there*.
      The first clause of this terrible sentence, *Depart from me,* is
pregnant with all that follows it, for taken in the absolute (as it
must be taken, now that ultimate issues are in view), it implies
whatever means are required to banish incorrigible sinners from
the presence of the Lord. Accordingly, the *goats* are addressed
as "ye cursed," and the construction of the verb is the same as
that used when the *sheep* are called "ye blessed [of my Father]."
It means, *ye who, having been cursed, are still under the curse.* It
does *not* say, "ye cursed *of my Father,*" for, whereas the "sheep"
owe their election to God, the "goats" have only themselves to
blame, having reprobated themselves by worshiping Antichrist
instead of Christ.
      Here, again, the King goes on to vindicate his sentence,
this time by pointing out the *absence* of any evidence of saving

---

faith:

> For I was hungry, and ye did not give me to eat;
> I was thirsty, and ye gave me no drink; I was a
> stranger, and ye took me not in; naked, and ye
> clothed me not; sick, and in prison, and ye vis-
> ited me not" (verses 42–43, ASV).

A telltale description of the unbelieving Gentiles' treatment of the Tribulation saints is this! They simply leave them at the mercy of Antichrist, doing nothing whatever to relieve their distress. This, at least, is the only indictment that is brought against the goats here, but it is enough to convict them of the only thing that really damns—sheer unbelief. As we are told in another place,

> For he that believeth not [that is, *disbelieves*] is
> condemned already, *because* he hath not believed
> [meaning, *he has refused to believe*] in the name of
> the only begotten Son of God (John 3:18).

Now, just as believers tend to deplore the weakness of their faith, unbelievers are prone to excuse their unbelief. So, as might be expected, the record goes on to say:

> Then shall they also answer, saying, Lord, when
> saw we thee hungry, or athirst, or a stranger, or
> naked, or sick, or in prison, and did not minis-
> ter unto thee? (verse 44, ASV).

Thus the goats reply to the Shepherd-King with virtually the same words the sheep have used; however, He is not deceived by their affected rhetoric. The *sheep* called Him "Lord" having demonstrated their sincerity in a practical way by ministering to His beleaguered brethren. The *goats*, having had and spurned the same opportunity, are only mouthing a complimentary title in an effort to draw attention from their guilt. True, they have never seen Him face to face beforehand; therefore, they could not have ministered to Him personally. Even so, even in His absence they have, by their works, denied Him.

On the same principle that moved Him to commend the sheep, the King now berates their wicked associates, "Verily I say unto you, Inasmuch as [or, *insofar as*] ye did it not unto one of these least, ye did it not unto me" (verse 45, ASV).

This brings us to our Lord's concluding statement. I say *our Lord's*, not merely *the King's*, for He projects Himself beyond the termination of the Millennial Kingdom, indeed, speaking as from the last great judgment bar. The sentence He pronounces *here* is executed *there* in all its awesome finality.

"And *these* shall go away into eternal punishment, but the righteous into eternal life" (verse 46, ASV, *italics added*). This statement, in actuality, pertains directly to only those Gentiles alive on earth at the end of the Great Tribulation. The word *these* refers to unbelieving Gentiles; the term *the righteous*, to believing Gentiles. But since the basic principles of judgment are everywhere and always very much the same, we may—indeed we must—assume that these two groups are, in the long run, representative of men in general.

As for the goats, the phrase *And these shall go away* answers the King's decree, *Depart from me*. According to the Apostle Paul, this means to be "punished with everlasting destruction from the presence of the Lord" (II Thessalonians 1:9). That, in turn, is the meaning of *eternal punishment*: "to be cut off from God and Christ eternally," or in other words to perish in the "second death" (cf. Revelation 20:6, 14).

As for the sheep, it answers to the King's invitation, "Come, ye blessed of my Father." That invitation in its broadest sense means not only to inherit the Millennial Kingdom, but also to enjoy the *summum bonum* of eternal life, here and hereafter—forevermore!

The basic theses of this interpretation are corroborated by the preview of our Lord's return in glory—an event witnessed by Peter, James, and John on the Mount of Transfiguration.

• There stood the King in all His beauty, as He will appear when He ascends His Messianic throne!

• There stood Moses, representing the righteous dead who

will be raised and glorified at the Rapture!
- There stood Elijah, representing the living saints who will be changed and caught up at that time!
- There stood the apostles, representing the Jewish remnant of the end-time.
- There, at the foot of the mountain, were teeming multitudes who, in this context, are suggestive of the living nations of the latter days.

Can it be that these remarkable points of correspondence are sheer coincidence, mere historical happenstance, without any significance? Or—shouldn't we see that Jesus had this tableaux in mind when, six days before His transfiguration, He remarked to His disciples, "Verily I say unto you, there be some standing here, which shall not taste of death, till they see the Son of man coming in his kingdom"? (See Matthew 16:28.)

50

An Expository Parable

THE TRUE VINE

The Realization of Our
Glorious Destiny in Christ

Primary text: John 15:1-8

*Jesus addressed this discourse to all of His apostles
except Judas—somewhere between the upper room
and Gethsemane—the night before the Crucifixion.*

Introduction. This passage, embracing the whole of John 15,
is an allegory, not a simple parable. However, as a forthright
statement of mystical truth in figurative language, it is most
eminently deserving of a place in a comprehensive treatment
of our Savior's illustrations. For our purposes, it will suffice to
use the first eight verses as our basic text. This is holy ground,
and should be trodden with unshod feet. It is also profound,
reflecting the Lord Jesus' firsthand knowledge of the entire
spectrum of Biblical truth.

Besides corroborating the message of the Bible as a whole,
it shows that He was totally familiar with all the "mysteries"
of which the prophets had enjoyed only fleeting glimpses—
and which were still to be more fully revealed in the Apostolic
Epistles (cf. I Peter 1:10-12). This fact compels anybody who
undertakes to interpret this passage to draw upon his overall
knowledge of the Scriptures, in particular, all that is revealed

about God's great redemptive purposes. Thus, what one finds here will depend largely on both the quantity and quality of the knowledge with which he approaches the endeavor.

First, one must perceive and evaluate those circumstances under which these words were spoken, and the nature of the ends they contemplate. All the information necessary for these tasks is found in the two immediately foregoing chapters, which record the beginning of Jesus' farewell message to His apostles in the upper room on the night before His crucifixion. Among other things, He had told them that He

- was going to die, but would still live on (cf. John 13:33; 14:19);
- was going away, but would not leave them alone (cf. John 14:18, 28);
- would return to them in the person of the Holy Spirit (cf. John 14:16-18) so that they might be in Him and He in them, even as He is in the Father and the Father in Him (cf. John 14:10, 20).

The wording of these promises was not mere rhetoric, but an intimation of a spiritual reality elsewhere revealed as the aim and end of God's eternal purpose: the creation, redemption, regeneration, and glorification of sons and heirs, that they might share His life and character in the same exalted milieu in which He Himself inhabits eternity. *That* is the purpose for which the world was created and the goal toward which all the processes of history move. God's original purpose, based on—dependent on—the mediatorial accomplishment of Christ, was the bringing of "many sons unto glory" (Hebrews 2:10).

God's eternal purpose and plan entailed—
- the *creation of men* in His image and likeness—as potential sons and heirs—so that they, as free moral agents, might be capable of realizing the destiny for which they were made.
- the inclusion in the creation process of *human fallibility,* which makes us needy of, and amenable to, impartation of grace, without which we could never realize our heavenly calling.

The Realization of Our Glorious Destiny in Christ

- the sacrificial *death of Christ* on our behalf, which alone makes it morally possible for a righteous God to lavish mercy on penitent sinners.

—and from that point onward, it entailed, and still entails—

- the *work of the Holy Spirit*, whereby He confronts us with the truth; convicts us of sin; enables, *inclines*, us to repent and believe the Gospel; regenerates our souls; unites us with Christ and one another in a mystical fellowship; dwells in our hearts; perfects us in holiness; and reconstitutes us in new, *immortal* bodies adapted to the environment of our eternal home (cf. II Thessalonians 2:13–14).

Jesus had *all* these concepts in mind when, on the eve of His death, He assured the apostles that the work He had begun would be continued and completed by the Holy Spirit. His death would lay the moral ground for the achievement of God's redemptive purposes. The Holy Spirit would consummate their execution thenceforth. God had been using natural Israel in the natural world to prepare the way for the manifestation and accomplishment of His spiritual aims.

Now the time had come for the natural to be superseded by the spiritual. From now on, the old Theocracy, which itself had failed but through which God had succeeded in *preparing the way for the new,* would vanish away (cf. Hebrews 8:13; 10:9). But a new, spiritual, abiding Theocracy would be in its ascendancy. All this lay before the Savior's mind as He began His discourse on "The True Vine."

Background. This discourse was delivered somewhere between the upper room and the Garden of Gethsemane on the night before the Crucifixion; of this much the record seems clear. We have no other definite information about the time and place of its utterance, and speculation is useless.

Many commentators, in an attempt to find a circumstantial occasion for Jesus' imagery, have surmised that He drew His metaphors from a grapevine on the local scene. However that may be, He did borrow His basic figures from the Scriptures. The Psalmist Asaph, as well as the prophets Isaiah (cf. 5:1-7), Jeremiah (cf. 2:21), Ezekiel (cf. 19:10-14), and Hosea (cf. 10:1) all had likened natural Israel to a once-noble vine which had become degenerate. This was common knowledge among the Jews, and they were reminded of it constantly on every hand. The vines in hundreds of vineyards in and around Jerusalem recalled the ancient prophecies; they were emblemized by a golden grapevine over the main gate of the temple. To Jewry, the vine symbolized the nation of Israel (that is, of Jacob and his descendants) as a holy Theocracy.

Now our Lord told His apostles that the natural vine was about to be superseded by a spiritual one. Christ Himself, not Jacob, was the "true Israel." His followers, regardless of their race, were the true "Israel of God." Actually, He had been the True Vine all the while, but now the natural branches were to be removed and the spiritual ones purged so that eventually the ideal envisaged by God's original purpose might be achieved.

Examination and interpretation. Jesus declared "I, and I alone, am the authentic, the archetypal Vine, and my Father is the Husbandman" (verse 1, revised). Natural Israel, Jacob and his descendants, was *a* vine, but Christ Jesus and His generation (cf. Psalms 22: 30–31; I Corinthians 12:12), is "*the* Vine, the true One" (KSW). It must therefore be said of Jacob's descendants (as of their carnal law) that they were "no more than a shadow of what was to come; the solid reality is Christ's" (Colossians 2:17, NEB).

Yet, in a sense much too important to be overlooked, Christ, as the True Vine, embodies the entire Adamic race in at least a provisional way. Through His birth and his life as a human, He identified Himself with *all* mankind; when He "tasted death for every man" (Hebrews 2:9), He redeemed us *all* alike. Apart from the question as to who are finally saved or lost, clearly Christ's identification with our humanity as a whole makes *every* human being a *potential* member of the True Vine. Nor is this a novel idea. It is just another way of saying . . .

• what the Lord Jesus Himself was to aver a few minutes later in His high priestly prayer: "Thou hast given [Me] power over *all* flesh, that [I] should give eternal life to as

The Realization of Our Glorious Destiny in Christ

many as thou hast given [Me]" (John 17:2, revised, *italics added*);

- what Paul means when he tells us that God "is the Saviour of *all* men, specially of those that believe" (I Timothy 4:10); and
- Paul's doctrine of the Federal Headship of Christ, as summed up by one sentence in his Epistle to the Romans:

> So then as through [Adam's] one trespass the judgment came unto *all* men to condemnation; even so through [Christ's] one act of righteousness the free gift came unto *all* men to justification of life (Romans 5:18, ASV).

The first Adam placed all of us under the sentence of death. The Second Adam, by redeeming our race as a whole from death, enrolled us all in the Book of Life. In that sense, all of us are members of the True Vine to begin with. But just as we are taught that the names of *willful disbelievers* are blotted out of the Book of Life (cf. Psalms 69:28; Revelation 22:19), leaving only those which are recorded in the Lamb's Book of Life (cf. Revelation 13:8), we shall presently see that such *unfruitful branches* are removed from the True Vine, leaving only the branches whose fruit yields evidential proof of saving faith.

First, let us consider what Jesus meant when He went on to say, "my Father is the husbandman." He did not call God the Father a mere *vine-dresser*, which may denote no more than an ordinary hired hand, but the *husbandman*, the Owner, who has complete control of the whole "plantation." This term *husbandman* is an obvious allusion to the sovereignty of God, who
- planned "the end from the beginning" (Isaiah 46:10);
- "worketh all things after the counsel of his own will" (Ephesians 1:11);
- causes "all things" to "work together for good" on behalf of those who love Him (Romans 8:28).

It is He who maintains the *vine* in its environment, removes the unfruitful branches and prunes the fruitful ones. He has definite ends in view and will accomplish "all his pleasure" (Isaiah 46:10).

Only what we have learned thus far enables us to understand our Lord's next statement:

> Every branch in Me not bearing fruit, He removes it; and every one bearing fruit, He prunes it in order that it may bear more fruit (verse 2, RV).

This utterance contemplates the True Vine as embracing, at least potentially and provisionally, *all* those with whom the Son of man identified Himself through His birth and death—in other words, as embracing *all humanity*.

1. The *unfruitful branches*, are ones that, like Judas and the whole of unbelieving Jewry, do not bring forth the fruit of faith because they are hopelessly unregenerate. Therefore, they are removed by judgment (cf. verse 6).

2. The *fruitful branches,* having been regenerated through faith in Christ, are gradually made to yield "the fruit of the Spirit . . . love, joy, peace, long-suffering, gentleness, goodness, faith, meekness, temperance" (Galatians 5: 22–23).

Thus, it is clear that . . .

- God makes salvation available to *all* of us alike,
- He eliminates those who render themselves unsavable by "doing despite unto the Spirit of grace" (Hebrews 10:29), and
- He disciplines the rest of us so that we may gradually be brought to realize our proper destiny.

Moreover, He disciplines us until . . .

- we are fully "conformed to the image of his Son" (Romans 8:29);
- we "all attain to the unity of the faith and the knowledge of the Son of God, to mature manhood, to the measure of the stature of the fullness of Christ" (Ephesians 4:13, RV);
- we are finally "presented faultless before the presence of his glory with exceeding joy" (Jude 24).

The Scriptures nowhere state how long it will take for such

The Realization of Our Glorious Destiny in Christ

discipline to be completed in any particular case. But we may, with the Apostle Paul, be "confident of this very thing, that he who began a good work in [us] will perfect it until the day of Jesus Christ" (Philippians 1:6). Then "we shall be like him" (I John 3:2).

That is the aim and end of God's eternal purpose! *That* is our destiny! Meanwhile, often pruned, we are never removed. God's pruning "yields the peaceable fruit of righteousness to those who have been trained by it" (Hebrews 12:11, RV), thus fitting us for the enjoyment of our heavenly inheritance.

Obviously, this pruning is not punitive, but disciplinary. It is not inflicted arbitrarily; no, it is brought about through self-judgment under the convicting and cleansing power of the Word of God (cf. I Corinthians 11: 31–32). That is why our Lord could say to His apostles, who had been under the influence of His preaching for the past three or more years, "As for you, you are already in sound condition on account of the Word which I have spoken to you" (verse 3, RV)—*the Word* evidently here comprising the whole course of His oral ministry. His teaching had disciplined their souls and pruned their carnal imperfections.

Even so, He urged upon them the necessity of persevering in communion with Him in order to keep on bearing fruit—in effect saying, *"Stay in communion with Me, as a definite, settled course of life, and [on that condition] I will stay in communion with you."*

> As the branch cannot keep on bearing fruit out of itself if it does not remain in the vine, so neither *can* ye if ye do not stay in Communion with Me" (verse 4, revised).

Here, our Lord is not addressing *fruitless* branches (like Judas and natural Israel) subject to *removal*, but those who have been pruned *because* they were fruitful (cf. verses 2–3). Hence, this passage must be taken as an admonition to real Christians to stay in fellowship with Christ in order to bear "more fruit" (cf.

verse 2). *Now* the danger was not that they might be cut off because of unbelief, but that, although believers, they might allow unfaithfulness to slow progress on their sanctification and, thus, defer the realization of their potential destiny.

As in a good many other Scriptures, there is an underlying assumption here that a real believer *will* persevere and that those who pretend to be believers but persist in an unspiritual state are actually still unregenerate. This our Lord and His apostles after Him were as careful to emphasize as they were forward to vouch for the security of those who are truly saved. Christ went on to reiterate two basic points of the foregoing analogy: namely,

• that regeneration always issues in spiritual fruit and
• that unbelief invariably leads to destruction.

"I, and I alone, am the Vine," He repeated, but this time He added, "ye are the branches." He, the Source of life; and they, dependent appendages through whom life produces fruit.

To emphasize the purpose, evidence, and indispensability of vital union with Himself, He continued: "He who stays in vital communion with Me, and I with him, this one bears much fruit; for apart from Me ye can do nothing" (verse 5, revised). Thus He poses two alternatives: to remain in union with Christ and bear much fruit or to spurn one's place in the federal Vine and become a sterile branch. Assuming the universal relevance and adequacy of Christ's redemptive ministry, this Scripture nevertheless shows the benefits of redemption are effectual only for those who believe. The disbeliever, who severs himself from his potential destiny in Christ, chooses death and destruction instead of life and immortality—this is plainly the meaning of Jesus' words:

> If anyone does not remain in *communion with* Me, he is cast forth once for all as a branch, and is completely dried up; such branches are gathered, cast into the fire, and burned" (verse 6, revised).

This verse proves the death knell of both universalism and the traditional notion of endless torment; moreover, it is borne out by numerous Scriptures, many transparently categorical.

1. The Psalmist David declared that "the wicked shall perish, and the enemies of the LORD shall be as the fat of lambs: they shall consume; into smoke shall they consume away" (Psalms 37:20).

2. Ezekiel, in pronouncing judgment upon Satan, declared that God would "bring forth a fire from the midst of thee, it shall devour thee . . . and never shalt thou be any more" (cf. Ezekiel 28:18, 19).

3. John the Baptist warned that Christ "will burn up the chaff" [that is, *the impenitent*] with unquenchable fire" (Matthew 3:12)

4. Our Lord Himself insisted that God "is able to destroy both soul and body in hell" (Matthew 10:28).

5. Paul tells us those who reject the Gospel will "be punished with everlasting destruction from the presence of the Lord, and from the glory of his power" (II Thessalonians 1:9).

Once we see this doctrine, we find it pervading the Scriptures, through and through. The unbeliever is everywhere forewarned that "the soul that sinneth, it shall die" (Ezekiel 18:4).

But "this is the record," as far as the believer is concerned, "that God hath given to us eternal life, and this life is in his Son" (I John 5:11). Or, to reduce the question to its simplest terms, "He that hath the Son hath life; and he that hath not the Son of God hath not life" (I John 5:12).

"For," Paul agrees with John, "the wages of sin is death; but the gift of God is eternal life through Jesus Christ our Lord" (Romans 6:23).

Just as God's eternal purpose envisages the elimination of those who are unsavable, it contemplates the ultimate perfection and glorification of those who can be saved. Incorrigible sinners resist the Holy Spirit's attempts to engender repentance and faith in their hearts, that resistance making them responsible for their nonelection and their doom. But equally undeserving sinners who do *not* resist the Holy Spirit are elected and saved.

Salvation is at first a *judicial* matter whereby the believer is justified from sin at the point of faith. Afterward, it is a matter of actually *becoming* what he was reckoned to be at the start: an incarnation of the life, the nature, and the character of God. This, our *sanctification,* can be accomplished only by the Holy Spirit, by means of the Word of God, in proportion as we are submissive and obedient. Its progress is measured by its *fruit* in terms of the spiritual graces we have mentioned before, and it is only as we cultivate these graces that we qualify ourselves to pray aright.

Prevailing prayer is evidence of spiritual growth, proof that we are rising to higher ground, for the more we become like Christ, the better we shall be able to pray the *kind* of prayer that God is pleased to grant. For this reason, Jesus went on to say,

> If ye abide in Me, and My words abide in you,
> ask for yourselves whatever you may wish, and
> it will come to pass for you" (verse 7, RV).

Knowing that communion conditions the soul for offering effectual prayer and that effective praying brings us more and more grace for greater and greater spiritual attainments, He challenged the apostles to exercise their faith to the utmost. Thus, it is clear that Jesus considered prayer essential to the achievement of Christian fulfillment, and every answer to prayer a divine accomplishment in human experience.

"By this is My Father glorified," He said, "that ye bear much fruit; and *by this* ye shall become My disciples" (verse 8, RV). In one sense, they were already His disciples, though still faulty and immature—but through constant communion, discipline, and prayer, they would advance from grace to grace and glory to glory until they were fully conformed to the image of Christ. So it is with us, for

> . . .all of us, with faces from which the veil is
> lifted, seeing, as if reflected in a mirror, the glory
> of the Lord, are being transformed into His like-
> ness, from glory to glory, as it is given by the

Lord, the Spirit (II Corinthians 3:18, TCNT).

In the realization of God's eternal purpose, divine sovereignty and human freedom coalesce in perfect harmony. Gradually we learn to want, and to ask for, what God is of a mind to give, until at last we find the answer to our prayers in the accomplishment of His will. Both He and we get *exactly* what we want:

> He, who created us for His glory, is glorified;
> we, who were created for glory, are satisfied.

BIBLIOGRAPHY

It is hereby gratefully acknowledged that, in addition to various translations, commentaries, and reference works too numerous to mention, the following volumes were consulted with considerable profit in preparing the material for this book.

Alford, Henry. *Alford's Greek Testament.* 4 vols (particularly Vol. 1). Revis. Everett F. Harrison. Chicago: Moody Press, 1958.

Broadus, John A. *Commentary on the Gospel Matthew.* First volume in *An American Commentary on the New Testament,* ed. Alvah Hovey. Philadelphia: American Baptist Publication Society, 1886.

Bruce, Alexander B. *The Parabolic Teaching of Christ.* New York: A. C. Armstrong, 1886.

Buttrick, George A. *The Parables of Jesus.* New York: Harper & Brothers, 1928.

Darby, J. N. *Synopsis of the Books of the Bible.* 5 vols. (particularly Vol. III). New York: Loizeaux Brothers, 1942.

Dodd, C. H. *The Parables of the Kingdom.* Revised edition. New York: Charles Scribner's Sons, 1961.

Dods, Narcus. *The Parables of Our Lord as Recorded in St. Matthew.* New York: Hodder and Stoughton, n.d.

Edersheim, Alfred. *The Life and Times of Jesus the Messiah.* New York: E. R. Herrick, n.d.

Fairbairn, Patrick. *The Typology of Scripture.* 2 vols. (particularly Vol. II, pp. 311–313, 388). New York: Funk & Wagnalls, 1900.

Fallows, Samuel, ed. *The Popular and Critical Bible Encyclopedia.* Chicago: Howard Severance, 1911, pp. 1283–1284; Appendix, pp. 52–55.

Farrar, Frederic W. *The Life of Christ*. New York: A. L. Burt, n.d.

Gaebelein, Arno C. *The Annotated Bible*. 9 vols.: (particularly N.T., Vol. I). New York: "Our Hope," c. 1913.

Geikie, Cunningham. *The Life and Words of Christ*. New York: John B. Alden, 1886

Godet, F. *Commentary on the Gospel of John*. Transl. 3rd French ed., Timothy Dwight. New York: Funk & Wagnalls, c. 1886.

Grant, F. W. *The Numerical Bible*. (Particularly N.T., Vol. I). New York: Loizeaux Brothers, n.d.

Henry, Carl F. H. *The Biblical Expositor* 4 vols. (particularly Vol. III). Philadelphia: A. J. Holman, 1960.

Jeremias, Joachim. *The Parables of Jesus*. New York: Charles Scribner's Sons. 1955.

Luccock, Halford E. *Studies in the Parables of Jesus*. New York Methodist Book Concern. 1932.

MacGregor, G. H. C. *The Gospel of John*. Vol. 4, *Moffatt New Testament Commentary*. New York: Harper and Brothers, c. 1928.

Meyer, H. A. W. *Meyer' s Commentary on the New Testament*. 11 vols. (particularly Volumes I, II, III). Transl. 6th Ger. ed., Peter Christie; ed. Frederick Crombie and William Stewart. New York: Funk & Wagnalls, 1884.

Morgan G. Campbell. *The Parables and Metaphors of Our Lord*. Westwood N. J.): Fleming H. Revell, 1943.

_____. *The Teaching of Christ*. New York: Fleming H. Revelle. 1913.

Renan, Ernest. *The Life of Jesus*. New York: A. L. Burt, n.d.

Robertson, Nicoll W., ed. *Expositor's Greek Testament* 5 vols. (particularly Vol. I). Sixth ed. New York: Dodd, Mead and Co., 1910.

Robertson, Archibald T. *Word Pictures in the New Testament* 6 vols. (particularly Vols. I, II, V). New York: Harper & Brothers, c. 1932.

_____. "The Four Gospels Paralleled" in *The System Bible Study* pp. 91–193). Chicago- The System Bible Co., 1927.

Sale-Harrison, T. *The Remarkable Jew*. London: Pickering & Inglis, n.d.

Stevens W. A. *A Harmony of the Gospels*. New York: Charles and

E. D. Burton–Scribner's Sons, c. 1904.

Thomson, William M. *The Land and the Book*. New York: Harper & Brothers. n.d.

Trench, Richard C. *The Parables of Our Lord*. New York: Appleton and Co., 1881.

Unger, Merrill F. *Unger's Bible Handbook*. Chicago: Moody Press, 1966.

Vincent, Marvin R. *Word Studies in the New Testament*. 4 vols. (particularly Vols. I, II). New York: Charles Scribner's Sons, 1906.

Weiss, Bernhard. *A Commentary of the New Testament*. 4 vols. (particularly Vols. I, II). Transl. G. H. Shodde and E. Wilson. New York: Funk & Wagnalls, 1906.